Groups of Companies in European Laws
Les groupes de sociétés en droit européen

Badia Fiesolana – Firenze

European University Institute
Institut Universitaire Européen

W DE G

1982

Walter de Gruyter · Berlin · New York

Foreword

The emerging law of multinational enterprises has been one of the major concerns in international business law over the last two decades. The phenomenon of the multinational enterprise is of course much older. Its origins can be traced to the big merchant companies of the 17th century or even to the merchant banks of the Italian Renaissance and of Southern Germany, such as the Fugger whose markets extended all over Europe and whose commercial interests reached beyond Europe to the New World. Yet, despite this long tradition, multinational enterprises in their modern form and especially with their present size and economic power are mainly a phenomenon of the period after 1950. The political attention given to multinational enterprises in Europe and the specific problems created by them both for home countries and host countries are highlighted by the catch phrase "le défi américain" which was coined by Servan-Schreiber in 1967. In the meantime, the United Nations, ECOSOC, UNCTAD, ILO, OECD, the Commission of the European Communities, the European Parliament and the Council of Europe, as well as most national states, for example France, Great Britain, Germany and the U.S.A., have tried to cope with these problems by countless hearings, reports and resolutions. Since March 1975 a special United Nations Commission on Transnational Corporations has been active. The Commission, which was created by ECOSOC, has established a Centre on Transnational Corporations in New York and is playing an important role in the preparation of the United Nations' Code on Transnational Corporations. In Europe, the OECD has succeeded in codifying and implementing guidelines for multinational enterprises and for home countries and host countries. These guidelines have just been revised in 1979. They have had a net impact on the behaviour of multinational enterprises, at least in specific cases, even though technically speaking they lack the binding force of law. The EEC on the other hand seems to rely more on legal instruments and on the harmonization of the laws of its member States. The harmonization of European company laws is a good example not only of the difficulties of any harmonization process which needs much patience, but also of the steadiness of these activities of the Commission of the European Communities and of their final results.

In parallel to these political developments the literature on multinational enterprises has grown at a breathtaking speed. Law and economics have been two of the more important sectors of this scientific development. The sheer number of books and articles in the field is such as to fill multi-volume bibliographies. The work of collection and enumeration surpasses the forces of the traditional one-man researcher in the humanities and has been taken over by such institutions as the OECD, the Centre on Transnational Corporations in New York, and specialized centers affiliated to business itself. The legal problems involved have long since gone beyond the traditional conflict of laws problems, such as the question of recognition of a foreign enterprise or the intricate problems of the applicable law. The elbow-room which the multinational enterprises enjoy, due to their activities in various countries with different legal and economic systems, is such as to affect a great number of areas of the law, for example antitrust law, corporate law, banking law, labour law, tax law, commercial law, currency law etc. While the multinational enterprises insist on being treated like national enterprises and on not being discriminated against by specific laws and regulations, the national states, both home states and host states, fear that multinational enterprises can evade the national laws more or less easily, since the force of the law ends at the state's frontier while the very essence of the multinational enterprises is their cross-frontier activities and their transnational organization.

After the many efforts of politics, law and economics at the national and the international level, it seems time to sum up the experience to date, and on this basis to concentrate on some more specific problems in the field. This was done by the participants in a *Colloquium on "Multinational Corporations in European Corporate and Antitrust Laws"* which I organized as Chairman of the Law Department at the European University Institute in *Florence*, Italy, from *28-31 May 1980*. Two problem areas in particular have attracted growing theoretical and practical interest in Europe, both of the nation states and the international organizations, as well as of the multinational enterprises themselves: the treatment of the multinational enterprise in antitrust law and, specifically, in the different merger control systems; and the emerging European laws on enterprise groups.

The acute problems involved in the first area – *European merger control* – stem from a basic conflict of interests. Modern business, and especially the multinational enterprises, want and need elbow-room for expansion and mergers. On the other hand, since the 1960's the naïve belief in the superiority of big business has faded away. Today in more and more European countries the public interest is conceived differently. In many cases, it is argued, economic performance may be achieved as well or even better by smaller or medium-sized enterprises, and efficient markets may be impaired by too much economic concentration and unreasonable enterprise mergers. One of the most far-reaching merger control systems in Europe is the *German* one, even though it does not rival the strictness of the merger control practised in the United States. *Great Britain* has also long since established its particular merger control system and continues improving and strengthening it. *France* introduced formal merger control in 1977, but there were many indirect ways of control long before. Other countries have not yet followed this trend – the *Dutch* Rules relating to mergers are not antitrust-oriented – but nevertheless in several of them economic concentration and its dangers are widely discussed, as for example in *Switzerland*. On the *European Economic Community* level, up to now the only general merger control measure is that which exists under Article 86 of the EEC Treaty. While this control has become famous through the European Court of Justice's *Continental Can* case, it is a mere abuse control and it is hardly able to cope with the problem of economic and enterprise concentration in a more general and systematic way, with a long term perspective of the European markets. A proposal for a Council Regulation on the control of concentrations between undertakings was made by the Commission in 1973. But even though there is the example of a full-fledged European merger control scheme under the European Coal and Steel Treaty, the member States are still debating on the proposal of the Commission. Meanwhile the Commission tries to exercise a certain control under the existing law, especially whenever joint ventures are involved. The multinational enterprises which tend to be in expansive markets and to be active in expansion and mergers are especially affected by these discussions and developments.

The second major problem area concerns the law of enterprise groups: *groups of companies in European laws.* The actuality and importance of this topic is reflected in the efforts of the Commission of the *European Communities* to have EEC directives concerning group accounts and a substantive law of groups adopted. Unlike *Germany* which already in 1965 introduced legislation on groups in its Stock Corporation Act, other European countries do not yet have codified laws of groups ("Konzernrecht"). But in practice, shareholders, creditors and enterprises are everywhere faced with similar problems and important court decisions have paved the way for dealing with at least some of these problems, as the experience in *France* and in *Great Britain* shows. A unique example of coping efficiently with these problems is given by *Belgium* where the *Commission bancaire* has taken over the role of an arbitrator respected by all sides of the economic community. In other countries still, for example *Sweden,* the trade unions seem to have played an important role in the field. But there are also countries such as *Switzerland* where, despite certain discussions by lawyers and politicians, there is still a basically uninhibited trust in the majority decision and its reasonableness and fairness for all those involved: majority, minority, individual shareholders and creditors. Shareholder and creditor protection is, of course, the core of the law of enterprise groups, but the problems of enterprise groups and specifically of multinational enterprises reach well beyond the interests of shareholders and creditors. They cannot be understood without taking into consideration the role played by banks, by labour and by taxation vis-à-vis such groups.

It is true that traditionally the control of enterprise merger and the law of enterprise groups have been discussed more or less separately. There are certain academic and other reasons for this which are pointed out in some of the contributions. Yet from the viewpoint of the enterprise the strict separation does not really make sense. For it is obvious that the restrictions of merger control and the requirements of the law on the affiliation of enterprises are part of the same difficult entrepreneurial decision: how to develop a multinational corporation or group. But also in the theory of corporate and antitrust law it is more and more apparent that both problem areas overlap and influence each other, as shown for example by the concepts of "enterprise" and of "merger" in both laws, or by the relevance of a relationship of control between two or more enterprises in both laws alike.

The leading idea in organizing the colloquium and in editing the reports was, beyond the choice of the topic, to achieve the right mixture of the participants, viewpoints and contributions. There would have been little challenge in holding yet another conference on the general problems of multinational enterprises or to add just another book to the many which already exist on this subject. Instead, concrete problems in the field are taken up from different angles. This is guaranteed by a triple mixture: First, of course, it would be hardly adequate to treat the problems of multinational enterprises and groups just from the viewpoint of one or two jurisdictions; a multinational phenomenon such as the multinational enterprise is bound to provoke a multinational, and by no means uniform, response. The choice of countries represented was, therefore, partly based on the respective contributions made by each to the problems involved, partly a practical compromise: they are Great Britain, France, Germany, Belgium, Switzerland and the Scandinavian countries. Of course the European Communities are not left out. It would have been challenging to include also the United States; but because of financial and technical problems this had to be postponed to another time. Second, not only academics were asked to present their theories and viewpoints. What counts in this field is the law in action. Therefore at the colloquium reports and oral contributions were presented by the general counsel of a multinational corporation; by an attorney at law and tax consultant dealing in private practice with the problems of multinational corporations; by several members of important commissions and regulatory agencies in the field; and by a judge in the antitrust division of the German *Bundesgerichtshof*. Finally, if business law is a means of influencing enterprise behaviour in order to further and to protect, for example, economic performance, competition, minority rights and creditors' claims, then it is dangerous to stick only to legal theories or legal precedents. It seems important also to know and to appreciate what other disciplines than law, especially economics, can contribute. Therefore the colloquium was and the publication is, if I may say so, a multinational joint venture between theory and practice in law and economics.

For the convenience of the readers, especially those in legal practice and in business and within the multinational enterprises themselves, it has been decided after thorough deliberation to split the publication into two volumes: *Volume I* deals with *European Merger Control; Volume II* treats *Groups of Companies in European Laws*. While both volumes have a common origin and belong together, it is perfectly possible to buy and to use just one of them according to each user's professional specialization or personal choice. This relative independence of both volumes is also shown in the fact that Volume I is only in English, while Volume II gathers contributions in English and in French. Each volume has its separate annex covering the necessary legal materials and giving a concise report about the discussion on the reports.

I thank here all those colleagues and friends who participated in the conference and who by their contributions and experience made it a memorable and fruitful undertaking. I also would like to mention and thank Brigitte Schwab, Nadine Magaud and especially Monica Seccombe for their great help in editing.

Florence/Italy April 1981
Tübingen/Germany Klaus J. Hopt

Table of Contents / Table des Matières (Volume II)

Table of Contents (Volume I)

Chapter III: Merger Control in the European Communities

Annex I: Discussion Report

Annex II: Relevant Legal Provisions

Chapter/Chapitre I

Horizontal Groups and Joint Ventures: The Practical Experience

Les groupes de sociétés horizontaux et les filiales communes dans l'expérience pratique

Horizontal Groups and Joint Ventures in Europe: Concepts and Reality

WILHELM F. BAYER
Wuppertal

I. The Historical and Factual Framework

Looking at the development of the organizational structure of industry in Europe, the formation of horizontal groups and joint ventures can certainly be considered as one of the most fascinating topics of the last decades. This subject has again and again inspired the phantasy of politicians, economists, trade unionists, journalists and last, but not least, of entrepreneurs and lawyers. It is for a relatively small number of groups and companies a matter of daily experience and reality.

European horizontal groups and *joint ventures* can be characterized as bi-national combines, which due to the lack of a uniform European law have been founded and are managed with the instruments and on the basis of the existing national laws. Since during the last two years and particularly during the last months some of these horizontal groups have undergone fundamental changes, the time has now come for a retrospective evaluation of and comparison between the ideas and perspectives of a developing body of European law on corporations and the actual experience of horizontal groups in Europe as they have been realized on the basis of concepts developed in the late 1950's and 1960's.

This will include, of course, some reference to the legal and practical difficulties facing these groups. Within this context it would be only too tempting to comment on a numer of interesting legal subjects and to elaborate on their development during the last decades. But the *main purpose* of this study is to *describe* the factual development and the *real situation of these groups and joint ventures*, and the environment and framework in which they operate, taking into account all economic, social, psychological and national elements which have contributed to the situation of *today*.

Concentrating on horizontal groups and joint ventures in Europe seems to be advisable: first of all because horizontal groups are a European phenomenon, whereas the headquarters of centralized multinational groups of companies are to be found in all major industrialized countries, with the United States and Japan at the top of the list. Furthermore, joint ventures on the international scenery outside Europe often take the form of investment in developing countries. It is obvious that joint ventures which are subject to national legislation on the control of foreign investments obliging the foreign investor to accept a minority or even majority shareholding either of nationals or of state-owned or state-controlled companies of the country in question, have quite a different character from joint ventures between industrial partners in Europe.

As already mentioned, the relatively small number of bi-national horizontal groups in Europe is actually undergoing a *phase of substantial changes*. Some of these groups have separated or are about to lose their bi-national character. Are we entitled to talk already of a phase of dissolution with regard to the horizontal groups formed in the late 1950's and 1960's? Is our subject only worth a nostalgic retrospective or do horizontal groups, in spite of the recent phenomenon described, still have a chance? Is this at least valid for specialized joint ventures run by two or more groups with domiciles in two or more countries, i. e., for joint ventures with a clearly defined but limited scope of activities? There can be little doubt amongst experts familiar with the European scene that the expectations shared by many, regarding the development of and progress towards a uniform or harmonized body of corporation and tax law in Europe have not been fulfilled. This is particularly true with regard to horizontal groups and joint ventures which – in a way – are more dependent on a positive European development than the more common traditional type of multinational organization with domicile and headquarters in one country and manufacturing or distributing affiliates in other countries. This latter type of organization, because it is clearly based on the available instruments offered by national legislation, has within the last decades developed and spread out almost without showing any interest in the European development. Industry has found that it is much easier to set up a multinational organization by setting up step by step affiliated companies in other countries, rather than by negotiating complicated horizontal partnerships comprising two or more countries. It is a fact, as we shall see, that considerable discrepancies have arisen between the expectations connected with the setting up of horizontal groups and the results actually achieved, between the organizational and strategical concepts formulated many years ago and the real structures and problems of these days.

Before reviewing the position of the individual horizontal groups, it should be said that there is no intention to dilate upon the firmly-established Dutch-English combines: The *Shell* Group (Royal Dutch Shell, formed in 1907) and the *Unilever* Group (formed in 1927). As these combines, the organizational and legal structure of which are well known, have their roots in a completely different phase of European industrial development, both groups already had such a firm and clearly defined organizational structure by the time the proposed body of European legislation began to materialize that neither Shell nor Unilever could be induced to change their existing structure and to adopt new possibilities offered by the European Community.

Consequently, this survey concentrates on and is limited to such horizontal groups and combines as were set up in the late 1950's and 1960's in anticipation of an expected progress with regard to the harmonization of European laws or with the view to a possible future uniform European corporation. The names of these horizontal groups are known only too well: *Agfa-Gevaert; Dunlop-Pirelli; Hoesch-Hoogovens-Estel; Fokker-VFW;* the bi-national management structure of the *Enka* Group within the *Akzo* Group of Companies, a phenomenon which can only be explained by historical reasons; the *Polygram* Group, a joint venture of the record business of Siemens and Philips; *Unidata's* venture with CII already dissolved; the intended but not realized cooperation and merger between *Fiat* and *Citroën;* and the already dissolved marriage between *Kléber-Colombes* and *Semperit.* Furthermore, there are a few bi- or tri-national groups in the aerospace and defense industry, as well as for research and development activities, the shareholdings being mainly in the hands of governments or government agencies or of companies in one way or another under governmental control. Private and public banks have set up a few jointly owned European banks for merchant bank or investment bank purposes, such as the *Banque Européenne de Crédit à Moyen Terme* in Brussels or the *Société Financière* in Paris. To round off the picture, a number of less known joint ventures should be mentioned, established by two or more industrial groups for special activities in the pharmaceutical and in the electronics industry as well as in the mechanic and equipment industry. Some of these joint ventures have been discussed in connection with the limited merger control exercised by the European Commission. The last of these cases was the joint venture between *ICI* and *WASAG Chemie* in the gunpowder field, a joint venture which was rejected by the Commission of the European Communities and which was not in fact realized.

II. The Relevant Questions

This brief survey leads to the relevant questions, to which we are in need of answers:

1. What were — in so far as is known — the motives behind the setting up of these horizontal groups and joint ventures and what were the objectives at which they were aiming?
2. With which organizational and legal means and instruments were they founded?
3. What relationship exists between the formation of these groups and the expected development of a European body of corporation and tax law, achieved either by uniform laws or by harmonization of national laws?
4. In what state and shape do we find these horizontal groups and joint ventures at the beginning of the 1980's?
5. To what extent will they be affected by the stagnation of the process of European political and further economic integration and the visible tendencies towards disintegration?
6. What are the reasons for the dissolution of horizontal groups and the structural changes to be observed within the last years?
7. Is there a chance of further development and survival in cases where the organizational and legal structures are well founded, proved and still appro-

priate to cope with the tremendous economic and social changes with which we have to live?

It is obvious that there are no general answers to the questions raised. The spectrum of premises, motives, objectives, possibilities and means, of business policies and strategies is much too manifold to permit of generalized statements. Nevertheless, an attempt will be made to give certain unavoidably subjective insights and to draw some conclusions. In any case, it can be taken for sure that the horizontal groups and joint ventures have contributed to the development of the European economy within the last decades to an extent which cannot be neglected. However, it has to be said that they have not turned out to be a successful device to cope with the problem of an increasing number of competitive companies within the Common Market, as had been anticipated and advertised during a certain period of time. It looks as if the main streams of the development of the last two decades have turned towards the expansion of national groups into other European and non-European countries by setting up manufacturing and distributing companies or acquiring participations. This has been done by using the traditional national instruments without paying too much attention to the development of a uniform or harmonized body of European laws in order to achieve an efficient and manageable group structure less complicated than the bi-national structure of horizontal groups and joint ventures.

III. Motives and Objectives for the Creation of Groups

What were the motives and objectives for the creation of bilateral horizontal groups in the late 1950's and 1960's?

There can be no doubt that the main impulse came from the foundation and the realization of a European common market as a consequence of the Treaty of Rome. Even in larger industrial groups, at that time, there was considerable uncertainty and fear that an existing national group even with affiliates abroad could not cope with the increased competition within the European Community, that other groups had a better start right from the beginning because of their technical or market position or because of cost advantages. We have almost forgotten that in the first years of the European Community economic exchange within Europe was very limited and since then has increased to a degree of market penetration which could not be anticipated at that time. It is a fact that during more than 20 years the growth rate of the internal trade within the European Communities (EC) has continuously been twice as high as the growth rate of the world trade, not to mention the huge investments which have been made by many companies from other than EC countries.

In the meantime, all major and most of the medium size and even many small companies have set up in most countries of the European Community a net of distributing companies and in many cases also of manufacturing companies or have acquired participations in corresponding enterprises in other European countries. This process of economic penetration and integration has reached a far advanced stage and in some branches of industry – although not, of course, in the banking and insurance businesses which still preserve their predominantly national character – this process towards a European branch structure has almost been completed. At the beginning, however, it was felt by many groups that a combination with another group in another European country might be the adequate response to the future demands of the developing European market and that it would be easier to establish such bi-lateral ties and links rather than setting up manufacturing companies in other European countries. This reasoning is certainly true for groups like *Dunlop-Pirelli* which had to face the competition of Michelin and the big American tyre manufacturers. A rather late response to the situation in the tyre and the rubber industry was the unsuccessful marriage between *Kléber Colombes* and *Semperit* by means of a Swiss holding company, also very much inspired by the growing pressure of cost increases and the need for rationalization of production by combining and streamlining production programmes. Improving the competitive structure is also the motive behind the merger between *AKU* and *Glanzstoff*, now an *Enka* Group part of the *Akzo* Group of Companies, because in spite of the very strong position of these two companies in the man-made fibre business, it was felt that it was necessary to amalgamate the existing German and Dutch facilities and the affiliates in a number of European countries, like Britain and Spain. The new uniform organizational structure was deemed to be required to be able to compete with such giants of the chemical industry as *ICI*, *Rhône-Poulenc*, *Bayer* and *Hoechst* – by the way, a very successful experiment if we look at the success of the Enka group in overcoming the fibre crisis of the recent years. The main impulse for the getting together of *Agfa* and *Gevaert* was not so much the fact that Gevaert with its plants in Belgium was and is concentrating on photographic films for technical applications, whereas Agfa with its German plants was more active in the making of photographic films for amateurs – of course an ideal situation for a combination – but rather the fear, not unjustified, that Kodak in the US might prove to be too strong to compete with and that Kodak might within a short time acquire a larger part of the European market. The dangers of the Japanese manufacturers of photographic products of all kinds were still far ahead.

In the case of *Fokker-VFW* the main objective of the combination was the hope, on the Dutch side, to get access to the defense budget of the Federal Republic of Germany, this being also the reason why the holding company controlling the operating Fokker-VFW company in the Netherlands and the operating VFW-Fokker company in Germany was set up and located in Düsseldorf. On the German side the main interest was to achieve a breakthrough in the business of commercial small aircraft, the traditional business of the Fokker Group. In the steel industry the Dutch-German merger of *Hoogovens-Hoesch*, now integrated into the *Estel* Group of Companies in Nijmegen, was a reaction to the fact that the steel industry in most European countries – Britain, Italy and in the meantime also France – is run by state-owned or state-controlled companies, with private enterprises left only in Germany and the Benelux countries. The strength of Hoogovens, as it was felt, was more in the steel making rather than in the making of steel products. Hoesch – on the other hand – had a strong foothold in many areas of steel products whereas its steel making units had natural cost disadvantages compared with the location of the Hoogovens steel plants on the sea-shore.

The 50:50 joint venture between *Siemens* and *Philips*, co-owners of the *Polygram* Group, was a reaction to the strong market position of the French, British and American manufacturers of records in Europe, certainly also influenced by the fact that the record industry – and this is true for classical records as well as for the wide range of popular music – is such a strange business that it hardly fits into the normal line of manufacturers of electrical and electronic equipment. Thus, it seemed to be logical to separate this business and to run it as an independent organisation, not connected with other lines of business.

If we look at this rather heterogeneous bundle of motives and objectives which brought about the horizontal groups in Europe of which we are talking, it can be said that these aims and objectives have not always been achieved successfully, as shall be demonstrated later. At least, many of them did not prove to be as stable a solution as anticipated at the moment of foundation. An exception has to be made for specialized joint ventures, such as the Polygram Group just mentioned, and many smaller and less known joint ventures with clearly defined but limited fields of activity.

IV. Concepts and Techniques of Realization

Bi-national horizontal groups and joint ventures in Europe have been founded using the traditional means and instruments of the national company and tax law of the member states of the European Community and with a body of contractual concepts and models of a very special nature. It is not the purpose of this survey to describe the various techniques and agreements which were necessary to form these horizontal groups. As is well known, each individual case varies from the other, not permitting direct comparisons. From an organizational point of view, however, it can be said that either by using one holding company as a link on a certain level of the structure or by using two legal units in two different countries tied together by cross-participations, some sort of joint management and joint supervision and a bi-national structure have been established by sometimes rather complicated agreements. As an insider, I could say that we all copied from each other and took elements of existing solutions and models inserting them into our own concepts and adjusting them to our specific requirements as we saw them. At the beginning there were doubts whether we could realize the intended concepts on the basis of the instruments and tools offered by the national laws.

Many misunderstandings arose. For instance, in the case of *Agfa-Gevaert*, the Belgian side, at that time enjoying a comparatively low corporation tax level of roughly 40 percent, did not realize the full scope of the tax burden in Germany of more than 60 percent. The German side was not aware of the difficulties and of the financial impact of the labour laws in Belgium, with high compensation to be paid to employees leaving the company. There was too little experience everywhere with the existing, and in many countries rapidly changing, rules governing industrial relations, works councils and co-determination systems – even between countries such as Germany and the Netherlands, in which it is believed that the situation is sufficiently clear.

V. Horizontal Groups and the Development of European Law

As these discrepancies and difficulties came to light and their significance was appreciated, great hopes and expectations arose that a harmonization of the European tax and company laws and laws governing co-determination would soon make progress, and that we would get a European law on groups; and last, but not least, that "a European company", as a new Europe-wide legal entity in which existing companies could be merged, would be put at the disposal of industry. Consequently, much backing and support came from these bi-national ventures for the development and realization of a European body of company and tax law. But for reasons well known, in more than 20 years only achievements of relative, if not secondary, importance have materialized. It is true that the Fourth Directive of the European Commission on the harmonization of accounting and reporting rules will mark some progress, but many important discrepancies will continue to exist due to the fact that differing national methods and rules have been declared as acceptable and of equal value. We are further away than ever from the realization of a *"Societas Europaea"* and there is only a faint hope that there will be a harmonized system of national laws on groups of companies and harmonized accounting and financial reporting for groups in Europe. It has to be said that many Presidents and General Counsels of those groups always were of and expressed the opinion that they would prefer their bi-national concepts to the concept of a European company and that they would not be inclined to transform the existing bi-national structures into a uniform European company. There can be no doubt that scepticism in industry towards the development of European integration in the field of *company and tax laws* and towards a concept of a European company has grown in recent years. This is mainly due to the fact that for years the European Community has been in a state of stagnation, if not disintegration, at least in some areas.

In industry there is wide-spread disappointment that the gap between the outstanding achievements of the economic integration of Europe – initiated and realized by the companies in industry, services, banking and insurance – as compared with the poor results in, if not the setbacks to, political integration and co-operation is widening continuously. In addition, there are the extremely detrimental effects of inflation and its repercussions on employment and social welfare, leading to the growing interventionism and dirigism of the individual national governments. Employment and restructuring policies of governments are a device and an excuse for national solutions leading to disintegration. Consequently, it is getting more and more difficult to run companies of the same group located in two or more countries on the basis of a uniform business policy and strategy. These difficulties are particularly evident in the field of *industrial and labour relations*, for instance with regard to employment and personnel policy, working conditions and systems of co-determination, but also in many fields of the economy, characterized by investment controls, foreign exchange controls, governmental aids and subsidies.

Very much to our regret, there is no trend visible towards harmonization of industrial and labour relations, working conditions and systems of co-determination in Europe. On the contrary, in the last two decades almost all European countries have followed their own co-determination policies in accordance with their specific conditions and necessities. It has also become clear to the supporters of European models for co-determination within the labour unions – it is well known that the German unions were amongst its strongest promoters – that these concepts cannot be realized and even should not be realized. Consequently, the German labour unions have given up their endeavours to convince others to move on the path towards parity co-determination in supervisory boards. If we look only at the development which has taken place within the last ten years in the Netherlands and in the Federal Republic of Germany, all we can state is that the newly introduced system of co-determination in the Netherlands – a system of co-optation to the supervisory board – cannot be compared at all in its procedures and effects to the German system of co-determination in supervisory boards which in 1976 was changed from a one third employees' participation to a nominal parity system for the major companies with more than 2000 employees.

VI. The Present Phase of Development

Looking at the present situation we find it full of inconsistencies and unclear. Let me first refer to the horizontal groups already dissolved or approaching dissolution.

A. Some Broken Marriages

After a married life of only 5 years, the co-operation between *Kléber-Colombes* and *Semperit*, by means of the Swiss holding company *Semkler* AG, came to an end in January 1979. In a joint statement both groups regretted the decision taken. They stressed the view that the original concept was still valid. Streamlined joint production programmes, improvements of the quality of the products by joint research and development, and exchange of products had brought about initial positive results. However, it had become clear that the detailed promising industrial and commercial plans already in an advanced stage of elaboration could not be realized due to unsurmountable difficulties within the two manufacturing companies in Austria and in France. Both companies were lacking the necessary structure to achieve a real international merger and to execute the existing plans. These somewhat delphic formulations are only a mild cover for the fact that the works councils of the Semperit plants strongly objected to the transfer of certain products to plants outside Austria in exchange for other products, as well as for certain measures of rationalization connected therewith. Taking into account the unions' influence on the Austrian Government and the dependence of Semperit on the financial support of its largest shareholder, Creditanstalt-Bankverein, owned and controlled by the Government, the venture could not survive the fact that no solution could be found to satisfy the Semperit works councils. Both groups continue to maintain a technical co-operation in some specific areas. In May 1980, plans for a majority share in *Kléber-Colombes* to be taken over by the German *Continental Gummi-Werke AG* were pending. In September 1980 the engagement was unexpectedly called off by Continental at the last moment. In 1979, Continental had absorbed the European tyre business of the US based *Uniroyal* group, thus becoming the second largest tyre manufacturer in Europe after *Michelin*. The rapid expansion and transformation of this German company into a European group by acquisitions in other European countries confirms the thesis that it seems to be easier and more efficient to follow this road rather than to create complicated horizontal groups.

Until a few months ago *Kléber-Colombes* was controlled by the Société Financière *Michelin*, and it should be mentioned, that in the 1960's the Michelin Group, which at that time also controlled Citroën, failed to bring about a joint Franco-Italian automobile group by combining *Fiat and Citroën*. The rather complicated concept of this planned horizontal group never reached the stage of realization. The pre-contractual agreements concluded, including a start-up shareholding of Fiat in Citroën, were vetoed by the French Government. Furthermore, it is likely that both sides became aware of the uneven balance between the automobile giant Fiat and its much weaker partner Citroën.

Another example of an unsuccessful cooperation is the *Fokker-VFW* case. In spite of a well defined and in some respects progressive organizational structure (which even aimed at a Dutch-German parity for the labour representatives in the Supervisory Board of the German holding company within the concept of the German Co-determination Act of 1976) the diverging interests of both sides could never be reconciled. It may be of interest that the High Court of Düsseldorf ruled on June 5, 1979 (Der Betrieb 79, 1451) that the workforce of a foreign subisidiary of a German holding company had no right to participate in the election of the labour representatives in the Supervisory Board of the German company. The Dutch *Fokker* Group wanted to exploit and expand its position in the Turboprop commercial aircraft field and to replace its successful F 27 and F 28 by a corresponding turbo-jet. This conflicted with the project of the German side to make a break-through with a new small economical 30 passenger and cargo jet for regional services and developing countries, an assumed gap in the market. The German side complained that the Fokker sales organisation – believed to be an important element from the German viewpoint – failed to promote the sale of the new VFW 614 jet because of its own long-term turbo-jet project. In fact, only very few planes could be sold. Finally, when additional problems arose concerning the choice of the engine, a costly flop was perfected. There was no chance of recovering the more than DM 500 million development expenditure, granted or financed by the German Government. From the VFW point of view, the Dutch side showed a lack of flexibility in integrating the manufacturing facilities and in rationalising production within the framework of a joint programme. Taking into account the losses as well as the tensions and the disagreement within the management, the Federal Government promoted the idea of a merger with the other German aircraft group MBB *(Messerschmitt-Bölkow-Blohm)*. The Dutch side at first refused to share the obligations incurred upon separation and played for time. As the VFW Bremen plant had by this time become fully engaged with activities for the airbus programme and had entered a positive phase, the divorce, being in the interest of both sides, was arranged for January 1st, 1979 on terms rather favourable for Fokker. The Fokker Group has now re-adopted its previous structure as a national manufacturer with links only in the field of technical co-operation, inter alia with a Japanese group. The restructuring and merger of the German aerospace-groups VFW and MBB has been negotiated in a long and difficult procedure under the guidance of the German Ministry of the Economy and was finished in December 1980 with MBB taking over VFW in exchange for 10 percent of its own shares and further consideration.

Reviewing the *Dunlop-Pirelli* development, it can be said, that the original concept via two holding companies to be shared on a 51:49 and 49:51 basis respectively could also not be maintained. Heavy losses in Italy since the venture was created in 1971 had to be shared by Dunlop (with a peak in 1973 of DM 300 million) and made the co-operation very difficult for the British side. Consequently, agreement was reached that Dunlop would abstain from participating in further capital investments in Italy. Dunlop's shareholding in Industrie Pirelli S. P. A. is now down to 30% and will decrease further to 19% as a consequence of a new rescue plan which became necessary in February of this year. A consortium of 7 Italian banks, with *Medio-Banca* at the top of the list together with the Italian mother company *Pirelli S. P. A.*, has subscribed the majority of a capital increase of approximately DM 150 million. The consortium has also consolidated substantial short-term borrowings and commitments of *Industrie Pirelli S. P. A.* As *Dunlop* did not contribute to the new capital injection its holding is now below 20%. It may be doubted whether the still existing Union Dunlop-Pirelli under these circumstances can be considered as a jointly managed and controlled horizontal group as originally planned. On the other hand, it has been stressed again and again that in spite of the losses and financial difficulties in Italy, the technical cooperation has proved to be efficient and fruitful. By April 1981 it had been decided that both holding companies should retransfer their respective minority participations in each other's subsidiaries; by the end of 1981 the marriage is to be finally dissolved.

B. Problem Marriages

Much to the surprise of business and of the public, the first horizontal group founded in the early 1960's is now also undergoing a drastic structural change. The so far very efficient and complementary co-operation of the *Agfa-Gevaert* Group will in the future not continue on the 50:50 basis originally agreed upon.

In spite of an upward trend in net sales (1978: DM 3.4 billion), investments (DM 206 million) and research and development expenses (DM 244 million), profitability remained always on a relatively modest level due to a highly competitive situation increasing within the last years, to unsuccessful marketing concepts and to rising raw material costs. Heavy losses incurred in 1979 (DM 118 million) led to the necessity of a substantial capital increase of DM 400 million. The shareholders of Gevaert were not prepared to contribute to this increase, for reasons which are not fully clear. By a first financial operation – increase of capital by DM 200 million – *Bayer's* share in the bi-national group will rise from 50% to 60%. This transaction has just been completed, after the necessary approval had been obtained from the German *Bundeskartellamt*. It is not very likely that the Belgian side will participate in a further capital increase already scheduled for 1981. In the event that *Gevaert Photo-Produkten N. V. Antwerpen* should fail to subscribe their 40% share, then Bayer's *Agfa* will have a call right that would gain it 100% of Agfa-Gevaert. For GPP, the consolation prize would be the acquisition of 2.5 million Bayer shares with an estimated value DM 325 million in exchange for their remaining 40% participation in *Agfa-Gevaert*. GPP would then become the largest single shareholder of Bayer owning about 6.5% of Bayer's equity. Adding to the current value of the Bayer shares of DM 325 million the two capital injections of DM 200 million each, the total cost of the transactions for Bayer would amount to DM 725 million. The first step of the operation already completed and the announcement of the possible future development has caused a storm of criticism inside Belgium, for Gevaert is a touchy symbol of Flemish industrial know-how and activity. Therefore, it is certainly feasible that considerable pressure will be exerted on the main shareholders of Gevaert to subscribe to the capital increase due this year or in early 1982. As the Belgian President of the joint Managing Board of Directors, Mr. Leysen, pointed out, there are barriers to a "Belgian solution" mounted by the Government and the use of State funds would unavoidably cause great problems for the Belgian-German partnership. It is intended to maintain the bi-national structure of the group in the management. Whether in the long run this is possible or not, will depend very much on the future economic development of the group (which in 1980 turned out to be unexpectedly good, with gains of DM 63 million) and the future attitude of the Belgian side with regard to the further capital injection required. The cost of moving closer to Bayer could, of course, as the Financial Times wrote, be "the end of what was Europe's first transnational merger". I should mention that Agfa-Gevaert have already announced in their Annual Report for 1978 that they would abstain in the future from publishing consolidated accounts of the group, for which a special scheme had been elaborated. It looks as if this decision was taken not only because of the evident difficulties of such an operation (with a number of special problems for a Belgian-German group) or with a view to the expected Seventh Directive of the European Commission on Consolidated Group Accounts, but rather in anticipation of the already planned change from a 50:50 to a 60:40 relationship of the partners.

The group *Estel–Hoogovens–Hoesch* was conceived as a complementary partnership: Hoogovens' steelplants on the seashore and Hoesch's converting and manufacturing capacities tied together to achieve optimal results. The group had to share the ups and downs of the development of the European steel industry of the 1970's. Initial substantial losses in steel-making in the Netherlands were followed by losses in converting and manufacturing of steel-products incurred by the German plants. As the organisational and legal structure seems to be well-founded the group has so far always been able to cope with changing and sometimes difficult circumstances. The question was raised from time to time whether the Dutch or the German side was favoured by the business policy followed by the joint group management. Inactivity in modernising certain steel units in Germany led to criticisms by labour unions and the press in 1979, particularly after the Estel Board had announced that it might become necessary to close down certain production facilities and dismiss 15,000 workers and employees, unless the German Government would be prepared to finance the setting up of a new oxygen-steelplant, in which case only 4,000 jobs would be lost. After lengthy discussions the Federal Government decided to grant an easy loan of DM 240 million to the group's operating company in Germany, a fact which was received badly by press and business because of its impact for the other private steel groups.

To round off the picture it can be said that only the less known specialized joint ventures are or seem to be really successful and stable. An outstanding example for this type of horizontal groups is the *Polygram* group, jointly run by *Siemens and Philips*. But the same partners made a mistake in trying to bring about a European co-operation in the computer industry, when in 1973 they founded *Unidata* together with the French *Compagnie Internationale pour l'Informatique* (CII). The French were hesitant because they feared that they might be dominated by their partners and started flirting with *Honeywell*. This again was unacceptable for Siemens. In addition, there was disagreement between CII and Siemens on the sale of CII computers and equipment in the Federal Republic. When the French Government announced a merger between *CII and Honeywell-Bull*, the co-operation came to an end in May 1975, after a lifespan of only two years.

VII. Conclusions and Prospects

What conclusions can be drawn from this rather gloomy picture. First of all, as an outline of the reasons for the unsuccessful development in Europe of most of the horizontal groups (excluding specialized joint ventures for the moment) the reasons for the relative failure are manifold and vary from case to case. They do not allow direct comparisons to be made. Nevertheless, it can be said that the lack of political integration within the European Community, and the growing interest, influence and interference of national governments and of national policies on the structure of industry, together with national aids and subsidies, certainly had a negative impact on the development of horizontal groups. Diverging economic and social developments between the Member States of the

European Community, characterized by entirely different inflation rates, completely different attitudes of labour unions with regard to wage policy, working conditions and codetermination rights and procedures, and, last but not least, differing financial results achieved and losses incurred in different countries, did a great deal to weaken the sensitive and complicated bi-national structures of horizontal groups in Europe. Generally speaking, the economic and social climate and environment in Europe has become considerably less favourable to horizontal groups since the first recession and oil crisis of 1974/75. It is interesting to note that since then no new bi-national horizontal groups have appeared on the European scene. On the contrary, the trend towards dissolution or towards far reaching structural changes with regard to the existing horizontal groups became visible in the middle of the Seventies. It cannot be excluded also that the slowing down, if not the temporary stagnation, of the development towards a harmonization of the European company laws and, even more so, tax laws has contributed to the process of dissolving existing horizontal groups and to the growing scepticism towards the setting up of new bi-national ventures. The relatively modest results of the Fourth Directive of the European Commission on the harmonization of accounts and annual reports which maintains many substantial differences – for example with regard to the treatment of fixed assets – cannot resolve the problems of uniform accounting methods with which bi-national groups are confronted.

There is another important element which seems to block the development of bi-national horizontal groups. After more than twenty years' experience with using the legal and fiscal instruments and institutions of other European countries, even medium and small size companies know how to proceed when the idea of a technical co-operation or the need for expansion by acquisition or foundation of an affiliate comes up. The economic, social and legal conditions of the other European countries are sufficiently known or can be made available by highly qualified lawyers, accountants, auditors and merchant banks. In addition, there is the experience of other companies, which can be consulted within the frame of the many associations of industry. Thus, the trend in industry is – in line with the development towards a Europe of Nations, in the sense of increasing national influences – in favor of the adjustment of varying national conditions in Europe rather than towards complex bi-national horizontal groups. For this reason in my view, horizontal groups are not a main subject for the projects of laws of groups of companies in Europe and for the Seventh Directive of the European Commission.

Recent announcements seem to illustrate and to confirm the general trend towards expansion on a national basis and towards specialized bi-national joint-ventures. A few examples may underline this: Europe's four largest helicopter makers have entered into or are preparing for a series of joint attacks on the world helicopter market, which is being expanded by rising military tension and a boom in offshore oil-drilling. There are new joint-ventures and joint projects between *British Westland Helicopter Ltd.* and *Augusta S. p. A.* of Italy; West-Germany's *Messerschmitt-Bölkow-Blohm AG* and *Aérospatiale S. A.*, the French state-owned combine. *Fiat* and *Peugeot-Citroën*, already collaborating in joint ventures in Southern Italy in the field of light commercial vehicles as well as in Argentina, have joined forces to set up a joint-venture for the manufacture of certain types of engines and gears. The objective, as announced, is to rationalize the manufacture of automotive components in order to obtain the necessary economies of scale. This special form of co-operation will include the acquisition of a participation of 5 per cent in the car manufacturing company of the Fiat Group and the acquisition of a 30 per cent participation in Iveco N. V., the Dutch Fiat holding company, in which the international activities of the Fiat Group in the field of heavy commercial vehicles are concentrated. As mentioned already, *Continental Gummiwerke AG* had plans to take over from the Michelin Group the majority of *Kléber-Colombes S. A.*, a clear case of expansion with no elements of a bi-national structure. Also the acquisition of a 20 per cent share in *Olivetti S. p. A.* by the French glass and computer giant *Saint Gobain S. A.* cannot be considered as a step towards a new bi-national horizontal group but rather towards integration of the financially weak Olivetti Group into the larger frame of the Saint Gobain Group. This is underlined by the fact that half the seats of the Board of Olivetti S. p. A. will be taken by representatives of Saint Gobain, whereas the President and co-owner of Olivetti S. p. A. will join the Board of Saint Gobain only "à titre personnel".

It looks as if the signals for the further development of industrial organisations in Europe are clearly set. Nevertheless, the possibility cannot be excluded that under special circumstances – maybe under the impact of the far-reaching structural changes with which industry in Europe will be confronted in the 1980's – new needs for fully integrated combines and not only for specialized joint-ventures may arise again.

Résumé:

Groupes horizontaux et filiales communes en Europe: concepts et réalité

Le rapport traite des groupes horizontaux et des filiales communes dans l'expérience pratique de la fin des années soixante-dix qui a transformé les bases du débat économique et juridique et a rendu périmé beaucoup de ce qui avait été dit et cru auparavant. Les groupes horizontaux et les filiales communes en Europe peuvent être caractérisés comme des entités bi-nationales qui, en raison de la carence d'une loi européenne uniforme, ont été créées et sont régies par les instruments et sur la base des lois nationales existantes. L'intention principale du rapport est de décrire le développement concret et la situation réelle de ces groupes et des filiales communes ainsi que l'environnement et le cadre dans lesquels ils fonctionnent (par exemple Agfa-Gevaert, Dunlop-Pirelli, Hoesch-Hoogovens-Estel, Enka, Polygram, Unidata etc.). En premier lieu les motifs et les objectifs de la création des groupes horizontaux bilatéraux à la fin des années soixante sont analysés ainsi que les concepts et les techniques de réalisation. Puis le rapport offre une évaluation et une comparaison rétrospectives des conceptions et des perspectives d'un corps de droit européen en expansion relatif aux sociétés et aux groupes horizontaux en Europe, tels qu' ils ont été réalisés en pratique. Nous avons ensuite une discussion détaillée sur la situation actuelle des groupes horizontaux. En général l'industrie approuve l'ajustement aux diverses conditions nationales en Europe plutôt que l'organisation de groupes horizontaux bi-nationaux complexes. La tendance générale va vers l'élargissement d'une base nationale et vers des filiales communes bi-nationales spécialisées. Enfin différentes perspectives sont proposées sur les développements futurs.

Chapter/Chapitre II

Groups of Companies in Major European Laws

Les groupes de sociétés dans les droits européens

The German Experience with the Law of Affiliated Enterprises

HERBERT WIEDEMANN
Cologne

I. Starting Point, Legal Rules and Legal Facts

A. Theoretical Foundations

1. The Concept of the Affiliated Enterprise

To understand the West German law on affiliated or combined companies (*Konzernrecht* in the broadest sense of the term) it is important to recall the concept of reality which statute, case law and legal theory take as their starting point: we shall view the law concerning affiliated enterprise as a *special law of conduct for a dominating enterprise in relation to the management of a controlled – usually through a majority participation – and therefore dependent commercial company.*

a) Internal Equilibrium Upset by Unequal Distribution of Participations and Control

The whole of West German company law proceeds upon the assumption that in an independent commercial company there exists an internal equilibrium among the shareholders, and that therefore ideally both the basic decisions and the conduct of management are oriented around the common company interest. The interests of creditors and employees are thereby simultaneously and indirectly protected. As is well known, such a pre-stabilized harmony is endangered as soon as one shareholder, or a coherent group of shareholders, acquires a majority of the shares, since they can then take advantage of their influence, which grows disproportionately large, to pursue their own interests at the cost of the other groups relevant under company law. These dangers are reinforced, firstly, by any increase in the number of shares owned; and secondly, if the controlling member is active in an enterprise outside of the company, i. e., when an outside enterprise gains a controlling influence. The dominant enterprise activity gives cause to fear that the dependent company will be made subservient to the outside enterprise's interests. It is especially likely, moreover, that a controlling enterprise-shareholder will use its opportunities for influence and authority to the disadvantage of the dependent company and its undertakings if it is itself engaged in an enterprise active in the same market or in an area of production or distribution in the neighbourhood of this market. The preservation of the dependent company's own interests becomes improbable or impossible if the controlling enterprise uses its influence not only to affect business decisions but also to transform the organizational structure and incorporates the operations of the dependent company as operational divisions into its own enterprise structure.

b) Protecting Dependent Enterprises While Maintaining Independent Units

At what point in the above spectrum of endangerment a cut should be made and a special right for the protection of the enterprise be developed, can be variously judged. The West German view, as expressed in the Stock Corporation Law of 1965 (AktG 1965),[1] is that the essential qualitative change lies in the company's potentially becoming dependent upon an outside enterprise (cf. sec. 17 AktG). Every controlling enterprise is not thereby automatically suspected of exploiting the subsidiary company: normally an enterprise-shareholder is interested in preserving and promoting dependent companies. The difference still remains, however, in that the direction of the enterprise is externally controlled and that the dependent company will in all probability conduct itself differently than if it were an independent company. The sharp division which German law draws between the (non-suspect) controlling individual shareholder and the (suspect) controlling enterprise is justified in that the latter brings about a change of policy.

The regulatory perspective which starts with the dependent enterprise, i. e., "*from below to above*", is fundamental for understanding the law on affiliated enterprises and the interpretation of the legislative provisions and influences even the interpretation of the individual sections of the Stock Corporation Law.[2] This regulatory perspective is made clearer through comparison with the Anglo-American legal system. The United States law relating to corporations perceived the problem of affiliated enterprises primarily as arising in connection with the acquisition by one company of a participation in another company, which was originally limited by the *ultra vires* doctrine. If one accepts this "from above to below" approach, the principal question is whether and in what way the organization and responsibility of the dominant enterprise are altered by its acquisition of participatory holdings. The question as to whether and, if so, which rights are created for the shareholders of the dependent company in view of this intrusion of an outside enterprise (which is thoroughly considered under the "from below to above" approach) arises only secondarily.[3]

[1] Most legislative provisions concerning affiliated Enterprises are contained in the *Aktiengesetz* 1965, (hereinafter referred to as AktG *or* Stock Corporation Law of 1965), which contains definitions concerning enterprise connections (*see* esp. secs. 15-19) and a special Book on associated enterprises (Book Three: Connected Enterprises, secs. 291-338) (referred to as the Law of Affiliated Enterprises or *Konzernrecht*). For an English translation of these special provisions, see *infra* Annex II.1, pp. 265 *et seq.*

[2] *Cf.* 62 BGHZ 193 at 197 ("Seitz AG").

[3] *See* M. A. Eisenberg, *Mega-Subsidiaries: The Effect of Corporate Structure on Corporate Control*, 84 HARV. L. REV. 1577 (1971).

The idea of affiliated enterprises, i.e. of a company (or companies) dependent upon another enterprise, contains at the same time both the notion of distinct units of organization and of property which remain legally independent. West German law in general rejects the economic or enterprise view of groups, which makes a distinction between, on the one hand, the independent companies which form a part of the group, and, on the other hand, the group, treating the latter as an independent unit with a separate identity. The *idea of unity*, or the entity concept, can sometimes determine whether certain provisions will be applied in a particular case, but recourse to this doctrine always retains the character of an exception.[4]

2. Legal Consequences

a) Neutrality Concerning Competition Policy

The Stock Corporation Law excludes from its consideration the consequences of the economic concentration which occurs in the competitive market as a result of the linking of enterprises. The norms of company law are drafted so as to be *neutral in respect of competition*.[5]

b) No Legal Recognition of Independent Organs of the Group

The Stock Corporation Law knows no separate organs of the combine *(Konzern)*; on the contrary, the duties of the combine are assumed by the competent organs of the dominant enterprise, depending upon its legal structure. The law provides for no participation by the subordinate companies or by their shareholders in the direction of the group enterprise.

c) Protection of Dependent Enterprises while Maintaining Independence of the Units

The Law of Affiliated Enterprises confines itself to protecting the parties relevant under company law of the *dependent company*, without making changes in the dominant enterprise. Within the dominant company, the management of company-held shares falls within the general duties of management; if the dominant company incorporates its production facilities into its subsidiary companies, organs of the dominant company, especially the shareholders' meeting, will thereby lose their power of influence over certain fundamental organisational questions – and possibly even their rights to information.[6] This

[4] *See* E. Rehbinder, Konzernaussenrecht und allgemeines Privatrecht, p. 50 *et seq.* (Bad Homburg, 1969); Bundesministerium der Justiz, Bericht über die Verhandlungen der Unternehmensrechtskommission, No. 1246 *et seq.* (Bonn, 1980). *See contra*, U. Bälz, *Einheit und Vielheit im Konzern*, in Festschrift für L. Raiser, pp. 287-338 (Tübingen, 1974).

[5] For a comparison of company and antitrust law *see* H. Wiedemann, Gesellschaftsrecht, Volume I, § 13 I, p. 712 *et seq.* (Munich, 1980).

[6] *See* M. Lutter, *Die Rechte der Gesellschafter beim Abschluß fusionsähnlicher Unternehmensverbindungen*, Supplement No. 21 to 1973 Betrieb; *id.*, *Zur Binnenstruktur des Konzerns*, in Festschrift für H. Westermann, p. 347 (Karlsruhe, 1974); W. Timm, Die Aktiengesellschaft als Konzernspitze (Cologne, 1980); U. Schneider, *Die Miterverwal-*

problem was overlooked by the legislator and it has only occasionally appeared in case-law.[7] Proposals to overcome this problem, e.g. by creating a special combine organ (the shareholders' committee) in the dominant enterprise, have so far not been widely discussed.

d) Failure to Cover the Process of Group Formation

The law concerning affiliated companies governs the *existing structure* of the affiliated enterprises rather than the *process of combine formation*. This accounts for the fact that important components of any law concerning the affiliation of enterprises are not covered by the statute and have been treated by scholars only sporadically (for example, insider trading, take-over bids, sale of control etc.). Legal control should begin earlier, i. e., already during the formation of the affiliated enterprise, in order, in the interest of other shareholders, creditors and employees, to make penetration by an outside enterprise impossible or at least dependent upon the fulfilment of certain conditions.[8]

B. The Legislative Framework

1. Companies Falling within the Scope of the Provision

a) Stock Corporations or Associations Limited by Shares

Only one sector of affiliated enterprises is governed by statute, since the relevant statute, the AktG 1965, is limited in its application to a stock corporation *(Aktienschaft)* or association limited by shares *(Kommanditgesellschaft auf Aktien)* which is dependent upon another enterprise. The provisions of AktG sections 15 et seq. and 291 et seq. thus presuppose that a stock company or association limited by shares is involved as a party, that is, in the party role established by the statute. It is sufficient for the other party that it be an "enterprise". For all those enterprises conducted under another form of business association (e. g., partnerships, limited partnerships, limited liability companies, co-operative associations) and which are dependent upon another enterprise there are no statutory provisions; at most the provisions of the Stock Corporation Law can be referred to by analogy.

b) Other Forms of Association

The Introductory Law to the Stock Corporation Law (EG AktG) contains a minor enlargement: it extends to certain cases of a combine directed by a limited liability company (GmbH) the duty to draw up a consolidated financial statement, as well as the examination and publication provisions (cf. sec. 28 EG

tungsrechte der Gesellschafter in der verbundenen GmbH in DER GMBH-KONZERN, p. 78 (Cologne, 1976); BERICHT DER UNTERNEHMENSRECHTSKOMMISSION, *supra* note 4, No. 1258 *et seq.*

[7] *Cf.* 25 BGHZ 115 at 118 (KG); BGH, 1973 WM 170 (KG).

[8] *Cf.* on this point, P. Behrens, 1975 ZGR 433; U. Immenga, 1970 BB 629; H. Wiedemann, 1978 ZGR 486.

AktG). However, proposals for a general law on limited liability company-combines have not been enacted.[9]

Special provisions for co-determination in combines are found in sections 5 and 32 MitbestG 1976 and in sec. 15 MitbestErgG. They provide that the rights incumbent upon a codetermined enterprise by virtue of a participation in another codetermined enterprise may be exercised, in the case of certain decisions on enterprise and personnel policy, by the organ of the enterprise authorized as legal representative only upon the basis of a resolution of the supervisory board.

2. *The System of the Statute Law*

a) General Definitions Concerning Connected Enterprises

Secs. 15-19 AktG contain definitions of forms of enterprise connection; the legal consequences of these various forms are elaborated elsewhere in the statute.[10] The *central concept* is *dependence (Abhängigkeit)*, which is defined in sec. 17 par. 1 AktG: a company is dependent if the possibility exists that a dominant enterprise can either directly or indirectly exercise influence upon it. The combine *(Konzern)*, the most intensive form of enterprise affiliation, presupposes that a dominant enterprise and one or more dependent enterprises be combined under the sole management of the dominant enterprise (*cf.* sec. 18 AktG). A dependent enterprise is presumed to have formed a combine with the dominant enterprise. In addition to this form of combine of subordination, sec. 18 par. 2 AktG also defines a combine of coordination; no difference exists in the legal consequences. Finally, in sec. 19 AktG the statute provides a definition of mutually participating enterprises.

b) Substantive Provisions

The provisions on affiliated enterprises in secs. 291-338 AktG form the heart of the statute. The structure of these provisions, however, is confused, because they deal partly with the acts of organization (such as enterprise contracts in secs. 291-307 and integration in secs. 319-327 AktG) and partly with the legal consequences resulting from the organizational structure already existing (power to direct in secs. 308-318 and mutual participation in sec. 328 AktG).

(1) Contracts of Control and/or of Transfer of Profits (Contractual Combines)

The most important enterprise contracts are the control and transfer-of-profits contracts. The conclusion of an agreement at any given time presupposes that the shareholders' meetings of both companies have agreed to its conclusion with a

[9] *Cf.* sec. 230 *et seq.* of the Government Proposal for a GmbH-Law of January 31, 1972. Critically on this ARBEITSKREIS GMBH-REFORM, *see* THESEN UND VORSCHLÄGE, Vol. II, *infra* note 16, at p. 47 *et seq.*

[10] Legal consequences of dependence are found esp. in secs. 18 par. 1, 20, 21, 56 par. 2, 71, 89 par. 2, 100 par. 2, 116 par. 1, 134 par. 1, 136 par. 2, 145 par. 3, 165 par. 4, 311, *et seq.* Legal consequences of forming a combine group are found, *inter alia*, in sec. 134 par. 1, 145 par. 3,160 par. 3, 165 par. 4 and in sec. 329 *et seq.* AktG.

majority sufficient to change the articles of incorporation. Moreover, the contract must be entered in the trade register to take effect. The contract of control empowers the dominant enterprise to take over control; the management of the dependent company is obligated to follow its directions unless they obviously do not serve the interests of the dominant enterprise or the enterprises affiliated with it.

A transfer-of-profits contract obliges the dependent enterprise to transfer its total profit to the dominant enterprise, so that after the conclusion of the agreement the dependent company no longer generates retained earnings. On the other hand, the dominant enterprise is then obliged to make up for accumulated losses of the dependent enterprise.

The statute also concerns itself with the modalities of the conclusion and termination of the contract, especially with the protection of creditors (secs. 300-303 AktG) and of so-called outside shareholders (secs. 304-307 AktG). Creditors are protected through the duty of the dominant enterprise to assume losses. Outside shareholders must be offered an exchange of shares for those of the dominant enterprise or a settlement in cash and in addition and at their election, a fixed or variable indemnity (dividend guaranty).

(2) De facto Combines

If there is no contract of control, the independence of the dependent company should be preserved as far as possible. For this reason the statute prohibits the dominant enterprise from prejudicing the interests of the dependent company. Directions of the dominant enterprise must, however, be followed, even when they involve detriment to the dependent company, if at the same time the dominant enterprise makes up for the detriment in question or, at least, gives a promise of early compensation (cf. secs. 311 AktG). In order to secure the duty to compensate for the detriment, every dependent company must report each year the measures of the dominant enterprise and, especially, the individual transactions with it; this so-called dependence report must be examined and confirmed by the auditor of the dependent company (*cf.* sec. 312 et seq. AktG). If the rules for detriment compensation and the dependence report are disregarded, the dominant enterprise and its organs become liable for the detriment to the dependent company in accordance with secs. 317 and 318 AktG.

(3) Integration

Integration in accordance with sec. 319 et seq. AktG presupposes that the dominant company possesses 95% or more of the dependent company's shares. Upon entering the integration in the trade register all shares pass over to the dominant company by operation of law and the outside shareholders must be compensated either with shares of the dominant company or in cash. The integrated stock corporation is no longer obligated to publish an annual report, but still remains in existence as an independent legal person with its own organs (management board and supervisory board).

(4) Mutual Participation

Mutually participating enterprises are not obligated, as in the French legal system, to sell their shares; they must, however, report to each other the exact amount of the mutual participation and any possible changes. Moreover, the voting and preemptive rights are suspended for both parties (cf., for details, secs. 19 par. 2, 136 par. 2 and 328 AktG).

(5) Group Accounts
If a contractual or de facto combine exists, then the dominant company, if it is a stock corporation or limited liability company, must prepare a consolidated financial statement (sec. 329 et seq. AktG). The consolidated financial statement proceeds upon the basis of the unity of the affiliated enterprises; consequently, intermediate gains or losses are disregarded and the actual economic situation of the total combine is presented.

(6) General Information Requirements
Irrespective of whether they are dependent or form a combine, enterprises which hold more than 25% of the shares of a stock corporation are obliged under sec. 20 AktG to keep the latter suitably informed. The corporation in question must in turn pass this information on to its own shareholders. The duty must be repeated if the 50% mark is exceeded.

C. Case Law

In the law of the limited liability company (GmbH) and of partnerships (civil partnerships/GbR, partnerships/OHG, limited partnerships/KG), the development of the law of affiliated enterprises is not extensive.

1. Dependent Limited Liability Companies

For the limited liability company dependent upon another enterprise there exist two leading cases of the Federal Supreme Court *(Bundesgerichtshof)*, which treat responsibility and liability.

In the *ITT* case,[11] the BGH (Commercial Law Division) ruled that it follows from the fact that it is possible for the majority, through the exercise of its influence upon management, to prejudice the interests of the co-shareholders that there is a duty on the majority to take due consideration of the interests of the minority (duty of good faith); upon violation of this duty through prejudicial directions the majority shall be liable to the minority in accordance with sec. 43 GmbHG; in addition, each GmbH-shareholder is granted a personal claim as shareholder.[12]

In *Typenhausbau-GmbH,*[13] the BGH (Civil Liability Division) refused to pierce the corporate veil of a dominant enterprise, even though the dependent

[11] 65 BGHZ 15.

[12] *Cf.* on this decision, K. Brezing, 1976 AG 5; E. Rehbinder, 1976 ZGR 386; W. Schilling, 1975 BB 1451; P. Ulmer, 1976 NJW 192; H. P. Westermann, 1976 GmbH-Rdsch 77; H. Wiedemann, 1976 JZ 392. *See also* BGH, 1981 WM 357.

[13] 68 BGHZ 312.

company was linked through property and personnel with the dominant enterprise and was, moreover, demonstrably undercapitalized.[14]

No uniform or even prevailing view has yet been formed in legal theory.[15] The proposals of the GmbH Reform Committee,[16] which worked out a scheme for the strict regulation of the qualified enterprises, are trail-blazing.

2. Dependent Partnerships

Even less developed is the law of the dependent partnership. So far there exists only one important case.

In *Gervais AG*,[17] the BGH held a dominant enterprise to be obligated to prove for its part that it had not used its influence on a dependent limited partnership in a manner contrary to good faith; moreover, a dominant enterprise shall generally be obligated to assume losses if it has incorporated the dependent company in such a manner that it can uncontrolledly encroach upon the partnership property.

Preliminary treatments of the law of affiliated partnership enterprises can now be found in the literature in this field.[18]

D. Legal Facts

1. Statistical Data

Reliable material on affiliated enterprises exists only concerning enterprise contracts with dependent stock corporations. According to the data of Huechting,[19] in 1971 there existed 287 contracts of control with stock corporations, of which 101 contracts were concluded after the enactment of the AktG 1965. A personal study conducted on the basis of the summaries contained in the magazine "*Die Aktiengesellschaft*" revealed the following statistics for the years 1970-79.

It can be determined from these figures that more than half of all the contracts concluded both annually and overall, are at one and the same time contracts both of control and for the transfer of profits. Since 1977 a decline in the conclusion of enterprise contracts can be ascertained; in 1978 and 1979 only half as many contracts were concluded as in previous years. This decline can be observed in all

[14] *Cf.* on this decision, V. Emmerich, 1977 NJW 2163; G. Kuhn, 1978 WM 598; M. Lutter and P. Hommelhoff, 1979 ZGR 31, 62 *et seq.;* K. Schmidt, 1977 NJW 1449; H. Wiedemann, Gesellschaftsrecht, Vol. I, pp. 225, 565 *et seq.* (Munich, 1980).

[15] *Cf.* on this point, the overview in F. Scholz & V. Emmerich, Kommentar zum GmbH-Gesetz, Appendix II (Die GmbH als verbundenes Unternehmen) with references contained therein (Cologne, 6th ed., 1978).

[17] BGH» 1979 WM 937.

[18] *Cf.* esp. U. H. Schneider, 1975 ZGR 253-293; *id.*, ZHR 485-521 (1979).

[16] Arbeitskreis GmbH-Reform of 31 Jan. 1972, (= Arbeitskreis Gesellschaftsrecht); Thesen und Vorschläge zur GmbH-Reform, Vol. II, pp. 45-70 (Heidelberg, 1972).

[19] H. J. Huechting Abfindung und Ausgleich im aktienrechtlichen Beherrschungsvertrag, p. 2 *et seq.* (Cologne, 1972).

Table 1
Number of Enterprise Contracts since 1970

Contracts to transfer profits	33
Contracts for partial transfer of profits	6
Contracts of control	20
Contracts to transfer profits and of control	110
Management and shop leasing contracts	20
Profit pools	3
Total enterprise contracts	192
Devoid of application or terminated	−59
Total additional enterprise contracts since 1970	133

Note: In this presentation only the enterprise contracts published (not: concluded) between 1970 and 1979 are included. Left out of consideration are contracts which could not clearly be categorized; they would slightly increase the total number of concluded contracts. Also left out of consideration are, finally, the alterations or extensions of already existing enterprise contracts.

kinds of enterprise contract, so that since 1978 some kinds have not been concluded at all; others (for example, the simultaneous contracts to transfer profits and of control) only appear in very much reduced scope (approximately one half of the earlier agreements). The introduction of the set-off procedure in the corporate tax reform in 1977 can be suspected as the cause.

We can assume that these contracts are concluded primarily by a few major enterprises. For example, there exist in the *Thyssen-Konzern* alone 89 control and transfer-of-profits contracts, which are, however, for the most part more than 10 years old.

For de facto dependent stock corporations and for the affiliated enterprise of the remaining types of companies reliable data are lacking. According to information given by Geßler,[20] in 1965 70% of all stock corporations and 20% of private liability companies were already dependent enterprises.

2. *Tax and Other Motives for the Formation of Enterprise Contract*

The motive for the conclusion of an enterprise contract is not only the intention to assume rights and duties under company law, in accordance with sec. 291 et seq. AktG, but also the desire to obtain tax advantages. The purpose of the special affiliated enterprise tax provisions is primarily to avoid multiple taxation.

In this regard the most important kind of tax is the corporate income tax, which concerns enterprise profits. Multiple taxation of the profits of the subsidiary corporation is avoided if the income of the subsidiary is first attributed to the dominant enterprise and is taxed there. The prerequisites for the

[20] E. Geßler, 1965 BB 677-681; *id.*, 1966 GmbH-Rdsch. 102 at 104.

recognition of such a consolidated group in tax law *(Organschaft)* are basically (according to sec. 14 KStG 1977):

(1) The existence of a contract for the transfer of profits; and,

(2) Organic incorporation, which in turn requires financial, economic and organizational incorporation.

The transfer-of-profits contract, which is concluded for five years and must be performed, thus represents a necessary, but not a sufficient, condition for the consolidated group in corporate income tax law. In addition, the incorporation of the consolidated subsidiary into the enterprise structure of the consolidated group representative, whose characteristics are only partially defined by statute, is necessary. A financial incorporation exists when the group representative possesses the majority of the voting rights in the shares of the consolidated subsidiary (cf. 14 Nr. 1 KStG 1977). Economic incorporation is present when the controlled company is incorporated into the enterprise structure of the consolidated group representative in the manner of a dependent operational division and, in this function, furthers or completes the industrial activity of the dominant enterprise (cf. sec. 14 Nr. 2 KStG 1977 and part 50 KStR). Organisational incorporation is irrebuttably presumed if a contract of control or an integration under company law are present; otherwise it must be guaranteed that the will of the group representative is actually executed (cf. sec. 14 Nr. 2 KStG 1977 and part 51 KStR). The tax law thus explicitly requires only the existence of a contract for the transfer of profits, but not a contract of control. The contract of control eases, however, the proof of the organic incorporation under tax law.

One legal consequence of the formation of a consolidated group in tax law is the attribution of the income under corporate income tax law (not the commercial law profit) of the dependent company to the income of the group representative, where it is taxed. In the separate determination of income, the goods and service transactions between the group enterprises are treated as those between unrelated third parties, and deemed profits resulting therefrom are accordingly assessed. In contrast, the transfer of profits under commercial law is ignored. Since, as a result of the set-off procedure introduced in the new corporate tax statute, corporate double taxation is eliminated, one reason for the legal structure of the consolidated group has disappeared. It has, however, been retained because it offers certain advantages as against the set-off procedure. On the one hand, the attribution makes possible a set-off of the losses of one enterprise against the profits of another in the same accounting period, without any need to use loss carry-backs or carry-forwards which are subject to time limitations (sec. 10 (d) EStG). On the other hand, tax-free income items of a consolidated subsidiary, which are subject to a dividend tax rate of 36% under the set-off procedure (sec. 27 par. 1 KStG 1977), are in the consolidated group passed on tax-free to the consolidated group representative. Additional advantages may arise for group representatives subject to the personal income tax regime (such as sole proprietors or partnerships); in this case the entire income of the dependent company and the group representative is taxed only at the personal income tax rate applicable to the group representative. If this lies beneath the top corporate tax rate of 56%, tax savings result. The same holds true for reserves of the consolidated subsidiary (sec. 14 Nr. 5 KStG 1977) and for expenses non-deductible under the corporate income tax (secs. 9, 10 KStG 1977).[21]

II. The Experience with the Law of Affiliated Enterprises of the Stock Corporation Law

A. Scope of the Law of Affiliated Enterprises

1. The Concept of "Enterprise"

Since the applicability of the special rules of company law is determined by the existence of a *dominant "enterprise"*, the definition thereof in the framework of company law is of great importance; the details are controversial in legal theory and have not yet been resolved by case law.

In the literature various definitions of the enterprise concept are offered, which one can characterize roughly as broad/narrow and uniform/differentiated. Concerning the first alternative, the broad or functional theory maintains that it is sufficient that a shareholder plans and determines the company's market strategy, for simply by doing so he, she or it becomes a dominant enterprise. Thus practically every majority shareholder is at the same time a dominant enterprise. In contrast, the narrow or institutional theory requires that the dominant enterprise be active in industry outside of the dependent company. Thus holding companies would be excluded a priori. The compromise, and prevalent, opinion tends today in the following direction: an enterprise is always present if a majority shareholder holds (potentially) a controlling participation in several companies and, in addition, is (actually) active as an entrepreneur in at least one enterprise.[22] The *pure investor-shareholder* is thus not a dominant entrepreneur, but certainly a holding company which in the case of even one subsidiary exceeds mere management of the participation interest will be. The discussion concerning the uniform/differentiated distinction centres around whether instead of a uniform enterprise concept, a definition differentiated

[21] The reasons for affiliated enterprises as such are a variety of business and market considerations. *See esp.* V. EMMERICH & J. SONNENSCHEIN, KONZERNRECHT, p. 6 *et seq.* (Munich, 2d ed. 1977); H. O. LENEL, URSACHEN DER KONZENTRATION (Tübingen, 2d ed., 1968). On the present state of economic concentration *see* MONOPOLKOMMISSION: HAUPTGUTACHTEN 1973/1975 [Monopolies Commission, Main Report 1973/1975] (Baden-Baden, 2d ed. 1977); HAUPTGUTACHTEN 1976/1977 (Baden-Baden, 1978); HAUPTGUTACHTEN 1978/1979, BTDrs 8/4404 (1980). *See also*, K. Hopt, *Merger Control in Germany: Philosophies, Experience, Reforms* in K. HOPT, ed., EUROPEAN MERGER CONTROL (Volume I of LEGALAND ECONOMIC ANALYSES OF MULTINATIONAL ENTERPRISES), pp. 71 *et seq.* (Berlin, New York, 1981).

[22] *See* E. Geßler in FESTSCHRIFT FÜR KNUR, p. 145, 148 (Munich, 1973); H. Wiedemann and K. J. Martens, 1976 AG 197, 201; W. Zöllner, 1976 ZGR 1, 17 *et seq.; contra,* V. EMMERICH & J. SONNENSCHEIN, *supra* note 22, at pp. 37, 38 (with references).

according to the purpose of the individual rules in question should not be utilized.[23]

Special problems appear for ***publicly owned enterprises,*** i. e., companies in which the Federal Republic of Germany, federal states or municipalities are shareholders. Contrary to the prevailing view in the literature, the Federal Supreme Court found for the enterpreneurial nature of the Federal Government and thus for the basic applicability of the entire law of affiliated enterprises.[24] In support of this finding, in the opinion of the Court, is the fact that a state-owned entity should be treated as a private economic enterprise if it employs the legal form of private law.

2. *The Concept of "Dependence"*

Dependence of the company upon its *majority shareholder* is presumed in law (cf. secs. 17 par. 2, 16 AktG). There are various responses to the question whether a relationship of dependence under the law of affiliated enterprises can in addition be based upon a debtor-creditor relationship or factual foundation, i. e., whether economic dependence should be relevant in company law. In case law and legal theory the concept of dependence is broadly conceived.[25]

Joint ventures (Gemeinschaftsunternehmen), i. e., companies in which exclusively other enterprises participate (cf. sec. 23 par. 2 sentence 3 GWB) also present special problems. Here we face the question whether a company can be dependent at the same time on several dominant enterprises (multiple parent consolidated group). Case law affirms the possibility of multiple dependence of joint ventures, if the coordination of the conduct of the parent enterprises is regularly guaranteed.[26] This case law is, on the whole, welcomed by legal theory. The provisions, which start from a dependence or consolidated group fact pattern, are thus valid for all dominant enterprises which have coordinated their influence upon each other.

[23] *Cf.* Bericht der Unternehmensrechtskommission, *supra* note 4, at p. 130 *et seq.*

[24] 69 BGHZ 334 ("Gelsenberg AG"); *cf.* M. Lutter and W. Timm, 1978 BB 836; H. P. Müller, 1978 WPg 61; H. Wiedemann and K. P. Martens, 1976 AG 232; W. Zöllner, 1978 AG 40.

[25] *Cf.* 167 RGZ 40 ("Thega"); J. Dierdorf, Herrschaft und Abhängigkeit einer Aktiengesellschaft auf schuldrechtlicher und tatsächlicher Grundlage, p. 97 *et seq.* (Cologne, Bonn, Munich, 1978); E. Geßler, in Gessler-Hefermehl-Eckardt-Kropff, AktG, sec. 17 AktG, 40, 56 (Munich, 1976); for a criticism of external dependence, *see* P. Ulmer, 1978 ZGR 457; H. Würdinger in Grosskommentar zum AktG, sec. 17 AktG, note 3 *et seq.*

[26] *Cf.* 62 BGHZ 193 ("Seitz-AG"): BAG AP No. 20 to sec. 76 BetrVG 195 (with a note by A. Hueck); *cf.* W. Gansweid, Gemeinsame Tochtergesellschaften im deutschen Konzern- und Wettbewerbsrecht, p. 119 *et seq.* (Baden-Baden, 1976); E. Geßler, 1974 ZGR 476.

B. Contractual Combines

It is very controversial whether the division in statute law between contractually combined enterprises and de facto combined enterprises is successful.[27] In my opinion the predominant reasons argue against such a division.

1. The Conclusion and Duration of the Contract

The *weakness* of the West German system, the so-called *dualistic system,* is already evident in that the enterprise contracts of secs. 291, 292 AktG are not freely negotiated, but dictated contracts; a contract exists only in form, but not in substance, since the dependent company has already become dependent before the conclusion of the contract. In most cases one encounters no arm's length transaction. This is especially apparent in the conclusion and termination of the contract and, to the extent freedom of contract exists, also in the formation of its terms.

In the first place the dominant enterprise can determine when the enterprise contract is to be entered into. Since controlling influence also can be, and is, enforced without conclusion of the contract, the dominant enterprise chooses a weak phase in the economic situation of the dependent company in order to produce through manipulations a low going-concern value and a correspondingly low settlement and compensation value.

The faults of the present law are even more apparent in the termination of enterprise contracts. Control and transfer-of-profits contracts are usually concluded for tax reasons for a period of five years, with a clause agreeing that they are to be automatically extended for a period of one year unless and until expressly terminated. The approval of the outside shareholders of the dependent company is not necessary.[28] The termination, moreover, can be utilized as an amendment termination, i. e., be combined with an offer to conclude a new enterprise contract with less favourable conditions for the outside shareholders. On the other hand, if the cooperation appears advantageous, through operation of the automatic extension of the contract the settlement initially determined for the remaining shareholders in the dependent company remains fixed for an unlimited period without renewed examination. Jointly realized advantages can be withheld by this method from the shareholders of the dependent company. Therefore it is sought to provide a remedy by requiring, in sec. 304 AktG, that the settlement is to be periodically reviewed at certain fixed determined intervals, and, if needed, adjustments made for inflation.

To make the protection of the outside shareholders more effective the legislator should have made it compulsory always to obtain a special resolution of the outside (independent) shareholders for the conclusion and termination of any enterprise contract. Unfortunately, secs. 295 par. 2 and 296 par. 2 AktG are too narrowly drafted and require a special resolution in only a limited number of situations.

[27] *Cf.* on this point, most recently, BERICHT DER UNTERNEHMENSRECHTSKOMMISSION, *supra* note 4, No. 1312 *et seq.*

[28] *Cf.* BGH, 1979 WM 770 ("Peine-Salzgitter AG").

2. Compensation and Indemnity Rights and Their Substantive and Procedural Weaknesses

Upon the conclusion of a control or transfer-of-profits contract the outside shareholders of the dependent corporation must, in accordance with sec. 304 AktG, be annually guaranteed an adequate compensation payment and, in addition, must be given the opportunity to withdraw from the company in return for a grant of the dominant enterprise's shares or for a cash indemnity (cf. 305 AktG). The adequacy of the compensation or indemnity can be reviewed in a court of law at the request of each shareholder in a procedure in accordance with sec. 306 AktG. This opportunity has often been used in the last few years.[29]

The compensation and indemnity claims of *outside shareholders* have many inherent weaknesses:

(1) The review procedure can drag out over several years. In one case this led to the plaintiff shareholders' receiving nothing at all, since the defendant dominant enterprise became bankrupt during the proceedings.

(2) The variable compensation offered according to sec. 304 par. 2, sentence 2, to the outside shareholders is not without risk: if the dominant enterprise does not distribute a dividend, the outside shareholders of the dependent company will accordingly go away empty-handed.[30] In legal scholarship the proposal has therefore been made to interpret the term "profit share" in sec. 304 par. 1 sentence 2 AktG as the "annual surplus".[31]

(3) To judge the adequacy of an indemnity offer according to sec. 305 AktG and to have the same reviewed by a court causes considerable difficulty. Theoretically a complete indemnity must be granted to the outside shareholders.[32] In practice they carry the burden of all the uncertainties, with which accountants are familiar, of valuing enterprises according to book value and productive value. The statements of experts differ from one to another, in some cases by more than 100%; in the case *VW/Audi/NSU* the indemnity sums actually paid amounted to three times the originally offered sums.[33] According to sec. 305 AktG, a dominant enterprise is obligated neither to reveal the basis for the amount of the indemnity offer nor to consult the opinion of a certified accountant.

(4) The dominant enterprise is – even after the conclusion of a control or

[29] *Cf.* the collection of actions made by G. Gössel and G. Hehl, 142 ZHR 19 at 42 *et seq.* (1978) as well as OLG Düsseldorf, 1978 AG 238 ("ATH/Rheinstahl AG"); OLG Celle, 1979 AG 230 ("Ilseder Hütte/Salzgitter AG"); BayObLG, 1979 AG 316 ("Erba AG/Glöggler"); LG Hannover, 1979 AG 234 ("Alsen-Breitenburg AG/Hannover AG").

[30] *Cf.* OLG Düsseldorf, 1978 AG 238, 239.

[31] *Cf.* K. H. Biedenkopf and H. G. Koppensteiner, in KÖLNER KOMMENTAR ZUM AKTG, sec. 304 AktG, No. 23; H. Würdinger in GROSSK, *supra* note 25, sec. 304 AktG, comment 15.

[32] *See,* most recently, OLG Düsseldorf, 1977 WM 797, 798; OLG Düsseldorf, 1978 AG 238, 239; OLG Celle, 1979 AG 230, 233 (note Forster, 1980 AG 45); LG Hannover, 1979 AG 234, 235.

[33] *Cf.* the description of the facts in 1976 JZ 325 *et seq.*

transfer-of-profits contract – not obligated to protect the interests of outside shareholders by duties of care and notice.[34]

(5) To these factual problems are added a number of procedural obstacles. The claim of the outside shareholder depends upon his being in possession of at least one share on the date of the shareholders' meeting which approved the contract of control, and thereafter uninterruptedly until the conclusion of the legal proceedings.[35] Finally, the question is still open whether outside shareholders who were indemnified before a final decision reviewing the adequacy of the amount are able to demand the difference if the court in the trial determines a larger indemnity in accordance with secs. 304 par. 5, 306 AktG. A supplementary claim upon the larger indemnity should accrue to the benefit of shareholders already indemnified.[36]

3. Exercise of Management Right

The management right, i. e. the right to direct the dependent corporation recognized in sec. 308 AktG, exists only against the management board of the dependent corporation, and therefore refers only to the sphere of responsibility of this body. Theoretically the right to direct could be further narrowed down in the contract of control; such clauses are, however, not common. Correspondingly, directives can be used in order to injure dependent companies in the – real or pretended – interest of the combine, in particular by removing liquid reserves or outstanding personnel. The prohibition on hidden dividend distributions laid down in secs. 57, 58 and 60 AktG, no longer applies in this case. If the dominant enterprise acts in violation of the broad scope of the principle of good business judgment for valid directives, then it is itself liable in accordance with the general principles of law on the basis of the contract of control.[37]

In accordance with sec. 308 par. 3 AktG when a transaction can only be executed with the approval of the supervisory board then the approval of the latter must be obtained and its absence must be reported to the dominant enterprise. The dominant enterprise is, to be sure, able to enforce its will through repetition of the directive but must, if it itself has a supervisory board, obtain its approval thereto. This time-consuming procedure serves above all to preserve

[34] *Cf.* BGH, 1976 JZ 561 ("VW/Audi-NSU"); for a criticism of this *see* M. Lutter, 1976 JZ 562; H. Wiedemann, 1976 JZ 392.

[35] *Cf.* KG, 1971 WM 764, 766; OLG Frankfurt, 1971 AG 369, 370; OLG Celle, 1974 WM 529; E. Geßler, in Gessler-Hefermehl-Eckardt-Kropff, *supra* note 25, sec. 304 AktG, No. 132; H. Würdinger in GrossK, *supra* note 25, sec. 304 AktG, Note 31.

[36] *See* V. Emmerich & J. Sonnenschein, *supra* note 21, at p. 183; E. Geßler, in: Gessler-Hefermehl-Eckardt-Kropff, *supra* note 25, sec. 305 AktG, No. 74; Kropff, 1969 WPg 3; W. Werner, 1972 AG 167 *et seq.; contra,* K. H. Biedenkopf and H. G. Koppensteiner, *supra* note 31, sec. 305 AktG, No. 22; H. G. Koppensteiner, 1978 BB 769 *et seq.*

[37] *Cf.* V. Emmerich & J. Sonnenschein, *supra* note 21, at p. 194; H. Wiedemann, *supra* note 14, at p. 350. For reform proposals, *cf.* Bericht der Unternehmensrechtskommission, *supra* note 4, No. 1324 *et seq.*

the codetermination rights of the employees, who should participate at at least one level in the measure to be decided.

According to sec. 302 par. 1 AktG the dominant enterprise must compensate every annual deficit of the dependent corporation to the extent that this is not already compensated for by transfers out of the freely disposable capital reserves of amounts which have been placed there during the duration of the contract. In practice the dominant enterprise will be allowed to cover the loss out of pre-contractual hidden reserves and will thereby be able to rob the dependent company not only of its hidden reserves, but also of its book value. Since there is no duty to maintain the book value, the dependent management board cannot defend itself against such measures.

4. The Foreign Dominant Enterprise

The Stock Corporation Law contains only by way of exception provisions for affiliated enterprises which are dependent upon a foreign enterprise (cf. e. g., secs. 305 par. 2 Nr. 3, 330 par. 2 and 334 par. 1 sentence 3 AktG). According to the general view an enterprise contract can also be concluded with a foreign company.[38] The number of control and transfer-of-profits contracts internationally concluded is small.

C. De Facto Combines

1. Dependence Report, Compensation for Disadvantages and Personal Liability

The Stock Corporation Law now in force distinguishes between on the one hand, companies simply dependent, but upon which no influence is exercised, and on the other, existing dependence relationships which are exercised occasionally or constantly. In the case of the second group the intention of the statute is nevertheless to preserve the independence of the company. For this purpose the statute fundamentally prohibits the dominant enterprise from prejudicing the dependent company. Yet to the extent that disadvantageous legal transactions are entered into or measures are taken, the detriment thereby caused to the dependent company must be compensated (cf., sec. 311 par. 1 AktG). A dependence report on the relations between the affiliated enterprises, to be examined by a certified accountant, must be annually prepared (cf. sec. 312 et seq. AktG).

The existing legal regulations permit the dependent company to be subjected in practice to constant and prejudicial directives.[39] The present law thus does not protect to a sufficient extent the legally approved interests of the outside shareholders, creditors and employees. It must first of all be determined that the prejudicial business act was "occasioned" by the dominant enterprise. In addition the point in time of the occasioning "ex ante" is determinative for

[38] *Cf.*, on this point, V. Immenga and D. Klocke, *Konzernkollisionsrecht*, 92 ZSR I 27 *et seq.* (1973). H. WIEDEMANN, *supra* note 14, at p. 799 *et seq.*

[39] *See contra*, E. Mestmäcker, in FESTGABE FÜR KRONSTEIN, p. 129, 139 *et seq.* (Karlsruhe, 1967) but this view has not found favour.

evaluating the detriment. After all, the detriment must be quantified, which becomes all the more difficult the longer and the more tenacious the influence exercised upon the dependent company.[40]

According to secs. 317, 318 AktG, the dominant enterprise is liable to the dependent company, as well as to the creditors and shareholders of the latter, for damages if compensation is not made for the transactions or measures it has occasioned. The plaintiff must prove that all these prerequisites are present. The claim becomes void if the management board of the dependent company declares that the combine management had not occasioned the transactions in question. Successful claims under secs. 317-318 AktG are for this reason unkown.

2. *Reform Proposals*

In the general opinion, the rules governing de facto combines are in need of reform, at least in those cases in which a dominant enterprise exerts a sustained and effective influence upon the management of the dependent company (so-called *qualified combine*).[41] Circumstances indicating loss of independence on the part of the dependent company are:

- the creation of an economic unit (consolidation of investment, financial, personnel and production policy):
- sustained prejudice to the entrepreneurial self-interest of the dependent company:
- a high percentage of shares owned (over 90% of the corporate shares in the hands of one person or group).

Proposals within the framework of the present law provide that the dominant enterprise be subject to an assumption of losses,[42] and that the outside shareholders be given a right to indemnity upon creation of a qualified combine.[43]

In the *Report of the Commission on Enterprise Law*[44] a new proposal for a reform of the West German Stock Corporation Law is submitted. Unlike the preliminary draft of a regulation for the assimilation of the law of affiliated enterprises in the European Communities, this proposal continues to provide for a distinction between a contractual and de facto combine. In the case of a de facto combine each shareholder or third party which can exercise a controlling influence upon the dependent company and which wants to subject that company to the combine management, can expressly declare this intention to the dependent company. The declaration must be made public by the dependent company and be submitted to the trade register. By the declaration the dominant

[40] *Cf.* L. Strohn, Die Verfassung der Aktiengesellschaft im faktischen Konzern, p. 65 *et seq.* (Cologne, 1977).

[41] Proposal of the Arbeitskreis GmbH-Reform, *supra* note 16, at 49 *et seq.*; critically, on this point, E. Geßler, 1973 Betrieb 48 *et seq.*; and, now approving, *id.*, in Festschrift für W. Flume, pp. 55, 63 *et seq.* (Cologne, 1978).

[42] Thus Bericht der Unternehmensrechtskommission, *supra* note 4, No. 1406.

[43] Thus H. Wiedemann, 1978 ZGR 477, 491 *et seq.*

[44] Bericht der Unternehmensrechtskommission, *supra* note 4, No. 1418 *et seq.*

enterprise is to be obligated to guarantee a dividend to the outside shareholders of the dependent company, the adequacy of which can be reviewed by a court. The dominant enterprise or the dominant shareholder, who has entered his name in the trade register, is to be obligated to assume losses in accordance with sec. 302 AktG. A dividend guaranty and a duty to assume losses make the dependence report superfluous. Every outside shareholder is to be given the right to have determined in a legal action whether the company in fact stands under the directions of a shareholder or third party.[45] After termination of the de facto combine relationship a compensation payment by the dominant enterprise to the dependent company must be made, in order to compensate the latter for detriments which it incurred during the combine membership but for which it has not yet been compensated. This proposal has, for the time being, little chance of being realized as a statute, since this would mean that other parts of the Stock Corporation Law would at the same time have to be reformed.[46]

III. The Law Concerning Affiliated Enterprises Having Other Organizational Forms

A. The Dependent Limited Liability Company (GmbH)

1. Lack of Specific Statutory Provisions

The position of a limited liability company dependent upon another enterprise is not governed by statute, although the limited liability company represents probably the most widespread form of dependent subsidiary.[47]

The application of the Stock Corporation Law to dependent limited liability companies is impermissible because of the structural dissimilarity between the two company forms. The limited liability company is typically a close corporation in which a few shareholders participate, who in turn themselves participate in management. The managing officer of the limited liability company is bound by directives of the shareholders' meeting; the limited liability company is, as a matter of principle, not required to have a supervisory board. Finally, the assets of the limited liability company are subject to a less narrow statutory control than those of the stock corporation: while in the stock corporation the total net assets are statutorily bound, and only retained earnings may be paid to shareholders as a dividend, sec. 30 GmbHG binds only those net assets of the limited liability company which correspond to the (lower) original capital.

[45] *Cf.*, in detail on this point, E. Geßler, *supra* note 41, p. 55, 64 *et seq.*

[46] On the (negative) position of the Enterprise Law Commission towards the Preliminary Draft of an EC Regulation, *cf.* BERICHT DER UNTERNEHMENSRECHTSKOMMISSION, *supra* note 4, No. 1449 *et seq.*

[47] The governmental proposal for a new limited liability company law and law of affiliated enterprises of 5 Nov. 1971, which is founded on the Stock Corporation Law, will not become law (BTDrs 595/71).

2. Definition of Dependence

The definitions of secs. 15-19 AktG are valid for all enterprises regardless of legal form, and therefore also for the dominant limited liability company.

3. Enterprise Contracts and De Facto Combines of Mere Dependence

The content of the law governing affiliated enterprises applicable to the limited liability company is characterized by *great uncertainty;* in some instances it is difficult to decide whether one is dealing with a presentation of the present law or proposals for development of the law.[48]

The most commonly found type of enterprise contract is the contract to transfer profits (cf. sec. 17 KStG 1977), and not the contract for control. According to the predominant view, the resolution of the shareholders' meeting for conclusion of an enterprise contract requires the approval of all the shareholders of the limited liability company, because the corporate purpose is thereby altered. If one adheres to this view, the outside shareholders can make their approval dependent upon special consideration (payment of compensation or indemnity). If they should, by way of exception, be obliged to agree by virtue of the operation of the duty of good faith, they then receive a claim for a cash indemnity in accordance with sec. 305 par. 2 AktG. In the case of a transfer-of-profits-and-control contract, creditors are protected by the obligation of the dominant enterprise to assume losses. For the performance and termination of enterprise contracts, considerations derived from the Stock Corporation Law can be consulted.

In the case of the de facto GmbH-combine, it has not yet been settled whether creditors are protected only in cases of fraud, in accordance with sec. 826 BGB,[49] and partners by the good faith and restitution duties of the "normal" GmbH-law,[50] or whether, at least in cases of a qualified combine, the rules of liability and indemnity automatically take effect. Case law favors the former, but commentators the latter alternative. In justification the principle of the unity of influence and responsibility can be cited: if the entrepreneurial self-interest of the dependent company is permanently endangered, then the common corporate purpose ceases to exist for the minority shareholders and the previous credit basis for creditors.

The Enterprise Law Commission has extensively discussed with a view to possible enactment a model law for the qualified de facto combine.[51] It is

[48] *Cf., inter alia,* Hachenburg & C. H. Barz, sec. 14 GmbHG, appendix II; K. P. Martens, Mehrheits- und Konzernherrschaft in der personalistischen GmbH (Cologne, 1970); F. Scholz & V. Emmerich, *supra* note 15, Appendix II (with further references).

[49] After the restrictive ruling in 68 BGHZ 312 ("Typenhausbau-GmbH"), *supra* note 13, recent case law has reverted to sec. 826 BGB; *cf.* BGH, 1979 WM 229 (GmbH & Co. KG).

[50] *Cf.*, BGH, 1981 WM 357 at 358; Ruwe, 1980 AG 21; on the general limits of majority rule, H. Wiedemann, *supra* note 14, at p. 405 *et seq.*

[51] *Cf.* Bericht der Unternehmensrechtskommission, *supra* note 4, No. 1662 *et seq.* and 1684 *et seq.*

apparently not impossible that the courts in the next few years will "enact" several of the individual elements of the proposed model as case-law.

For the cases of mere dependence of a limited liability company, or of simple incorporation into the combined enterprises of the dominant enterprise, no rules diverging from the usual GmbH-law are in force. The dominant enterprise is liable in the same way as every majority shareholder for prejudicial directives or for special benefits for non-corporate purposes.[52] At the same time it is unresolved whether a majority shareholder must be liable also for an intentionally prejudicial exercise of his voting right. According to the general view, sec. 311 et seq. AktG do not take effect in such circumstances.

B. The Dependent Partnership

The structure and scope of dependent partnership arrangements are not known in detail, since partnership contracts are not subject to publication. According to existing information, two types of dependent partnership can be distinguished. In the first group, the managing general partner is also an entrepreneur outside of his partnership: he runs or manages another enterprise. In the second group, a general partner-limited liability company is dependent upon a third enterprise; the partner is thus made an indirectly dependent enterprise. The second group arises especially through penetration by large enterprises of small businesses, in which the former owners become outside limited partners. In both alternatives control and transfer-of-profits contracts are seldom found; the dependence relationship can take effect, however, through the partnership contract of the dependent partnership.

For the conclusion, performance and termination of partnership enterprise contracts the statements made earlier in respect of the dependent limited liability company are mutatis mutandis valid.

Moreover, one can demand that the partners of a (closed) partnership agree not only to the contractual, but also to the de facto combine. In other words, the union of the dependent partnership with a dominant enterprise requires consent by all parties. For this reason the managing partner is obliged to notify partners not involved in management about existing or potential outside enterprise interests; it is precisely a concealed seizure of influence which would especially endanger the dependent partnership. If this understanding exists, there is nothing which opposes the introduction of a combine – also of a qualified combine. The management is, however, obligated to inform the partners of the enterprise connection. In addition the dominant enterprise becomes subject to a duty to assume losses.

The typical partnership form of the GmbH & Co. KG (limited partnership with private liability company as general partner), which is widespread in West Germany and in which the entrepreneurial interest of the limited liability company is limited to the general partnership, does not constitute a combine fact

[52] On the question of "consolidated" liability of the dominant enterprise as majority shareholder, *cf.* H. WIEDEMANN, *supra* note 14, at pp. 349-350.

pattern. The element of a dominant enterprise is lacking here; rather, the GmbH & Co. KG connects two legal structures in order to carry on one enterprise.

C. The Registered Co-operative

The law of affiliated enterprises plays only a minor role for the registered co-operative. A contractual combine cannot be established with a dependent co-operative. Control through a voting or capital majority is, to be sure, theoretically possible, but fails in practice because multiple voting rights or a capital majority can be acquired only in a very limited scope.[53]

IV. Features of Co-Determined Combines

A. The Present State of the Law

The influence of the law relating to co-determination upon the law governing combined enterprises varies according to the different kinds of co-determination under the present law.

1. Simple Co-Determination

Co-determination according to secs. 76, 77 of the Plant Co-Determination Law *(BetrVG 1952)* requires that one-third of the supervisory board of the companies in question be filled with employees; the provisions apply, irrespective of the number of employees, to all enterprise parent companies having the form of a corporation (AG) or of a limited partnership organized on a shares basis (KGaA); and, in addition, to any limited liability company (GmbH), co-operative and mutual insurance union, of which the parent enterprise employs more than 500 employees. If only one employee is to be elected, then he must belong to the dominant enterprise; if two or more are to be elected then at least one must be a worker belonging to the enterprise, and a second an office employee belonging to the enterprise.

The Federal Labour Court has developed special rules for the election of the employee representatives in a combine. According to sec. 76 par. 4 BetrVG 1952, the employees of plants of the other enterprises in the combine are also to take part in the election of the employee representatives for the supervisory board of the dominant enterprise. Here the principles of group membership and enterprise membership must certainly be observed. It is, however, disputed and questionable whether the combine structure must be considered in such a way that, of the combine-linked employee seats, at least one must be held, respectively, by an employee of the dominant enterprise and one by an employee of the dependent enterprise. The Federal Labour Court has asserted this in a series of decisions.[54]

[53] *Cf.*, on this in detail, Merle, *Die eingetragene Genossenschaft als abhängiges Unternehmen*, 1979 AG, 265-274.

[54] *Cf.*, most recently, BAG AP No. 22 and 23 on sec. 76 BetrVG 1952, note by H. Wiedemann and L. Strohn; and, generally, K. FITTING, F. AUFFARTH & H. KAISER,

2. *Expanded Co-Determination*

The recent co-determination law, the *MitbestG* 1976, provides that half of the seats of the supervisory board of the company in question are to be filled with employees. These provisions apply to any representative enterprise of a combine having the legal form of a stock corporation, limited liability company or co-operative, if such an enterprise usually employs more than 2000 employees. The president of the supervisory board and his deputy are elected by the supervisory board by a qualified majority; if neither obtains a majority, then the shareholder representatives elect the president of the supervisory board out of their own members, and the employee representatives elect the deputy from their own group (cf. sec. 27 MitbestG). The president of the supervisory board is given a tie-breaking vote in case of a draw in the voting. The shareholders thereby obtain the opportunity – if they are all present and vote in unison – normally to prevail in personnel and material questions against the employee representatives; their predominance is, however, not guaranteed.

In the combine, the employees of an indigenous dependent company count in the same way as employees of the dominant enterprise (cf. sec. 5 MitbestG). Because of this, the scope of application of the MitbestG is expanded in several aspects: first, a co-determined supervisory board must be formed for the dominant enterprise, even when the enterprise taken on its own has fewer than 2000 employees; second, the employees of a *dependent* combine enterprise which, because of its legal form or of its small number of employees, does not fulfill the requirements of Sec. 1 par. 2 MitbestG are nevertheless given rights of representation in the *dominant* combine enterprise under the co-determination provisions. Conceptually sec. 5 MitbestG signals a step towards the unity of corporate enterprises. In West Germany, as well as abroad, a trend has emerged from labour and social law towards a unified view of the combine.[55] In the context of the application of sec. 5 MitbestG it is especially controversial whether inside a combine further combine relationships can exist, i. e., whether a dependent combine enterprise can itself be a dominant enterprise vis-à-vis one or more dependent combine enterprises. If one agrees with this, the employees of dependent combine enterprises participate in co-determination not only at the top of the combine, but also in the subordinate combine.[56]

The same trend toward the formation of a general enterprise law is shown in sec. 32 par. 1 sent. 2 MitbestG. It contains a shift of authority to, and at the same time provides for the creation of, a special supervisory board with a reduced membership. Sec. 32 MitbestG transfers to the supervisory board of the dominant enterprise management decisions regarding the use of participation rights, which belong under normal corporation law to the management board/

Betriebsverfassungsgesetz, sec. 76 BetrVG 1952, No. 79 *et seq.* (Munich, 12th ed., 1977).

[55] *Cf.*, on this point, K. P. Martens, *Das Arbeitsverhältnis im Konzern*, in 25 Jahre Bundesarbeitsgericht, pp. 367-391 (Munich, 1979).

[56] *Cf.*, on this point, K. Fitting, O. Wlotzke & J. Wissmann, Mitbestimmungsgesetz, sec. 5 MitbestG, No. 30 *et seq.* (Munich, 2d ed. 1978).

president. The decision-making organ is, however, not the complete supervisory board, but only the panel of shareholder representatives. This complicated provision is to prevent the influence of the employees from multiplying at every level of the combine.

3. Mining Co-Determination

The principle of equal co-determination under the Mining Co-Determination Law, *MontanMitbestG 1951*, provides that the supervisory board seats are distributed equally to shareholders and employees. The importance of mining co-determination is declining; presently it applies only to one combine, namely the *Salzgitter* firm.

B. Future Legal Developments

The ideologically motivated doctrine of the unified and integrated "*social union enterprise*" attempts to develop the supervisory board of the head company of the combine (on which there is equal representation) into an independent and central combine organ, to be granted not only supervisory rights, but also management authority, as against the management board, and fundamental decision-making rights, as against the shareholders' meeting.[57] To what extent a disintegration of previous corporate law is occuring here cannot yet be determined.[58]

[57] *Cf.* BERICHT DER UNTERNEHMENSRECHTSKOMMISSION, *supra* note 4, No. 1476 *et seq.*

[58] *Cf.*, on this point, T. Raiser, in FESTSCHRIFT FÜR R. FISCHER, p. 561 *et seq.* (Berlin, 1979); *id.*, 144 ZHR 206 *et seq.* (1980).

Résumé:

L'expérience allemande avec le droit des sociétés affiliées

Cet article traite du droit allemand des sociétés affiliées ("Konzernrecht"), qui établit des règles de conduit spéciales pour une entreprise dominante quant à la gestion d'une société commerciale contrôlée, habituellement par une participation majoritaire, et par conséquent dépendante. Une telle société subordonnée n'étant plus capable de préserver ses propres intérêts ainsi que ceux de tous ses actionnaires et créanciers, le droit des sociétés affiliées vise à protéger ces intérêts contre l'entreprise dominante. Dans la première partie de l'article nous avons une brève description des dispositions de la loi allemande sur les sociétés de 1965, du système législatif et de la jurisprudence sur ce sujet ainsi qu'une présentation des faits économiques et des statistiques disponibles. La seconde partie de l'article passe en vue l'expérience faite depuis 1965. Tout d'abord, le but de la loi n'est pas encore déterminé, la notion d'entreprise étant très controversée. Cela est également vrai pour la notion de dépendance, spécialement pour la question si une simple dépendance économique suffit, par exemple la dépendance dans la relation créancier-débiteur. Selon la jurisprudence, les filiales communes peuvent dépendre en même temps de différentes entreprises dominantes. Nous trouvons alors une discussion critique de ce qui est appellé le système dualiste du droit allemand. La question de savoir si la division du droit législatif entre les entreprises affiliées contractuellement ou de facto doit être considérée comme satisfaisante, est répondue par la négative. Différentes faiblesses du système allemand sont mises en évidence. Elles concernent la conclusion et la durée des contrats des entreprises, les compensations et droits à indemnité, l'exercice du droit de gérer et le problème d'une entreprise dominante étrangère. De plus le droit des groupes "de facto" est considéré comme ayant besoin d'être transformé , au moins pour les cas dans lesquels une entreprise dominante exerce une influence soutenue et effective sur la gestion de la société dépendante. Différentes propositions de réformes sont décrites et évaluées. Une brève troisième partie traite du droit des sociétés affiliées ayant d'autres structures, par exemple la société à responsabilité limitée dépendante, la société en nom collectif et la société coopérative inscrite. Nous avons enfin une brève étude des systèmes différents de cogestion des salariés (simple, élargie et minière).

Les groupes de sociétés en droit français

ROGER HOUIN
Paris

Depuis la seconde guerre mondiale on a assisté dans l'économie française à des concentrations très importantes d'entreprises qui ont été favorisées par le Gouvernement, notamment par des avantages fiscaux et par des aides ou subventions financières. Pendant assez longtemps ces concentrations se sont réalisées au moyen de fusions de sociétés, de scissions, d'apports partiels d'actif. Mais, depuis un certain nombre d'années se sont formés d'importants groupes de sociétés, soit pour des raisons de commodité, soit à raison de l'expansion hors de France, en Europe et dans le monde. Ces groupes réunissent non seulement des sociétés par actions, mais aussi des sociétés à responsabilité limitée et même des sociétés en nom collectif ou des sociétés civiles. Ces groupes s'établissent essentiellement par des participations au capital des sociétés; beaucoup plus rares sont les conventions ou accords de dépendance, le droit fiscal français n'accordant aucune faveur à de telles conventions, à la différence de ce qui se passe en Allemagne.

Nous ne traiterons que du droit de ces groupes en laissant de côté aussi bien les fusions que les groupements entre entreprises demeurant sur un pied d'égalité: joint venture, filiales communes, groupements d'intérêt économique, coopératives, etc.

La législation française est très pauvre en matière de groupes de sociétés. La loi du 24 juillet 1966 sur les sociétés commerciales, aussi bien que celle du 4 janvier 1978 sur les sociétés civiles, ignorent presque totalement cette matière. Tout au plus contiennent-elles quelques règles sur certaines relations entre des sociétés dont l'une possède une participation dans le capital de l'autre.

La *loi du 24 juillet 1966* ne donne pas de *définition* du groupe de sociétés mais seulement de la société filiale et de la participation. La *filiale* est la société dont le capital est possédé pour le plus de la moitié par une autre société qu'on appelle en pratique une société-mère, ou une holding lorsqu'elle n'a pas d'activité industrielle ou commerciale propre. Le mot *»participation«* est réservé au cas où une société possède entre 10% et 50% du capital d'une autre société.[1] Ces définitions, et notamment celle de la filiale, sont donc très simplistes: peu importe le lien de dépendance et l'unité de direction entre les sociétés. Mais il convient de noter que ces définitions n'ont d'utilité que pour l'application d'un nombre limité de règles

[1] Art. 354 loi 24. 7. 1966.

qui s'y réfèrent plus ou moins expressément: informations à donner aux actionnaires, limitation des participations réciproques, incompatibilités pour les fonctions de commissaires aux comptes, etc. Dans tous les autres cas, ou bien la loi définit le pourcentage de la participation au capital d'une des sociétés par l'autre pour que la règle s'applique, ou — beaucoup plus rarement — elle utilise une formule plus vague et générale faisant état d'un lien de dépendance. Par exemple, le *droit fiscal* contient diverses règles pour éviter qu'une société établie en France ne cherche à transférer une partie de ses bénéfices soumis à l'impôt des sociétés ou une partie de ses recettes de chiffre d'affaires à une société-mère ou à une filiale établie hors de France; le droit fiscal parle alors d'*»entreprise dépendante«* et définit cette entreprise comme étant »toute entreprise dans laquelle directement ou par personne interposée une autre entreprise exerce en fait le pouvoir de décision.«[2] Mais il s'agit alors d'une définition particulière au droit fiscal et qui ne saurait s'appliquer telle quelle dans le droit des sociétés.

Les lacunes du droit français relatives aux groupes de sociétés ont été comblées, dans une certaine mesure, ainsi qu'on le verra plus loin, par la jurisprudence. Mais celle-ci est encore hésitante, notamment en ce qui concerne les conflits qui peuvent surgir entre l'intérêt global du groupe et l'intérêt particulier d'une société-mère. Il faudra sans doute qu'un jour la loi française soit complétée. Mais le Gouvernement paraît attendre que soit prise la Directive en matière de Groupes de sociétés que prépare depuis quelque temps la Commission des Communautés européennes. Il ne semble pas très pressé, car les milieux d'affaires sont généralement hostiles à une législation du genre de celle qui est en vigueur en Allemagne. Cependant, certains parlementaires, et tout particulièrement un député, M. Cousté, ont déposé une proposition de loi — remaniée à plusieurs reprises — sur les groupes de sociétés.

Nous commencerons par étudier les quelques dispositions législatives et leurs compléments jurisprudentiels qui s'appliquent aux filiales et participations. La seconde partie exposera brièvement la proposition de loi de M. Cousté.

I. Droit positif français

A. Formation des groupes

1. La notion de société

On rappelera d'abord qu'en France la société d'une seule personne n'a qu'une existence limitée: il faut au moins deux associés pour qu'une société puisse exister; il en faut même sept pour la société anonyme et quatre pour la commandite par actions. Mais, depuis la loi du 24 juillet 1966 sur les sociétés, et en vertu de son article 9, la réunion de toutes les parts ou actions entre les mains d'un seul associé n'est plus une cause de dissolution automatique de la société comme auparavant; l'associé unique dispose d'un délai d'un an pour »régulariser« la situation en cédant des parts ou actions à un ou plusieurs autres associés; il peut aussi dissoudre la société. A défaut, tout intéressé, notamment tout

[2] Art. 57 Code général des impôts.

créancier, peut demander cette dissolution après l'expiration d'un an et il est alors procédé à la liquidation dans les conditions ordinaires, avec droit de préférence au profit des créanciers sociaux. Les mêmes règles jouent lorsque le nombre des actionnaires d'une société anonyme descend au dessous de sept. Cette disposition du droit récent est une application de la deuxième directive de la C. E. E. sur l'harmonisation du droit des sociétés. Mais il n'en demeure pas moins que la *société d'une seule personne* est en situation irrégulière et que sa survie est temporaire. Par suite, dans les groupes de sociétés, les filiales dont 100% du capital sont détenus par la société-mère sont irrégulières; bien que la loi de 1966 soit muette sur ce point il semble qu'il faille en déduire que la société-mère est alors tenue de toutes les dettes de sa filiale à 100%; notamment si la filiale est mise en faillite, la société-mère pourra se voir imputer tout le passif de la filiale, celle-ci étant considérée comme purement fictive.

En fait cependant les *filiales à 100%* existent et sont même nombreuses dans les groupes de sociétés; il suffit de faire souscrire ou acheter les actions par plusieurs sociétés du groupe ou par plusieurs dirigeants de la société-mère ou holding. Le seul risque est que, si la filiale fait de mauvaises affaires, la société-mère risquera d'avoir à régler son passif.

2. Le contrôle d'une société par une autre

a) La constitution d'une filiale n'est soumise à aucune règle particulière sauf si elle se réalise par l'acquisition d'actions en bourse. Si une société veut créer une filiale, par exemple, pour diversifier ses activités ou ses risques, elle peut le faire en souscrivant les actions de numéraire de la nouvelle société qu'elle crée. Elle peut aussi apporter en nature à une société nouvelle une partie de ses actifs; cette scission ou apport partiel d'actif peut être assujetti aux règles concernant les fusions et scissions totales ce qui assure une meilleure protection des associés et des créanciers.[3] Cette création de filiale par constitution d'une société nouvelle est soumise purement et simplement aux règles du droit commun des sociétés.

b) Il en est de même de la *prise de contrôle* d'une société existante par une autre société qui devient sa société-mère. Cette prise de contrôle peut résulter de la souscription par cette dernière à une augmentation de capital de la première ou de l'apport partiel d'actif rémunéré par des actions de la société bénéficiaire de l'apport. On applique alors les règles ordinaires sur l'augmentation de capital.

La prise de contrôle peut aussi résulter de *l'acquisition* par la société-mère d'un paquet d'*actions* qui lui donnera la majorité et le contrôle de la société qui a émis ces actions. Mais, ici, il faut faire une distinction fondamentale selon que les actions cédées sont ou non cotées en bourse.

Si les actions *ne* sont *pas cotées en bourse,* la jurisprudence a décidé qu'il s'agit d'une simple cession d'actions entre actionnaires, qui obéit aux règles générales de la vente. A cet égard, elle ne fait aucune différence entre une cession d'un petit nombre d'actions à titre de placement et la cession d'un bloc d'actions conférant le contrôle; les organes de la société dont les actions sont cédées n'ont donc pas à intervenir puisque ce sont les actionnaires et non la société elle-même

[3] Art. 387 loi 24. 7. 1966.

qui vend les actions; tout au plus la Cour de cassation tient compte du fait qu'aucun abus de droit de la majorité ne peut être reproché à celle-ci lorsque ce sont les organes majoritaires qui ont discuté les conditions de la cession; elle tient compte aussi du fait que l'offre d'achat avait été faite à tous les actionnaires et de façon à respecter l'égalité de ceux-ci.[4] Il n'est pas certain que ces solutions assez peu protectrices des actionnaires minoritaires se maintiendront longtemps alors que, comme on va le voir, cette protection est remarquablement assurée pour les cessions d'actions cotées en bourse. D'ailleurs dès maintenant, et à d'autres égards, la jurisprudence considère que des cessions de contrôle portant sur des actions cotées ou non en bourse, présentent des caractères particuliers, distincts de ceux d'une simple cession d'actions, en ce qu'elles intéressent la vie de la société. Elle en déduit notamment qu'il faut en informer le Comité d'entreprise de la société et recueillir son avis; elle en déduit aussi que ces actions sont des actes de concurrence, que les litiges auxquels une cession de contrôle peut donner lieu sont de la compétence du tribunal du siège de la société et que la prescription extinctive applicable est la prescription commerciale.

Lorsque les actions d'une société sont *cotées en bourse*, une série de mesures ont été prises pour assurer la protection de ceux qui se livrent à des opérations de bourse, notamment pour assurer une certaine égalité devant les fluctuations du marché. En premier lieu, depuis une loi du 23 décembre 1964, les cessions directes d'actions cotées en bourse entre une société et une personne physique ou morale, doivent obligatoirement être réalisées par l'intermédiaire d'un agent de change qui n'admet qu'un prix voisin du cours moyen de bourse; une dissimulation d'une partie du prix réel serait une cause de nullité de la cession; toutefois, cette règle ne s'applique pas pour les cessions entre une société et une filiale à plus de 20%.

D'autre part et surtout, une réglementation de plus en plus stricte est intervenue depuis 1970 pour les offres publiques en bourse d'achat ou d'échange d'actions cotées en bourse (*O. P. A.* et *O. P. E.*) et pour les cessions de blocs de contrôle; cette réglementation résulte, d'une part, de dispositions insérées dans le Règlement des Agents de change[5] et d'autre part, d'une sorte de Code de bonne conduite des dirigeants des sociétés concernées, qui a été rédigé par la Commission des opérations de bourse. Le régime des O. P. A. et des O. P. E. est inspiré, dans une certaine mesure, par le régime des "take-over bids" du Stock Exchange de Londres; il commence par une »phase secrète« dans laquelle une banque présente, au nom de la société acheteuse, à la Chambre syndicale des Agents de change, l'offre d'acheter, ou d'échanger contre ses propres actions, un certain nombre d'actions d'une autre société cotées en bourse, dont le montant est au moins de 15% du capital de celle-ci; il peut même s'agir d'une fraction inférieure

[4] Cass. com. 21. 1. 1970 ("Cassegrain c. Saupiquet"), J. C. P. 1970, II, 16541, note B. Oppetit; Cass. com. 24. 2. 1975, Rev. Soc. 1976, p. 92.

[5] Modifié par un arrêté ministériel en 1978. V. arrêté 7 août 1978, J. O. 1978, p. 3060. Pour l'homologation des articles du règlement général de la Compagnie des agents de change relatives aux offres publiques d'achat ou d'échange v. J. O. 1978, pp. 3060-3062.

permettant à la société offrante d'acquérir le contrôle de l'autre société. La Chambre syndicale examine si l'offre est recevable et la transmet au ministre des Finances qui peut s'y opposer pour des raisons tirées du contrôle des investissements étrangers en France ou du contrôle des concentrations d'entreprises. Commence alors la phase publique: une publicité est faite qui porte sur une note d'information qui doit être visée par la Commission des Opérations de bourse qui vérifie notamment la véracité des renseignements fournis. Les dirigeants des deux sociétés concernées doivent s'abstenir de faire des opérations dépassant celle de l'administration courante; ils doivent aussi déclarer les opérations auxquelles ils se livrent sur les actions soumises à l'offre d'achat. Ces actions continuent, en principe, d'être cotées en bourse. Un délai est fixé aux actionnaires pour qu'ils se décident ou non à présenter leurs titres à la société offrante; pendant ce délai des offres concurrentes à des conditions plus avantageuses peuvent encore être présentées. Dans la pratique ces procédures sont surtout utilisées pour permettre à une société d'acquérir le contrôle d'une autre société cotée en bourse; trés souvent, les dirigeants des deux sociétés sont d'accord pour cette procédure, mais parfois ils s'opposent ce qui peut entrainer des surenchères et des litiges (O. P. A. dites »sauvage«).

La procédure de *cession de »blocs de contrôle«* a pour but de protéger les actionnaires minoritaires d'une société dont la majorité des actions est cédée par des dirigeants sociaux à de nouveaux dirigeants à qui le contrôle de la société est ainsi cédé; on a voulu éviter que cette cession se fasse à un prix élevé dont ne profiteraient pas les minoritaires. La Chambre syndicale des Agents de change apprécie s'il s'agit bien d'une cession d'un bloc de contrôle, compte tenu du nombre d'actions cédées, du nombre total des actions et du nombre d'actions répandues dans le public. Si elle estime qu'il s'agit bien d'un bloc de contrôle, un avis, visé par la C. O. B., est publié et l'acquéreur du Bloc est alors obligé d'offrir à tout autre actionnaire de lui acheter ses actions pendant 15 séances de bourse au même prix que celui prévu dans la cession du bloc de contrôle. Ainsi est assuré une sorte de »maintien des cours« pendant ce délai de 15 jours. L'acheteur, s'il le préfère, pourrait aussi proposer une O. P.A.

Ces mesures sont évidemment très protectrices des petits actionnaires. Elles montrent la différence considérable qui existe, à cet égard, entre les actions non cotées en bourse et les actions cotées en bourse.

B. Régime juridique des groupes

1. Nationalité

En principe, en droit français, une société a la »nationalité« du pays dans lequel elle a son *siège social réel*, c'est-à-dire le lieu de sa direction; ce lieu coincide, en général, avec celui du siège social indiqué dans les statuts. Cette règle s'applique, en principe, aux filiales et notamment à celles qui dépendent d'une société étrangère et qui ont leur siège en France; il en résulte que ces filiales sont régies, quant à leur constitution et à leur fonctionnement, par le droit français des sociétés. Mais, en ce qui concerne les droits dont elles peuvent se prévaloir en France, la jurisprudence a parfois décidé que les sociétés dont le siège est en

France, ne peuvent pas invoquer certains droits réservés aux nationaux français, lorsqu'elles sont sous le contrôle de personnes de nationalité étrangère. Cette jurisprudence qui est intervenue à propos des lois sur l'interdiction du commerce avec les personnes ennemies en temps de guerre, ou sur la réparation des dommages de guerre, a été confirmée par diverses textes législatifs qui concernent essentiellement la jouissance de droits de caractère public. Et ces solutions s'appliquent notamment à des filiales qui sont sous le contrôle direct ou indirect de sociétés-mères étrangères; elles sont alors considérées comme ayant la même nationalité non-française que celles-ci.

2. Domicile

Pour l'inscription d'une société au registre du commerce, les dirigeants de cette société doivent justifier que celle-ci a son siège social dans un local dont elle est propriétaire ou locataire; cependant, si l'inscription concerne une société filiale à 50% au moins, le domicile de celle-ci peut être commun avec celui de la société-mère. Par ailleurs, si une filiale n'a pas d'indépendance réelle et se trouve sous la dépendance absolue de la société-mère la jurisprudence a tendance à considérer que son siège social réel se confond avec celui de la société-mère (même si son siège statutaire est distinct) et il en résultera des conséquences importantes pour la compétence ratione loci des tribunaux; ces solutions sont notamment admises fréquemment pour les déclarations de faillite.

3. Participation au capital des sociétés-mères et filiales

Pour éviter la fictivité du capital et, dans une certaine mesure l'autocontrôle d'une société par l'intermédiaire d'une filiale qui participerait au capital de la société-mère, le droit français, depuis 1943, contient des dispositions sur la limitation des *participations réciproques ou croisées.*[6] Toute société dont une fraction du capital égale ou supérieure à 10% est la propriété d'une autre société, ne peut pas posséder d'actions de cette dernière société. Il en résulte que deux sociétés peuvent participer au capital de chacune d'elles dans une proportion inférieure à 10%. Mais, dès qu'une société détient plus de 10% du capital d'une autre société elle doit informer celle-ci et cette dernière, en principe, ne peut plus détenir aucune fraction du capital de l'autre, même au-dessous de 10%; elle doit vendre dans un délai d'un an les actions qu'elle peut détenir dans le capital de l'autre. Si une société par actions détient plus de 10% du capital d'une société d'un autre type (S. A. R. L. ou société en nom collectif) c'est toujours cette seconde société qui doit vendre les participations qu'elle peut détenir dans le capital de la société par actions. Ces règles sont assorties de sanctions pénales; mais elles ne jouent presque jamais dans la pratique car, dans les groupes de sociétés, il est très facile de les tourner en faisant intervenir une troisième société et en réalisant ce qu'on appelle des *participations circulaires* qui parviennent aux mêmes résultats, en ce qui concerne l'autocontrôle, que les participations réciproques ou croisées. Un projet de loi prévoit des modifications sur ce point à la législation en vigueur.

[6] Art. 358 et seq. loi 24. 7. 1966.

4. Information des associés ou du public

Diverses mesures ont été prises pour développer l'information des associés et des usagers de la Bourse de valeur sur les groupes de sociétés. Elles sont cependant encore assez timides. Tout d'abord, le rapport annuel que les dirigeants sociaux présentent aux actionnaires ou associés doit:

- signaler toute acquisition ou aliénation de plus de la moitié du capital social d'une autre société (filiale) française
- signaler toute prise de participation supérieure à 10% dans le capital d'une autre société
- rendre compte des activités des filiales par branche d'activité et faire ressortir les résultats obtenus; un tableau est annexé au rapport du Conseil, qui donne les résultats de chaque filiale française dont la valeur des actions dépasse 1% du capital de la société, ainsi que les résultats globaux par catégories des autres filiales et des participations françaises et étrangères; ce tableau doit aussi mentionner les prêts et garanties fournis par la société-mère à ses filiales et participations.

Ce dernier compte-rendu des résultats des filiales et participations n'est pas nécessaire si la société-mère tient des comptes consolidés et remplace dans son bilan la valeur des titres de participation en portefeuille par la situation nette de chaque société émettrice et indique la méthode d'établissement de ses comptes consolidés. Pour le moment, de tels *comptes consolidés ne* sont *pas imposés* par la législation française; mais il en sera autrement si la directive de la C. E. E. sur les comptes de groupes de sociétés est adoptée. Cependant, dès maintenant, la C. O. B. exige que la société qui demande que ses titres soient cotés en bourse ou qui entend faire appel à l'épargne publique et qui soumet une "note d'information" à la C. O. B. pour obtenir le visa de celle-ci, fournisse à l'appui des comptes consolidés de groupe, contresignés par le commissaire aux comptes.

Le rapport annuel des commissaires aux comptes dans les sociétés par actions doit aussi signaler les prises de participation survenues au cours de l'exercice. On notera que les commissaires aux comptes ont le droit de se faire communiquer les comptes de toutes les filiales, ainsi que de la société-mère de la société qu'ils contrôlent, mais non pas ceux des autres filiales de cette société-mère.

Par ailleurs, les sociétés dont les titres sont cotés en bourse et qui ont un bilan supérieur à dix millions de francs, ainsi que leurs filiales (même non cotées en bourse) qui ont aussi un bilan supérieur à ce chiffre, doivent publier chaque année au Bulletin des annonces légales obligatoires (B. A. L. O.) 45 jours après l'approbation des comptes par l'assemblée générale, le tableau des renseignements concernant les filiales et participations qui est annexé au rapport du conseil d'administration.

Mais, pour le moment, rien n'impose à une société d'indiquer à ses actionnaires ou associés, ni à fortiori de publier, la liste de ses principaux actionnaires; un projet de loi tend à la fourniture d'un tel renseignement, mais il se heurte à la résistance de la pratique.

5. Incompatibilités

Une société ne peut pas exercer les fonctions de président du conseil d'administration, de directeur général, de membre du directoire, de président du conseil de surveillance d'une société anonyme, ni de gérant d'une société à responsabilité limitée, car ces fonctions sont réservées à des personnes physiques; mais il est facile pour une société-mère de faire exercer de telles fonctions dans ses filiales par ses propres dirigeants sociaux ou par des cadres salariés soumis à son autorité. En revanche, une société peut être administrateur ou membre du conseil de surveillance d'une société anonyme et il suffit alors qu'elle désigne un "représentant permanent" qui siège en son nom dans ces conseils.

Pour faciliter la gestion des groupes de sociétés, la loi admet qu'une personne physique ou morale qui exerce les fonctions d'administrateur ou de membre du conseil de surveillance dans une société anonyme peut cumuler ces fonctions avec celles d'administrateur ou de membre du conseil de surveillance dans cinq autres sociétés dont la première détient plus de 20% du capital social, en plus des huit autres postes admis par le droit commun dans toutes autres sociétés.

Les articles 101 et suivants et 141 et suivants de la loi du 24 juillet 1966 sur les sociétés commerciales, contiennent des dispositions pour soumettre à contrôle les contrats conclus entre une société et un de ses dirigeants afin d'éviter les excès auxquels pourraient conduire les conflits d'intérêts. Ce contrôle (autorisation préalable du conseil d'administration ou de surveillance, rapport du commissaire aux comptes, approbation a posteriori de l'assemblée générale des actionnaires) ne s'appliquent pas de plein droit aux contrats conclus entre sociétés appartenant au même groupe; mais il en est autrement lorsque ces sociétés ont des dirigeants communs, notamment des administrateurs communs, ce qui est assez fréquent. Ces textes contiennent d'ailleurs une règle de faveur pour les groupes de sociétés; alors qu'en droit commun, une société anonyme ne peut pas consentir des prêts ou des cautions et garanties à un de ses administrateurs, elle le peut lorsque l'administrateur est une société, ce qui suppose que cette société est la société-mère ou possède du moins une participation dans le capital.

Les dirigeants de la société anonyme dont les titres sont cotés en bourse doivent mettre au nominatif ou déposer en compte spécial en banque les actions de la société qu'ils dirigent ainsi que de toutes les sociétés du groupe, afin que la C. O. B. puisse exercer un contrôle sur les opérations en bourse ou hors bourse que ces dirigeants peuvent faire avec leurs titres. Par ailleurs si ces dirigeants et toutes autres personnes »initiées« à raison de leurs fonctions, profitent de renseignements acquis avant que le public n'en ait eu connaissance pour réaliser des opérations en bourse, ils encourent des sanctions pénales.[7]

Les commissaires aux comptes d'une société peuvent aussi exercer leurs fonctions dans les sociétés-mère ou filiales de cette société. Mais des mesures sont prises pour que le commissaire aux comptes d'une société ne cumule pas ses fonctions avec celles de dirigeant d'une société-mère ou filiale (à 10%) de celle-ci; et il ne peut pas être nommé dirigeant d'une société-mère ou filiale moins de cinq ans après avoir abandonné ses fonctions de commissaire aux comptes.

[7] Art. 162-I et seq. loi 24. 7. 1966.

6. *Gestion abusive*

En droit commun, le dirigeant d'une société anonyme ou à responsabilité limitée, commet un délit pénal sanctionné d'amende et/ou d'emprisonnement, s'il utilise abusivement les biens sociaux dans son intérêt personnel ou dans l'intérêt d'une autre entreprise qu'il dirige, ou s'il utilise abusivement ses pouvoirs ou ses droits de vote dans un intérêt autre que l'intérêt social. Ces sanctions sont en principe applicables dans les groupes de sociétés, de telle sorte que si le dirigeant de la société-mère ou de la société holding utilise les biens d'une filiale contrôlée par celle-ci ou utilise les droits de vote attachés aux actions détenues par la société-mère ou la holding, dans l'intérêt du groupe tout entier et au préjudice de la filiale, les actionnaires minoritaires de la filiale peuvent poursuivre ce dirigeant devant les tribunaux repressifs pour délit d'abus des biens sociaux ou d'abus des pouvoirs et votes. Cependant, la jurisprudence récente tient compte, dans une certaine mesure, de l'intérêt légitime du groupe pour écarter le délit.[8] Elle prononce notamment le relaxe si le groupe de sociétés repose sur des bases non artificielles et si les transferts d'actif d'une filiale à la société-mère (notamment les avances) concourent à la politique d'ensemble et à l'équilibre du groupe, sans faire courir des risques trop importants à la filiale et au moyen de contreparties suffisantes.

Cette jurisprudence tient donc compte – dans une certaine mesure – de la réalité des groupes de sociétés pour admettre des transferts d'actif ou de bénéfices entre les sociétés du groupe; mais le délit serait retenu si la filiale était utilisée par le groupe de façon abusive et au préjudice de ses actionnaires minoritaires.

On peut encore citer un autre effort de la jurisprudence pour protéger la filiale et ses associés minoritaires (outsiders) contre les excès commis par la société-mère dans le contrôle de la filiale, l'affaire *Fruehauf*.[9] Dans cette affaire, la société-mère américaine avait interdit à sa filiale française de produire des remorques de camion à destination de la Chine; mais les actionnaires minoritaires estimaient que cet ordre – pris sous la pression du Gouvernement des U. S. A. – risquait de conduire la filiale à la ruine et leurs représentants au conseil d'administration démissionnèrent et demandèrent au Tribunal de désigner un administrateur judiciaire provisoire chargé notamment d'exécuter le contrat litigieux. Il fut fait droit à cette demande, la position des dirigeants américains étant considérée comme abusive et de nature à nuire aux minoritaires.

En droit commun et malgré certaines atténuations jurisprudentielles, les dirigeants de la société-mère ou de la holding ne sont donc pas les maîtres de la société et s'il existe des minoritaires, leur responsabilité peut être engagée à leur égard.

[8] Trib. corr. Paris 26. 11. 1968, Rev. Trim. Dr. Com. 1968, 1080, note R. Houin; Paris, 16. 5. 1974, Rev. Soc. 1975, p. 657.

[9] Trib. corr. Paris, 22. 5. 1965, J. C. P. 1965, II, 14274 bis.

7. Obligation aux dettes de la filiale

En principe, la société-mère n'est pas tenue des dettes de sa filiale, car il s'agit de deux personnes morales et de deux patrimoines distincts.[10] Mais la solution est inverse si la filiale a une personalité morale fictive, par exemple si tout son capital est entre les mains de la société-mère ou si elle a été constituée dans un but de fraude; la solution est encore inverse lorsqu'il existe une *confusion* totale des activités et des patrimoines des deux sociétés du groupe et si celles-ci apparaissent comme une société unique. Ces solutions sont principalement relevées lorsque la filiale est mise en faillite: la *faillite* pourra être *"étendue"* à la société-mère (et plus généralement à toutes les sociétés d'un groupe); elle pourra aussi être étendue de la filiale à la société-mère lorsque celle-ci a dirigé en fait ou en droit la première et a abusé des actifs sociaux de la filiale dans son intérêt propre ou dans l'intérêt du groupe.[11] Dans de telles hypothèses et spécialement en cas de confusion des patrimoines, une seule masse sera constituée, réunissant tous les actifs des sociétés du groupe et tous les créanciers des diverses sociétés du groupe.

Mais, encore une fois, il s'agit de dérogations au principe d'après lequel les personnalités et les patrimoines de chaque sociéte du groupe sont distincts.

8. Situation des salariés

Les règles qui viennent d'être dégagées pour l'obligation aux dettes s'appliquent aussi à la situation des salariés des sociétés faisant partie d'un même groupe. En principe, si les diverses sociétés demeurent nettement distinctes dans leur activité et leur patrimoine, le salarié n'est lié par son contrat de travail qu'avec la société avec laquelle il l'a conclu; s'il en conclut successivement avec deux sociétés d'un même groupe, son ancienneté prise en considération pour le calcul d'une indemnité de licenciement ne s'additionnera pas et si, dans la première société, il bénéficiait d'une convention collective, il ne pourra pas invoquer celle-ci dans la seconde société dans laquelle il est entré.[12]

Mais on considère au contraire que les diverses sociétés du même groupe qui ont employé le salarié doivent être considérées comme un employeur unique, notamment du point du vue du calcul de l'ancienneté et des indemnités, si toutes ces sociétés, malgré leur forme juridique particulière, avaient des activités confondues et ne constituaient qu'une seule et même entreprise.[13] Dans cette hypothèse, on tiendra compte du nombre total des salariés du groupe pour apprécier si ce nombre était supérieur à celui prévu par la loi pour l'exercice des fonctions des délégués du personnel ou du comité d'entreprise.

On peut encore noter que les textes qui favorisent l'actionnariat des salariés au

[10] Cass. 3ème civ. 22. 5. 1975, Rev. Trim. Dr. Com. 1975, p. 866, obs. C. Champaud; Cass. com. 15. 10. 1974, ibid. 1975, p. 530; Rev. Soc. 1975, p. 495.

[11] Art. 101 loi 13. 7. 1967.

[12] Cass. soc. 7. 2. 1973, Bull. cass. civ. V, n° 507; Cass. soc. 8. 7. 1975, Bull. civ., V, n ° 382.

[13] Cass. soc. 10. 5. 1972, Rev. Soc. 1973, p. 139; Cass. soc. 23. 6. 1960, Dr. Soc. 1961, p. 600.

moyen d'attribution d'actions ou d'options d'achat ou de souscription d'actions,[14] prévoient que ces attributions ou options peuvent profiter à tous les salariés des sociétés d'un même groupe et porter sur des actions de l'une ou l'autre de ces sociétés.

9. *Droit fiscal*

Le droit fiscal qui est toujours le premier à s'adapter à la réalité économique, ne manque pas de tenir compte de l'existence des groupes de sociétés, tantôt pour leur concéder des avantages, tantôt au contraire pour parer aux fraudes qui peuvent en résulter.

Les avantages concernent surtout l'impôt des sociétés sur les bénéfices réalisés par celles-ci. Afin d'*éviter une double imposition*, au niveau de la *filiale* et au niveau de la *société-mère*, des bénéfices réalisés par la première et transmis à la seconde, le droit fiscal exonère la société-mère de l'impôt sur les dividendes qui lui sont versés par la filiale. Ce règime joue même lorsque la participation au capital ne dépasse pas 10% et peut parfois descendre au-dessous de ce seuil. D'autre part, pour les sociétés-mères qui ont des filiales à l'étranger, le droit fiscal admet une imposition du bénéfice global réalisé par toutes les sociétés du groupe (système du bénéfice mondial), ce qui permet de déduire de la société-mère française les pertes subies par des filiales étrangères. Enfin, si une société-mère a plus de 95% du capital de sa filiale, elle peut, avec l'autorisation de l'administration, intégrer complètement les résultats de sa filiale dans ses propres résultats comme si cette filiale n'etait qu'une succursale.

Inversement, le droit fiscal prend des mesures pour éviter une évasion fiscale qui résulterait d'un *transfert* plus ou moins clandestin de bénéfices *entre une société-mère et une société-filiale* placée sous sa dépendance et sa direction et dont le siège serait *à l'étranger*. Il est trop facile, en effet, en ce cas, de pratiquer entre la société française et la société filiale des prix tels que la première ne fasse jamais de bénéfice et que tous les bénéfices soient reportés sur la filiale. Ces dispositions intéressent surtout la taxe à la valeur ajoutée et le régime des importations.

En conclusion de la première partie, on voit que le droit français ne connait pas un régime général des groupes de sociétés. On trouve quelques dispositions éparses et non coordonnées dans le droit des sociétés et le droit du travail, complétées par la jurisprudence, encore que celle-ci ne puisse tenir compte de l'existence d'un groupe de sociétés que lorsque l'autonomie des diverses sociétés du groupe disparait derrière une activité commune, sinon une confusion des patrimoines.

C'est ce qui explique le mouvement qui se dessine – non sans hésitation – pour introduire dans le droit français des règles sur les groupes de sociétés, plus ou moins inspirées du droit allemand, en attendant la directive de la C. E. E. sur les groupes de sociétés.

[14] Art. 208-3 et seq. loi 24. 7. 1966, modifiée par lois 31. 2. 1970 et 27. 12. 1973.

II. Projets de réforme

Le Gouvernement français, devant l'hostilité des milieux d'affaires, n'a pas encore mis à l'étude la réforme du droit des groupes de sociétés; à plusieurs reprises, il a fait connaître qu'il attendrait l'adoption par la Commission des Communautés européennes, du projet de directive sur les groupes de sociétés fondée sur l'article 54, § 3 (g) du Traité de Rome. Attitude prudente car on ne sait pas encore à quelle date cette directive qui a soulevé d'importantes réserves, sera adoptée.

Cependant une initiative parlementaire d'un député, *M. Cousté*, a abouti au dépôt devant l'Assemblée nationale, d'une proposition de loi "sur les groupes de sociétés et la protection des actionnaires, du personnel et des tiers". Cette proposition a été déposée d'abord le 19 février 1970[15] puis reprise dans les mêmes termes le 2 avril 1973 après des élections générales. Elle a de nouveau été reprise le 1er août 1974[16] mais avec des modifications sensibles. En effet, dans sa première formulation, cette proposition reprenait la distinction du droit allemand entre les groupes de droit (résultant d'un contrat d'affiliation) et les groupes de fait qui ne sont assujettis aux règles des groupes de sociétés que sur une décision judiciaire à la demande notamment des actionnaires minoritaires. Dans sa forme de 1974, la proposition Cousté admet l'existence de contrats d'affiliation par lesquels les groupes se soumettent *volontairement* à des règles protectrices des actionnaires "outsiders" et des créanciers; mais, à défaut d'un tel contrat, le régime juridique des groupes serait exclu et les sociétés du groupe ainsi que leurs dirigeants demeureraient soumis aux règles du droit commun des sociétés; certaines de ces règles seraient même aggravées, puisqu'à défaut de contrat d'affiliation, les dirigeants du groupe n'auraient nullement le pouvoir de donner des ordres aux filiales dans l'intérêt du groupe, d'imposer des prix entrainant des pertes, de procéder à des transferts d'actif de société à société ou à des glissements de bénéfices, de consentir des avances ou des prêts, etc.

La proposition définit le lien de groupe par, d'une part, la dépendance d'une société qui peut résulter d'une participation au capital ou de tout autre accord ou contrat, et d'autre part, de l'unité de direction. Les règles concernant les groupes de sociétés supposent l'intervention d'un contrat d'affiliation entre les deux sociétés qui prévoit un "règlement terminal" pour protéger les actionnaires: ceux-ci doivent avoir une option entre le retrait de la filiale avec paiement d'une indemnité ou échange d'actions de la société-mère ou d'une autre société du groupe et, d'autre part, le maintien dans la filiale avec une allocation compensatrice annuelle consistant soit en une allocation fixe calculée sur le rendement actuel, soit en une fraction des résultats du groupe.

Diverses obligations sont imposées à la société tête de groupe. Elle doit tenir des comptes consolidés; les participations doivent être publiées; chaque année la

[15] Ass. Nat. n° 1055.

[16] N° 1-211; P.-B. Cousté, *Vers un nouveau statut des groupes de sociétés*, GAZ. PAL. Nos. 145-147, 25.-27. 5. 1975, p. 5. La dernière version date du 28 juin 1978, n° 522, et est reproduite *infra*, annexe II n° 2, pp. 296 et seq.

société-mère doit compenser intégralement les pertes de la filiale affiliée, ce qui peut être très lourd.

Pour la protection des créanciers, la société dominante est obligée solidairement avec sa filiale. Quant aux salariés, le projet est assez vague et prévoit seulement la création d'un Comité d'entreprise de groupe.

En l'absence de contrat d'affiliation, le droit commun continue de s'appliquer avec la rigueur des règles sur l'abus des biens sociaux: l'intérêt du groupe ne suffit pas à justifier le préjudice qui peut être causé à l'intérêt d'une filiale. Il n'y a pas de règlement terminal; rien n'est prévu pour le retrait des actionnaires, ni pour le versement d'indemnités précises. Mais, si les dirigeants de la société dominante nuisent à une filiale dans l'intérêt du groupe, les actionnaires minoritaires peuvent demander des indemnités à la société dominante et agir en responsabilité civile et même pénale contre les dirigeants du groupe. On espère que ce régime s'étendra à la conclusion du contrat d'affiliation.

On notera enfin que le projet contient une disposition intéressante, inspirée du droit allemand et du droit anglo-américain, qui permettrait à une société détenant plus de 95% du capital d'une autre, de racheter les quelques actions demeurant entre les mains d'actionnaires, pour intégrer complètement une telle filiale.

Cette proposition est intéressante bien qu'assez timide. Il n'est pas du tout assuré qu'elle ait une chance d'être adoptée. Le Gouvernement et le Parlement, devant l'hostilité des milieux d'affaires, attendront sans doute de se faire "forcer la main" par la C. E. E.*

* Note bibliographique:

M. van Haecke, Les groupes de sociétés (Paris, 1959); C. Champaud, Le pouvoir de concentration de la société par actions (Paris, 1962); R. Rodière, *Groupement et société en droit français*, in P. Verrucoli, ed., Evolution et perspectives du droit des sociétés, tôme II p. 377 (Milan, 1968); Conseil supérieur de l'ordre des experts comptables et des comptables agréés, Les groupes et groupements de sociétés (Paris, 1968); D. Schmidt, Les droits de la minorité dans la société anonyme (Paris, 1970); Droit des groupes de sociétés analyse – propositions, Colloque á l'université de Rennes (Paris, 1972), *v. spéc.* R. Houin, *Rapport de synthèse*, p. 209; A. Petitpierre-Sauvain, Droit de sociétés et groupes de sociétés (Genève, 1972); Les groupes de sociétés, Une politique législative, Étude du centre de recherche sur le droit des affaires (Paris, 1975); M. Béjot, La protection des actionnaires externes dans les groupes de sociétés en France et en Allemagne (Bruxelles, 1976); C. Champaud, *Les méthodes de groupement des sociétés*, Rev. Trim. Dr. Com. 1967, 1003; R. Rodière, *La protection des minorités dans les groupes de sociétés*, Rev. Soc. 1970, 243; J. Paillusseau, *Les groupes de sociétés*, Rev. Trim. Dr. Com. 1972, 813. *Cf.* aussi les indications bibliographiques données par Y. Guyon, *Examen critique des projets européens en matière de groupes de sociétés: le point de vue français*, *infra* pp. 155 et seq. *Cf.* en langue allemande, G. Brachvogel, *Die neuere Entwicklung des Konzernrechts in Frankreich*, ZGR 1980, 486.

Summary:

Groups of Companies in French Law

The report deals with the French law concerning enterprise groups. In France such groups are usually set up by means of participations and only in rare cases by enterprise contracts, since there are no tax privileges for such contracts under French tax law. Even though the phenomenon of enterprise groups is quite important in France, the pertinent French law is poor. This is especially true for the statutory law, while there is a certain body of relevant case law. There is no general legal definition of what constitutes an enterprise group, but there are definitions of a participation (possession of 10% to 50% by one company of the capital of another company) and of a subsidiary (participation of more than 50%). In the first part of the report the widely dispersed provisions and rules concerning enterprise groups, the problems of a 100%-held subsidiary and of the constitution of a subsidiary by the purchase of shares which are quoted on the stock exchange are discussed. As far as the juridical regime of enterprise groups is concerned, there are several peculiarities. They concern the nationality of the subsidiary, its domicile, reciprocal participations or cross-holdings, disclosure to the shareholders and the public, certain incompatibilities, the problem of abusive management and of a possible justification on the grounds of the interest of the group as a whole, the liability of the dominating enterprise for the debts of its subsidiary, the legal status of the workers within the enterprise group and finally some specific tax law problems. In the second part the reform discussion is mentioned. There have been repeated Parliamentary initiatives (project "Cousté"), but so far they have been without success. It seems that the French Government as well as the Parliament, aware of the hostility of business towards such plans, would rather wait for the EEC to force the Member States by a directive to enact statutory provisions on enterprise groups.

Les groupes de sociétés et l'expérience du droit belge

PIERRE VAN OMMESLAGHE
Bruxelles

I. Introduction

1. Importance de la question et l'expérience belge en ce domaine

La vie économique et sociale en Belgique est, dans une large mesure, dominée par des groupes de sociétés dont certains sont très puissants et jouissent de pouvoirs économiques considérables. Le développement économique du pays est d'ailleurs assuré en grande partie par ces groupes. La plupart des entreprises industrielles ou même commerciales de quelque importance dépendent, de manière plus ou moins étroite, d'un groupe de sociétés. A la tête de ces groupes, se trouvent le plus généralement des entreprises financières; les groupes à caractère purement industriel ou commercial sont rares ou sont d'importance limitée.

Même s'il est difficile de donner une description complète du phénomène, son évidence frappe tous les juristes qui pratiquent le droit des affaires. Une enquête, qui permet de se faire une certaine idée du phénomène, a été récemment menée à l'initiative de la Commission Droit et Vie des Affaires de l'Université de Liège.[1] Les tentatives destinées à dessiner la «géographie» ou encore la «morphologie» des groupes financiers, demeurent fragmentaires, et sans caractère scientifique suffisant pour servir de base à une étude juridique.

L'enquête menée par les collaborateurs de la Commission Droit et Vie des Affaires met particulièrement en lumière la variété et la complexité des relations entre les sociétés d'un même groupe et la prudence avec laquelle il convient d'aborder toute réglementation, si l'on veut tenir compte de la vie économique réelle.

C'est sans doute ce qui explique le caractère très pragmatique de l'«approche belge» en ce domaine. Ce pragmatisme et l'importance du phénomène au niveau national expliquent que l'étude du droit belge puisse présenter un certain intérêt, particulièrement pour les petits pays. Nous verrons en effet que certaines des

[1] *Cf.* les documents distribués à l'occasion des journées d'études de la Commission Droit et Vie des Affaires le 19, 20 et 21 octobre 1972, à Liège. Une partie de la documentation et des études a fait l'objet d'un volume intitulé «Les Groupes de sociétés» (Fac. Lettres, Liège, 1973), cité ci-après comme LIÈGE, LES GROUPES DE SOCIÉTÉS. On y trouve la synthèse de l'enquête menée, à p. 30 *et seq.*

solutions auxquelles la Belgique est arrivée ne sont applicables de manière efficace que dans le cadre d'une communauté nationale relativement restreinte.

2. *Définition des groupes de sociétés*

La doctrine récente parait se rallier assez nettement à une conception générale commune du groupe de sociétés – malgré des nuances dont il convient naturellement de tenir compte.

Chacun reconnaît qu'il y a lieu de définir le groupe de sociétés et la concentration en les opposant notamment aux cartels, aux ententes et aux méthodes de coopération entre entreprises qui demeurent indépendantes non seulement juridiquement mais encore économiquement.[2] Suivant ce courant, nous proposons de considérer qu'il existe un groupe de sociétés lorsque plusieurs sociétés juridiquement indépendantes se trouvent réunies sous une direction économique unique, quels que soient les instruments qui permettent d'imposer cette direction unique.[3]

Cette direction économique unique peut résulter d'un contrôle exercé par une société sur une ou plusieurs autres. Elle peut également résulter de l'influence exercée par des administrateurs communs ou des actionnaires communs à plusieurs sociétés, sans que l'une domine nécessairement l'autre. Chacun sait que ce critère est inspiré de la doctrine puis de la loi allemande où il correspond à la notion de *Konzern* appliqué tant dans la loi sur les sociétés que dans la loi sur la concurrence (GWB).

3. *Les méthodes de groupement de sociétés*

Dans la pratique belge, la plupart des techniques usuellement décrites pour la formation des groupes de sociétés se rencontrent.[4]

[2] Sur la définition du concept de groupes de sociétés dans la doctrine de langue française récente, *cf.* G. Keutgen, Le droit des groupes de sociétés dans la CEE, p. 5 *et seq.* et les réf. (Louvain, 1973;) A. Petitpierre-Sauvain, Droit des sociétés et groupes de sociétés, n° 73 *et seq.* et les réf. (Genève, 1972); liège, les groupes de sociétés, spécialement les rapports de A. Jacquemin, p. 27, et l'intervention de O. Penard, p. 55, ainsi que le rapport général de R. Houin, p. 227. *Cf. aussi* les ouvrages classiques de C. Champaud, Le pouvoir de concentration de la société anonyme (Paris, 1962); de J. Paillusseau, La société anonyme technique d'organisation de l'entreprise (Paris, 1967), ainsi que de M. Vanhaecke, les groupes de sociétés (Paris, 1962). En Allemagne, H. Würdinger, Aktien- und Konzernrecht, p. 252 *et seq.* (Karlsruhe, 3e éd., 1973); H. G. Koppensteiner, Internationale Unternehmen im deutschen Gesellschaftsrecht (Frankfurt, 1971); E. Rehbinder, Konzernaussenrecht und allgemeines Privatrecht, p. 33 *et seq.* (Bad Homburg, 1969).

[3] Pour les besoins de l'analyse du droit belge, il n'est guère nécessaire d'envisager l'hypothèse d'un groupe comprenant des entreprises qui n'auraient pas la forme de sociétés. Du point de vue théorique, cela serait possible, mais ne se rencontre guère, sinon jamais, en pratique.

[4] Pour une description des méthodes de groupements de sociétés en droit belge v. J. Van Ryn, *Les méthodes de groupement des sociétés en droit belge,* dans Rapport au VIIe Congrès international de droit comparé (Centre Universitaire de droit comparé, Bruxelles, 1966). Nous ne reprenons pas cette description ici. *Cf. aussi,* Keutgen, *supra* note 2, p. 15 *et seq.*

Sans qu'il soit possible de faire ici un inventaire détaillé de toutes les méthodes utilisées en Belgique pour constituer des groupes de sociétés, on peut mentionner les techniques suivantes.

Le moyen le plus usuellement utilisé pour la constitution des groupes, consiste naturellement dans *la prise de participations*. Les sociétés dominantes assurent leurs pouvoirs sur les sociétés filiales grâce à une participation dans le capital de celles-ci qui leur procure un pouvoir de vote déterminant à l'assemblée générale.[5] Tantôt il s'agit d'une participation majoritaire; tantôt les sociétés dominantes se contentent d'une majorité de fait à l'assemblée générale, assise sur une participation inférieure à 50% du capital social. Cette dernière situation se rencontre notamment lorsque les actions sont répandues dans le public et repose sur la constatation de la désaffection bien connue des actionnaires pour les assemblées générales. On rencontre aussi des participations qui portent sur la quasi totalité du capital social.[6]

Très souvent, les liens de domination fondés sur une participation sont complétés par des *conventions* conclues entre *les groupes d'actionnaires* ou entre des actionnaires qui conviennent de se réunir pour assurer la domination sur la société et la stabilité de sa gestion. Ces conventions portent sur la concertation entre les actionnaires dominants, sur la répartition des mandats au sein des conseils d'administration et des organes exécutifs des sociétés, sur l'appui à apporter éventuellement par ces actionnaires à la filiale notamment sur le plan des moyens de financement, sur la détermination des grandes lignes de la politique de la société filiale. Ces conventions, extrêmement fréquentes dans la pratique, sont cependant dans l'état actuel du droit belge, sans valeur juridique, car elles portent atteinte au libre exercice du droit de vote aux assemblées générales et au fonctionnement de la société anonyme telle que la détermine la loi.[7] Néanmoins, elles sont très généralement respectées même s'il n'apparait pas possible de leur

[5] En droit belge, le droit de vote dans les assemblées générales de sociétés anonymes est nécessairement proportionnel à la participation au capital social, sous réserve des réductions du droit de vote individuel d'un même actionnaire qu'imposent les articles 75 et 76 des lois coordonnées. Le droit belge actual ne connaît ni les actions à vote plural, ni les actions sans droit de vote ou à droit de vote conditionnel. Le projet de réforme du droit des sociétés autorise, en revanche, l'émission d'actions privilégiées sans droit de vote qui pourraient jouer un rôle important notamment dans la structure des groupes de sociétés.

[6] Rappelons que selon le droit belge, la société anonyme doit comprendre au moins sept actionnaires, mais en pratique on rencontre des sociétés filiales dans lesquelles six personnes détiennent chacune une action, tandis que le solde est détenu par la société-mère. Le projet de réforme actuellement déposé au Parlement autorise dans ce cas la constitution d'une société d'une personne.

[7] Sur la nullité des pactes syndicataires, lorsqu'ils impliquent notamment un accord sur l'exercice du droit de vote aux assemblées générales *v.* J. Van Ryn et P. Van Ommeslaghe, *Examen de jurisprudence sur les sociétés commerciales*, R. C. J. B. 1967, p. 345, n° 57 et les références à la doctrine et à la jurisprudence constantes. Sur ce point encore, le projet de réforme des lois sur les sociétés propose de modifier le droit positif et de ne condamner les pactes de l'espèce que lorsqu'ils deviennent l'instrument d'un abus de majorité.

donner une sanction par un recours au tribunal ou l'allocation de dommages-intérêts en cas d'inexécution.

Un autre moyen classique de réaliser une domination entre sociétés ou de les inclure dans un groupe soumis à une politique unique, consiste à assurer des liens personnels par la ***désignation d'administrateurs communs.*** Cette pratique est très fréquente en Belgique. Elle est souvent consacrée par des conventions du type de celles décrites au paragraphe précédent. Par exemple, à la suite d'un regroupement lorsqu'elles aboutissent à dessaisir les conseils d'administration des sociétés d'électricité, une politique commune est assurée par la complète identité dans la composition de conseils d'administration et de comités de direction de certaines de ces sociétés — en vertu d'un protocole intervenu entre les sociétés holding qui les contrôlent.

On rencontre encore des groupes reposant sur l'utilisation de *la technique contractuelle*. Une certaine propension à accroître le recours à ces méthodes peut être observée dans la pratique. La légalité de ces conventions, tout particulièrement lorsqu'elles aboutissent à dessaisir les conseils d'administration des sociétés membres de leur pouvoir de décision et à aliéner l'autonomie des sociétés regroupées est très douteuse,[8] mais les nécessités de la pratique sont souvent plus fortes que les considérations proprement juridiques. Ainsi, on utilise parfois la forme de l'association en participation pour réunir diverses sociétés qui demeurent juridiquement indépendantes, mais, qui par leur participation à l'association, deviennent associées et en arrivent à former un groupe. L'association en participation est un moyen d'arriver économiquement aux mêmes résultats qu'une fusion, mais sans aliénation patrimoniale et en maintenant l'identité juridique distincte des sociétés regroupées.[9] Dans d'autres cas, on conclut des contrats de concession des installations et du fonds de commerce, ou encore des contrats de gestion pouvant se traduire par une véritable aliénation du pouvoir de décision.[10]

4. Etat de la législation belge

La loi belge sur les sociétés ignore la notion de groupes de sociétés et la doctrine classique en la matière n'y fait guère allusion. La société est toujours considérée comme si elle demeurait isolée et indépendante — ce qui, de toute évidence ne correspond pas à la réalité. Toutefois, des études récentes tiennent compte de ce phénomène fondamental et tentent d'en décrire les effets et d'en cerner les contours.[11] Des journées d'études et des cours approfondis lui sont maintenant consacrés.[12]

[8] J. Van Ryn, ***supra*** note 4.

[9] J. Van Ryn, ***supra*** note 4.

[10] Les contrats de gestion se traduisant par une aliénation du pouvoir de décision ont appelé des critiques de la part de la Commission bancaire: rapport 1973-74, p. 81. Par ailleurs, on rencontre dans la pratique de groupes déjà constitués, des contrats de gestion limités à des aspects techniques ou administratifs des activités des sociétés filiales qui ne peuvent appeler de critiques.

[11] *Cf.* notamment, LIÈGE, LES GROUPES DE SOCIÉTÉS, ***supra*** note 1, et KEUTGEN, ***supra*** note 2, où l'on trouvera une bibliographie à ce propos.

[12] Outre les journées d'études de la Commission Droit et Vie des Affaires en 1972, ***supra***

Le projet de réforme des lois coordonnées sur les sociétés commerciales propose une définition de la société dominante et de la société dépendante et, partant, dans une certaine mesure, du groupe de sociétés – mais uniquement à des fins limitées: il s'agit d'éviter que, par le biais de sociétés filiales ou de sociétés dominantes, on n'élude des dispositions relatives au fonctionnement de la société anonyme comme telle.[13] On ne trouve pas dans ce projet une organisation des groupes de sociétés quoique la Commission appelée à l'élaborer à la demande du Ministre de la Justice, en ait examiné l'opportunité.[14]

La définition donnée dans le projet de réforme a inspiré d'une part les avant-projets de directives actuellement en cours d'élaboration à la C. E.E. et, d'autre part, le législateur belge qui l'a utilisée dans diverses lois particulières qui contribuent à l'organisation progressive du groupe de sociétés: il s'agit notamment de l'arrêté de pouvoirs spéciaux n° 64 du 10 novembre 1967 organisant le statut des sociétés à portefeuille, et leur association à la programmation économique, modifié par une loi du 20 janvier 1978 et de la nouvelle législation comptable instituée par une loi du 17 juillet 1975 et par ses arrêtés d'application dont particulièrement un arrêté royal du 29 novembre 1977 sur les comptes annuels des sociétés à portefeuille (pris en exécution de l'article 73 d'une loi du 30 juin 1975, concernant le statut des banques, des caisses d'épargne privées et d'autres institutions financières).

On peut donc relever une évolution très nette dans ce domaine - non seulement dans les conceptions des juristes ou des praticiens des sociétés, mais encore dans les interventions du législateur.

5. *L'entreprise multinationale*

Le droit belge n'a pas considéré jusqu'à présent que l'entreprise dite "multinationale" présentait un caractère spécifique sur le plan juridique. Certes, ces entreprises, par leur puissance et par la variété de leurs moyens d'actions, peuvent donner lieu à des préoccupations sur le plan politique, mais celles-ci ne

note 1, *cf. aussi* le séminaire postdoctoral de l'Université Catholique de Louvain, sous la direction du regretté Professeur Renaud, REV. PRAT. SOC. 1972, pp. 1 à 102, et le cycle de cours donné à l'Université de Gand, en 1972, publiés sous le titre EKONOMISCH EN FINANCIEEL RECHT VANDAAG, II; *cf. aussi* notre cours à l'Institut Universitaire International à Luxembourg, *v.* les recueils de cours: les groupes de sociétés, les sociétés multinationales–Company Systems and Affiliation, Multinational Enterprises, directeur du programme U. Immenga.

[13] Ce que j'appelais dans un rapport introductif destiné aux autorités de la C. E. E. le «premier objectif» d'une réglementation des groupes de sociétés (*cf.* pour le texte de ce rapport REV. PRAT. SOC. 1965, p. 153 *et seq.*) par opposition à un «second objectif» visant à l'organisation du groupe à partir de la reconnaissance des ses caractéristiques spécifiques. On sait que le projet de directive actuellement en cours d'élaboration à la C. E. E. a pour objet l'organisation des groupes comme tels.

[14] La Commission, après diverses consultations, a estimé, au moment de la clôture de ses travaux, que la question n'était pas encore suffisamment «mûre» en Belgique pour proposer un tel projet. Ces travaux de la Commission se sont terminés voici plusieurs annéees, et les choses ont évolué depuis lors. On ne peut exclure que le Parlement souhaite que le texte soit complété sur ce point.

sont pas spécifiques aux entreprises dites «multinationales». Elles concernent plus généralement la détention du pouvoir économique et les rapports entre ce pouvoir et le pouvoir politique. Notamment des entreprises étrangères sont souvent mises en cause, qu'elles soient ou non «multinationales».

Nous pensons donc que l'entreprise dite «multinationale» constitue simplement un groupe de sociétés, caractérisé par le fait que certaines cellules de ce groupe sont des sociétés étrangères. Parfois, il s'agit d'une société unique qui possède des établissements ou des succursales dans plusieurs pays. Les seuls problèmes *juridiques* spécifiques qu'elle soulève relèvent du droit international privé et sont étrangers au présent rapport.[15]

6. *Inventaire sommaire des questions soulevées par une étude des groupes de sociétés*

Nous indiquons ci-après les domaines dans lesquels, à notre avis, se traduit, sur le plan juridique, le phénomène du groupe de sociétés.

On songe en premier lieu, naturellement, au *droit des sociétés*. Le groupe de sociétés, caractérisé par une direction unique, aboutit normalement à gauchir considérablement les règles de fonctionnement des sociétés membres du groupe dans toute la mesure où il existe un risque – éventuellement admis et reconnu en droit positif moyennant des garanties appropriées – que les sociétés composant le groupe soient gérées dans l'intérêt du groupe pris dans son ensemble, et non point en considération de l'interêt individuel de chacune des sociétés isolées qui composent le groupe. Il peut en résulter des préjudices pour les actionnaires étrangers au groupe (minoritaires ou même majoritaires mais sans exercice du contrôle), pour les autres titulaires de valeurs mobilières émises par la société (et spécialement pour les obligataires) et éventuellement pour les créanciers. Le groupe entraine souvent aussi une altération plus ou moins complète du mode de fonctionnement normal des sociétés anonymes.[16]

La puissance atteinte par les groupes de sociétés, grâce à l'extraordinaire pouvoir que cette technique de concentration permet de mettre en œuvre, soulève la question de leur action au regard de *l'intérêt économique général* et de leur association, à la politique économique générale d'un pays, voire de la surveillance de leurs décisions ainsi que de leurs interventions dans la vie économique ou sur le marché des produits et services ou des capitaux.

Les groupes de sociétés sont encore pris en considération en matière de *droit des ententes*, particulièrement lorsque les législations relatives au droit anti-trust entendent réglementer la concentration indépendamment des ententes propre-

[15] *Cf.* Centre d'études juridiques européennes de l'Université de Genève, Colloque international sur le droit international privé des groupes de sociétés (Genève, 1974).

[16] Nous parlons ici exclusivement des sociétés anonymes, car la société anonyme est en pratique la seule forme réellement utilisée dans le cadre des groupes de sociétés. On peut y ajouter quelques cas de sociétés en commandite, mais ils deviennent rares. La S. A. R. L., en revanche, n'y apparait jamais pour des raisons tenant aux conditions imposées en Belgique à la constitution des S. A. R. L. Celles-ci notamment ne peuvent comprendre de personnes morales parmi leurs membres.

ment dites. C'est en ce domaine que la distinction entre les accords de coopération et les procédés qui aboutissent à la formation d'un groupe est la plus délicate à tracer et la plus importante en raison de ses conséquences concrètes.

En *matière fiscale*, le législateur et la pratique fiscale sont amenés à tenir compte des relations entre sociétés d'un même groupe pour en déduire certaines conséquences, moyennant des ajustements appropriés. Parfois, ils se méfient des groupes de sociétés qui peuvent être les instruments d'une réduction de la matière imposable, sinon d'une évasion fiscale, et ils prennent à leur encontre des mesures particulières.

En *droit du travail*, enfin, les groupes de sociétés doivent aussi être pris en considération tant au niveau individuel de la protection des relations d'emploi pour les salariés qui sont engagés par une société dépendant d'un groupe, qu'au niveau collectif lorsqu'il s'agit d'organiser soit la représentation des travailleurs à des fins de contrôle, d'information, voire même de cogestion.

7. Vue générale des réponses données à ces questions par le droit belge, objet du présent rapport

En droit des sociétés, comme nous le disions ci-dessus, la loi sur les sociétés ne fait aucune mention des groupes de sociétés et la jurisprudence des tribunaux ordinaires ne comporte que de rares décisions qui concerneraient cette matière. Mais l'adaptation du droit belge au phénomène a été réalisée de manière pragmatique par la Commission bancaire, à la faveur de la jurisprudence prétorienne qu'elle a élaborée depuis 1935 dans les conditions très particulières que nous décrirons sommairement ci-aprés.

D'autre part, le législateur a institué, par un arrêté royal de pouvoirs spéciaux, n° 64 du 10 novembre 1967, modifié par une loi du 20 janvier 1978, une certaine surveillance des sociétés holding – c'est-à-dire en pratique des sociétés financières qui se trouvent à la base des plus importants groupes de sociétés.

La législation comptable récente tient compte des relations de groupe; elle prescrit l'établissement de comptes consolidés par les sociétés à portefeuille.

Sur le plan de l'intérêt général, la loi assure l'association des sociétés holding à la programmation économique. Les prises de participation de contrôle par des sociétés étrangères d'abord, puis par toute espèce de sociétés – qui bien souvent servent de base à la constitution des groupes – font l'objet de certaines interventions gouvernementales.

En matière de droit des ententes, la loi belge est d'application très exceptionelle et l'on ne signale aucune intervention en matière de groupe de sociétés.

En droit fiscal, l'attitude adoptée par le droit belge est fondamentalement inspirée par une méfiance à l'égard des groupes de sociétés qui se traduit par diverses mesures destinées à éviter des évasions de matière imposable. Le droit fiscal belge se refuse toujours à reconnaitre le groupe de sociétés comme tel et rejette toute taxation de groupe ou toute consolidation des résultats du groupe au niveau de la société-mère. Les relations entre sociétés du groupe, sous la forme de distributions de dividendes, ne donnent lieu qu'à une double imposition réduite. Les relations dites «anormales» entre sociétés d'un même groupe peuvent donner lieu à des taxations particulières. Dans notre domaine donc, contrairement à ce que l'on peut observer en d'autres matières,[17] le droit fiscal belge ne contribue nullement à l'élaboration des notions du droit privé.

Le droit du travail ne tient guère compte des groupes de sociétés – sauf en ce qui concerne certaines décisions de justice relatives à la résiliation de contrats d'emploi et en ce qui concerne des informations à donner aux conseils d'entreprise. Ce problème affleure aussi à propos de la composition des conseils d'entreprise.

Nous ne traiterons, dans le présent rapport, que des questions de droit des sociétés, sans étudier les questions de droit des ententes ou de droit de la concentration ou de droit fiscal ou social.

II. La Commission bancaire

1. Rôle de la Commission bancaire en Belgique

Le rôle particulier joué par la Commission bancaire dans la vie économique belge et l'originalité de ses interventions et de son organisation, nous obligent à donner, à propos de cette introduction, quelques indications sommaires sur cette institution.[18] Il serait impossible de se faire une idée de la vie des groupes de sociétés en Belgique en omettant cet aspect fondamental de la vie pratique juridique et économique belge qui en fait d'ailleurs l'originalité.

Instituée en vertu d'un arrêté royal n° 185 du 9 juillet 1935, à la suite des crises financières consécutives aux catastrophes économiques de 1929, la Commission bancaire est un établissement public *autonome*, dotée de la personnalité morale et complètement indépendante des pouvoirs politiques. Elle dispose d'un budget propre et jouit d'un certain pouvoir réglementaire dans les limites précisées par le texte dont elle tire son existence. Elle est composée de dix membres, et d'un président, désignés par le Roi, pour une durée de six années. Elle se réunit pratiquement tous les quinze jours et délibère comme un organe collégial. Actuellement, la Présidence a pris une importance considérable, par suite de la permanence acquise en fait par la fonction et surtout en raison de la très haute qualité des présidents successifs, qui ont pris une place prépondérante dans la vie économique du pays.

Le *président* est assisté de fonctionnaires, jouissant d'un statut autonome défini par la Commission elle-même et rétribués par elle. Ceux-ci forment l'armature permanente de l'institution. Ils sont au nombre d'une quinzaine sous la direction quotidienne du président et assurent le fonctionnement des services

[17] Par exemple, c'est le droit fiscal qui a contribué à élaborer les concepts de droit des sociétés de fusion ou de scission de sociétés à tel point que ces institutions ne sont pas régies par des dispositions écrites de la loi sur les sociétés et que leur régime juridique s'est précisé sous l'influence du droit fiscal.

[18] Pour une étude condensée, mais très complète, et parfaitement informée, sur la composition, les compétences et l'action de la Commission bancaire, *v.* A. Bruyneel, [dans la Revue française] Banque 1972, n° 303 à 305; *cf. aussi*, J. L. Le Brun, La Protection de l'épargne publique et la Comission bancaire (Bruxelles, 1979).

et la préparation des dossiers en vue des décisions à prendre par la Commission elle-même. La personnalité des différents présidents (au nombre de six depuis 1935) et la qualité de leur état-major ont assuré à la Commission bancaire une indépendance totale tant à l'égard des pouvoirs politiques qu'envers les banques (que la Commission doit régir en ordre principal), la Banque Nationale et les groupes économiques et financiers.

Ses *méthodes d'action* ont été telles qu'elle est parvenue le plus souvent à faire accepter ses points de vue par la persuasion sous la forme de recommandations, à tel point qu'elle n'a pratiquement jamais été contrainte de faire un usage des pouvoirs formels — mais très réduits — que la loi lui a conférés en matière d'émissions publiques de valeurs mobilières notamment.[19] On peut penser que le caractère très limité des mesures coercitives que la Commission peut prendre dans ce domaine, la contraint en quelque sorte à user de la persuasion et à recueillir l'adhésion des milieux intéressés pour faire triompher ses points de vue, avec toute la mesure nécessaire. Ces moyens d'action n'excluent pas que la fermeté dans la détermination des principes et l'action générale de la Commission sur le fonctionnement des marchés et sur les modes de gestion des entreprises, a été déterminante depuis 1935. Mais ces méthodes ne sont efficaces que dans une communauté nationale relativement restreinte, en dehors de tout pouvoir formel, de toute coercition directe, où les moyens indirects de persuasion sont nombreux.[20]

La Commission bancaire a été chargée, au fil du temps, de quatre *missions* fondamentales, dont deux sont étrangères à notre sujet: elle assure l'application des règles organiques du commerce de banque (agréation des banques de commerce, surveillance de celles-ci, mise en œuvre du statut bancaire, surveillance des réviseurs de banque et analyse des rapports que ces derniers doivent lui faire sur des points particuliers, mise au point des règles de formes régissant les comptes sociaux des banques et leur publication, élaboration de coefficients relatifs à la structure financière des banques et surveillance de l'application de ceux-ci, police générale des banques afin d'éviter les accidents financiers, etc.). La Commission bancaire exerce des fonctions analogues en ce qui concerne les

[19] Le dernier rapport de la Commission fait état cependant d'un groupe de sociétés qui a refusé de se ranger à ses avis à propos d'une opération et de sa comptabilisation (Rapport 1978-79, p. 139). Dans le cas d'espèce, l'opinion de la Commission et celle différente des dirigeants du groupe, ont été toutes deux publiées en détail dans le rapport du conseil d'administration et l'annexe aux comptes sociaux. Moyennant quoi, la Commission bancaire a renoncé à publier séparément son avis comme la loi le lui permet lorsque l'opinion de la Commission bancaire n'est pas suivie (article 6, al. 2 de l'A. R. n° 64 du 10 novembre 1967).

[20] Les entreprises et leurs dirigeants sont fréquemment appelés à avoir des rapports avec la Commission bancaire pour toutes sortes de matières et ils sont soucieux dès lors de ne pas se l'aliéner. La Commission peut exercer des actions indirectes auprès des banques, des institutions publiques de crédit, des services gouvernementaux, voire des parquets qui la consultent fréquemment en matière de droit pénal des affaires — dont il n'est pas possible en pratique de ne pas tenir compte. Mais cela implique que l'action de la Commission soit acceptée en règle générale par le milieu auquel elle s'adresse.

fonds communs de placement (loi du 27 mars 1957), les caisses d'épargne privées et les sociétés qui recueillent par appel au public des fonds remboursables à un terme ou moyennant un préavis excédant six mois (loi du 10 juin 1964).[21]

2. La Commission bancaire et les émissions de valeurs mobilières

La Commission bancaire a ensuite été chargée de la *surveillance* des émissions publiques de valeurs mobilières par toutes les sociétés, quelle que soit leur activité. Elle a, dans ce domaine, le pouvoir de vérifier si les informations publiées à l'occasion des appels au public sont complètes et si elles ne sont pas de nature à induire les souscripteurs en erreur sur «la nature de l'affaire et les droits attachés aux titres» (article 29 de l'arrêté royal n° 185 du 9 juillet 1935). Si elle juge que tel est le cas, la Commission doit en avertir la société émettrice et ses administrateurs et formuler des recommandations pour que les informations publiées soient modifiées. Si celles-ci ne sont pas suivies, elle peut interdire l'émission, mais pour une période de trois mois au plus, et elle peut publier sa décision. Elle n'a donc aucun pouvoir pour se prononcer sur le fond de l'opération — qu'il s'agisse de son opportunité ou de ses chances de succès ou de ses conditions, telles qu'elles sont proposées par la société émettrice, pour autant que les informations données soient de nature à éclairer complètement les souscripteurs à tous égards.

La Commission joue également un rôle de régulateur du marché financier et elle peut suspendre pendant trois mois au plus des opérations qui en provoqueraient le déséquilibre si ses suggestions à ce sujet n'étaient pas suivies (article 28 de l'arrêté royal n° 185).

Ses interventions concernent pratiquement toutes les formes d'appel public à l'épargne portant sur des valeurs mobilières. Cette notion a été définie très largement par une loi du 10 juillet 1969. Sont notamment visées toutes les formes d'offres publiques d'achat ou d'échange. Cette même loi a habilité le Roi à donner une définition du concept de «public» et, faisant usage de cette habilitation par un arrêté royal du 28 novembre 1969, le Roi a étendu considérablement cette notion en y comprenant notamment toute sollicitation pour compte propre ou pour compte de tiers de plus de cinquante personnes, ainsi que toute opération impliquant une publicité par annonce ou, sauf certaines exceptions, l'intervention d'un intermédiaire professionnel.[22] L'intervention de la

[21] Il résulte pratiquement de cette loi du 10 juin 1964 et des autres dispositions légales en matière de droit financier, que toutes les entreprises qui font appel au public pour recevoir des fonds remboursables à vue, à terme ou à préavis, sont nécessairement soumises à un contrôle, qu'elles soient des banques, des caisses d'épargnes ou des entreprises soumises au régime particulier prévue par la loi du 10 juin 1964, ou encore qu'il s'agisse de certaines entreprises publiques. Une entreprise qui recevrait de tels fonds sans observer les règles organiques de ces contrôles, se rendrait coupable d'une infraction pénale.

[22] Quel qu'en soit l'intérêt pratique, nous ne pouvons naturellement nous étendre ici sur les aspects techniques de la définition de l'appel au public ou du concept de «valeur mobilière». *Cf.* à ce propos, A. Bruyneel, *supra* note 18, p. 128 *et seq.*, ainsi que les rapports de la Commission bancaire. Adde, R. Wtterwulghe, *La loi du 10 juillet 1969*

Commission bancaire s'étend donc bien au-delà des demandes d'inscriptions à la cote d'une Bourse du Royaume, et même des expositions ou offres en vente publique ou en souscription publique «classique». Elle embrasse notamment les sollicitations émanant de conseillers en placement ou d'intermédiaires financiers dès lors que ceux-ci utilisent certains moyens décrits par l'arrêté royal ou sollicitent plus de cinquante personnes. Bien entendu, ces pouvoirs concernent aussi les valeurs mobilières étrangères qui seraient offertes sur le territoire belge.

En pratique, et cela est essentiel, les attributions légales de la Commission bancaire, très limitées quant à l'objet des mesures qu'elles autorisent, ont été utilisées par elle avec une grande parcimonie puisque jamais elle n'a été contrainte de suspendre une émission par application de l'article 29 de l'arrêté royal n° 185.

Et pourtant, la Commission a considérablement étendu, dans sa jurisprudence administrative, le champ de ses interventions. Partant d'une interprétation extensive de la notion d'information, elle s'est montrée sévère quant à l'étendue des indications à donner aux épargnants, inspirée par une philosophie de la «disclosure» inspirée de la pratique des pays anglo-américains. Elle a rendu pratiquement obligatoire l'établissement d'un prospectus très développé — dont la loi ne parle nulle part — et elle a soigneusement vérifié le contenu de celui-ci. Elle a exercé une grande influence — en l'absence de dispositions légales suffisantes — sur les règles relatives à l'établissement et à l'articulation des comptes sociaux y compris les comptes consolidés.[23] Elle veille aussi aux informations soit occasionelles, soit permanentes, données par les sociétés, même en l'absence d'émission publique, pour tenir leurs actionnaires, et plus généralement le public, au courant de certaines opérations projetées ou en cours.

Mais en outre, la Commission bancaire a élaboré une *jurisprudence prétorienne* considérable concernant des problèmes de fond du droit des sociétés, en marge de la loi et «praeter legem» en réalisant ainsi de manière souple et progressive une adaptation des lois coordonnées sur les sociétés commerciales aux exigences de la vie moderne des sociétés, même en l'absence d'intervention formelle du législateur. Elle a ainsi anticipé sur plusieurs questions, réglées par le projet de réforme des lois coordonnées. Pratiquement, elle use de ses techniques habituelles de persuasion et de contrôle des informations données aux souscripteurs, pour obtenir des sociétés commerciales qu'elles acceptent ses vues. Elle est ainsi intervenue en de multiples matières que nous ne pouvons songer à énumérer ici. Elle publie ses prises de position dans ses rapports annuels.

sur la sollicitation de l'épargne publique notamment en matière de valeurs mobilières, J. T. 1970, p. 291; J. L. Le Brun, *supra* note 18, n° 613 *et seq.*

[23] Après avoir patronné l'élaboration d'une doctrine comptable sous la forme de recommandations sans force obligatoire directe (Recommandations élaborées en 1968 par une Commission qu'elle avait réunie), la Commission bancaire a joué de facto un rôle considérable dans l'élaboration du nouveau droit comptable belge. La loi du 17 juillet 1975 a institué une Commission des normes comptables, actuellement présidée par un haut fonctionnaire de la Commission bancaire et avec laquelle la Commission demeure en rapports étroits.

A titre d'exemple, elle est intervenue dans les domaines suivants qui touchent évidemment le fonds du droit: tantièmes et rémunérations des administrateurs, droit de souscription préférentiel des actionnaires, émissions de parts sociales sans mention de valeur nominale au-dessous du pair comptable des parts existantes de même catégorie, acquisition par une société de ses propres actions, participations réciproques, cession de participation de contrôle, offres publiques d'achat, comptabilisation d'opérations, régime des primes d'émission, régime des obligations convertibles, participations prises par l'Etat dans les sociétés sidérurgiques, etc. . . . Elle a parfois, lorsque besoin en était, provoqué l'intervention du législateur.[24]

Enfin, la Commission a servi d'organe de recours et d'intervention permanent dans la vie des sociétés commerciales – à tel point qu'il est devenu usuel de s'adresser à elle pour tous les conflits de quelque importance qui concernent la vie des sociétés, plutôt que de recourir aux tribunaux, et qu'elle se manifesta ainsi dans nombre de litiges de manière préventive, en vue de concilier ou d'arbitrer les intérêts en présence, préalablement à un recours éventuel aux tribunaux ordinaires. Cette mission est devenue tellement importante qu'elle s'exerce non seulement pour les sociétés ayant fait publiquement appel à l'épargne, mais aussi pour des sociétés privées. Ces interventions sont d'autant plus importantes que la désaffectation à l'égard des tribunaux ordinaires, pour trancher les litiges importants en matière économique, a été, pendant le même temps, en s'accroissant.

L'action de la Commission bancaire a ainsi représenté la première expérience d'une *magistrature économique*, à l'action souple, et dégagée d'un juridisme excessif que d'aucuns appellent de leurs vœux dans d'autres domaines du droit des affaires également. Mais le caractère extrêmement délicat de la mise en œuvre de tels pouvoirs apparait immédiatement: dénuées de sanctions directes, les interventions de la Commission bancaire peuvent rester lettre morte si ses «justiciables» ne les acceptent pas spontanément; d'autre part, intervenant sans texte précis et par une interprétation souple certes, mais parfois arbitraire, du droit des sociétés, elle n'offre pour ces justiciables que des garanties de sécurité réduites, si son président et les collaborateurs qui l'assistent n'étaient pas animés d'un sentiment du bien public particulièrement élevé et d'une compétence exceptionelle. Par ailleurs, les conditions de l'intervention de la Commission bancaire expliquent à la fois l'autorité morale dont elle dispose avec les sociétés belges, mais l'incompréhension qu'elle rencontre parfois auprès des dirigeants de sociétés étrangères et notamment d'entreprises «multinationales» qui, habitués à davantage de légalisme, aperçoivent mal les motifs de se soumettre à ses décisions.

On ne saurait comprendre le développement des droits des sociétés et des groupes de sociétés en Belgique sans tenir compte de ces facteurs.

[24] Par exemple, en matière d'obligations convertibles, de transformations de sociétés commerciales sans solution de continuité de leur personnalité morale, d'unification de titres de catégories différentes.

3. *Le rôle de la Commission bancaire en matière de sociétés à portefeuille*

Une mission de la Commission bancaire, qui intéresse particulièrement notre matière, concerne la surveillance des sociétés à portefeuille, qui lui a été confiée par un arrêté royal de pouvoirs spéciaux n° 64 du 10 novembre 1967. La Commission est chargée de vérifier les informations diffusées par les sociétés à portefeuille d'une certaine importance qui appartiennent à des groupes ayant fait publiquement appel à l'épargne, soit au niveau de la société à portefeuille, soit au niveau de sociétés filiales: nous sommes au coeur des groupes de sociétés puisque, en Belgique, les groupes sont généralement contrôlés par des sociétés financières.

Dans l'exercice de cette tâche, la Commission a évidemment adopté la même philosophie qu'en matière d'émission de valeurs mobilières: à la faveur du contrôle des informations diffusées, elle a exercé un magistère sur les aspects les plus divers de l'administration des sociétés à portefeuille, et tout particulièrement sur les relations entre sociétés faisant partie d'un même groupe. Nous examinerons ces interventions plus en détail ci-après.

III. Les groupes de sociétés en droit des sociétés

La notion de direction économique unique et les rapports de dépendance qui caractérisent les groupes de sociétés peuvent être considérés sous deux angles dans le droit des sociétés, suivant les objectifs poursuivis.

Selon un *premier ordre* de préoccupations, il faut éviter que le recours à des sociétés dépendantes ou à des sociétés appartenant au même groupe, *ne permette d'éluder* trop aisément *des règles relatives au fonctionnement de la société anonyme*. Dans cette optique, le groupe de sociétés est considéré avec suspicion et si le droit le prend en considération, c'est pour des motifs de police des sociétés.

Mais le droit positif peut aller au-delà et admettre que, dans la réalité, les *groupes de sociétés* constituent l'un des éléments importants de la vie économique, pour en *reconnaitre l'existence et la légitimité tout en remédiant*, le cas échéant, *aux abus* auxquels ils peuvent occasionnellement donner lieu. C'est ce que j'ai proposé d'appeler le *«second objectif»* d'une réglementation des groupes de sociétés.[25]

[25] *Cf.* rapport précité, supra note 13, rédigé pour la Commission de la C. E. E. en 1964, publié en 1965, où l'on trouvera des indications sur la réponse donnée en droit comparé à ces deux ordres de question et sur les interventions possibles au niveau communautaire. *Cf. aussi* P. Van Ommeslaghe, *Les objectifs d'une organisation des groupes de sociétés en droit comparé*, dans Liber amicorum en l'honneur de Louis Frédéricq, t. II, p. 1023 (Gent, 1966). Les mêmes conceptions se rencontrent d'ailleurs en droit fiscal: celui-ci peut, comme c'est le cas en Belgique, utiliser diverses techniques destinées à combattre une évasion fiscale que les groupes de sociétés pourraient favoriser sous diverses formes. Il peut également, comme en Allemagne par exemple, reconnaître le phénomène du groupe de sociétés pour soumettre, à ce groupe, un régime fiscal particulier.

Section 1: Le droit belge et le premier objectif

A. Application du droit commun

En droit belge, on peut évidemment appliquer les règles du droit commun lorsque des dispositions organiques du fonctionnement des sociétés anonymes prises comme telles sont éludées par le recours à des filiales ou à des sociétés du même groupe, ou encore lorsque la société-mère profite de sa position au sein de sa filiale pour imposer un gauchissement illégal des règles qui régissent cette dernière.

C'est ainsi que les principes de droit commun concernant le prête-nom et la simulation frauduleuse peuvent être invoqués si une société fait accomplir pour son compte par une filiale ou une société de son groupe, des opérations qu'elle ne pourrait accomplir elle-même.

B. Applications dans la jurisprudence de la Commission bancaire

Dans l'élaboration de ses règles prétoriennes concernant le fonctionnement des sociétés, la Commission bancaire tient naturellement compte des liens d'affiliation qui peuvent exister entre ces sociétés.

C'est ainsi que lorsqu'elle proscrit en principe les participations réciproques, elle veille à ce que l'on ne puisse éluder cette règle par le jeu de participations en cascades à l'intervention de sociétés filiales.[26] Il en est de même en ce qui concerne l'interdiction de principe, édictée par la Commission bancaire, concernant l'acquisition par une société de ses propres actions.[27] Elle n'admet pas davantage qu'une société filiale souscrive au capital de la société qui la domine.[28]

Défenseur attentif des actionnaires et plus généralement des épargnants, la Commission bancaire a particulièrement veillé au respect de leur droit de souscription préférentiel en cas d'augmentation de capital ou d'émission d'obligations convertibles. En certaines circonstances, elle a imposé que le droit de souscription préférentiel dans une augmentation de capital d'une société filiale, soit rétrocédé à ses propres actionnaires par la société-mère qui n'entendait pas l'exercer.[29]

Il s'agit là d'exemples qui illustrent que, de façon générale, la Commission bancaire est attentive aux conséquences qui s'attachent aux liens d'affiliation à un groupe, en ce qui concerne le fonctionnement des sociétés qui en font partie.

[26] D. Ponlot, Le statut légal des banques et le contrôle des émissions de titres et valeurs, p. 313 (Court-St-Etienne, 2e éd., 1969) et les extraits des rapports de la Commission bancaire à ce propos.

[27] Ponlot, *supra* note 26.

[28] *Id.*, p. 277 *et seq.*

[29] *Id.*, p. 285 et les réf. aux rapports de la Commission bancaire.

C. Projet de réforme des lois coordonnées sur les sociétés commerciales (projet n° 387, session 1979-1980)

Comme nous l'avons indiqué ci-dessus, le projet de réforme des lois coordonnées sur les sociétés commerciales, déposé récemment par le Gouvernement à la Chambre, prend en considération les liens d'affiliation entre sociétés mais uniquement dans le but d'éviter que le recours à des sociétés filiales ne permette d'éluder l'application de règles relatives au fonctionnement de la société anonyme considérée isolément. A cet effet – et à cet effet seulement comme l'indique l'exposé des motifs – l'article 36 du projet donne une définition de la société dominante fondée sur le pouvoir – de droit ou de fait – de disposer du patrimoine d'une autre société ou de diriger l'activité de celle-ci. Cette définition générale est accompagnée d'une première présomption – juris et de jure – selon laquelle une société est considérée en tout cas comme la filiale d'une autre lorsque cette autre société dispose, au sein de son assemblée générale, d'un nombre de voix dépassant la moitié des voix attachées à l'ensemble des titres ou parts, ou de titres représentant plus de la moitié de l'avoir social, ou encore lorsqu'elle dispose du droit de désigner la majorité des membres de l'organe de gestion et de représentation de la société.

En outre, le lien d'affiliation est présumé – mais sous réserve de la preuve contraire – lorsqu'une société a disposé en fait au sein de l'assemblée générale d'une autre, par elle-même, par ses filiales ou personnes interposées, de la majorité des voix à deux assemblées générales. Cette présomption est destinée à appréhender l'hypothèse, fréquente en pratique où la domination est assise sur une simple majorité de fait, compte tenu notamment de la dispersion des titres de la société dominée.

Cette définition reçoit des applications dans les cas suivants:

- à propos des participations réciproques, qui doivent être dénouées dans un délai de rigueur dès qu'elles dépassent un certain seuil: les participations détenues à l'intervention de filiales sont prises en considération;
- à propos de l'interdiction de l'achat par une société de ses propres actions: une filiale ne peut jamais acheter des actions de la société qui la domine indépendamment de toute participation réciproque;
- à propos de la définition elle-même du lien d'affiliation tel qu'il est donné ci-dessus;
- à propos des règles qui interdisent ou limitent les prêts et les crédits consentis par une société aux membres de son organe d'administration ou de surveillance;
- à propos de l'interdiction des prêts garantis par la mise en gage des actions de la société;
- à propos de l'interdiction faite à une société filiale de souscrire au capital de la société qui la domine;
- à propos des pactes relatifs à l'exercice du droit de vote qui sont désormais autorisés en principe, mais demeurent interdits lorsqu'ils aboutissent à subordonner le droit de vote aux instructions données aux actionnaires par la société elle-même ou par les sociétés du même groupe;

– à propos des mandats de vote aux assemblées générales, qui ne peuvent être donnés à des sociétés filiales.

Ces applications particulières s'analysent le plus généralement en des présomptions d'interposition de personnes qui facilitent l'application de la règle de droit commun qui interdit de recourir à des personnes interposées pour éluder une règle légale. Elles ne font pas obstacle à l'application du droit commun dans tous les autres cas que le législateur n'aurait pas spécialement visés.

Comme indiqué ci-après, il en est fait encore application en matière de comptes sociaux.

Section 2: Le droit belge et le second objectif

Ni le droit belge positif, ni le projet de réforme n° 387, n'acceptent le postulat de base qui doit présider à toute organisation des groupes de sociétés comme tels, – à savoir qu'il serait licite de diriger l'ensemble des sociétés du groupe dans l'intérêt supérieur de celui-ci au besoin en sacrifiant tel ou tel intérêt particulier des sociétés membres du groupe moyennant, s'il y a lieu, l'application de mesures appropriées en faveur des actionnaires étrangers au groupe ou des tiers. En principe l'intérêt de chaque société prise isolément, doit rester la mesure des pouvoirs de la majorité et du conseil d'administration.

Le second élément essentiel du groupe de sociétés – à savoir *le droit* pour la société dominante ou ses organes de donner des instructions aux organes des sociétés dominées – est également étranger au droit belge positif et contraire aux dispositions de la loi: un conseil d'administration ne peut aliéner au profit d'un tiers son pouvoir de décision et les administrateurs restent en toute hypothèse responsables des mesures qu'ils prennent, sans pouvoir se soumettre aux injonctions qui viendraient de l'extérieur.

Toutefois, dans la pratique des groupes de sociétés, il est bien évident que ces deux caractéristiques fondamentales des groupes se rencontrent, avec plus ou moins d'intensité suivant le degré d'intégration des sociétés formant le groupe et suivant la nature des décisions prises. Les sociétés membres du groupe jouissent souvent d'une autonomie variable selon les groupes et selon l'objet des décisions à prendre. Dans certains groupes, les filiales sont gérées à tous égards par des services de la société-mère, et elles ne disposent pas de plus d'autonomie que des divisions d'une même entreprise. Dans d'autres groupes, suivant les circonstances, la centralisation porte sur les décisions relatives à la politique générale, aux investissements, à la conclusion d'opérations particulièrement importantes et parfois à la centralisation de services juridiques, fiscaux ou des services du personnel, tandis que les questions commerciales et techniques et, naturellement la gestion ordinaire, restent de la compétence des sociétés filiales. Ces répartitions de compétence peuvent être adaptées de manière très différente suivant les circonstances, notamment suivant que des actionnaires étrangers au groupe doivent ou non être pris en considération, suivant qu'ils sont organisés et forment une minorité plus ou moins associée à la gestion ou, qu'au contraire, ils demeurent purement passifs.

Si le législateur belge, comme tel, ignore les groupes de sociétés, les difficultés qui peuvent en résulter ne sont évidemment pas inconnues du *droit* belge et notamment de la pratique de la Commission bancaire.

Ces difficultés peuvent concerner la protection des actionnaires et des épargnants d'une part, et celle des créanciers d'autre part.

A. La protection des épargnants et des actionnaires

1. Les moyens juridiques traditionnels

Lorsque la société dominante d'une société filiale prétend imposer à celle-ci des mesures qui seraient contraires aux intérêts de cette filiale, et qui lèseraient les droits des autres actionnaires de celle-ci (qu'ils soient, comme il est dit ci-dessus, majoritaires ou minoritaires), ou encore les droits d'autres titulaires de valeurs mobilières émis par cette filiale, les personnes lésées peuvent avoir recours aux principes qui régissent ***l'abus de majorité***.

Suivant le droit commun, les organes des sociétés commerciales ne peuvent utiliser les compétences que la loi leur donne dans un intérêt étranger à celui de la société en lésant les droits de la société, des actionnaires et éventuellement des autres titulaires de valeurs mobilières conférant des droits sociaux émis par la société. La doctrine et la jurisprudence se fondent sur les concepts d'abus de droit, de détournement de pouvoirs, ou encore, mais de manière plus discutable, sur la bonne foi qui préside à l'exécution de toute convention ou encore sur le principe de l'égalité entre les actionnaires. Parfois même ces diverses notions sont utilisées conjointement.[30] La Cour de Bruxelles a considéré que ces règles s'imposent non seulement aux assemblées générales, suivant la jurisprudence et la doctrine traditionnelles, mais aussi aux conseils d'administration.[31] L'abus de majorité suppose un élément objectif consistant dans le préjudice porté aux actionnaires minoritaires et un élément intentionnel particulièrement mis en lumière par le Professeur Coppens.[32]

Les cas d'application de ces règles à des groupes de sociétés sont cependant rares dans la jurisprudence judiciaire. On peut citer un jugement du tribunal de Bruxelles du 28 juin 1955 relatif à une fusion, critiquée par un actionnaire minoritaire qui se plaignait des conditions de l'opération imposée selon lui de manière abusive par une société dominante.[33] L'action a été rejetée dans ce cas d'espèce.

Une espèce très intéressante a été soumise au Tribunal de commerce de Bruxelles, récemment, à propos d'un contrat conclu entre deux sociétés ayant des actionnaires et des administrateurs communs. Ces deux sociétés avaient progressivement intégré leurs activités et certains de leurs services, et elles formaient un

[30] P. Coppens, L'abus de majorité dans les sociétés anonymes (Louvain, 1947); P. Coppens, *Du caractère intentionnel de l'abus de majorité*, Rev. prat. soc. 1955, p. 292; J. Van Ryn et P. Van Ommeslaghe, *Examen de jurisprudence sur les sociétés commerciales*, R. C. J. B. 1958, p. 61, n° 27 et R. C. J. B. 1967, p. 344, n° 56.

[31] Bruxelles, 13 janvier 1971, Rev. prat. soc. 1971, p. 116.

[32] Coppens, *Du caractère intentionnel de l'abus de majorité, supra* note 30.

[33] J. T. 1956, p. 71.

groupe. L'une d'entre elles se trouva en graves difficultés financières. L'autre société conclut alors des conventions complexes qui avaient notamment pour objet d'apporter une certaine assistance à la premiére société. Des actionnaires minoritaires de la société prospère critiquèrent ces décisions, en faisant valoir qu'elles n'étaient pas prises dans l'intérêt de la société, et qu'elles pouvaient même l'entrainer dans la déconfiture de la société en difficulté. Après une analyse circonstanciée de l'affaire, le tribunal rejeta l'action par un jugement du 27 avril 1978, en considérant notamment qu'en raison de l'intégration des activités des deux sociétés, et des répercussions de la défaillance de la seconde sur les activités de la première, cette dernière pouvait légitimement juger nécessaire d'apporter un concours à la société en difficulté, sans que l'on puisse y voir une méconnaissance de l'intérêt social et un abus de majorité. On peut donc relever que le tribunal a tenu compte, en l'espéce, des relations de groupe, mais sans considérer qu'il existerait un intérêt supérieur du groupe distinct de l'intérêt de chacune des sociétés le composant.[34]

Un jugement du Tribunal de commerce de Bruxelles du 6 juin 1977,[35] rejette une action introduite par des actionnaires minoritaires, fondée sur l'abus de majorité, critiquant les modalités d'une fusion intervenue entre sociétés faisant partie d'un même groupe.

Si les actions soumises aux tribunaux sont assez rares, la menace de telles actions fondées sur l'abus de majorité est plus fréquemment invoquée dans des litiges, notamment à propos de groupes de sociétés, même lorsque ces litiges se résolvent par des transactions ou des «armistices» sous les auspices, par exemple, de la Commission bancaire. Ces règles jouent dans cette mesure un rôle qu'il ne faut pas minimiser. Il serait erroné de conclure de l'absence de toute décision judiciaire importante en ce domaine à leur inefficacité complète. Certaines «batailles financières» récentes en témoignent.

Parmi les recours judiciaires les plus efficaces en pratique, il faut signaler *les actions devant le juge des référés* — lorsque la compétence de ce magistrat peut être justifiée par l'urgence suivant les règles ordinaires de la procédure civile. Les présidents des tribunaux de commerce sont, ces dernières années, plus accueillants en ce domaine. Sans doute, les actions ne peuvent tendre qu'à des mesures provisoires, mais elles aboutissent à clicher des situations acquises tant que les conflits au fond ne seront pas tranchés, — ce qui bien souvent empêche des coups de force et amène les parties en présence à composition. Le caractère rapide et immédiat de ces mesures — par opposition à la lenteur des procédures au fond — les rend efficaces et explique que l'on ait eu recours à plusieurs reprises à ce moyen - encore qu'il ne se soit guère agi de contestations relatives à de grands groupes de sociétés. On peut citer, cependant, une décision relative à une fusion dont un actionnaire minoritaire demandait la suspension,[36] une décision récente

[34] Rev. prat. soc., 1978, p. 276. Ce jugement est actuellement déféré à la juridiction d'appel. Il est également intéressant en ce qu'il tranche une question de responsabilité d'administateur et en ce qu'il définit la manière dont les tribunaux doivent exercer leur contrôle sur les décisions critiquées au nom de la théorie de l'abus de majorité.

[35] Rev. prat. soc. 1977, p. 202.

[36] Prés. Comm. Bruxelles, 21 juin 1968, Rev. prat. soc. 1968, p. 268.

dans un litige intéressant une société belge incorporée dans un groupe multinational anglais,[37] et une décision désignant un expert pour vérifier des paiements et transferts de fonds opérés par une société envers une société-sœur.[38]

L'article 191 des lois coordonnées sur les sociétés commerciales, organise ***un droit d'enquête*** en matière de sociétés anonymes. L'enquête peut être demandée au tribunal par des actionnaires représentant un cinquième au moins du capital social, s'il existe une présomption de graves irrégularités au sein de la société. L'investigation doit s'exercer dans les livres et dans les comptes de la société et le tribunal doit déterminer les points précis sur lesquels elle portera. Les commissaires investigateurs rédigent un rapport à l'intention du tribunal, mais la loi ne donne aucune indication sur l'usage qui pourrait être fait de ce rapport. Il pourrait servir de base à des poursuites pénales, si des infractions étaient révélées ou encore à une action en responsabilité civile. En pratique, les tribunaux se montrent rigoureux avant d'ordonner — de telles investigations et ce moyen est peu utilisé pour ce motif mais on peut relever une tendance à accueillir ce recours plus aisément.[39]

Les actionnaires lésés par une société dominante pourraient aussi avoir recours à ***l'action en responsabilité de droit commun***. Encore celle-ci est-elle difficile à mettre en œuvre pour des minoritaires.

Une action en responsabilité fondée sur les dispositions de droit commun prévue par le Code civil, serait possible si des actionnaires subissaient un préjudice personnel par suite du comportement illicite de l'actionnaire majoritaire ou de ses représentants dans les organes sociaux (C. c., art. 1382 et 1383). Une telle action pourrait notamment être invoquée en cas d'abus de majorité, soit que l'annulation des mesures abusives soit impossible, notamment par suite de l'acquisition de droits par des tiers de bonne foi, soit qu'elle ne suffise pas à réparer le préjudice subi par les actionnaires lésés.

En revanche, ***l'action en responsabilité sociale***, dirigée contre les membres du conseil d'administration de la société par suite de fautes de gestion ou de violation de la loi sur les sociétés ou des statuts (art. 62, alinéa Ier et 2 des lois coordonnées sur les sociétés commerciales), n'est pas ouverte aux actionnaires minoritaires ou aux actionnaires agissant individuellement, dès lors que le préjudice subi consiste dans une atteinte apportée au patrimoine social dans son ensemble. Le législateur a, en effet, suivant l'interprétation de la jurisprudence et de la quasi-unanimité de la doctrine, supprimé l'action sociale minoritaire ou individuelle en 1913.[40]

[37] Prés. Comm. Bruxelles, 2 octobre 1970, Rev. prat. soc. 1971, p. 132.

[38] Plus généralement sur les interventions du juge des référés dans la vie des sociétés, *v.* notamment, G. Horsmans, *Le juge des référés et le droit des sociétés*, Rev. prat. soc. 1969, p. 47.

[39] *V.*, par exemple, Bruxelles, 6 décembre 1979, Rev. prat. soc. 1980, p. 13, confirmant Comm. Bruxelles, 6 novembre 1978, *ibid.*, 1978, p. 260.

[40] En ce sens, consultez J. Van Ryn, Principes de droit commercial, t. I, n° 610 (Bruxelles, 1954); C. Resteau, Sociétés anonymes, t. II, n° 983 (Bruxelles, 2e éd., 1934/35). La thèse contraire, isolée, a été soutenue par J. Kirkpatrick, *La responsabilité des*

Parmi les mesures de protection des actionnaires minoritaires qui trouvent application notamment lors de la constitution de groupes de sociétés, notamment par la voie de conventions ou de clauses statutaires, on peut encore citer la règle, établie actuellement en droit positif belge, selon laquelle les pactes relatifs à l'exercice du droit de vote aux assemblées générales ou dans les organes d'administration des sociétés, sont nuls. Ces pactes sont souvent les instruments de la constitution de groupes de sociétés soit isolément, soit, le plus souvent, complémentairement à d'autres éléments. Leur *nullité* permet aux parties de ne point les observer sans encourir le risque de devoir payer des dommages-intérêts. Les clauses pénales ou les moyens de contrainte indirects parfois imaginés pour tenter de les rendre efficaces, sont également sans valeur. Nonobstant leur absence de valeur juridique, ces pactes sont cependant très fréquents et dans la plupart des cas, ils sont observés par leurs signataires qui craignent les atteintes à leur réputation qui résulteraient d'un refus d'honorer leur signature.

Sont également considérées comme nulles, car elles contreviennent au principe de l'égalité des actionnaires, les clauses oligarchiques imaginées par la pratique néerlandaise pour constituer notamment des groupes de sociétés en assurant la haute main d'une société sur la formation des organes d'administration ou de surveillance d'une autre société sans y détenir la majorité. Ces constructions ingénieuses — que certains auraient voulu introduire en Belgique — ont été jugées sévèrement par la Commission bancaire et ne se rencontrent pas dans la pratique.[41]

La protection des actionnaires est encore assurée par la jurisprudence relative à *l'intervention obligatoire de l'assemblée générale* pour la conclusion de certaines conventions qui sont de nature à aboutir indirectement à la modification de l'objet social d'une société en changeant radicalement son mode d'exploitation, alors que les statuts ne le prévoyaient pas. La concentration entre entreprises sans fusion est parfois réalisée par le biais de conventions d'amodiations, de dation à bail des installations, de gestion de l'ensemble des biens d'une société et de ses affaires par une autre, de la cession de la totalité de son patrimoine ou de parties essentielles de celui-ci. Suivant la manière dont les statuts sont rédigés, de telles opérations peuvent requérir l'intervention de l'assemblée générale et être ainsi clairement portées à la connaissance des actionnaires qui peuvent se prononcer sur leur conclusion.[42]

Tel est l'inventaire — assez limité, il faut bien le dire — des moyens "classiques" qui s'offrent, le cas échéant, au praticien en présence d'une domination abusive instaurée par un ou plusieurs actionnaires au préjudice d'autres actionnaires qui leur sont étrangers.

La difficulté majeure réside dans la collecte des informations qui permettent de se rendre compte d'un éventuel abus de majorité et sur ce point, le droit belge

administrateurs de société anonyme à l'égard de chaque administrateur en droit positif belge, Rev. prat. soc. 1964, p. 1.

[41] H. Biron, *Les clauses oligarchiques en droit néerlandais,* Rev. prat. soc. 1961, p. 273; *cf.* rapport de la Commission bancaire 1962, p. 95 *et seq.*

[42] *Cf. supra* § 1, 3.

n'offre pas de solutions très satisfaisantes. Les actionnaires agissant individuellement n'ont guère d'autre droit que celui de prendre connaissance des documents sociaux dans les conditions prévues par l'article 73 des lois coordonnées à l'occasion des assemblées générales, mais la mesure dans laquelle il doit être répondu à ces questions, n'est pas très clairement définie par la doctrine et la jurisprudence. Il n'existe pas d'exemples publiés de recours à des tribunaux qui auraient abouti à contraindre une société à donner à ses actionnaires des informations déterminées[43] et le seul moyen d'obtenir de telles informations paraît bien résider dans l'intervention de commissaires investigateurs désignés en vertu de l'article 191 des lois coordonnées (cfr. supra). Encore faut-il faire état de présomptions selon lesquelles des irrégularités graves auraient été commises, ce qui est exceptionnel. Le droit d'investigation et d'information individuel des membres du conseil d'administration a été défini par la jurisprudence et par la doctrine.[44]

2. *Interventions de la Commission bancaire*

On comprend que les actionnaires qui s'estiment lésés par le comportement d'une société dominante, commencent par s'adresser à la Commission bancaire plutôt que de recourir aux tribunaux d'emblée.

La Commission bancaire intervient, comme il a été dit, de manière occasionnelle dans la vie des sociétés lorsqu'un conflit surgit et que l'une ou l'autre partie (et bien souvent les deux) porte la question devant elle. Si ces interventions concernent surtout les sociétés ayant fait publiquement appel à l'épargne, il n'est pas rare, en pratique, que des contestations à caractère purement privé, dès lors qu'ils revêtent une certaine importance, lui soient soumises également. Son rôle est de pure conciliation, mais il s'est avéré efficace dans les grands conflits qui ont surgi ces dernières années et dont les tribunaux n'ont guère eu à connaître – sauf par quelques incidents en référé.

Par ailleurs, dans le cadre général de sa mission de surveillance des émissions de valeurs mobilières, la Commission bancaire a été parfois appelée à intervenir pour mettre fin à des *situations abusives,* notamment en matière de conventions conclues entre sociétés appartenant à un même groupe. Citons par exemple: la vérification du caractère équitable des conditions des conventions de gestion dans le secteur – très concentré – de la production et de la distribution de l'énergie électrique;[45] des interventions dans une espèce où l'augmentation de

[43] Comp. en France l'espèce ayant donné lieu à l'arrêt rendu par la Cour de Lyon le 22 mai 1951, JOURNAL soc. 1952, p. 267, détaillant une série d'informations qui n'apparaissaient pas dans les comptes et que la Cour a estimées devoir être données aux actionnaires.

[44] L. Simont, *L'administrateur d'une société anonyme agissant isolément a-t-il un droit d'investigation individuelle?*, REV. PRAT. SOC. 1963, p. 189, Prés. Comm. Bruxelles, 2 octobre 1970, REV. PRAT. SOC. 1971, p. 132.

[45] *Cf.* rapport de la Commission bancaire 1958-59, p. 98: elle impose la mention de ces conventions de gestion dans les prospectus. En pratique, la Commission scrute également les conditions auxquelles elles ont été conclues. *Cf. aussi,* le rapport 1955-56,

capital d'une société filiale s'était faite dans des conditions inéquitables pour les actionnaires minoritaires de celle-ci;[46] des interventions pour que des sociétés contrôlantes respectent les promesses faites dans des prospectus antérieurs quant à leur politique envers les actionnaires étrangers au groupe;[47] la vérification du caractère équitable et normal des conventions par lesquelles une grande entreprise de distribution avait pris à bail les immeubles dans lesquels elle poursuivait son exploitation et qui appartenaient à une autre société du même groupe (non publié); des interventions à propos de commissions, et d'autres avantages alloués par une société à une autre société du même groupe en reconnaissance de services rendus;[48] les objections de principe contre les contrats qu'elle qu'en soit la forme par lesquels une société se place sous la dépendance d'une autre.[49] Il existe bien entendu de nombreux autres cas qui montrent le caractère concret et efficace de ces interventions, suivant des méthodes que les tribunaux ordinaires ne pourraient pas appliquer.

Les recommandations de la Commission bancaire en matière d'*informations proprement dites* sont nombreuses et elles concernent souvent les relations entre sociétés faisant partie d'un même groupe. A ce propos, la loi belge prescrit la communication par les sociétés à leurs actionnaires, à l'occasion des assemblées générales annuelles, de la liste de leur portefeuille. En pratique, les sociétés qui publient leurs comptes comprennent cette liste dans les brochures contenant leurs bilans, leurs comptes de profits et pertes et les rapports de conseil d'administration. Ils s'agit d'une source très importante d'informations concernant la composition des groupes de sociétés et la Commission bancaire veille naturellement à l'exactitude et au caractère complet des données ainsi publiées. Elle s'assure à cette occasion que les prises de participations rentrent bien dans l'objet social des sociétés qui les détiennent.[50]

Mais il ne suffit pas de publier la liste des participations et la Commission veille à ce que les sociétés donnent des informations sur les activités et la situation de leurs principales filiales tant dans leurs prospectus d'émission que dans leurs rapports annuels. Elle intervient parfois aussi à propos des *communications occasionelles* relatives à des prises de participation significatives.

Lorsque des contrats très importants sont de nature à influencer le jugement que l'on peut se former sur une société, la Commission s'assure que les informations nécessaires sont données au public notamment dans les *prospectus*. Celles-ci doivent porter non seulement sur les contrats qui sont de nature à

p. 12, à propos des conventions de gestion et des autres accords contractuels qui servent de base à la formation de groupes.

[46] Rapport 1951-52, p. 76.

[47] Rapport 1970-71, p. 150 *et seq*.

[48] Rapport 1970-71, p. 189.

[49] Rapport 1973-74, p. 181. Si les observations de la Commission à ce propos sont dans l'ensemble conformes à l'état du droit belge positif, on peut cependant ne pas partager son opinion sur les contrats dits «organiques» en général, s'ils s'accompagnent de dispositions permettant d'éviter de léser les actionnaires et les tiers.

[50] Rapport 1950-51, p. 63.

conduire à la formation de groupes de sociétés parce qu'ils instituent des communautés d'intérêts totales ou partielles,[51] mais même sur des conventions de fournitures ou d'approvisionnements susceptibles, en raison de leur importance, d'exercer une influence sur la rentabilité de l'exploitation.[52]

L'on aperçoit par là toute l'importance que revêt la technique de la divulgation d'informations relatives aux groupes de sociétés sur le comportement de ceux-ci et l'effet préventif considérable que cette méthode exerce sur des abus possibles. Il s'agit là d'un des aspects fondamentaux de la philosophie générale de l'action de la Commission bancaire.

3. Interventions particulières de la Commission bancaire en matière de cessions de participation de contrôle

La Commission bancaire a élaboré progressivement une *doctrine* concernant la cession d'une participation de contrôle — dont elle veille à assurer l'application — et qui pénètre dans le droit positif belge encore qu'elle soit contestée par une partie de la doctrine et que la jurisprudence des tribunaux ordinaires n'ait pas été appelée à se prononcer à son propos.[53] Cette question est évidemment essentielle pour ce qui concerne la formation des groupes de sociétés.

Cette doctrine est appliquée de manière souple et en tenant compte des circonstances de chaque espèce. Dans la pratique, diverses solutions peuvent être proposées à la Commission et être mises sur pied de commun accord avec elle. Après avoir été précisée au fil de nombreux cas d'espèce, la position de la Commission a été synthétisée dans son dernier rapport[54] sous la forme de recommandations.

Fondamentalement, la Commission considère que les actionnaires qui cèdent une majorité de contrôle ne peuvent en tirer profit pour obtenir un prix supérieur à celui qui serait offert aux autres actionnaires. Le fondement juridique de ce postulat demeure assez incertain: la Commission a le principe de l'égalité des actionnaires et l'«affectio societatis». Puis, elle a insisté sur la circonstance que les administrateurs sont tenus d'obligations non seulement envers la société, mais encore envers les actionnaires individuellement dont ils devraient sauvegarder l'intérêt commun et l'égalité. En d'autres circonstances, elle met l'accent sur l'abus que commettraient des administrateurs ou des actionnaires prépondérants qui profiteraient de leur position pour faire connaître aux acquéreurs toutes les informations requises par ceux-ci en vue de l'acquisition de la participation de contrôle, alors que les actionnaires étrangers au groupe dirigeant ne jouissent pas

[51] Rapport 1955-56, p. 112.

[52] Rapport 1968-69, p. 149.

[53] *V.* sur la question, C. Lempereur, *Cessions de majorité et protection des actionnaires minoritaires en droit comparé,* REV. PRAT. SOC. 1978, p. 91; et P. Van Ommeslaghe, *Les devoirs des administrateurs et des actionnaires prépondérants envers les actionnaires d'une société en cas de cession de contrôle de cette société en droit belge et en droit comparé,* dans FESTSCHRIFT FÜR BÄRMANN, p. 1014 *et seq.* (Munich, 1975); G. Keutgen et M. Huys, *La cession de contrôle,* REV. BANQUE 1974, p. 774.

[54] Rapport 1978-79, p. 101 *et seq.; v. aussi* dans les rapports récents: 1977-78, p. 116 *et eq.;* 1976-77, p. 102 *et seq.;* 1975-76, p. 77 *et seq.;* 1974-75, p. 168 et 170 *et seq.*

de cette possibilité. Les premiers ne doivent pas pouvoir en tirer un profit particulier. Suivant la Commission bancaire, la valeur particulière qui résulte du pouvoir de direction et de commandement lié à la détention d'un portefeuille majoritaire (en droit ou en fait) ne constitue pas un avantage dont les majoritaires puissent tirer personnellement un bénéfice, car ce pouvoir résulte de l'organisation même de la société et d'un ensemble d'éléments qui doivent profiter à tous les actionnaires et non point seulement à certains d'entr'eux.

Sur le plan *pratique*, la Commission en déduit essentiellement les conséquences suivantes: en premier lieu, elle n'admet pas que des conditions différentes soient pratiquées dans les relations entre l'acquéreur et les actionnaires majoritaires d'une part, et les actionnaires minoritaires d'autre part. Le même prix et les mêmes avantages doivent donc être offerts à tous les actionnaires. Ainsi, dans l'hypothèse d'une offre publique d'achat, il n'est pas admis que les offrants acquièrent préalablement ou parallèlement à l'offre publique, un ensemble de titres des actionnaires majoritaires à des conditions particulières, notamment pour les inciter à recommander l'acceptation de l'offre à la généralité des autres actionnaires. De même, elle veille à éviter qu'une partie du "surprix" liée au contrôle, soit en réalité payée aux actionnaires majoritaires qui détiennent des postes de direction dans la société sous la forme d'indemnités anormales pour la résiliation de leur contrat d'emploi ou l'obtention de leur démission d'administrateurs.[55]

Dans le dernier état de sa réflexion, la Commission a admis que certaines différences de prix puissent, le cas échéant, être justifiées par des obligations spécifiques assumées par les seuls actionnaires titulaires du contrôle, par exemple en acceptant de donner à l'acquéreur des garanties non supportées par les autres actionnaires et qui dépasseraient les garanties de droit commun liées à la vente. La pratique de telles garanties s'est fortement développée en Belgique, notamment sous l'influence anglo-américaine et elles peuvent être génératrices d'obligations très lourdes pour les cédants qui les souscrivent. Encore que faut-il, selon la Commission bancaire, que d'éventuelles différences de prix restent proportionnées aux obligations ainsi assumées.

Dans cette hypothèse, en effet, la situation est particulièrement choquante puisque ce "surprix" est mis à la charge de la société elle-même. Bien entendu,

[55] En droit belge, les administrateurs de sociétés anonymes sont révocables à chaque instant par l'assemblée générale et il n'est pas licite de leur assurer, par contrat ou par des clauses statuaires le paiement d'une indemnité en cas de cessation de leurs fonctions, car il en résulterait une restriction au droit absolu de révocation reconnu à l'assemblée générale. Cette règle s'applique même aux administrateurs titulaires de délégations spéciales telle la gestion journalière. Toutefois, il est assez fréquent en pratique que l'on accorde, au moment de la cessation des fonctions d'un administrateur exerçant des fonctions permanentes à temps plein dans une société, une indemnité comparable à celle que la loi reconnait aux cadres supérieurs de la société. Parfois, les administrateurs concluent un contrat d'emploi avec la société, mais pour être valable, celui-ci doit se rapporter à des fonctions distinctes de celles que l'administrateur exerce en cette qualité et il faut que le lien de subordination caractéristique du contrat d'emploi existe réellement.

des indemnités normales, suivant les usages et la pratique des affaires, ne peuvent être critiquées. Dans d'autres cas où la Commission est intervenue, il existait plusieurs catégories d'actions: si le prix offert pour les actions ordinaires était normal et égal pour tous les actionnaires, un prix exceptionnellement élevé était offert parallèlement pour des actions privilégiées qui se trouvaient toutes aux mains de la majorité.

Lorsque l'acquisition doit préluder à une fusion ultérieure, la Commission vérifie aussi que les conditions faites aux actionnaires majoritaires ne soient pas trop différentes de celles qui seront ensuite offertes, dans le cadre de la fusion, à la généralité des actionnaires.

Lorsqu'un groupe décide de faire l'acquisition d'une participation de contrôle dans une société, la Commission bancaire insiste souvent pour que ce groupe étende son offre à tous les actionnaires de la société, en pratiquant une offre publique d'achat — naturellement aux mêmes conditions que celles offertes aux détenteurs de la majorité. Cette exigence n'est pas absolue. Dans certains cas, il est arrivé que la Commission bancaire, après avoir obtenu des garanties de la part du groupe acquéreur quant au régime qui serait réservé aux minoritaires après l'acquisition, se contente de la surveillance de ces garanties — généralement à l'intervention d'administrateurs représentant la minorité. Il faut que la Commission soit persuadée que l'acquisition n'a pas pour objet d'intégrer la société dans un groupe où elle serait dorénavant gérée en fonction des intérêts du groupe et sans égard pour les minoritaires. C'est donc une question d'espèce — mais le plus fréquemment la Commission invite le groupe acquéreur à faire une offre générale spécialement dans le dernier état de sa jurisprudence. D'autres techniques permettant d'assurer l'égalité de traitement des actionnaires peuvent aussi être utilisées.

Les critières à prendre en considération, selon la Commission bancaire, pour déterminer dans quelle mesure il y a lieu de requérir l'extension de l'offre à tous les actionnaires sont notamment les suivants: l'importance de la participation et le pouvoir de vote qu'elle confère en fait, compte tenu de la dispersion des titres aux assemblées générales ordinaires ainsi qu'à celles appelées à se prononcer à des conditions spéciales de présence et de majorité; l'opposition d'intérêts qui peut exister entre l'acquéreur et les autres associés; l'orientation que le nouvel actionnaire majoritaire se propose d'imprimer à la vie sociale; l'existence ou l'absence d'un marché effectif pour la négociation des actions ainsi que le rapport entre les cotations qui s'y forment, le prix des cessions et la valeur de l'action telle qu'elle peut être appréciée sur base d'autres critères.

La Commission bancaire a condamné avec une particulière vigueur des administrateurs qui avaient été saisis en cette qualité d'une offre d'acquisition de la majorité de contrôle par un groupe tiers, intéressé par la société et qui avaient fait usage de cette offre au profit de leur groupe ou de certains actionnaires choisis par eux. La Commission considère que les administrateurs doivent nécessairement faire profiter tous les actionnaires des occasions qui se présentent dans ces conditions.

La Commission bancaire considère même que l'actionnaire majoritaire — indépendamment de sa qualité éventuelle d'administrateur ou de sa représentation au conseil d'administration — est tenu envers les actionnaires minoritaires de se préoccuper des conséquences de la cession de la participation de contrôle, dans la mesure où celle-ci implique le transfert d'un pouvoir susceptible d'avoir des conséquences pour les actionnaires étrangers à l'opération. La Commission bancaire admet, certes, qu'elle ne peut agir dans ce domaine particulièrement que par voie de recommandations puisque, par définition même, la cession d'une participation de contrôle est une opération entre actionnaires qui échappe à sa compétence légale. Le plus souvent cependant ces recommandations sont suivies pour les raisons indiquées ci-dessus.

Enfin, la Commission édicte des devoirs d'information: il faut d'abord l'avertir de toute opération de ce genre intéressant une société soumise à sa juridiction. Il faut ensuite que les cessions de contrôle soient portées à la connaissance du public dans leur principe et dans leurs conditions et que, si une offre publique est en préparation, la cotation des titres soit suspendue pour éviter des spéculations.

On peut assurément se demander dans quelle mesure les thèses de la Commission bancaire sont conformes au *droit belge positif* tel qu'il existe actuellement. En effet, le principe de l'égalité des actionnaires paraît bien ne concerner que le fonctionnement de l'institution que constitue la société anonyme et son contenu technique est bien limité: les décisions prises par les organes de la société doivent en principe avoir pour tous les actionnaires une incidence proportionellement égale, compte tenu de leur participation au capital social. Il parait très douteux qu'il concerne des opérations étrangères au mécanisme de l'institution. De même, le droit belge positif n'a pas reconnu l'existence d'une obligation personnelle des administrateurs envers les actionnaires individuellement et un tel devoir n'est pas sanctionné par la loi, puisque l'action individuelle en responsabilité, pour des actes accomplis par les administrateurs dans l'exercice de leurs fonctions, n'est pas admise en principe — indépendamment de violations de la loi qui pourraient être constitutives de fautes quasi-délictuelles de droit commun. On ne trouve pas, en droit belge positif, d'équivalent de la «fiduciary relationship» à l'égard des actionnaires, individuellement admise par exemple en droit américain. A fortiori est-il difficile d'admettre, sur le plan des principes généraux du droit des sociétés, l'idée qu'un actionnaire majoritaire serait tenu à des devoirs particuliers envers les autres actionnaires, du fait même de sa position et du pouvoir qu'elle implique.

Mais la Commission contribue ainsi à créer le droit et les applications qu'elle fait de ses théories, même si la justification précise en demeure incertaine, qui aboutissent à introduire, dans le droit positif, *par voie prétorienne*, des principes qui en étaient absents. Il faut reconnaître à cette jurisprudence le grand mérite d'appréhender avec réalisme le phénomène du groupe de sociétés par son aspect essentiel — à savoir l'existence d'un intérêt de groupe distinct de l'intérêt commun des actionnaires de chaque société membre de groupe et la recherche d'une protection en présence de cette situation. Elle présente aussi l'avantage considérable d'éviter, en ces matières délicates, tout dogmatisme et toute solution a priori identique dans chaque cas puisque la Commission se réserve précisément la faculté d'examiner toutes les circonstances propres aux espèces qui lui sont soumises et d'adapter les solutions à ces circonstances.

Il faut reconnaître, en revanche, que la formation des groupes de sociétés n'est ainsi abordée que de manière fragmentaire puisque, comme la Commission l'a elle-même reconnu, la cession d'une participation de contrôle ne constitue que l'un des modes possibles d'institution d'un lien de dépendance.

4. Interventions particulières de la Commission bancaire en matière d'offres publiques d'achat

La Commission bancaire a des pouvoirs importants en matière d'offres publiques d'achat ou d'échange et elle en fait un très large usage. Elle a progressivement élaboré, au fil des cas successifs dont elle a eu à connaître, un véritable *code des bonnes pratiques* à suivre en ce domaine et elle le fait respecter à la faveur de ses pouvoirs en matière d'information conformément à sa technique habituelle. La Commission est particulièrement favorable à l'offre publique comme mode d'acquisition d'un contrôle, car elle implique la mise en œuvre de mécanismes qui permettent d'assurer l'information des intéressés et qui éliminent au maximum les risques d'abus grâce au code de bonne conduite dont le respect peut être imposé plus aisément que dans les opérations occultes, telles les cessions de participations de contrôle.

Les offres publiques sont d'ailleurs fréquentes en Belgique, et la technique en est connue depuis de longues années. Les offres agressives sont exceptionnelles et l'on peut citer un cas célèbre qui avait pour objet la société Sofina. Plus récemment, des contre-offres ont été faites à la suite d'une offre faite par la Cie d'assurances La Royale Belge portant sur les actions de la Cie U. P. B., convoitée également par des compagnies d'assurances britanniques.[56]

La Commission jouit en ce domaine d'une compétence légale, puisque son intervention est requise pour toute offre d'achat ou d'échange de valeurs mobilières adressée au public, en vertu de l'arrêté royal n° 185 du 9 juillet 1925, interprété par la loi du 10 juin 1964 et complété par la loi du 10 juillet 1969.

Tant le concept de «valeur mobilière» que celui de «public» ont été interprétés très extensivement par la loi du 10 juin 1964 et par la loi du 10 juillet 1969 et son arrêté royal d'application du 12 novembre 1969.[57]

[56] *Cf.* G. Guelders, *Les offres publiques d'achat,* dans Conférences d'études bancaires et financières (1970); R. Wtterwulghe, L'offre publique d'acquisition au service d'un marché des sociétés (Bruxelles, 1973); G. Schrans, *L'offre publique d'achat d'actions au porteur,* Rev. Banque 1965, p. 494.

[57] Rappelons que l'opération est «publique» dès que l'on sollicite pour compte propre ou pour compte de tiers de plus de cinquante personnes ou que l'on utilise, pour annoncer ou recommander l'opération, une quelconque insertion dans la presse ou que l'on a recours à l'envoi de lettre circulaires ou d'autres documents relatifs à l'opération, même adressés individuellement ou sur demande des destinataires, ou que l'on s'adresse à un quelconque intermédiaire (sauf s'il s'agit d'une banque ou d'un agent de change), ou encore si une banque ou un agent de change agit comme «organisme guichet» ou comme mandataire des auteurs de l'opération. Il existe certaines exceptions en faveur des banques et des agents de change, lorsqu'ils établissent que leur intervention en Belgique est demeurée limitée à un »cercle restreint de personnes physiques ou morales».

La Commission impose la rédaction d'un prospectus qui doit comprendre des informations circonstanciées par la société faisant l'objet de l'offre, sur les auteurs de l'offre, leurs intentions, et les conditions qu'ils proposent. La «philosophie de l'information» qui caractérise l'action de la Commission bancaire, se développe naturellement en ce domaine particulier également.

Dans l'élaboration des règles normatives destinées à régir le comportement des parties à l'offre, la Commission s'est fréquemment inspirée du *«City Code on Take-overs and Mergers»* de 1968, révisé à plusieurs reprises, sans négliger les solutions préconisées par la Commission française des Opérations de Bourse, encore que cet organisme soit beaucoup plus récent et moins expérimenté que la Commission bancaire et que les conditions de fonctionnement et les pratiques du marché français soient assez différentes de celles du marché belge.

Plusieurs principes de base guident la Commission dans la détermination des règles de bonne conduite à appliquer en matière d'offres publiques d'achat.

D'abord, elle applique *la règle de l'égalité* entre les actionnaires, même au-delà du contenu usuellement assigné à cette règle, puisque, ici encore, il s'agit d'opérations étrangères au fonctionnement même de la société, et en déduit de multiples conséquences concrètes.[58] Ainsi, elle prescrit que le droit à l'information soit le même pour tous les actionnaires, sans aucun privilège pour ceux qui exercent le contrôle. Elle s'assure que les conditions faites à tous les actionnaires soient bien les mêmes et elle proscrit tout régime discriminatoire en faveur de certains d'entre eux sous quelque forme que ce soit. Elle interdit à l'offrant de faire des achats en bourse ou hors bourse pendant le cours de l'offre à des conditions différentes de celles proposées.

Elle condamne aussi les dirigeants ou les actionnaires qui, en vue d'une offre imminente, s'empressent de faire l'acquisition de titres auprès d'autres actionnaires, ignorants de l'opération, à des conditions peu avantageuses pour ces derniers. Plus généralement, elle condamne toute utilisation par les «initiés» de leurs informations particulières à l'occasion d'une offre publique.

Ensuite, la Commission se fonde sur l'idée que, dans cette matière au moins, *le conseil d'administration* a des *obligations envers les actionnaires individuellement* et qu'il ne peut se borner à se préoccuper de la société considérée indépendamment de la collectivité de ses actionnaires, ni des seuls intérêts personnels de ses membres ou des actionnaires qu'il «représente». Il en résulte que le conseil d'administration de la société faisant l'objet de l'opération doit être averti de celle-ci alors que, – stricto jure – cette société, et par conséquent son conseil d'administration, sont étrangers à l'offre. Le conseil doit alors informer les actionnaires de la société dont les actions font l'objet de l'offre, de la position que prendront les membres du conseil, de l'importance de leur participation, de la situation qui leur sera faite par l'offrant éventuellement. Il doit donner son

[58] *V.* par exemple dans le rapport de la Commission 1978-79, p. 112 *et seq.* le cas d'un offre publique dans laquelle l'égalité de traitement des actionnaires avait été violée à la faveur d'une convention secrète avec le détenteur du contrôle. *Cf.* aussi diverses interventions récentes dans les rapports 1973-74, p. 116 *et seq.*; 1976-77, p. 105 *et seq.*; 1977-78, p. 116 *et seq.*

opinion sur l'offre et notamment sur les conditions proposées, ainsi que sur les objectifs que l'offrant se propose d'atteindre s'il réussit dans sa tentative. Dans ce rôle, le conseil doit mettre les informations dont il dispose à la disposition des actionnaires. Lorsqu'il existe plusieurs offres, il ne peut avantager l'une au détriment de l'autre, mais il doit faire connaître son choix et son opinion personnelle de manière motivée. Les administrateurs ne peuvent rien faire qui entraverait les actionnaires dans leur libre choix. Ils ne pourraient, par exemple, conclure, pendant le cours de l'offre, des conventions nouvelles qui modifieraient fondamentalement la situation, comme par exemple augmenter le capital social en faveur de l'un des offrants ou en faveur d'un tiers pour faire échouer l'offre en modifiant les conditions de majorité. Ils ne pourraient même, suivant les prescriptions les plus récentes de la Commission bancaire, faire usage d'une clause d'agrément figurant dans les statuts pour mettre l'offrant dans l'impossibilité de réaliser l'opération — du moins s'ils faisaient usage de cette clause au bénéfice des actionnaires majoritaires et non en considération des intérêts de la collectivité des actionnaires.

Une troisième idée fondamentale consiste à imposer aux offrants des *règles du jeu* qui soient *«fair»*. Ils doivent d'abord coopérer au respect des règles inspirées par les deux principes ci-dessus énoncés et ils ne pourraient se livrer à des manoeuvres dont l'effet serait de violer le principe de l'égalité entre les actionnaires ou de leur donner des informations incomplètes ou insuffisantes. Ils ne pourraient agir dans des conditions qui mettraient le conseil d'administration de la société en cause dans l'impossibilité d'exercer son rôle de conseil des actionnaires. Ils doivent aussi respecter l'égalité des actionnaires dans les conditions de leur offre: par exemple, si une réduction des offres est prévue, elle doit être proportionnelle et non point organisée discrétionnairement par l'offrant. Les délais et les mesures d'information doivent être suffisants pour que tous les actionnaires aient une chance de se prononcer. Si une contre-offre est pratiquée, l'offrant doit accepter de dégager les actionnaires qui auraient déjà accepté son offre pour les remettre en situation de choisir entre les deux offres.

Les offres doivent être libellées de manière telle que les conditions dans lesquelles l'offrant peut se rétracter n'apparaissent pas comme purement potestatives (conditions relatives à la quantité de titres à recevoir en vertu de l'offre ou conditions concernant la modification des circonstances fondamentales de l'opération). L'offrant doit indiquer de manière claire ses objectifs et la Commission n'accepte que les opérations qui tendent à obtenir une majorité permettant d'assumer les responsabilités de gestion de l'entreprise en cause, à l'exclusion par exemple d'offres qui viseraient à la formation d'une minorité de blocage. Une contre-offre n'est recevable que si elle compacte une contrepartie (en espèces ou en actions) d'une valeur plus élevée que celle prévue dans la première offre. La surenchère doit être suffisamment importante pour éviter des marchandages anormaux. En pratique, dans les cas d'espèces qui lui furent soumis, la Commission a exigé que la première surenchère soit d'au moins 5% et qu'en cas de surenchères ultérieures, l'amélioration de la contrepartie atteigne au moins 2,5%. Mais il ne s'agit pas d'une règle absolue, car tout dépend des autres éléments qui permettent d'assurer la comparaison des offres en présence. La question serait plus complexe, par exemple, en cas d'offre publique d'échange, puisque les caractéristiques des titres offerts en échange devraient alors aussi entrer en ligne de compte. L'offrant doit justifier du caractère sérieux de son offre et notamment établir qu'il dispose des fonds nécessaires et que ceux-ci sont disponibles notamment au regard de la réglementation relative au contrôle de changes. S'il s'agit d'une offre publique d'échange, les conditions requises pour l'émission des actions offertes en échange doivent avoir été accomplies. L'offrant ne peut, pendant la durée de l'opération, pratiquer des achats en bourse ou des achats directs étrangers à la procédure d'offre à des conditions différentes de celles de l'offre.

La Commission n'exclut pas que l'acquisition d'une participation de contrôle puisse avoir lieu par les mécanismes boursiers — dont ce peut être l'une des raisons d'être. Mais il faut alors que les règles relatives à l'offre publique d'achat soient observées suivant les circonstances. En effet, l'opération soulèverait des objections si les principes relatifs à l'information exacte des intéressés et la règle de l'égalité des actionnaires n'étaient pas respectés. L'application de la réglementation propre aux offres publiques d'achat permettrait précisément d'éviter tout reproche.

5. *Rôle de la Commission bancaire en matière de sociétés holding*

Comme dit ci-dessus, une compétence particulière a été attribuée à la Commission bancaire par l'*arrêté royal* de pouvoirs spéciaux n° 64 du 10 novembre 1967, *concernant les sociétés à portefeuille*, modifié par une loi du 20 janvier 1978. Ces sociétés se trouvent genéralement à la base des groupes de sociétés en droit belge. Ce rôle s'inspire de la philosophie générale qui préside aux interventions de la Commission bancaire en matière de sociétés — c'est-à-dire qu'il est fondé sur un contrôle des informations et sur l'intervention de réviseurs d'entreprises spéciaux mais que, à travers la surveillance des informations, la Commission bancaire est amenée à jouer, avec prudence et souplesse un véritable rôle normatif.

Le législateur s'est inspiré, dans une certaine mesure, de la définition des liens de domination et de dépendance donnée dans le projet de réforme des lois sur les sociétés commerciales (supra, n° 4), pour déterminer le champ d'application du «statut des sociétés à portefeuille». Alors que, dans sa version initiale, de 1967, le texte visait les sociétés «dont l'activité se fonde principalement sur la détention de participations dans une ou plusieurs filiales», cette condition a été supprimée en raison des discussions qu'elle avait fait surgir notamment à propos de sociétés ayant des activités mixtes.

Les sociétés qui sont soumises à un régime spécifique de surveillance, par une autorité, ne sont pas soumises au régime des sociétés à portefeuille; tel est le cas par exemple des compagnies d'assurances ou des caisses d'épargne privées.

Sont soumises à ce statut, les sociétés de droit belge qui possèdent des participations dans une ou plusieurs filiales belges ou étrangères, leur conférant en droit ou en fait le pouvoir de diriger l'activité de celles-ci, pour autant que soit les sociétés-mères, soit encore certaines de leurs filiales ou sous-filiales, aient fait appel à l'épargne publique et pour autant que la valeur de ces participations atteigne au total 500 millions de francs belges, ou représente au moins la moitié des fonds propres de la société-mère. Y sont également soumises, les sociétés de droit belge ayant fait appel au public (ou dont des filiales ou sous-filiales ont fait appel au public) et qui sont elles-mêmes filiales ou sous-filiales de sociétés ou d'institutions étrangères possédant dans des sociétés de droit belge des participations atteignant au total 500 millions de francs belges, ou représentant la moitié de leurs fonds propres. On prend en considération les participations détenues directement ou indirectement.

Une présomption irréfragable d'affiliation est déduite de la détention, directe ou indirecte, ou par interposition de personnes, d'une participation représentant la moitié au moins du capital social ou d'une participation à laquelle est attaché un pouvoir de vote égal à la moitié au moins des voix attachées aux titres émis par la société dominée. Une présomption juris tantum d'affiliation est déduite de la détention, dans les mêmes conditions, d'une participation à laquelle est attaché un nombre de voix égal à la moitié au moins des voix présentes ou représentées à la dernière assemblée générale.

Une seconde présomption juris tantum d'affiliation repose sur une constatation d'une domination assurée par un mécanisme «contractuel ou non» ou «établie sur une quelconque situation de fait». Ces derniers termes paraissent bien incertains et vagues.

Lorsque les contrôles sont assurés par plusieurs sociétés suivant l'un ou plusieurs de ces mécanismes, le lien de filiation existe à l'égard de toutes les sociétés dominantes.

Ces sociétés doivent être inscrites sur une liste dressée par la Commission bancaire et elles doivent faire choix d'un réviseur investi de missions particulières. La Commission a déterminé de manière pragmatique la liste des sociétés en cause, en collaborant aussi étroitement que possible avec les intéressés. Un recours peut être introduit contre la décision d'inscription devant le Ministre des Finances.

L'inscription sur la liste entraîne un contrôle de la Commission bancaire, portant sur les informations diffusées par les sociétés à portefeuille et particulièrement sur leurs bilans et comptes de profits et pertes, ainsi que sur les rapports des conseils d'administration. Ces documents doivent donner une vue «complète et correcte de la situation de la société, de ses charges, de ses revenus et de son activité« notamment en ce qui concerne les relations existant entre elle et ses filiales et les autres sociétés du groupe et les opérations dans lesquelles ses administrateurs peuvent avoir des intérêts personnels.

La Commission peut faire à ce sujet des recommandations et, s'il n'est pas tenu compte de celles-ci, elle peut rendre son avis public. Elle n'a été amenée à faire, jusqu'à présent, usage de ce droit qu'une seule fois.[59]

Par ailleurs, la Commission bancaire peut demander aux réviseurs désignés, avec son accord, dans les sociétés holding, de lui faire des rapports spéciaux concernant les comptes sociaux, les rapports faits aux organes sociaux, les relations entre les sociétés du groupe, les modifications apportées à la composi-

[59] *V. supra* II 1 et note 19.

tion des portefeuilles de la société, de ses filiales ou de ses sous-filiales, ainsi que les opérations et décisions dans lesquelles un administrateur aurait des intérêts personnels. Ces réviseurs envoient, en outre, des rapports réguliers à la Commission.

La Commission bancaire doit publier chaque année, dans ses rapports, une analyse de l'application faite par elle de ces dispositions.

La Commission a élaboré une *circulaire*, adressée en janvier *1972* aux réviseurs des sociétés holding, leur indiquant les points sur lesquels devront porter les rapports circonstanciés que ces réviseurs doivent lui adresser. Il s'agit particulièrement:

- des méthodes d'évaluation et des critères d'imputation comptable retenus pour l'établissement des comptes sociaux;
- de l'attestation de la sincérité des informations ainsi publiées;
- de la description détaillée des méthodes de consolidation éventuellement suivies en cas d'établissement d'un bilan consolidé.

Une série d'informations doivent également être données en ce qui concerne les filiales et les sous-filiales, concernant notamment les relations financières entre les sociétés du groupe, ainsi que l'économie des accords organiques conclus entre la société holding et ses filiales ou sous-filiales. Le rapport doit encore comporter des précisions sur la modification de la composition des portefeuilles et sur les contreparties obtenues en cas de cessions de participations, notamment entre sociétés du même groupe.

Une autre circulaire du même jour, adressée aux sociétés à portefeuille, organise les modalités de la transmission par ces dernières, à la Commission bancaire, des informations dues en vertu de l'arrêté royal n° 64.

Pratiquement la Commission bancaire a utilisé, dans ce domaine, l'expérience qu'elle avait acquise en matière d'émission publique de valeurs mobilières. Ses *interventions* concernent fréquemment le fond du droit sous couleur de vérifier les informations données aux actionnaires et aux épargnants. Les recommandations et les discussions personnelles avec les dirigeants des sociétés holding — c'est-à-dire en fait en Belgique, des groupes de sociétés — sont fréquentes.

On peut signaler des interventions notamment sur les points suivants, outre celles que nous avons mentionnées ci-dessus:[60]

- une convention d'assistance technique avec une autre société dissimulant le paiement de rémunérations supplémentaires à un administrateur;[61]
- des opérations de cessions de participations entre sociétés faisant partie d'un même groupe, dans des conditions que la Commission a jugées critiquables;[62]
- des interventions assez nombreuses sur la manière de présenter les comptes et les principes de la consolidation;[63]

[60] *V. supra* III § 2A-4.

[61] Rapport 1976-77, p. 133.

[62] Rapport 1976-77, p. 134.

[63] Rapport 1976-77, p. 134 *et seq.;* 1975-76, p. 105; 1977-78, p. 145; 1978-79, p. 136 et 142, 146 *et seq.*

- la critique d'avantages particuliers accordés à des actionnaires prépondérants, représentés au conseil d'administration, ou de conventions avec des actionnaires;[64]
- la détermination des tantièmes et rémunérations proportionnelles,[65] compte tenu de modifications apportées à la loi fiscale;
- la critique d'opérations de fusion et de scission, avec dégagement de plus-values opérées entre sociétés d'un même groupe;[66]
- le sort à réserver à la distribution gratuite d'actions de bonus au sein d'un groupe;[67]
- le paiement injustifié d'une commission à une société-mère, et des opérations dommageables imposées à une filiale par sa société dominante.[68]

B. La protection des créanciers

1. Application des règles du droit commun

La protection des créanciers contre les abus qui pourraient résulter des pratiques des groupes de sociétés est assurée uniquement par l'application des règles du droit commun. La Commission bancaire n'intervient guère en ce domaine qui sortirait de sa compétence, même entendue de manière très extensive.

Il semble cependant que ces dispositions aient généralement donné satisfaction, car l'on n'enregistre guère de plainte concernant une insuffisance des moyens d'actions ouverts aux créanciers – même si la politique récemment suivie par l'une ou l'autre société «multinationale» étrangère, ayant abandonné sa filiale belge à une faillite sans gloire, en se refusant à se porter à son secours, a été vivement critiquée. En réalité, le droit commun aurait vraisemblablement permis des recours, mais les créanciers se seraient heurtés aux grandes difficultés matérielles qu'implique l'exécution d'un jugement belge aux Etats-Unis.

Le droit commun comprend essentiellement les règles applicables en matière de faillite et, le cas échéant, en matière de banqueroute.[69] On y trouve les règles usuelles relatives à la protection des créanciers, notamment en cas d'actes accomplis pendant la période suspecte qui précède la déclaration de faillite.[70] Le

[64] Rapport 1975-76, p. 107. *V.* aussi 1977-78, p. 144.

[65] Rapport 1973-74, p. 215.

[66] Rapport 1978-79, p. 139.

[67] Rapport 1978-79, p. 145.

[68] Rapport 1970-71, p. 193.

[69] La banqueroute comprend en droit belge une série d'infractions pénales commises par un commerçant en état de cessation des paiements (même en l'absence d'une déclaration formelle de faillite par la juridiction commerciale), définies par le Code de commerce (art. 573 à 578 du livre II du Code de commerce).

[70] La période suspecte est fixée en droit belge à 10 jours avant la date de la cessation des paiements qui peut être, en matière commerciale, fixée à six mois au plus avant la date du jugement déclaratif de faillite, sauf exceptions. Cette limite ne s'applique pas aux infractions pénales de banqueroute. *Cf.* J. Heenen, *Les nullités de la période suspecte, dans les pays de la Communnauté économique européenne*, dans Liber amicorum Baron Frédéricq, *supra* note 25, t. I, p. 557.

droit pénal sanctionne les détournements d'actifs, l'utilisation de biens sociaux en faveur de tiers, qui peuvent être des sociétés du même groupe, ou encore les avantages accordés à certains créanciers (notamment applicables en matière de relations financières entre sociétés d'un même groupe). Nous n'insistons pas ici sur ces règles, dont il est fait fréquemment application, mais qui ne concernent pas spécialement les relations entre sociétés faisant partie d'un même groupe.

Le droit belge positif ne connaît pas d'infraction spéciale pour les abus de biens sociaux – et cette matière demeure régie par le droit pénal commun. Le projet de réforme des lois coordonnées sur les sociétés commerciales, s'inspirant à cet égard dans une certaine mesure de l'exemple français, propose d'ériger en infraction pénale spéciale, l'usage des biens ou du crédit de la société, dans un intérêt contraire à celui de la société ou des actionnaires, à des fins personnelles ou pour favoriser une autre société ou entreprise dans laquelle les auteurs de l'infraction étaient intéressés, directement ou indirectement (article 402 du projet). Cette disposition pourra trouver application en matière de groupes de sociétés, mais son objet se trouve relativement limité par la nécessité d'un intérêt direct ou indirect des auteurs de l'infraction dans la société ou l'entreprise en faveur de laquelle l'abus a été commis.

2. *L'extension de faillite ou de passif*

Les tribunaux belges ont développé une jurisprudence considérable sur l'extension de faillite ou du passif d'une société à celui qui apparaît comme étant son «maître» – sans qu'un texte spécial ait été nécessaire à cet effet.[71] Ceux-ci sont protégés non seulement en cas de faillite – par l'extension de la faillite sociale au «maître de l'affaire» — mais encore, indépendamment de toute faillite, par la condamnation du maître de l'affaire à supporter le passif social. Deux idées servent de base à la sanction des abus de la personnalité morale commis au détriment des créanciers. Les tribunaux considèrent parfois la société comme *fictive* — en sorte qu'elle ne peut se prévaloir de la responsabilité limitée et de l'existence d'un patrimoine distinct. Dans d'autres cas, suivant les circonstances, ils jugent la société, quoique réelle, comme ayant agi en tant que prête-nom pour une personne qui, la dominant, a exercé une activité commerciale sous son couvert. La théorie générale du *prête-nom* permet alors de rendre cette personne responsable du passif et éventuellement même de la déclarer en état de faillite.

Depuis l'entrée en vigueur de la loi du 6 mars 1973, qui a déterminé de manière limitative les cas de nullités de sociétés anonymes, et qui a assimilé les effets de la nullité à ceux d'une liquidation, il semble bien que l'explication fondée sur le caractère fictif de la société ne puisse plus guère être retenue.[72] A notre avis, le fondement le plus exact à donner à cette jurisprudence consiste dans l'abus de la personnalité morale; cet abus est sanctionné par l'inopposabilité de la personnalité morale — en tout ou en partie — à ceux qui en sont les victimes.

[71] Comp. la situation en France où les décrets-lois de 1937 ont confirmé une jurisprudence antérieure, créée à l'aide des instruments du droit commun.

[72] P. Coppens et F. t'Kint, *Examen de jurisprudence sur les faillites et les concordats*, R. C. J. B. 1979, n° 6, p. 300, spéc. p. 303.

Lorsque les circonstances caractéristiques de l'abus se rencontrent, la faillite de la société peut être étendue à celui dont elle dissimulait les activités personnelles. Parfois, sans étendre la faillite, les tribunaux condamnent ces personnes à supporter le passif social qui est considéré comme le leur propre.

La jurisprudence, sur ces questions, est très abondante et fait preuve d'une grande sévérité.[73] Les circonstances dans lesquelles il a été fait application de cette jurisprudence, sont assez variées: sociétés constituées par une seule personne assistée par d'autres fondateurs agissant sans affectio societatis; sociétés créées avec un capital et des moyens d'action manifestement insuffisants; sociétés dans lesquelles les organes sociaux ne fonctionnent pas et où toutes les décisions sont prises et exécutées sur ordre du «maître de l'affaire», lequel ne respecte pas les «règles du jeu»; confusions entre le patrimoine social et celui du «maître de l'affaire» sous diverses formes; utilisation par le «maître de l'affaire» d'actifs appartenant à la société et vice versa; confusions créées à l égard des tiers entre l'activité sociale et celle du maître de l'affaire; comptabilité tenue d'une manière irrégulière et ne permettant pas de faire le départ entre les biens sociaux et ceux des associés; prêts ou avances consentis par le «maître de l'affaire» en dehors de toute décision valable des organes sociaux. Le seul fait d'une participation prépondérante d'un actionnaire ou encore des fautes de gestion commises par des administrateurs, ne suffisent pas à justifier l'application de ces règles.

En pratique, la plupart des décisions qui concernent cette matière, ont trait à des personnes physiques qui dominent une société. Les quelques décisions qui étendent une faillite à une autre société ou mettent le passif d'une société à charge d'une autre, sont relatives à des petites sociétés et elles ne peuvent être considérées comme significatives pour le droit des groupes de sociétés. Toute fois, ces règles pourraient naturellement être appliquées sans aucune difficulté à des groupes de sociétés et les motifs qui les inspirent seraient parfaitement valables en pareille occurrence.

Plusieurs litiges sont actuellement pendants devant les tribunaux belges relatifs à des sociétés holding très importantes, visant à les faire déclarer responsables du passif de sociétés filiales tombées en faillite. Ces principes pourraient recevoir application en matière de groupes de sociétés.

Une *loi du 4 août 1978,* dispose que, en cas de faillite d'une société et

[73] *Cf.* sur cette question, P. Coppens, *La faillite personelle du maître de l'affaire,* REV. PRAT. SOC. 1967, p. 195 et les réflexions suscitées par cette question dans IDÉES NOUVELLES DANS LE DROIT DE LA FAILLITE, p. 135 (Journées d'études organisées par l'Université catholique de Louvain, 1969); J. VAN RYN & J. HEENEN, PRINCIPES DE DROIT COMMERCIAL, t. IV, n° 208 (Bruxelles, 1965); A. Cloquet, *Les faillites et les concordats,* dans LES NOVELLES, DROIT COMMERCIAL, t. IV, n° 110 *et seq.* (Bruxelles, 1965). Sur les applications en jurisprudence, *v.,* J. Van Ryn et P. Van Ommeslaghe, *Examen de jurisprudence sur les sociétés commerciales,* R. C. J. B. 1958, p. 61, n° 5; et R. C. J. B. 1967, p. 316, n° 29; et R. C. J. B. 1973, p. 358, n° 20. P. Coppens et F. t'Kint, *Examens de jurisprudence sur les faillites et les concordats,* R. C. J. B. 1974, p. 376, n° 7; R. C. J. B. 1979, p. 300, n° 6; Y. Dumon et M.-F. Maussion, *Propos sur la notion d'extension de la faillite et sur les mesures analogues en droit belge et en droit comparé,* J. C. B. 1974, p. 180.

d'insuffisance de l'actif, s'il est établi qu'une faute grave et caractérisée a été commise par eux et a contribué à la faillite, tout administrateur ou ancien administrateur ainsi que toute autre personne qui a effectivement détenu le pouvoir de gérer la société, peuvent être déclarés personnellement obligés, avec ou sans solidarité; de tout ou partie des dettes sociales à concurrence de l'insuffisance d'actif. Si cette disposition concerne au premier chef les personnes qui exercent les fonctions d'administrateur, elle pourrait cependant être interprétée de manière extensive, en sorte qu'elle s'appliquerait à une société-mère qui aurait effectivement exercé le pouvoir de gestion de sa société filiale. Il n'existe pas de cas d'application en ce sens, compte tenu du caractère récent de la loi nouvelle.

Il faut encore faire mention d'une pratique des tribunaux de commerce des grandes villes qui, à l'image du tribunal de commerce de Bruxelles, ont institué un *«service des enquêtes commerciales»* parfois appelé *«service de dépistage»*.[74] Ce service examine la situation des entreprises qui paraissent en difficulté, même si elles ne sont pas en état de cessation des paiements et si leur crédit n'est pas ébranlé. Le tribunal est informé de ces situations par le Parquet, par la consultation des rôles d'audience, par les prôtets publiés, par les saisies pratiquées, par l'examen des bilans de sociétés publiés aux Annexes du Moniteur et enfin par les plaintes dont il est rapidement saisi lorsqu'une société cesse de faire face à ses engagements de manière normale. Le tribunal intervient auprès de sociétés-mères actionnaires prépondérantes de sociétés dont la trésorerie apparaît étroite ou encore dont la structure de bilan est anormale,[75] pour que la société-mère accepte de cautionner les engagements de sa filiale envers les créanciers, par une déclaration unilatérale en ce sens, ou pour qu'elle transforme ses propres créances en apports en capital, ou encore pour qu'elle accepte que ses créances soient payées après celles des autres créanciers et se transforment en «prêt subordonné». Le remède doit naturellement être approprié aux circonstances. Ces pratiques sont intéressantes par leur souplesse et par la variété des solutions qu'elles permettent. Elles se développent – comme les interventions de la Commission bancaire – en marge du droit commercial traditionnel et en l'absence de texte précis, en vertu d'une interprétation extensive de la compétence particulière accordée aux tribunaux de commerce en matière de faillite.

C. Les groupes de sociétés et le droit comptable

1. Le droit comptable en Belgique

Le droit comptable belge est resté pendant longtemps embryonnaire. Tant la loi sur les sociétés que le Code de commerce, ne comprenaient que des dispositions tout à fait insuffisantes sur la comptabilité. On se référait aux bonnes pratiques comptables, qui n'étaient guère définies. Comme dit ci-dessus, sous le patronna-

[74] *Cf.* IDÉES NOUVELLES DANS LE DROIT DE LA FAILLITE, *supra* note 73, p. 363 *et seq.*

[75] Par exemple, en raison d'une disproportion entre les capitaux apportés par la société-mère et ceux qu'elle prête ou met simplement à la disposition de la société filiale.

ge de la Commission bancaire, une commission de spécialistes avait élaboré des «recommandations» assez circonstanciées pour pallier ces insuffisances et celles-ci étaient largement suivies. Il y était tenu compte des relations d'affiliation pouvant exister entre plusieurs sociétés.

Le projet de réforme des lois sur les sociétés comprenait des dispositions beaucoup plus circonstanciées – inspirées notamment des propositions de directives européennes alors en cours d'élaboration.

A partir de ces diverses sources, le législateur a promulgué une *loi du 17 juillet 1975*, qui constitue maintenant une base solide pour un développement très complet du droit comptable. Cette loi est complétée par des textes d'application sous la forme d'arrêtés royaux. Elle trace un cadre général au droit comptable et il appartient aux arrêtés royaux d'édicter les règles précises qui en forment le tissu.

Une *loi du 24 mars 1978* a modifié les lois sur les sociétés, pour tenir compte de l'application des dispositions nouvelles. Celles-ci concernent non seulement les sociétés, mais plus généralement, les entreprises, suivant diverses distinctions dans le détail desquelles il n'y a pas lieu d'entrer ici.

Les principaux *arrêtés d'application* sont les suivants:

- un arrêté royal du 8 octobre 1976, modifié par un arrêté royal du 27 décembre 1977, édicte des règles circonstanciées concernant l'articulation des bilans, des comptes de résultats et de l'annexe à ces documents, ainsi que des principes d'évaluation des articles actifs et passifs de ces comptes;
- un arrêté royal du 23 décembre 1975, modifié par un arrêté royal du 3 avril 1979, concerne la tenue des livres;
- un arrêté royal du 12 novembre 1979, concerne les comptes annuels des compagnies d'assurances;
- un arrêté royal du 29 novembre 1977, régit les comptes annuels des sociétés à portefeuille; il a été pris en vertu d'un article 73 de la loi du 30 juin 1975.

Une Commission des normes comptables a été instituée par la loi du 17 juillet 1975. Elle peut formuler des recommandations générales et se prononcer par voie d'avis non obligatoires, sur les cas qui lui sont soumis. Elle publie un Bulletin où elle donne ses avis et contribue ainsi à élaborer de manière pragmatique le droit comptable à partir des textes légaux et réglementaires.

2. *Les groupes de sociétés et le droit comptable*

L'arrêté royal du 8 octobre 1976 impose que le bilan, le compte de résultat et l'annexe donnent diverses informations, sous des rubriques particulières concernant les relations avec les entreprises liées: dettes et créances, participations, transferts entre entreprises liées.

Les entreprises liées sont définies par le texte comme étant d'une part les filiales et les sous-filiales, et d'autre part les sociétés-mères ainsi que les filiales et les sous-filiales de ces sociétés-mères.

Quant au lien d'affiliation, il est défini en s'inspirant du projet de réforme des lois sur les sociétés:[76] est considérée comme une filiale ou une sous-filiale d'une

[76] *Cf. supra* III § 1 C.

entreprise, toute autre entreprise, lorsque la première est en mesure, en droit ou en fait, d'exercer une influence décisive sur la désignation de la moitié au moins des dirigeants de la seconde, ou sur l'orientation de la gestion de celle-ci et ce, soit en vertu de conventions, soit en raison des participations détenues dans la seconde, directement par la première ou indirectement à l'intermédiaire des ses filiales ou sous-filiales.

Si ces participations représentent la moitié au moins du capital de cette autre entreprise, ou si le pouvoir de vote qui y est attaché représente la moitié au moins des voix attachées à l'ensemble des actions et parts émises par celle-ci, cette autre entreprise est irréfragablement réputée être la filiale ou la sous-filiale de la première.

Si le nombre des voix attachées à ces participations représente la moitié au moins du nombre des voix présentes ou représentées à la dernière assemblée générale de cette autre entreprise, celle-ci est réputée, sauf preuve contraire, à mentionner dans l'annexe au bilan, être la filiale ou la sous-filiale de la première.

Cette définition correspond donc à la conception générale du groupe que nous mentionnions au début du présent rapport. On observera qu'elle prévoit expressément l'hypothèse du groupe contractuel. C'est donc par le biais du droit comptable que le groupe de sociétés fait ainsi sons apparition dans la législation positive. La définition n'est pas identique cependant à celle que donne la loi organisant le statut des sociétés à portefeuille, sans que ces différences puissent s'expliquer très rationnellement.[77]

L'*arrêté royal du 28 novembre 1977* étend aux sociétés à portefeuille[78] les principes consacrés par l'arrêté royal du 8 octobre 1976, concernant l'articulation des bilans et des comptes de résultats, la présentation de l'annexe ainsi que les règles d'évaluation, sous réserve de diverses modalités et adaptations.

La définition de la filiale ou de la sous-filiale y est adaptée pour correspondre à la définition quelque peu différente contenue dans la législation sur les sociétés à portefeuille précisément.[79]

En outre, l'arrêté prescrit que les sociétés à portefeuille devront établir et rendre publics, complémentairement à leurs comptes sociaux, des comptes consolidés comprenant un bilan consolidé, un compte de résultats consolidé et une annexe. L'annexe doit comprendre l'indication des sociétés comprises dans la consolidation et la liste des participations évaluées selon la méthode des équivalences dans les comptes consolidés, les critères adoptés pour les déterminer, ainsi que l'énoncé des méthodes mises en oeuvre pour l'établissement des comptes consolidés.

L'arrêté ne prévoit pas quelles seront les méthodes de consolidation. Le rapport au Roi précédent l'arrêté, contient d'intéressantes considérations sur cette question, et énonce quelques règles tout en recommandant de se référer aux

[77] Cf. *supra* III § 2 A 5.

[78] Telles que définies par l'arrêté royal du 10 novembre 1967, modifié par la loi du 20 janvier 1978, *supra* III § 2 A 5.

[79] *Ibidem.*

normes dégagées par l'*«International Accounting Standards Committee»* en 1976. En réalité, la mise au point progressive et pragmatique des méthodes de consolidation doit avoir lieu sous les auspices de la Commission bancaire, puisque celle-ci exerce sa surveillance sur les sociétés à portefeuille. Suivant le rapport au Roi, un nouvel arrêté pourra intervenir ultérieurement pour codifier les normes de bon comportement qui se seront ainsi progressivement dégagées. Il faut d'ailleurs remarquer que, antérieurement à l'entrée en vigueur de l'arrêté royal du 22 novembre 1977, plusieurs groupes publiaient déjà volontairement des comptes consolidés et avaient donc acquis une expérience en ce domaine complexe. Mais c'est actuellement que s'opère cette codification progressive, ce qui explique l'importance des développements consacrés à la consolidation des comptes par les derniers rapports de la Commission bancaire.

D. Conclusions

Les développements qui précèdent, montrent que si le droit belge des sociétés ne comprend pas une organisation complète et normative des groupes de sociétés, il s'est néanmoins adapté dans une certaine mesure à ce phénomène par le jeu de la jurisprudence et grâce à l'intervention d'institutions, comme la Commission bancaire, les services spéciaux du tribunal de commerce et le droit comptable, qui peuvent innover de manière souple même au-delà des règles bien arrêtées du droit positif.

L'efficacité de ces méthodes est évidemment liée à une mentalité particulière et à la taille réduite du monde économique et financier dans lequel elles s'exercent. Mais l'on peut comprendre que les justiciables préfèrent la souplesse et le pragmatisme qui en résultent, à une organisation normative rigide, même plus rationnelle, telle celle de certains modèles étrangers. Ceux-ci engendrent un certain effroi parmi eux.

Il reste qu'une adaptation du droit positif à cette réalité, apparaît maintenant comme nécessaire, sans abandonner les avantages et les vertus de la souplesse. Le droit positif devrait reconnaître le phénomène du groupe de sociétés, admettre la licéité d'un intérêt de groupe distinct de celui des sociétés qui le composent et éventuellement prescrire des règles générales de protection applicables aux groupes qui voudraient faire prévaloir cet intérêt de groupe. Il devrait aussi étendre l'éventail des instruments permettant la formation d'un groupe notamment en autorisant le recours à la technique contractuelle en ce domaine – dont la souplesse et l'adaptabilité a fait ses preuves en droit économique. Actuellement, la constitution de groupes contractuels a lieu le plus généralement en dehors de la loi – ce qui engendre une insécurité juridique très inconfortable.

Il faudrait également permettre, à l'instar de certains droits étrangers, l'expulsion, moyennant indemnisation, de très petites minorités dont la présence fait obstacle à l'inclusion complète d'une société dans un groupe et à sa subordination intégrale à l'intérêt de groupe.

Pratiquement, il paraît indispensable que cette matière donne lieu à l'élaboration de régles communes au niveau de la C.E.E. On sait qu'une directive est en cours de négociation à ce propos. La difficulté majeure consiste naturellement à trouver un commun dénominateur acceptable pour tous.

Summary:

Groups of Companies and the Experience of Belgian Law

The experience of Belgian law and practice with enterprise groups is discussed in this contribution. In its introductory part the importance of enterprise groups for the economic and social life in Belgium is underlined, a definition of enterprise group is sought and the methods of formation of these groups are summed up. Another short part deals with the Belgian Banking Commission. The Belgian rules on enterprise groups cannot be understood without an appreciation of the role which the Banking Commission plays, especially in the fields of issuance of corporate securities and regulation of portfolio companies. The main part of the article deals with enterprise groups in Belgian corporate law. Two basic objectives in the law are distinguished: first that of preventing the general corporate law from becoming meaningless in situations where one corporation controls another; second, to acknowledge the existence and function of enterprise groups and to develop an adequate special set of rules for them. As to the first objective, the company law reform project of 1979/80 would introduce a definition of a controlling corporation and certain provisions concerning such situations. As to the second objective, while the legislator has so far ignored the phenomenon, the Banking Commission has dealt with it extensively. Three main problems arise in the case of enterprise groups: protection of the investors and shareholders, protection of the creditors, and group accounting. The report shows in detail what rules the Banking Commission has developed in order to achieve the investor and shareholder protection needed, for example in the case of the transfer of controlling interests or in the case of take-over bids. As for creditor protection, a doctrine of the extension of bankruptcy to the so-called master of affairs has been developed. While up to now such an extension has only been granted by the courts in the case of a physical person controlling an enterprise, it seems possible — and is being tried in several pending cases — to have this doctrine extended also to the case of controlling corporations. Finally the Belgian law on accounting and new regulations concerning group accounting are discussed. On the whole, the Belgian experience shows that despite the lack of a statutory law of groups, the problems have been dealt with by an administrative agency in a smooth and efficient way.

Groups of Companies: The English Experience

D. D. PRENTICE
Oxford

I. Introduction

To a large extent this is an essay in speculation and synthesis. Although the phenomenon of corporate group activity is a familiar characteristic of United Kingdom commercial life,[1] and is recognised both in judicial opinions and the Companies Acts,[2] the principles of company law do not address themselves in any coherent way to the problems to which this form of doing business can and does give rise. The treatment of these problems is both fragmented and incomplete and there is no distinct doctrinal category dealing with parent-subsidiary relations. In English company law there is no technical definition of what constitutes a group, but for the purposes of this essay a group will be taken to exist where one company, or a number of companies, is a subsidiary, or are subsidiaries, of another. A company is treated as being a subsidiary of another (the parent) where the parent company (a) is a member and controls the composition of the former's board of directors[3] or (b) where it controls half in nominal value of the former's voting share capital.[4] This is a very undemanding test of control and as Berle and Means[5] and other empirical studies have

[1] For example, it has been estimated that in 1975, in 23 out of the top 250 British non-financial companies, another industrial company held a controlling block: J. SCOTT, CORPORATIONS, CLASSES AND CAPITALISM at 67 (London, 1979). *See also* CMND. 6706, REPORT OF THE COMMITTEE OF INQUIRY ON INDUSTRIAL DEMOCRACY (H. M. S. O., London, 1977), at p. 130, where the report states that in the United Kingdom the "738 *enterprises* employing 2,000 or more people . . . will . . . translate into a larger number of separate *companies* employing 2,000 or more. No precise figure can be given, but the number is likely to be of the order of 1,800".

[2] *See, e. g.*, Companies Act 1948, s. 149 (group accounts); Companies Act 1980, s. 74 (power to provide for employees of a subsidiary on cessation of business).

[3] Companies Act 1948, s. 154 (1) (a). A subsidiary may not hold shares in its parent, Companies Act 1948, s. 27, and this precludes some of the problems arising with respect to directors maintaining themselves in control by intracorporate holdings.

[4] This is a somewhat loose interpretation of Companies Act 1948, s. 154 (1) (b), but it will suffice for present purposes.

[5] A. BERLE & G. MEANS, THE MODERN CORPORATION AND PRIVATE PROPERTY at 70 (New York/Chicago, 1932).

indicated,[6] control (particularly in large public companies where shareholdings are dispersed) can be exercised by possession of a holding which falls well below de iure control. However, for present purposes a corporate group enterprise will be taken to exist where the legal relationship between the constituent members of the group is that of parent and subsidiary as this at least provides a paradigm with respect to which the legal problems of group activity can be examined.

II. The Entity Doctrine

A. The Principle

The starting point for any discussion in English company law of the legal problems arising from corporate group activity is the corporate entity doctrine by which a company on incorporation becomes a legal entity which is separate and distinct from the members who compose it. As a result, a company "is capable of enjoying rights and of being subject to duties which are not the same as those enjoyed or borne by its members"[7] and this doctrine applies whether or not the members of the company are individuals or another company or companies. A forceful example of the operation of this doctrine is provided by the recent decision of the English Court of Appeal and House of Lords in *Lonrho Ltd. v. Shell Petroleum Co. Ltd.*[8] In that case the plaintiff company

[6] Scott, *op. cit. supra*, note 1, at 67, gives the following statistics:
"Table 20 Major shareholders in the largest British non-financial companies (1975)

Proportion held by a single large interest or by directors	No. of companies	% of companies
No dominant interest	98	39.2
0-5%	15	6.0
5-10%	10	4.0
10-20%	32	12.8
20-30%	12	4.8
30-40%	11	4.4
40-50%	8	3.2
More than 50%	22	8.8
Unquoted	16	6.4
Unkown	26	10.4
Totals	250	100.0

Source: Nyman and Silberston (1978), table 1; see also Francis (1977).
Note: In the 10-20 per cent category I have included six companies which had in excess of 10 per cent of their shares held by single interests but for which the authors could give no precise figures."

[7] L. C. B. Gower, Principles of Modern Company Law at 97 (London, 4th ed., 1979).

[8] [1980] 2 W. L. R. 367 (C. A.); affirmed [1980] 1 W. L. R. 267 (H. L.). The leading authority on this is Salomon v. Salomon & Co. Ltd. [1897] A. C. 22 in which the House of Lords recognised the separate identity of the "one-man company".

sought compulsory disclosure of documents which were in the possession of the South African subsidiaries of companies controlled by the defendants and which were relevant to litigation between the plaintiff and defendant companies; some of their subsidiaries were wholly owned while others were controlled to a lesser extent.[9] The plaintiff was only entitled to obtain compulsory disclosure of the documents in question if it could demonstrate that the documents were within the "possession, custody or power" of the defendant companies. The Court, applying the corporate entity doctrine, refused to grant the order on the grounds that the documents were under the control of the defendant companies' subsidiaries which were separate and distinct legal entitities and the defendant companies had no enforceable legal right to obtain inspection of the documents.[10]

B. The Exception: Piercing the Corporate Veil

Although the courts will on occasions pierce the corporate veil and examine the underlying economic and commercial factors, it is impossible to predict with any degree of accuracy when they will do so. The cases in which the courts have pierced the corporate veil are a wilderness of principle and are devoid of any consistent policy. Professor Gower has valiantly attempted to synthesise the cases but concludes that the courts' "haphazard" approach to this problem "smacks of palmtree justice rather than the application of legal rules".[11] Two points can be made on this issue at this point, although the topic will have to be returned to later. First, what is at stake in piercing the corporate veil is more often than not the doctrine of limited liability: the court is being asked to hold those persons who are members of the company liable for the company's debts. When the issue of veil piercing arises with respect to groups the problem takes on a slightly different form. In this situation (for example, where an attempt is being made to hold a parent responsible for the debts of a subsidiary) the principle of limited liability will still apply to the parent, and the individuals who compose the membership of the parent company will not forfeit the protection of the limited liability doctrine. Secondly, as far as groups are concerned, there would appear to be a greater willingness on the part of the courts to ignore the separate legal identity of the various companies making up the group and treat the group as a single entity. As was stated by Lord Denning, M. R. (adopting the words of Professor Gower), "there is evidence of a general tendency to ignore the separate legal entities of various companies within a group, and look instead to the economic entity of the whole group".[12]

[9] In actual fact the defendants did not control the subsidiaries directly but controlled them through other companies: [1980] 1 W. L. R., at 834B. This has no immediate relevance for the point under discussion.

[10] The doctrine can also work to the disadvantage of companies within a group: *see* Woolfson v. Strathclyde Regional Council (1979), 38 P. & C. R. 521 (H. L.).

[11] Gower, *op. cit., supra,* note 7, at 138.

[12] D. H. N. Food Distributors Ltd. v. Tower Hamlets [1976] 1 W. L. R. 852, at 860

C. Legal Consequences

There are certain legal consequences which flow from the entity doctrine and which have a direct bearing on the topic under discussion:

1. No Liability of Constituent Members

Prima facie no constituent member of a group of companies will be liable for the debts or obligations of any other constituent member of the group. Thus a parent will not be liable for the debts and obligations of its subisidary and should a subsidiary be wound up on the grounds of insolvency the parent will not be obliged to come to its rescue or to satisfy its creditors.

2. Directors' Fiduciary Duties

As part of the fiduciary ideology of directors' duties, directors are treated as owing their duties to their company and not to individual shareholders (although this aspect of the doctrine is in a state of flux[13]) or, where a group of companies is involved, to any other member company within the group. (Thus the directors of a parent company will owe their duty to the parent and likewise the directors of a subsidiary will owe their duties to the subisidiary.) Theoretically, directors must consider only the economic welfare of the company which they direct and cannot take into consideration the economic welfare of the constituent members of the group, or the overall economic health of the group, except in so far as it has a bearing on the fortunes of their own company.

3. Directors' Powers and Shareholders' Rights

It will be the directors of the parent company who will exercise the votes attached to the shares held in the subsidiary this being a normal consequence of the vesting of the powers of management in the board.[14] In so far as there has been a move to subject directors' powers to greater shareholder control this policy can be subverted by the parent-subsidiary set up. For example, if it is considered proper to require shareholder consent for the sale of all, or substantially all, of a company's assets,[15] this policy could be subverted by the directors of a parent company exercising the votes attached to the parent's holdings in a subsidiary to get the subsidiary to dispose of its assets. Also, it will be the directors of the parent who will decide whether any action should be commenced against a subsidiary's directors for breach of duty and it follows from this that shareholders in the parent company will have no standing to commence derivative actions with respect to wrongs done to the subsidiary

(C. A.). Just to illustrate the unpredictability of the court's attitude, it was the same judge who declined to pierce the veil in Lonrho v. Shell Petroleum Co. Ltd. [1980] 2 W. L. R. 367. Of course, the legislature can always ignore the corporate entity doctrine if it so wishes: *see* Gower, *op. cit. supra*, note 7, at 112-123.

[13] *See* Coleman v. Myers [1977] 2 N. Z. L. R. 225.

[14] *See* Companies Act 1948, Schedule 1, Table A, para. 80.

[15] This presently is not the law, but it was recommended by the Jenkins Committee. *See* Cmnd. 1749, Report of the Committee on Company Law Reform, at para. 117 (H. M. S. O., London, 1962).

company even though these may have a direct and detrimental bearing on the value of their holdings.[16]

D. Practical Implications

A clear implication of the consequences of the application of the entity doctrine to groups is that the separate companies within the group should be run so as to maximise the economic interests of that particular company and not with a view to the enhancement of the economic performance of the group. This assumption, to put it mildly, is one that is commercially questionable as there are theoretically reasons to suggest, and fragmented evidence to support, the proposition that, in the case of corporate groups, corporate decisions will be made with "a view to overall return on investment rather than the profitability or viability of a particular corporate unit; and the concomitant danger that any given entity will not be operated as a separate profit-making firm with a realistic potential for profitability".[17] As was stated by Scott,[18]

> Because corporations are frequently related to one another in a hierarchical way as parents, subsidiaries and associates, it follows that the strategies of the various corporations will be hierarchically arranged. For example, a wholly owned subsidiary may have its strategy totally determined at the level of the parent company . . .

[16] In certain limited circumstances shareholders can commence an action on behalf of their companies: see GOWER, *op. cit. supra*, note 7, Ch. 26.

[17] J. Landers, *Another Word on Parents, Subsidiaries and Affiliates in Bankruptcy*, 43 U. CHI. L. REV. 527 (1976) at 528. Posner challenges this thesis: *see* R. Posner, *The Rights of Creditors of Affiliated Corporations*, 43 U. CHI. L. REV. 499 (1976). But Landers' position appears to be theoretically more convincing and empirically more accurate. In operating groups of companies there are no economically compelling reasons why the profit centres within the group should correspond with the centres of legal right and entitlement, namely, the individual companies. Cases would also suggest that the individual companies are operated with a view to the overall welfare of the group: *see, e. g.*, Charterbridge Corp. Ltd. v. Lloyds Bank Ltd. [1970] Ch. 62; B. P. Exploration Co. (Libya) Ltd. v. Hunt (No. 2) [1979] 1 W. L. R. 783, at 820G: "It was pointed out . . . that no interest was in fact charged to B. P. by the B. P. group in respect of the very substantial sums of money advanced to B. P. . . ."; Eastern Airlines Inc. v. Gulf Oil Corp., 415 F. Supp. 429 (1975) at 440: "The "transfer? prices at which Gulf "sells" its foreign oil to its domestic subsidiaries are set by a pricing committee in Gulf's Pittsburgh home office. Intra-company profit can be and is allocated among these 400-plus corporate subsidiaries of Gulf, largely through the transfer price device, to optimise overall benefit to the corporation . . .". *See also* O. E. WILLIAMSON, MARKETS AND HIERARCHIES: ANALYSIS AND ANTITRUST IMPLICATIONS (New York, 1975) where it is argued persuasively at p. 29-30 that even though divisions within an internally integrated firm "have profit centre standing, this is apt to be exercised in a restrained way."

[18] SCOTT, *op. cit. supra*, note 1, at 35. *See also* THE REPORT OF THE COMMITTEE OF INQUIRY ON INDUSTRIAL DEMOCRACY, *supra*, note 1, at p. 130; THE IMPACT OF FOREIGN DIRECT INVESTMENT ON THE UNITED KINGDOM, 135-160 (Department of Trade and Industry, 1973).

Coupled with this there is the danger that the assets of the various companies within the group will be indiscriminately commingled (something which could plausibly flow from the economies of group activity); that the distribution of economic opportunities to the various companies within the group will be effected on the basis of the group's overall economic welfare and not with a view to the individual needs of the constituent legal components of the group; that creditors may be mislead as to the creditworthiness of the individual companies in the group by relying on the credit of the group rather than the individual debtor company; and finally the possibility that subsidiaries will be initially capitalised inadequately because of the expectation that the group's resources will be made available should the need arise.[19]

This functional interdependence and fusion of a group's commercial activities (involving as it does the ignoring of the separate legal identities of the constituent companies within the group) theoretically gives rise to a number of problems in company law. These problems broadly speaking fall into three distinct areas: problems of creditor protection, especially with respect to the protection of creditors of an insolvent subsidiary (*infra* § III); problems of the protection of the minority shareholders in a subsidiary (*infra* § IV); and problems of the accountability of directors, especially with respect to the power of a parent's board of directors to control the affairs of the subsidiary (*infra* § V).

III. Groups and Creditor Protection

A. The Principle of Non-Liability of the Parent

The corporate entity doctrine involves as one of its consequences the non-liability of a parent for the debts of a subsidiary which is wound up on the grounds of insolvency. The only liability of a parent (like any other shareholder) is to pay the amount it has agreed to pay on subscription for the shares in the subsidiary.[20] Coupled with this, incorporators under English company law have considerable autonomy as to the form of the capital structure of the company and, in particular, the debt/equity composition of a company's capital structure is left to the discretion of the incorporators, something not without significance with respect to the question of the protection of a subsidiary's creditors.[21] Because a parent has a relative autonomy to make its investment in the subsidiary in the form of debt (which it can also secure), rather than equity, it will be tempted to do this so as to be at the head of the queue of creditors should the

[19] *See* Landers, *supra*, note 17, at 528, where these points are made in greater detail.
[20] Companies Act 1948, s. 212 (1) (d).
[21] This is because under English company law creditors are paid off in full, so far as a company's assets permit, in order of seniority. Roughly speaking, the assets of an insolvent company will be distributed in the following order: (i) secured creditors; (ii) unsecured creditors; (iii) preference shareholders; and (iv) lastly the common shareholders who are entitled to all a company's residual values, if any.

subsidiary be wound up on the grounds of insolvency.[22] This result, which is perceived as being inequitable, is one of the reasons why the decision in *Salomon* v. *Salomon & Co. Ltd.*[23] has come in for criticism, because the dominant shareholder in that case was claiming in the winding up of an insolvent company to have his claim as a secured debenture holder satisfied in priority to the company's unsecured creditors.[24]

B. The Position of the Creditors

1. Preferential Position of the Parent

Of course, whether creditors of a subsidiary *are* in fact prejudiced depends to a large extend on whether they contract around the increase in the riskiness of their loan caused by the fact that the parent is, or may be, in a preferential position should its subsidiary be wound up. This could be done either by charging more for the provision of credit to reflect its increased riskiness, or by an agreement with the parent to subordinate its claim to that of the other creditors. Whether this as a matter of fact occurs, it is difficult to say.[25]

In an insolvency, corporate creditors fall roughly into four large groupings: (1) involuntary creditors (e. g., victims of tortiously inflicted injuries), (2) quasi-involuntary creditors (the revenue authorities and employees for unpaid wages),[26] (3) unsecured trading creditors and (4) secured creditors (e. g., sophisticated lenders such as banks).

It is clear that the creditors falling into (1) cannot, and creditors falling into (2) normally do not, contract for the contingency that a subsidiary may be capitalised in a way which unduly favours a parent in the event of its insolvency.

Creditors falling into (3) also would appear normally not to make contractual provision for the pro-parent skew of a subsidiary's capital, as to do so would

[22] *See, e. g.*, In re Southard & Co. Ltd. [1979] 1 W. L. R. 1198 (C. A.) where a parent petitioned to have its subsidiary wound up in circumstances where the parent claimed all the assets of the subsidiary to satisfy a secured debenture of which it was the assignee. As Templeman, L. J., stated: "English company law possesses some curious features, which may generate curious results. A parent company may spawn a number of subsidiary companies, all controlled directly or indirectly by the shareholders of the parent company. If one of the subsidiary companies, to change the metaphor, turns out to be the runt of the litter and declines into insolvency to the dismay of its creditors, the parent company and the other subsidiary companies may prosper to the joy of the shareholders without any liability for the debts of the insolvent subsidiary" (at 1208).

[23] [1897] A. C. 22. *See supra* note 8.

[24] This has been more of an American criticism of the case than an English one: *see* H. W. Ballantine, Corporations, 301-302 (Chicago, 1946). The result is to place part of risk of promoting new companies on creditors for which they may not be compensated.

[25] *See* Posner, *supra*, note 17, at 501-505.

[26] Under English company law such creditors are given a preference: *see* Gower, *op. cit., supra*, note 7, at 731.

probably be disproportionately expensive in relation to the face value of the type of transaction an unsecured creditor would customarily enter into.[27]

In addition, creditors of a subsidiary may be misled into relying on the total credit worthiness of the group because of the natural tendency to look upon the enterprise as a whole as the natural trading unit.

Creditors in (4) are in a position to, and often do, protect themselves by ensuring that their claims against the subsidiary have priority over any security interest of the parent company. In fact complaints have been voiced that in this respect banks often put themselves in a preferential position as compared with other corporate creditors and, for reasons which are far from clear, this was felt to be an unacceptable practice.[28]

Although it is not possible to be dogmatic about this because of the non-existence of satisfactory data, creditors of a subsidiary do not generally appear to require compensation for the risks associated with the fact that a parent can arrange the nature of its capital investment in a subsidiary in such a way that on the subsidiary's winding up the parent is in a position superior to that of other creditors. The effect of this is to minimise the parent's risks, and to transfer some of the costs of forming the company onto the shoulders of the subsidiary's creditors for which they will not be compensated.

2. *Undercapitalization of the Subsidiary*

Another way in which a subsidiary's creditors might be prejudiced is that the company may be inadequately capitalised at its inception. This is, of course, a possibility with respect to any company, but arguably it is more likely in the context of groups of companies. Firstly, a parent may be somewhat casual in estimating the capital needs of its subsidiary, or at least providing it with the capital necessary to finance its business adequately because of the assumption that the resources of the group can always be called upon.[29] Secondly, a subsidiary's creditors will more often than not consider that they are doing business with the group and that in the last resort the group will stand behind the

[27] "Unsecured creditors" have attempted in the last few years to protect themselves against secured creditors by the use of title reservation clauses which hitherto had not been a very common feature of English commercial practice. This device has only afforded limited protection to unsecured creditors: *see* Aluminium Industrie Vaassen B V v. Rompola Aluminium Ltd. [1976] 1 W. L. R. 676; Re Bond Worth Ltd. [1979] 3 All E. R. 919; Borden (U. K.) Ltd. v. Scottish Timber Products Ltd. [1979] 3 All E. R. 1961.

[28] *See* Business Computers Ltd. v. Anglo-African Leasing Ltd. [1977] 1 W. L. R. 578, at 580. To deprive banks and other lenders of the ability to secure fully their loans would merely increase the cost of the loan because of its increased riskiness and probably the net position of all corporate creditors would overall not be altered. However, the increased servicing costs of more risky loans could exacerbate the cash flow problems of borrowing companies.

[29] For example, the parent may initially finance the subsidiary's activities through interest free loans: *see* B. P. Exploration (Libya) Ltd. v. Hunt [1979] 1 W. L. R. 783, at 820G.

debts of its constituent members, a not unreasonable assumption, as a company's commercial standing would scarcely be enhanced by a reputation for abandoning its subsidiaries when they get into financial difficulty.[30] The only situation where English company law stipulates any minimum capital requirements is with respect to public companies which now have to possess a nominal paid up capital of £50,000.[31] But this will have little bearing on the problem of groups as the private company is by far the most common type of company, and anyhow £50,000 is a derisively small sum for guaranteeing economic viability (assuming that this is theoretically possible).[32]

C. Strategies of Creditor Protection

A number of different policies could be adopted to deal with the protection of the creditors of companies which are part of a group: First, the creditor claims of any company in the group against another group member could be postponed to the claims of the creditors of the debtor company in the event of its insolvency. For example, any creditor claims of a parent (secured or otherwise) against its subsidiary could be postponed in the subsidiary's winding up on the grounds of insolvency until the claims of the subsidiary's other creditors had been fully satisfied. Second, a parent might be made absolutely liable in all circumstances for the debts of a subsidiary, or it might be made liable only in certain defined situations. This solution differs from the first in that in the former situation the parent's claims are merely postponed and the subsidiary's creditors still have to look exclusively to the assets of the subsidiary for the satisfaction of their claims. Whereas under this second solution the parent would become an equal, if not the primary, source of satisfaction for the debts of the subsidiary and to that extent the subsidiary's assets would be increased.

1. Postponing the Claims of Group Members: Priority to Outside Creditors

English company law has no doctrine of postponement; the status of parent is not a legally significant category with respect to the enforceability of the debts of a company and to the proof of creditor claims in a company's winding up.

Under English company law there are a cluster of doctrines designed to set aside certain transactions entered into by insolvent companies prior to the winding up. Broadly speaking these doctrines are aimed at transactions whereby a company fraudulently prefers one creditor at the expense of other creditors thus departing from the general principle of parity of treatment of creditors of the same class in the distribution of an insolvent company's assets.[33] These

[30] It may be that when the subsidiary is created it does not have a great need for risk capital; for example, it is set up merely to hold a patent. However, such a company could become liable to involuntary creditors (employees injured at work) and it would not itself possess sufficient resources to satisfy these claims.

[31] This was introduced by the Companies Act 1980, s. 3 (2) and s. 85 (1).

[32] For example, there are only about 4,000 companies registered on the Stock Exchange out of a total of about 700,000 companies.

[33] *See* Gower, *op. cit., supra*, note 7, at 733-734; Companies Act 1948, s. 302; British Eagle

fraudulent preference provisions are transaction specific; they merely upset certain types of transaction and their operation is not dependent upon the status of the creditor; they directly affect questions of priority and the treatment of creditors *inter se*, but do not increase the total pool of assets available for the satisfaction of creditor claims. Also, the fraudulent preference rules under English company law are arguably not sufficiently robust to guarantee parity of treatment of an insolvent company's creditors. As has been stated by one commentator,[34] "the rules as to fraudulent preference are too weak. The test is not the conduct of the creditor, but the motive of the debtor. If he does not give the security voluntarily but responds to pressure, the grant of a security does not constitute a preference".

Because the focus of these doctrines is towards certain types of transaction they do not address themselves to the problems under discussion, namely, a corporate capital structure which favours parent claims in the insolvency of its subsidiary and thin capitalization of the subsidiary. In light of the inadequacy (if not irrelevancy) of the principles of fraudulent preference, and because of a parent's strategic position in controlling the level and nature of the capitalization of subsidiaries, a strong argument can be made for at least to postpone all parent claims on the dissolution of its insolvent subsidiary.[35]

2. *Holding Parents Liable for Subsidiaries' Debts*

The second strategy designed to deal with the protection of creditors of companies which are part of a group is, either absolutely, or in certain limited circumstances, to make a parent liable for the debts of insolvent subsidiaries. This would for all intents and purposes treat the subsidiary as the agent of the parent and would operate to swell the assets available for satisfying the claims of the subsidiary's creditors by giving them access to the parent company's resources. In English company law there are two doctrines which could operate to render a parent liable for the debts of a subsidiary; the first relates to piercing the corporate veil, the second is embodied in s. 332 of the Companies Act 1948.

a) Piercing the Corporate Veil

As was stated earlier, although English company law recognises the principle of piercing the corporate veil, it is impossible to extract from the cases in which the corporate veil has been pierced principles of any predictive quality. Also,

International Airlines Ltd. v. Compagnie Nationale Air France [1975] 1 W. L. R. 758.

[34] R. Goode, *The Death of Insolvency Law*, 1 Co. Law 123, at 125 (1980).

[35] *See* J. Landers, *A Unified Approach to Parent, Subsidiary, and Affiliate Questions in Bankruptcy*, 42 U. Chi. L. Rev. 589 (1975) at 597-606 where the problem of subordination is extensively dealt with. This would not solve all the problems. Others remain, such as the treatment of the claims of a subsidiary on the dissolution of its parent or on the dissolution of another subsidiary within the group. But once the general principle of postponement is conceded then these problems can be worked out.

although the recognition of the "reality" of group enterprises has constituted the basis on which the entity doctrine has been ignored in a number of cases, in none of them was the thin capitalisation of a subsidiary, or the specific features of its capital structure, adopted as a basis for piercing the corporate veil.[36] The entrenched position of the corporate entity principle has meant that parent companies run little risk of being held liable for the debts of insolvent subsidiaries. Also, even if the courts were more favourably disposed to piercing the corporate veil in the context of groups, it is difficult to see how a satisfactory operational rule could be formulated for doing so assuming, as we are, that the veil piercing is not going to be done on an indiscriminate basis in all situations involving subsidiaries. "Domination" by the parent as the triggering event is scarcely helpful as this will be the state of affairs with respect to the vast majority of parents and subsidiaries. "Thin capitalization" or "economic viability" of the subsidiary are scarcely more helpful. Although they focus on the problem, it is difficult to give them any operational content except in cases of flagrant abuse. Unless viability is interpreted to mean success, which would have the effect of making a parent the guarantor of its subsidiary's success, there are no criteria of economic viability (applicable *ex ante* or *ex post*) which would suit the plethora of types of companies and markets in which they operate.

b) Statutory Fraud

The Companies Act 1948, s. 332 (1) provides that:

> If in the course of the winding up of a company it appears that any business of the company has been carried on with intent to defraud creditors of the company or creditors of any other person or for any fraudulent purpose, the court . . . may, if it thinks proper so to do, declare that any persons who were knowingly parties to the carrying on of the business in manner aforesaid shall be personally responsible, without any limitation of liability, for all or any of the debts or other liabilities of the company as the court may direct.

It can be seen that this provision abrogates the principle of limited liability in limited circumstances so as to make persons potentially liable for the debts of an insolvent company. For the section to apply, firstly, the company must be being wound up; secondly, the person on whom liability is to be imposed must have "knowingly" been a party to the carrying on of the company's business; and, thirdly, the company's business must have been conducted "with intent to defraud creditors" or for a "fraudulent purpose". Obviously, the second and the third conditions are the most critical as the first is a straight forward question of fact. As to the second, there has been little jurisprudence interpreting it, but what there is clearly indicates that a parent which dominates the management of its subsidiary would be considered to have been a party to the carrying on of the subsidiary's business, a conclusion which is clearly mandated by the terms of

[36] For a particularly flagrant example of thin capitalisation (rather non-existent capitalisation) involving a non-corporate shareholder *see* Henry Browne & Sons Ltd. v. Smith [1964] 2 Lloyd's Rep. 476.

section.[37] The major limitation with respect to using s. 332 to protect creditors of insolvent subsidiary companies, is the interpretation which has been placed on the third condition – the requirement of showing an intent to defraud or a fraudulent purpose. The courts require "actual dishonesty involving, according to current notions of fair trading among men, real moral blame"[38] and have held that there would not be a breach of the section "even if the chances of payment of all a company's creditors in full were so remote that it belonged to the realms of hope rather than belief".[39]

This strict standard for proving fraud greatly attenuates the effectiveness of the section as a means of providing an insolvent subsidiary's creditors with access to the parent's assets. Parents will always have an incentive to gamble on the minimal chance of being held liable under s. 332, not only because of the demanding requirements for proving fraud but also because of the evidential difficulties of showing intent to defraud on the part of the company.[40] Proposals for the reform of s. 332 to make it easier to find persons liable for the debts of an insolvent company were mady by the Jenkins Committee on the Reform of Company Law.[41] Before having a cursory look at these, some reference needs to be made to recent proposals mooted in Parliament for extending in a quite dramatic way the liability of a parent for the debts of its subsidiary.

D. Proposals for Reform

1. Liability in Absence of Express Disclaimer for Subsidiary's Debts

During the debates on the Companies Act 1980 a proposal was put forward by the spokesman for the Labour Party that a holding company should be made liable for the debts of its insolvent or defaulting subsidiary unless the holding company had given specific notice to the subsidiary's creditors excluding such

[37] In In re Gerald Cooper Chemicals Ltd. [1978] 1 Ch. 262 Templeman, J., held that on the facts of that case a creditor who knowingly received payment of its debts out of funds obtained fraudulently from an insolvent company's creditors was liable under s. 332 (1). In the course of his judgement he stated:

> I agree that a lender who presses for payment is not party to a fraud merely because he knows that no money will be available to pay him if the debtor remains honest. The honest debtor is free to be made bankrupt. But in my judgement a creditor is party to the carrying on of the business with intent to defraud creditors if he accepts money which he knows full well has in fact been procured by carrying on the business for the very purposes of making the payment ... a man who warms himself with the fire of fraud cannot complain if he is singed (at 268).

This obviously would cover a parent who pressed for payment of intra-corporate debts knowing it to be a fraud on its subsidiary's creditors. *See also* Re Sarflax Ltd. [1979] 2 W. L. R. 202; Re Maidstone Buildings Provisions Ltd. [1971] 1 W. L. R. 1085.

[38] Re Patrick Lyon Ltd. [1933] Ch. 786, at 790; Hardie v. Hanson (1960), 105 C. L. R. 451 (Aust. H. C.); GOWER *op. cit., supra,* note 7, at 115.

[39] Hardie v. Hanson (1960), 105 C. L. R. 451, at 467. *Cf.* Re William Leitch Bros. Ltd. [1932] 2 Ch. 71.

[40] *See* Belmont Finance Corp. Ltd. v. Williams Furniture Ltd. [1979] Ch. 250 (C. A.).

[41] CMND. 1749 (1962), *supra,* note 15, at para. 503 (b).

liability.[42] The precipitating cause for the proposal was a series of incidents involving solvent parents who had abandoned their insolvent subsidiaries and also, at least one case, where a parent took steps to appoint a receiver to recover its loan while the debts of the insolvent subsidiary's trade creditors went unsatisifed.[43] This was considered particularly iniquitous in light of the alleged widespread practice of subsidiary companies exploiting the relationship with their parent companies to obtain credit:

> Small firms become impressed by the connection of a subsidiary with a substantial, highly prestigious holding company, a connection that is often mercilessly exploited by the subsidiary for its own commercial purposes to give the impression that it has backing from the parent company.[44]

The Government rejected these proposals,[45] primarily (although there were other reasons) because it was uncertain as to their impact on the willingness of parent companies to become involved in high risk ventures; a point which, at least theoretically, has much validity as the result of the proposals would be to put all the parent's resources at risk with respect to the trading activities of its subsidiaries.[46]

2. *Modification of s. 332 of the Companies Act 1948*

However, a less sweeping solution to the problem of protecting subsidiary company creditors has been proposed and this is to modify s. 332 to make it more readily available against parent companies (or for that matter any others) who misuse the corporate form. One way of achieving this is to make a parent company liable for debts of a subsidiary where the subsidiary has traded in a fraudulent manner.[47] This would for all intents and purposes make a parent company vicariously liable for the fraudulent activities of its subsidiaries,

[42] Parliamentary Debates, House of Commons Official Reports (Hansard), Vol. 979, 1980, cols. 1249-1272. For the purpose of the proposed provision, a holding company-subsidiary relationship would exist where one company held one-quarter of the shares in the other. The extreme example of the capital structure of the companies in Investment Trust Corp. Ltd. v. Singapore Traction Co. Ltd. [1935] 1 Ch. 615 was cited to support this broad definition of control. In that case one share was capable of out-voting the remaining 399, 999 shares.

[43] *Ibid.*, col. 1253. *See also, supra*, note 22.

[44] *Ibid.* No evidence was cited for this, but it is intuitively appealing. Also, even those who call into question the theoretical justification for piercing the veil between parent and subsidiary, concede that the entity doctrine should be ignored where a creditor is led to believe that the parent's assets will be available to satisfy a subsidiary's debts. *See* Posner, *supra*, note 17, at 521.

[45] There are examples of this type of proposal on the statute book: *see* Aircraft and Shipbuilding Industries Act 1977, s. 53.

[46] Under the proposed legislation a parent could disclaim, but the mechanics for doing this were unclear. Also, the disclaimer mechanism is not without its flaws as it will be available not only with respect to the high risk venture but equally to the unscrupulous.

[47] See Parliamentary Debates, *supra*, note 42.

something which is scarcely likely to have any material impact on socially desirable decisions to become involved in high risk ventures. Also, as the Jenkins Committee on Company Law Reform recommended, s. 332 should be amended to make it applicable to cases where a company's affairs have been carried on "in a reckless manner", and an argument could be made to extend the reach of the section to parent companies who negligently conduct the business of a subsidiary.[48] This last reform in particular would provide parent companies, who are (or at least should be) better informed than others of the riskiness of their subsidiaries' activities, with an incentive to seek a winding up of subsidiaries immediately it becomes clear that they are economically non-viable. As the law now stands a parent only has an incentive to do this when its investment (both in terms of capital and loss of reputation) is put at risk, but for other creditors this may be much too late.

3. Allowing the Parent's Directors to Consider the Interests of Subsidiaries

The above suggestions for reform are far from uncontroversial, but there is one defect in the law the elimination of which is probably less contentious. Because of the entity doctrine, the directors of a parent company owe their fiduciary duties (i. e. their obligation to act bona fide in the interests of the company) to the parent and not to the subsidiary: theoretically they can only take the interests of the subsidiary into consideration in so far as this contributes to the economic welfare of the parent. Not only does this not oblige the parent's directors to have regard for the interests of a subsidiary's creditors, but it may positively oblige them to abandon such creditors to the unappetising prospects of a claim in a winding up. For example, in one incident involving a parent company and its subsidiary, damages of £2.1 million were awarded against the subsidiary and the parent company alleged that it had a duty to the shareholders of the parent company to wind up its subsidiary in order to escape any potential liability or claims on its assets. Arguably, if the parent company had come to the assistance of the subsidiary this would have been a breach of duty on the part of the parent company's directors. This state of affairs has little to commend it and parent company directors should be free to consider the interests of subsidiaries, something which, they undoubtedly do now as a matter of practice.

IV. Directors' Fiduciary Duties and Minority Shareholder Protection

It is a direct consequence of the entity doctrine that directors of a company owe their fiduciary duties to their company and not to other members of the group; thus the directors of a parent or a subsidiary will owe their duties to their respective companies and they will be entitled to take into consideration the interests of other constituent members of the group only to the extent that this furthers the interests of their own companies. This commitment to corporate individuality belies commercial reality and, as we have already seen, the affairs of

[48] Cmnd. 1749 (1962), *supra*, note 15, at para. 503 (b).

the constituent companies in a group will be conducted so as to further the overall interests of the group. Where there are no minority shareholders in a particular subsidiary then the only persons who might be prejudiced by the practice of giving pre-eminence to the interests of the group are the subsidiary's creditors and some aspects of this problem have already been examined.[49] Where, however, there is a minority shareholder interest in a subsidiary company (i. e., the subsidiary is not wholly owned) there is the added likelihood that the interests of this minority could be prejudiced by the directors of the subsidiary making decisions on the basis of overall group economic welfare. For example, the parent may no longer have any need for its subsidiary and may wish to run down its activities;[50] the group may pursue a dividend policy which as regards the group is optimum but which is not in the interests of the subsidiary;[51] in allocating business opportunities between the group members, the parent may unduly favour its own interests or that of other member companies in the group;[52] lastly, there are the problems of pricing policies to be followed in parent-subsidiary transactions (which are not arm's length) and the allocation of any tax savings[53] and other economies which may flow from carrying on business in group form. Theoretically, the directors of the subsidiary are supposed to protect the subsidiary's interests, but as we have already noted it is highly problematical if they do this with any consistency.

It is proposed to examine this problem of minority interest prejudice under the following headings:

A. prevention of the creation of minority shareholder interests;
B. oppression remedies available for minority shareholders;
C. the right of the majority (i. e. the parent) to acquire the minority shareholder interest;
D. the right of the minority to compel the majority to acquire their interest;
E. directors' fiduciary duties, in particular, the application of the "corporate opportunity" doctrine.

A. Prevention of the Creation of Minority Shareholder Interests

This is a difficult and relatively unexplored issue and, although somewhat tangential to the topic under discussion, some comment needs to be made on it. Theoretically it would be possible to order things so as to preclude the

[49] There are also the interests of employees, but that is a story for another day.

[50] *See* Scottish Co-operative Wholesale Society Ltd. v. Meyer [1959] A. C. 324.

[51] *See* Sinclair Oil Corp. v. Levien 280 A. 2d 717 (1971). There will, or course, be constraints on the amount of dividend payable (Companies Act 1980, s. 39 and s. 40) but what is legally permissible may not necessarily be commercially desirable as an optimal dividend policy involves a trade off between pay out and growth: *see* E. F. Brigham, Financial Management: Theory and Practice, Ch. 17 (Caterham, 1979). In other words, the legal rules do not necessarily protect minority shareholders.

[52] Schreiber v. Bryan 396 A. 2d 512 (1978); Sinclair Oil Corp. v. Levien 280 A. 2d 717 (1971).

[53] *See* TWA Inc. v. Summa Corp. 374 A. 2d 5 (1977).

possibility of a minority shareholder interest being created in a subsidiary company; in other words, all subsidiaries would have to be wholly owned. No one has seriously put forward such a proposal, which is not surprising in light of its practical difficulties and theoretical shortcomings, not the least of which is that it would preclude companies from entering into joint ventures unless perhaps there was equality of participation between the participants. However, there are certain rules regulating take-over bids in the United Kingdom which are designed to protect shareholders in a company against the possible prejudice to their interest which might be caused by a merger with another company resulting in them ending up as a minority group in a subsidiary company. These rules, contained in the City Code on Take-overs and Mergers,[54] relate to partial bids and mandatory bids.

1. Partial Bids

A partial bid is a take-over offer by one company to purchase something less than all the shares of another company. The attitude to such bids embodied in the City Code on Take-overs and Mergers, while not one of outright hositility, has been one of "suspicion", the reason for this being that as a result of a partial bid "conferring voting control . . . the remaining shareholders are left as a powerless minority (or even, where the bidder acquires only effective control, an effectively powerless majority). By a successful partial bid . . . the new controller places itself in a position to exercise control over net assets considerably exceeding in value the financial stake of the controller in those assets".[55] These objections have not been considered sufficiently weighty to justify an outright prohibition on partial bids (i. e., only bids for the whole of the target company's share capital would be permitted), and arguably such an embargo would constitute an unacceptable interference with the market for corporate control.[56] Instead, broadly speaking, the City Code provides that a partial offer for shares carrying more than 30 per cent of the voting rights of the shares in the offeree company must be "conditional upon the approval of the shareholders [of the offeree company] in respect of over 50 per cent of the voting rights [of the shares

[54] It is not possible in the limited space available to go into detail on the nature and scope of this Code for regulating take-overs. Broadly speaking, this is a self-regulatory code of conduct, promulgated by the major institutions active in the securities industry, which is enforced by an administrative body and which (although opinions on this differ) has enjoyed a fair measure of success. If takeovers were to be regulated by statutes, the City Code would undoubtedly provide the basis for such legislation. *See* M. A. Weinberg, Take-overs and Mergers, Ch. 12 (London, 1979); P. Davies, The Regulation of Take-overs and Mergers, 37-46 (London, 1976); A. Johnston, The City Take-over Code (Oxford, 1980).

[55] Weinberg, *op. cit., supra,* note 54, at 116.

[56] *See* R. K. Winter, Government and The Corporation (American Enterprise Institute, Washington, 1978), at 18-28 and articles cited therein. *See also,* Cmnd. 7937, Committee to Review the Functioning of Financial Institutions (H.M.S.O., London 1980): "Share price movements operate to provide sticks and carrots for those who manage listed companies" (at para. 658).

of the offeree company] not held by the [offeror] or persons acting in concert with it."[57] The details of the mechanics of partial bids are of no great concern to us here, but what the procedure as set out in the City Code does, is to protect shareholders against ending up as a minority in a subsidiary without at least having an opportunity to express their views on the matter. The extent to which dispersed and not particularly well informed shareholders can, in the face of the pressures exercised by a take-over offer,[58] realistically protect themselves is problematical, but at least this arrangement provides them with some protection against ending up in an unwanted minority position. Coupled with this, the Code requires the board of an offeree company to circulate to the offeree shareholders "its views on the offer",[59] a requirement which fills a gap in the law as there is no legal obligation on directors of an offeree company to comment on the merits of a take-over offer. This can be an even more critical requirement where a parent company makes a take-over offer to buy out a minority interest in its subsidiary, on which something more will be said at a later point.

2. Mandatory Bids

Some comment must also be made on mandatory bids, but this can be brief. Broadly speaking where a person, together with any other persons acting in concert with him, acquires shares in a company which carry 30 per cent of the voting rights in that company, then he must make a mandatory bid to acquire the shares of the other shareholders in the company.[60] This rule is also inspired in part by a suspicion of persons who acquire control over assets at a price which may be considerably below the value of those assets. Likewise it has the effect of preventing shareholders from ending up in an unwanted minority position by providing all shareholders with an equal opportunity to sell their shares where control of a company is transferred either by market purchases or private agreement. This is particularly important if the market values the shares of the target company at a lower price after the acquisition of control by the new controllers than it did before. The net effect of the mandatory bid procedure, like that relating to partial bids, is to provide some protection to shareholders against ending up in an unwanted minority position in a group of companies where this is prejudicial to their interests.

[57] WEINBERG, *op. cit., supra*, note 54, at 159. *See also* JOHNSTON, *op. cit., supra*, note 54, at 253-257.

[58] This pressure is somewhat minimised by the fact that in partial bids acceptances must be made on a *pro rata* basis. WEINBERG, *op. cit., supra*, note 54, at 163-164.

[59] City Code on Take-overs and Mergers, Rule 10.

[60] City Code on Take-over and Mergers, Rule 34. This is a very simplified version of the rule: *see* WEINBERG, *op. cit., supra*, note 54, at 118-156, for a more detailed treatment.

B. Oppression Remedies Available to Minority Shareholders

1. The Potential for Oppression

It is clear that the affairs of a subsidiary could be conducted by a parent in such a way as to prejudice the interests of the minority shareholders in the subsidiary. A good example of this is provided by the facts in *S. C. W. S.* v. *Meyer:*[61] there the Scottish Co-operative Wholesale Society (S. C. W. S.) set up a subsidiary company in order to manufacture rayon. The respondent Meyer was a minority shareholder in the subsidiary company and initially his presence was essential to enable S. C. W. S. to obtain a licence to manufacture rayon which at the time the company was formed was subject to Government controls which were subsequently discontinued. When Meyer refused an offer for the purchase of his shares, the appellant company (S. C. W. S.) attempted to squeeze him out: orders were diverted from the subsidiary company, the directors of the subsidiary (who were S. C. W. S. appointees) did nothing to find alternative customers and the strategy of the parent company was to run down its subsidiary's affairs.

2. The Remedies and Their Failures

Where oppression like that in *S. C. W. S.* v. *Meyer* occurs, English Company Law provides the aggrieved minority with a remedy. This remedy is now embodied in section 75 of the Companies Act 1980 which provides that a member of a company may apply to the court for relief on the grounds that the "affairs of the company are being conducted in a manner which is unfairly prejudicial"[62] to his interests. Although this section has a long legislative pedigree, and its predecessor was invoked successfully in *S. C. W. S.* v. *Meyer* to protect the interests of minority shareholders in a subsidiary company,[63] it does not provide a very satisfactory solution to the problem of protecting minority shareholder interests in a group situation.

The reasons for the relative failure of the sec. 75 remedy are the following: Firstly, this remedy (which applies to all situations of shareholder oppression and is not confined by any means to parent-subsidiary situations) applies predominantly in the context of "private" companies because there will be no conveniently available market for the shares of such a company and it is this absence of liquidity which facilitates the oppression of minority shareholders. Where there is a market for a company's shares, a disgruntled shareholder will normally sell even if he has suffered some wrong at the hands of the majority as he will have to weigh the quantum and probability of recovery against the costs

[61] [1959] A. C. 324.

[62] Companies Act 1980, s. 75 (1).

[63] *See generally,* D. D. Prentice, *Protection of Minority Shareholders,* 25 C. L. P. 124 (1972). In *Meyer* the court found that the petitioner had been oppressed by the directors of the subsidiary adopting a policy of "uniform silence in face of the progressive deterioration in the [subsidiary's] activities; of the failure to disclose to the petitioners the explanation of the deterioration; unwillingness to encourage the [subsidiary] to seek other . . ." customers: [1959] A. C. 324, at 362.

of seeking legal redress and what he would obtain in selling his shares in the market. Because the costs of access to the legal system are so prohibitive, most shareholders will choose to sell rather than fight.[64]

Secondly, the concept of "unfairly prejudicial treatment" or "oppression" is not particularly well suited to deal with the type of prejudicial treatment a minority shareholder in a group situation is likely to suffer. It will no doubt pick up flagrantly outrageous behaviour, but this probably is atypical and does not address itself to what is a more widespread but subtle type of "oppression". The minority's complaint will be that things would have been better if the subsidiary's directors had single-mindedly pursued the subsidiary's interests rather than making them subservient to the overall interests of the group. In the absence of some illegality on the part of the parent company, or the minority shareholders being treated in a discriminatory manner, it will be difficult for minority shareholders to show that they have received unfairly prejudicial treatment.

Thirdly, where a shareholder succeeds in proving oppression, the normal remedy is to compel the majority shareholders to purchase the shareholder's shares at their pre-oppression value, i. e., the value they would have had had there been no oppression. The method of valuation (which is self-evidently correct), however, raises extremely difficult problems in the parent-subsidiary context to which the courts have not addressed themselves. It requires the court to assess in some way what the position would have been had the parent not been there, no easy matter.

Accordingly, although the oppression remedy provides some protection to minority interests in a group situation it is not a perfect strategy for dealing with the problem: (1) the plaintiff shareholder bears the responsibility of initiation and prima facie must shoulder the costs; (2) the test of oppression is blunt and may be too broadly meshed to provide an adequate safety net for minority shareholders in group situations; and (3) there are difficult problems of valuing the minority interest.[65]

[64] The issue of costs in corporate litigation is worthy of a conference by itself. But a recent example may give some flavour of the problem. In what will undoubtedly become a cause célèbre, a major institutional investor (Prudential) brought an action against the directors of a company in which it had investments. Prudential's investment was valued, at £ 88,642 but its legal expenses were reputed to be £ 300,000. *See* The Sunday Times, Feb. 24, 1980, p. 54. *See also*, Financial Times, Wed., Feb. 20, 1980, p. 26; Prudential Assurance Co. Ltd. v. Newman Industries Ltd. [1980] 2 W. L. R. 339 (which involved earlier proceedings in the case); Prudential Assurance Co. Ltd. v. Newman Industries Ltd. (No. 2) [1980] 2 All E. R. 841.

[65] It is also possible for administrative procedures to be used to protect minority shareholders. This involves the appointment of inspectors to investigate a company's affairs under the Companies Act 1948, s. 165. The procedure, however, is cumbersome, dilatory, expensive and only really suitable where shareholders lack information necessary to mount their own action: *see* Gower, *op. cit., supra*, note 7, at 671-680.

C. The Right of the Majority to Acquire the Minority Interest

The simplest way for a parent company to acquire a minority holding in its subsidiary is to acquire them by way of contract and there will often be very sound reasons why it would wish to do so. The elimination of the minority would provide the maximum latitude to integrate the group's activities without having to consider the interests or possible response of the minority. A negotiated solution is the optimum solution to the problem provided there is no fraud or misrepresentation and (although this is not presently the position) the directors of the subsidiary and the parent company should be obliged to disclose to the selling shareholders all relevant information relating to the value of the shares.

If the parent and minority shareholders of a subsidiary are unable to reach agreement for the purchase of the latter's shares the question arises as to whether or not the parent (as majority shareholder) can compulsorily acquire the shares of the minority. This requires an analysis of: (1) the rules relating to alterations of a company's constitution; (2) s. 206 of the Companies Act 1948; (3) s. 209 of the Companies Act 1948.

1. Alterations to the Corporate Constitution

English company law recognises a strong doctrine of majority rule: control of a company is exercisable by the shareholders by majority vote (of varying pluralities) and a shareholder's vote is perceived in very Victorian terms as an item of property which a shareholder may exercise so as to maximise his own economic self-interest.[66] This renders minority shareholders vulnerable to oppressive majority action, a vulnerability which is enhanced by a modern tendency to treat proprietary interests in general as being contingent and defeasible.[67]

As a corollary of the principle of majority rule, majority shareholders can alter a company's constitution. But if this power were untrammelled it would leave minority shareholders in an intolerably exposed position. As a result, the courts have formulated the rule that shareholders in effecting an alteration to the corporate constitution must act "bona fide for the benefit of the company as a whole"[68]. It is not possible here to go into a detailed examination of this doctrine, which places extremely indeterminate constraints on the majority, but it has been

[66] North-West Transportation Co. Ltd. v. Beatty (1887) 12 App. Cas. 589. This perception of property is now under considerable attack: *see* P. S. Atiyah, The Rise and Fall of Freedom of Contract, at 727-729 (Oxford, 1979).

[67] *See* Manning's perceptive observation that we are moving from a "law centering on ownership to a law centering on claim" in B. Manning, *Shareholder's Appraisal Remedy: An Essay for Frank Coker*, 72 Yale L. J. 223 (1962) at 229-230. This is of critical importance in company law because it results in a shareholder's interest being perceived as a fungible which is interchangeable with what it represents, *i. e.*, money.

[68] Allen v. Gold Reefs of W. Africa Ltd. [1900] 1 Ch. 656, at 671 *per* Lord Lindley M. R. *See also* Greenhalgh v. Arderne Cinemas Ltd. [1951] Ch. 286.

applied in a number of cases to strike down alterations to a company's constitution enabling the majority to acquire compulsorily the shares of a minority shareholder.[69] Where, however, some overriding corporate interest is adduced to justify such an alteration, for example, the need to oust a minority shareholder carrying on a business competing with that of the company, then the alteration may be upheld.[70]

There are at least two distinct situations where a majority may wish to have the power to acquire compulsorily the shares of the minority; these relate to a majority in a public or private company seeking to acquire the minority's shares, and a parent-subsidiary relationship where the parent wishes to eliminate a minority holding in the subsidiary. Although this division (or something along these lines) has not been recognised either by the legislature or the courts, there are more compelling reasons for permitting an alteration to a company's constitution to empower a parent majority shareholder to acquire the minority's shares in its subsidiary than to permit this in the other situations. This is because in the parent-subsidiary situation there is the possibility of overall efficiency gains from the elimination of the minority interest.[71] The elimination of the minority in this situation would not constitute a mere re-allocation of the interests within the company where there is a strong likelihood that the re-allocation will be of a type "whose benefits are presented to the controllers and whose costs are visited on those frozen out".[72] Because of these possible efficiency gains in the parent-subsidiary context, an alteration of a subsidiary's constitution empowering a parent to acquire a minority's shares, should perhaps receive a cautious but more ready acceptance by the courts.

[69] *See* Brown v. British Abrasive Wheel Co. Ltd. [1919] 1 Ch. 290; Dafen Tinplate Co. Ltd. v. Llanelly Steel Co. Ltd. [1920] 2 Ch. 124; Gower, *op. cit., supra,* note 7, at 620-623.

[70] *See* Sidebottom v. Kershaw Leese & Co. Ltd. [1920] 1 Ch. 154.

[71] *See* V. Brudney and M. A. Chirelstein, *A Restatement of Corporate Freezeouts,* 87 Yale L. J. 1354 (1978) at 1371, where the potential gains are stated to be as follows:

> In many instances, the merger of a partly held subsidiary into its parent is designed to achieve operating economies or other economic gains that are unavailable, or less readily available, when the two firms are maintained as separate entities. Elimination of duplicated functions, tax savings and financial and stock market gains are among the benefits commonly cited as potentially realizable through unification of parent and subsidiary . . . Even if "synergistic" gains of the sort just described were minimal in a particular instance, there is a sound and creditable reason for management to want to reduce to *one* the number of stockholder constituencies to which it is legally responsible. The difficulty of placing intercompany dealings on a fair basis, of allocating overhead costs and (where relevant) tax benefits between the companies, and in particular the nearly impossible task of attributing opportunities for growth and diversification to the "appropriate" unit – these and related fiduciary problems present issues of practical day-to-day administration that are notoriously hard to solve.

Somewhat similar arguments can be made in favour of allowing a parent to acquire a minority interest in a subsidiary.

[72] V. Brudney, *A note on "Going Private"*, 61 Va. L. Rev. 1019 (1975) at 1032.

Where a parent does propose to use its voting power to alter the constitution of its subsidiary so as to eliminate a minority holding, English company law does not recognise that it is subject to any special obligations. Also, the directors of the subsidiary theoretically have little role to play in this situation as the alteration involves primarily shareholder interests and not corporate interests. Anyhow, it would be difficult to see what could realistically be expected from the subsidiary's directors as they would be nominees of the parent company and could scarcely be relied upon as an independent source of advice on the transaction. Because the elimination of a minority group may have valid business justifications, it would be undesirable to completely prohibit the ouster of a minority interest in a subsidiary. However, the price for being able to do this should be an obligation on a parent to act with fairness towards the minority interest.[73] This would be some improvement on the present position where, although the courts' adopt a frosty attitude to alterations to a company's constitution empowering a majority to acquire the minority's interest, the onus of proof is still on the dissentient minority to show that the alteration is not bona fide in the best interests of the company.[74]

2. Company Act 1948, s. 206

This is a far reaching section which enables a company to enter into arrangements and compromises with its shareholders and creditors. Although primarily used to re-organise the capital structures of companies which have run into financial difficulties, but which nevertheless remain viable, it can also be used to eliminate a minority in a group situation. For the section to apply two conditions must be satisfied: (a) the class of creditors or shareholders in question must, by "a majority in number representing three fourths in value" of the class affected, approve the scheme; and (b) the scheme must also be sanctioned by the court. As regards the latter requirement, the courts treat approval by the statutory majority as strong (almost conclusive) evidence of a scheme's overall fairness and broadly speaking they will only refuse their consent if the scheme is discriminatory or such that a reasonable man could not approve it.[75] One general point can be made on the involvement of the court. In general, the locating of a discretionary power in the courts as a way of protecting shareholders' interests has not in English company law proven to be particularly successful. The primary reason for this is that the courts have shown an excessive deference to the views of the majority and, while appreciating that the interests of the holders

[73] What constitutes fairness raises a host of difficult problems. For an excellent discussion on this *see* V. Brudney and M. A. Chirelstein, *Fair Shares in Corporate Mergers and Takeovers*, 88 HARV. L. REV. 297 (1974).

[74] It should also be noted that there is no legal prohibition on a company inserting a compulsory acquisition clause in its constitution when initially incorporated: *see* Phillips v. Manufacturers Securities Ltd. (1917) 116 L. T. 290. There is no jurisprudence on the problems surrounding the operation of these provisions.

[75] *See* Re Alabama, New Orleans, Texas and Pacific Junction Rly. [1891] 1 Ch. 213; Re English, Scottish and Australian Chartered Bank [1893] 3 Ch. 385; Re N. F. U. Development Trust Ltd. [1972] 1 W. L. R. 1548.

of a class of shares may be anything but identical, they have done little to deal with the problem of intra-class diversity of interests. If the integrity of any given exchange were measured on a continuum running from arm's length bargaining to self-interested dealing, English company law perceives majority approval of any scheme by a class of securities as evidencing the former whereas in actual fact it might be more likely to evidence the latter.

As well as court approval, the approval of the class in question is also necessary for the scheme to be effected under s. 206. *Re Hellenic & General Trust Ltd.*[76] illustrates how "class" is defined for this purpose and also how s. 206 might be used to eliminate a minority interest in a group situation. More importantly, it involves a fundamental principle at the root of the treatment of minorities in group situations and therefore no apology is needed for examining the case in some detail.

Hellenic & General Trust Ltd. was an investment company in which MIT (another company) held 53% of the shares. MIT was in turn the wholly owned subsidiary of Hambros (H. Ltd.). As a result the companies were linked in the following manner:

H. Ltd.
↓
MIT ——→ Hellenic & General Trust Ltd.
(53%)

It was proposed to effect a re-organisation of the capital of Hellenic & General Trust Ltd. whereby its shares were to be cancelled, new shares issued to H. Ltd., and the other shareholders would be paid 48 pence as compensation for their shares. The net result of this would be that Hellenic & General Trust Ltd. would end up as a wholly owned subsidiary of H. Ltd. and the minority shareholders would be eliminated. A meeting of the shareholders of Hellenic & General Trust Ltd. was summoned to approve the scheme, which MIT attended, and the scheme was endorsed by the necessary majority. As the Court found, the votes of MIT were critical in obtaining the vote of approval: "[I]f they had not attended and voted the requisite majority could not have been achieved against the opposition of the objectors."[77] The Court, however, found that the procedure for effecting an arrangement under s. 206 had not been duly complied with. Two separate meetings of shareholders should have been summoned to approve the scheme as the shareholders in Hellenic & General Trust Ltd. fell into two distinct classes: the shares held by MIT (H. Ltd.'s wholly owned subsidiary) fell into one class, and the remaining shareholders fell into another.[78]

[76] [1975] 3 All E. R. 382.

[77] *Ibid.*, at 384.

[78] In the following dictum Templeman, J., recognises the theoretical shortcomings of the law dealing with group enterprises (*ibid.*, at 385-386).

> In the present case on analysis Hambros are acquiring the outside shares for 48p. So far as the MIT shares are concerned it does not matter very much to Hambros whether they are acquired or not. If the shares are acquired a sum of money moves

The importance of this decision does not resides merely in the fact that the Court required the shareholders of a particular class to be independent; more importantly, it establishes the principle that in the context of groups of companies a minority interest in a subsidiary can now only be eliminated if the parent company acquires the shares by agreement. This constitutes an abandonment of the principle of majority rule, whether the views of the majority are to be tested against some abstract principles of fairness or otherwise. In fact, one of the interesting features about *Re Hellenic & General Trust Ltd.* was that the price offered for the shares was more than fair in that it was well above what the shares would have fetched in the market.[79] The case illustrates graphically the central policy issue in dealing with the elimination of a minority interest in a group situation, namely, "whether the majority is to be given the unique power to affect the terms of a break-up which flows from the right to maintain the

from parent to wholly owned subsidiary and shares move from the subsidiary to the parent. The overall financial position of the parent and the subsidiary remains the same. The shares and the money could remain or be moved to suit Hambros before or after the arrangement. From the point of MIT, provided MIT is solvent, the directors of MIT do not have to question whether the price is exactly right. Before and after the arrangement the directors of the parent company and the subsidiary could have been made the same persons with the same outlook and the same judgment. Counsel for the company submitted that since the parent and subsidiary were separate corporations with separate directors, and since MIT were ordinary shareholders in the company, it followed that MIT had the same interests as the shareholders. The directors of MIT were under a duty to consider whether the arrangement was beneficial to the whole class of ordinary shareholders, and they were capable of forming an independent and unbiased judgment, irrespective of the interests of the parent company. This seems to me to be unreal. Hambros are purchasers making an offer. When the vendors meet to discuss and vote whether or not to accept the offer, it is incongruous that the loudest voice in theory and the most significant vote in practice should come from the wholly owned subsidiary of the purchaser. No one can be both a vendor and a purchaser and, in my judgment for the purpose of the class meetings in the present case, MIT were in the camp of the purchaser. Of course this does not mean that MIT should not have considered at a separate class meeting whether to accept the arrangement. But their consideration will be different from the considerations given to the matter by the other shareholders. Only MIT could say, within limits, that what was good for Hambros must be good for MIT.

[79] *See* [1975] 3 All E. R. 382, at 388:

The shares of the company are listed on the stock exchange and in common with other investment trust companies normally stand between 20 per cent and 25 per cent below the net asset value of the company's assets. Thus the offer price of 48p, if it represents the true net asset value of the shares, is 20 per cent to 25 per cent more than the shareholders can now obtain elsewhere. The assets of the company consist largely of cash and stock exchange investments, so that the ordinary shareholders, if they receive 48p instead of their existing shares, can follow the same outline of investment and will have roughly 48p to invest instead of a share worth on the stock exchange 36p. There has been independent advice provided to shareholders and I am quite satisfied that the offer is extremely fair.

enterprise and merely pay off the others, or whether the terms of the break-up should be bargained out, with neither group having the legal advantage which flows from the right to freeze out the other."[80] With respect to the elimination of a minority by an alteration to a company's constitution empowering a parent to buy them out (discussed earlier) the law's response is indecisive and the "bargaining chips" are, if anything, evenly distributed. However, with respect to the use of s. 206 to eliminate a minority interest in a group situation, the allocation of legal entitlements clearly favours the minority shareholders.[81] Of course, it carries with it the ability of the minority to hold out for better terms, something which the minority had an incentive to do in *Re Hellenic & General Trust Ltd.* because their liability to capital gains tax exceeded (apparently) the premium offered for their shares. This "hold out" tactic may also, of course, abort otherwise beneficial mergers.[82]

3. Companies Act 1948, s. 209

Where a parent company wishes to eliminate a minority interest in a subsidiary it can make a direct take-over offer to the minority shareholders to buy out their interest. In this situation the offeree shareholders would be harbouring unreal expectations if they were to expect independent advice from the directors of the subsidiary. The Panel on Take-overs and Mergers has been sensitive to this problem and in its 1977 Report is stated that the Code requirement, that the board of an offeree company obtain competent independent advice on any offer,[83] "is of particular importance in cases where the controlling shareholder is making an offer to the outstanding minority holders".[84]

If a parent does decide to proceed by way of a formal take-over offer, then it can utilise the Companies Act 1948, s. 209, which confers a right on a take-over bidder in certain circumstances to buy out dissentient shareholders who do not accept the offer. Broadly speaking, where a take-over offer is made for the shares of a company, and the offer is accepted by ninety per cent of the offeree shareholders, the offeror may acquire the shares of the dissentient shareholders (i. e., those who do not accept the offer)[85] at the offer price.[86] This section is

[80] Brudney, *supra,* note 72, at note 38.

[81] On the way in which the law's allocation of entitlements can affect a negotiated settlement *see* R. H. Mnookin and L. Kornhauser, *Bargaining in the Shadow of the Law: the Case of Divorce,* 88 YALE L. J. 950 (1978).

[82] The bargaining position of the minority will be weakened by the fact that they are dispersed, the directors control the proxy machinery and the majority control the timing of the alteration, all considerations of some importance.

[83] *See* City Code on Take-over and Mergers, Rule 4.

[84] THE PANEL ON TAKE-OVERS AND MERGERS, ANNUAL REPORT 1977, at 9. It continued that the adviser's "independence from the parties involved should be beyond question".

[85] The Companies Act 1948, s. 209 (5), defines a dissenting shareholder as one who has either refused or has not assented to the scheme, thus inertia works against the offeror.

[86] On the mechanics of the section *see* WEINBERG, *op. cit., supra,* note 54, at Ch. 14. The courts have gone out of their way to guarantee parity of treatment as between accepting

clearly committed to a policy favouring take-overs and also to the principle referred to earlier that majority acceptance is one of the more reliable hallmarks of the fairness of any particular scheme. This latter policy is not unreasonable where the parties are at arm's length, but it ceases to have credibility where the parties are connected. S. 209 directs itself to this problem and it provides that where an offeror already owns ten per cent of the shares in the offeree company the compulsory acquisition procedures can only be invoked if the offer is accepted by ninety per cent of the independent shareholders representing not less than three fourths in number of the holders of the shares. Thus where a parent is making a bid for a minority interest in its subsidiary, the mathematics produced by this qualification puts the minority in a virtual "hold out" position and the parent will be compelled to offer a considerable premium for the shares to guarantee success.[87]

D. Right of Minority to Compel Parent to Purchase Their Shares

Minority shareholders in a subsidiary company will not be slow to appreciate the unattractiveness of their position particularly if there is no ready market for their shares. The question therefore arises whether they should be given some means to liquidate their investment other than by agreement. It is always possible for them to reach agreement with the parent company for the disposal of their shares but the parent will be in a strategic bargaining position and its dominant position within the group will entail that it has access to all the relevant information pertaining to the value of the shares in its subsidiary and it will accordingly have considerable informational advantages over the selling minority. Were minority shareholders in a subsidiary to sell their shares directly to the directors of that company, a strong argument can be made that the directors do (and definitely should) owe them fiduciary duties which would oblige the directors to disclose all relevant information in their possession pertaining to the value of the shares.[88] If this is the position (and a compelling policy argument can be made that it should be), then a similar obligation should be imposed on a parent company which enters into an agreement to purchase a minority holding in its subsidiary. This would oblige the parent to disclose all information in its possession relevant to the value of the shares.

The above rule would only apply where the parties voluntarily agree to the

and non-accepting shareholders: *see* Re Carlton Holdings Ltd. [1971] 1 W. L. R. 918.

[87] On this problem *see* WEINBERG, *op. cit., supra*, note 54, at p. 106. The parent could resort to face to face transactions but this itself has problems.

[88] The accepted rule is that directors do not owe fiduciary duties to shareholders, but owe their duties exclusively to the company: *see* Percival v. Wright [1902] 2 Ch. 421. This rule, however, has been much criticised and may no longer reflect the prevailing position: *see* Coleman v. Myers [1977] 2 N. Z. L. R. 225. While insider trading is now proscribed, Companies Act 1980, s. 68, the legislation only makes it a criminal offence and it does not give use to any civil liability.

minor exceptions, by which a minority shareholder in a subsidiary could compel the parent to acquire his shares. The two exceptions are as follows. Firstly, if a minority shareholder can show oppression in the way in which the subsidiary's affairs have been conducted then a court can order, by way of relief, that the minority's shares be acquired by the majority.[89] An argument can be made that the oppression remedy[90] in general is a costly and inefficient pricing mechanism and that it should be replaced with a provision which gives a minority shareholder the right to compel the majority to purchase his shares without the need to show oppression.[91] Such a reform is especially apposite in the parent-subsidiary context. Secondly, if the conditions for the operation of s. 209 of the Companies Act 1948 have been satisfied, a minority shareholder can compel a successful bidder to purchase his shares. Outside these two provisions, a minority shareholder in a subsidiary is powerless to compel the purchase of his shares by the parent company.

E. Directors' Fiduciary Duties

As was pointed out earlier a consequence of the entity doctrine is that directors owe their fiduciary duties to the company on whose board they sit and, at least theoretically, they can only take into consideration the overall interests of the group in so far as these contribute to the interests of their own company. The fiduciary duties imposed on directors prohibit them from making secret profits from their position and, more importantly for our purposes, they must act in the best interests of their companies and not subject themselves to conflicting loyalties. One particular aspect of these fiduciary obligations is that directors must not appropriate for their own personal use "corporate opportunities" which fall within the general line of business of the company or in which the company has developed an expectancy.[92] The application of this doctrine to individual directors gives rise to few troublesome difficulties. However, the same cannot be said with respect to the application of the doctrine in the context of groups.

The allocation of corporate opportunities between the various companies of a group gives rise to vexing (and as yet relatively unexplored) problems, particularly as in this situation there will be no obvious element of improper directorial profit-making to taint the whole transaction. Where the parent and the subsidiary are in different lines of business then, if the group's activities remained static, few difficulties would arise as the opportunities could be allocated in light

[89] Companies Act 1980, s. 75 (dealt with earlier); S. C. W. S. v. Meyer, *supra*, note 50.

[90] For completeness' sake mention must be made of the Companies Act 1948, s. 222 (f), which also enables a shareholder (among others) to have a company wound up where its affairs are being conducted oppressively.

[91] *See* J. A. Hetherington and M. P. Dooley, *Illiquidity and Exploitation: A Proposed Statutory Solution to the Remaining Close Corporation Problem*, 63 VA. L. REV. 1 (1977).

[92] *See* Canadian Aero Service Ltd. v. O'Malley (1973) 40 D. L. R. (3d) 371; Industrial Development Consultants Ltd. v. Cooley [1972] 1 W. L. R. 443.

of the type of activity historically carried on by the various constituent members of the group. But this will seldom be the case. Assume that,[93]

> (1) P[arent] and S[ubsidiary] are in different businesses and an opportunity arises to acquire a business different from either of those; or (2) P and S are in the same business, which can now be profitably expanded; or (3) P and S are in the same business and an opportunity arises to acquire a different business.

Clearly in allocating these various opportunities between the parent and its subsidiary (or other subsidiaries within the group) the historical trading activities of the constituent members of the group will be of little assistance. Also, it would be extremely difficult for a minority interest to show breach of duty on the part of the directors of the subsidiary as what they will be alleging is frustration of their expectations of future growth, a type of breach of duty which fits awkwardly into the traditional fiduciary doctrines. At the minimum in this situation a parent should be treated as owing a fiduciary duty to its subsidiary and as under an obligation to treat its subsidiary with fairness.[94]

V. Directors' Accountability and Groups

A. Accountability of Directors of Subsidiaries

The last problem to be discussed in connection with groups is that of directors' accountability in a group situation. As regards the directors of subsidiaries, minority shareholders (like the shareholders in any company) will be able to bring an action in those limited circumstances where English company law permits a shareholder to initiate a derivative action alleging breach of duty on the part of the directors. All things considered (costs, the procedural hurdles to the bringing of such an action, ignorance, and the difficulties posed by a parent company's hostility), the chances of such an action being brought are remote. The only glimmer of hope for minority shareholders is that if directors act as nominees of the majority shareholder (i. e. the parent company) then they will be liable for abdicating their discretionary powers should the majority shareholder loot the company.[95]

B. Rights of Shareholders in the Parent Company

A slightly different problem arises with respect to the ability and entitlement of shareholders in a parent company to exercise effective control over the company's management. It is possible for a parent company to be merely a

[93] Brudney and Chirelstein, *supra*, note 73, at 327.

[94] *See* Sinclair Oil Corp. v. Levien 280 A. 2d 717 (1971); TWA Inc. v. Summa Corp. 374 A. 2d 5 (1977); *Note, The Fiduciary Duty of Parent to Subsidiary Corporation* 57 VA. L. REV. 1223 (1971). *See* Brudney and Chirelstein, *supra*, note 73, at 325-331 who argue for a much more stringent rule in favour of the sharing of opportunities among the group members.

[95] *See* Selangor United Rubber Estates Ltd. v. Cradock (No. 3) [1968] 2 All E. R. 1073.

holding company whose primary trading and business activities are carried on through subsidiaries. As Eisenberg states,[96]

> Under the corporate system which prevails . . . ultimate ownership of business assets is once typically removed from the assets themselves. Within the last two decades, however, the process has gone a step further: a significant proportion of our business assets is now held, not by corporations whose stock is principally owned by investors, but by massive subsidiaries – megasubsidiaries – whose stock is principally owned by parent corporations.

Where a company does conduct a major part of its business through subsidiaries its shareholders face a more difficult task than usual in exercising the limited ownership functions which still remain to them. If their complaint relates to directoral wrongdoing in the conduct of the subsidiary's affairs, they will have no standing to bring an action as they are not shareholders in that company and the decision as to whether or not the parent company should bring an action will normally be vested in the parent board. Should the parent board decide not to bring an action it would be difficult to show that they had abused their discretion. One simple way of dealing with the problem would be to permit a shareholder in a parent company to bring a derivative action on behalf of a subsidiary, thus in effect vesting in the parent company's shareholders the right of the parent to bring an action in connection with the subsidiary's affairs.[97]

C. Powers of the Parent Board and Shareholder Control

Even if the reform discussed above (§ B) were to be introduced, other problems remain. The structure of the governance of companies normally, although this is not a legal requirement, vests the powers of management in the board of directors. Concern has been expressed that this vests in the board powers that are unduly wide; in particular, the power to allot shares or to dispose of all, or substantially all, of a company's assets should (it is argued) be exercisable only with the approval of the shareholders.[98] Some tentative reforms along these lines have been made,[99] but if it is intended to pursue this matter seriously then allotments of shares or sales of assets by a subsidiary must also be dealt with. Failure to do so would result in shareholder control being circumvented where a company carried on its business through subsidiaries. One way of preventing the frustration of any such reforms designed to enhance shareholder control is to "pass through" the votes of the shares held by a parent in a subsidiary so that the

[96] M. A. Eisenberg, The Structure of the Corporation, 277 (Boston, 1976).

[97] *See* W. H. Painter, *Double Derivative Suits and Other Remedies with Regard to Damaged Subsidiaries*, 36 Ind. L. J. 143 (1961). The converse might also be introduced, minority shareholders in a subsidiary being able to bring an action against the parent's directors.

[98] *See* Cmnd. 1749, *supra*, note 15, at paras. 122(e) and 122(h). The basis on which such proposals can be justified is that these transactions resemble basic constitutional changes and therefore should be located in the shareholders in general meeting.

[99] Companies Act 1980, s. 14.

right to vote "is exercisable by the body of the parent's shareholders, or passes through the parent directly to the parent's shareholders".[100] This technique (for which there are precedents) could be used for all those corporate transactions which cannot be carried out by management alone and which require the approval of the company's ultimate owners.

D. Self-Perpetuation of Group Boards

In dealing with the problems of groups, the assumption has been made that a parent-subsidiary relationship exists and, as a subsidiary under English company law is prohibited from owning shares in its parent,[101] no problem is posed of the parent board maintaining itself in power by voting in its own favour the shares held in it by its subsidiary. Where a group exists, but the holdings of the dominant company fall short of creating a parent-subsidiary relationship, this problem, however, does arise. The point was succinctly posed, but not answered, by a Canadian judge as follows:[102]

> Suppose corporations A and B are public companies whose shares are listed on a stock exchange. May the directors of A properly maintain themselves in positions of influence and advantage in B by virtue of A having "working control", through share ownership of B, which has, in turn, working control of A? It is argued that as a practical matter the directors of A, unless the Court intervenes, will be able to maintain perpetual control of both A and B and, in effect, stultify the votes of the "outside" shareholders of both companies.

One way of dealing with this problem of directors perpetuating their control by cross or circular holdings is to pass through the votes attached to shares held by one company in another to the shareholders of the company, at least with respect to those matters which are treated as falling legitimately within the jurisdiction of shareholders.

VI. Conclusions

The reality of commercial life obliges English company law to deal with the problems that corporate group activity gives rise to, although, as can be seen, the principles it uses have to be cobbled together in a somewhat makeshift fashion. Central to the issue are two questions which are indeed fundamental to company law in general. What are the underlying economic purposes of limited liability and do they justify or require that the doctrine apply in the context of groups? What is the nature of a shareholder's interest: should it be treated as property which a shareholder owns in a significant sense and is therefore not defeasible

[100] Eisenberg, *op. cit.*, *supra*, note 96, at 283. M. P. Curzan and M. L. Palesh, ***Revitalizing Corporate Democracy: Control of Investment Managers' Voting on Social Responsibility Proxy Issues***, 93 Harv. L. Rev. 670 (1980) at 694.

[101] Companies Act 1948, s. 27.

[102] Re Goldhar and Quebec Manitou Mines Ltd. (1976) 61 D. L. R. (3d) 612, at 614 (Ont. H. C.) *per* Reid, J.

without its owner's consent? Or is it a fungible, a money claim which can be replaced, without altering its intrinsic nature, by its equivalence in cash? The answer to these questions would go a long way to solving some of the problems relating to groups.

Résumé:

Les groupes de sociétés: l'expérience anglaise

Bien que l'activité des personnes morales sous forme de groupe soit un trait reconnu de la vie commerciale anglaise, le droit des sociétés anglais ne possède pas de corps autonome de doctrine juridique sur ce phénomène. La doctrine sur les entités morales, qui est un domaine bien établi du droit anglais des sociétés, implique que les sociétés doivent être dirigées de manière à permettre l'épanouissement économique maximum des sociétés, hypothèse qui ne correspond pas à la réalité de la situation des personnes morales. L'activité des personnes morales soulève deux catégories de problèmes distincts: (a) la protection des créanciers et (b) la protection des actionnaires minoritaires. En ce qui concerne la protection des créanciers, il est possible pour une société-mère de faire valoir toute action qu'elle pourrait diriger contre une filiale si bien que, si la filiale est liquidée en raison de son insolvabilité, les demandes de la société-mère sont prioritaires sur celles des créanciers qui n'ont pas de garanties. Ainsi, il se peut qu'une filiale soit improprement capitalisée dès ses débuts, les créanciers de celle-ci considérant que l'actif de tout le groupe sera disponible pour satisfaire toute demande contre les membres du groupe. Aucun de ces problèmes n'est traité de manière cohérente soit en subordonnant les demandes de la société-mère en cas de liquidation de sa filiale, soit en perçant le voile de la société-mère afin de la rendre responsable des dettes de sa filiale.

Avec une personne morale existe également le danger que les intérêts des actionnaires minoritaires d'une des sociétés du groupe soient défavorisés par ce que les intérêts particuliers de leur société seront subordonnés aux intérêts généraux du groupe. Théoriquement, les dirigeants de la société devront exercer leurs pouvoirs de manière à maximaliser les intérêts de la société dont ils sont les dirigeants, mais il s'agit d'une hypothèse guère réaliste dans le cas des groupes. Une certaine satisfaction sera accordée aux actionnaires minoritaires par des remèdes statutaires contre des oppressions des minorités. Néanmoins le droit des sociétés anglais ne s'est pas consacré de manière cohérente aux problèmes de la protection des actionnaires minoritaires dans les groupes de sociétés.

Company Groups in Swiss Law

Jean Nicolas Druey
St. Gall

I. Groups in Swiss Economic Life

A. Facts and Development

Sporadic holding companies were known in the 19th Century when they were used for purely investment purposes. After World War I, this sort of company was increasingly established with the purpose of enabling other companies to be directed from a place which was advisable for tax or other reasons. Soon the subsidiary became the typical model for the establishment of the more important interests of Swiss enterprises *abroad*. At a later stage, companies also started to organize their internal structure *within the country* on a group basis, for various reasons, amongst which the following might roughly be given equal weight: tax advantages (cf. § II.B below); the conservation of the good-will of acquired companies; the "naturalization" of an outlet in a region; and considerations of organizational autonomy.

Foreign companies almost always use the form of the subsidiary for their settlement in Switzerland, even if they are very small in size.

As a whole, it is estimated that up to 70% of all Swiss companies are connected with a group, the total number of registered companies being above 100,000.

B. Group Structure and Group Accounts

The power of parent companies is almost exclusively based on a majority participation in the subsidiaries. Domination or earnings derivation contracts in the sense of German Law are unknown. Control of direction is very rarely excercised with less than 50% of the voting rights, and parent companies tend, and to a large extent successfully, to broaden their participations to 100%. The rights of minority participations may, however, well be honoured by the granting of a certain influence and privileges.

The form of company involved is almost always that of the *company limited by shares* (hereinafter "limited company") *(société anonyme)*, this being the form generally most favoured by far for the formation of companies in the country, although the simple limited company, the GmbH (S. A. R. L.) and other forms of enterprise are known as well. The law of the limited company provides anonymity for the shareholder, in particular when bearer-shares are used. Furthermore, it allows the holder of the majority of voting rights to dominate almost without limits. The rights of the minority to dividends or to information, and their possibilities to act against decisions of the general assembly or the board are very restricted in their practical impact. In theory, the shareholders meeting should not be used as the body to determine a company's policies, this function being reserved to the board and its delegates, but nevertheless the board usually behaves in the way indicated by a majority shareholder and board members may even validly be bound to follow his instructions by a mandate agreement.

The organizational structure of groups can be of any degree of centralization or of decentralization. The boards of subsidiaries often have no real material function within the enterprise group as a whole. Sometimes they act as a controlling instrument, with high ranking employees of the parent company taking chairs; or they can be token bodies, with well-known personalities sitting on them.

As to ***publicity***, statistics show that a majority of important groups publish *consolidated financial statements*. These, however, are of differing value due to the variety of consolidation methods adopted. Some of them entirely eliminate the hidden reserves contained in the statements of the individual companies, whereas others continue the practice of concealing reserves – which has a deep-rooted tradition in Switzerland – to some degree (which is difficult to evaluate) in the consolidation. The problem of transformation of foreign currencies (which, of course, is of preeminent importance given the very strong foreign ties of the big groups headed in Switzerland) is much discussed.

II. The Statute Law

Swiss law has very few provisions explicitly referring to company groups or at least essentially aimed at such.

A. The Company Law

Only the Law concerning one specific form of company, this being the limited company, contains any provisions concerning holding companies. The relevance of the provisions contained therein is, however, very restricted:

Sec. 671 para. 4 of the Swiss Code of Obligations (CO) provides that companies "the aim of which essentially consists in participating in other enterprises (holding companies)" are exempted from certain obligations to retain earnings.

Sec. 711 para. 2 CO sets forth that companies of this sort do not have to comply with a rule which otherwise obliges Swiss corporations to have a majority of board members of Swiss nationality and domicile. The exception may apply where a holding company has a majority of participations abroad.

The first rule obviously is based on the consideration that a holding company has no activity as an enterprise and therefore has no need to safeguard the interests of employees etc. against bad times by creating reserves. The other provision reflects the thought that a company, although of Swiss nationality, may be of less relevance to the Swiss economy if its assets mainly lie abroad. It cannot be determined whether it is intended to limit this rule to holding companies, thereby excluding the case where the foreign operation is a mere *branch* of the Swiss company; the case where such a branch really would have importance is rare.

B. Tax Law

Swiss tax law is strictly based on the Civil Law structures. Since company law does not recognize groups as having a particular form of legal personality, tax law in turn only recognises the specific companies as relevant entities. There is no possibility of fiscal consolidation.

Given the split of taxing authority in Switzerland between the 25 Cantons and the Confederation, a certain race has developed since World War I among the Cantons in offering privileged tax status to holding companies to encourage them to set up in the Canton, comparable to some degree to the situation in the United States. This brought about the so-called holding privilege, realized in two forms:

(1) The status of a "pure holding": the company is exempt from taxes on revenue and capital. The condition is that the assets and the source of revenue must mainly consist of participations.

(2) The "deduction for participations": in the case of participations (at least 20% of the share-capital) the revenue resulting therefrom is entirely or partly exempt.

Other aspects of the tax system have been of influence in furthering company groups. Firstly, the multitude of tax territories within the country has brought about a tendency to establish subsidiaries rather than branches in order to avoid a situation where factors relevant for tax purposes in one Canton are also relevant in others. Thus a parent company e. g. located in Basle would not have to reveal its capital and revenue to the authorities of the Canton of Aargau where it runs a factory legally formed as a subsidiary. Secondly, the Federal authorities raise a 1% tax on the value of assets formally merged into another company. This brings about a hesitation to merge acquired companies into the parent, and therefore these acquired entities remain formally independent companies, despite by their total organizational integration.

C. Trademark Law

The Swiss law on trademarks is one of the very few other bodies of law containing an allusion to groups. Sec. 6bis provides that producers having "narrow economic ties" with each other may, as an exception, deposit identical trademarks for the same categories of goods, according to the resolution of the London Conference to implement the Paris Union.

III. The Position of the Courts

A. General Conservative Approach

Swiss courts in matters of economic law tend to be conservative. Beyond the specific subject of groups, they draw a rather strict line between the legal viewpoint and an economic evaluation, as for instance is shown by the rule established by the Swiss Federal Court (the supreme jurisdictional body) saying that the courts are not to substitute their own discretion in judging corporate opportunity for that of the leaders of the company.[1] Nevertheless, groups have been recognized in some decisions as a phenomenon having an independent existence, be this in the sense that the Courts have recognized that the formal division between a company and its principal shareholders can be disregarded in particular circumstances (cf. § B below); or that the close relationship in group (and other) cases can be regarded as a motive for special interpretation of certain rules (cf. § C below), or even that the group can in certain circumstances be treated as an independent entity (cf. § D below).

However, any such recognitions of the group phenomenon have so far been understood as tied to the very special circumstances of the particular case and do not allow generalization. The prevailing attitude is illustrated by a recent decision of the Zurich Superior Court: A Swiss holding company held property on the island of Mallorca through a local real estate corporation *(société immobilière)*. In negotiations for the sale of this property all contacts with the buyer went through the holding company which concluded the contract on behalf of the Mallorca company. The court held that all the legal ties of the buyer were exclusively with the Mallorca company. It argued that if one were to look at the actual economic set-up and not at the form alone "any fairly reasonable and practicable business would not be possible any longer", because of the uncertainty of the criteria which this would bring about.[2]

B. Piercing the Corporate Veil ("Durchgriff")

The Swiss Civil Code has in Sec. 2 para. 2 a provision stating that the manifest abuse of a right will not be protected. This was the basis for a number of decisions which looked beyond the corporate form, in the sense that a main shareholder (usually holding 100% of the shares) was identified with his company. This general principle, of course, is not only applicable to groups, but also to private shareholders and to companies not carrying out any enterprise activity of their own.

This piercing of the corporate veil has, for instance, been upheld where a person tried to avoid a contractual duty not to compete by establishing a separate

[1] *See* BGE/RO [Official collection of decisions of the Swiss Federal Court, vol.] 99 (1973) [part] II [p.] 62 (with precedents cited).

[2] Commercial Court of Zürich in Blätter für Zürcher Rechtssprechung [hereinafter ZR] [vol.] 77 (1978) no. 112.

company,[3] or in order to determine the number of employees for the purposes of a labour protecting law in the case of two companies held in common by one person and closely cooperating in common premises.[4] In particular, this rule has been applied in cases where it was sought to avoid liability by advancing a separate corporation.[5] Consequently, in accordance with the principle underlying the rule, courts refuse to let a main shareholder invoke it for his own personal benefit.[6]

C. Influence of the Group Phenomenon on the Interpretation of Rules

In certain fields the courts grant groups of companies special treatment, in the sense that they treat them as an instance (if not the case "par excellence") of a narrow relationship between companies deserving exemption from standards otherwise applicable to companies. This approach obviously goes beyond the one mentioned above under § III.B, since it is not limited to mere abuse, but has more general validity for certain legal provisions.

One field in which this occurs is tax law, where the court and administrative practice has elaborated a body of rules for "closely related persons".[7] The same is true for the law of trademarks where, on the basis of the legal provision mentioned above (§ II.C), it was extrapolated that the obligation concerning the use of a registered trademark which Swiss law provides can be fulfilled for one company by another company of the same group;[8] and, similarly, it was admitted that a trademark licence could be used throughout a group of companies without inducing errors as to the source of the products.[9] In respect of other aspects of trademark law, however, the Federal Court seems to hesitate in qualifying the group as a unit in the sense of being one single producer of the labelled goods.[10]

A related area is that of the corporate name. The courts seem to admit lower standards in respect of the risk of confusion of firm names, if the firms involved belong to a group; this follows particularly from the consideration, often spelled out by the Federal Court, that similar names in fact induce one to presume such a relationship.[11]

[3] BGE/RO 71 (1945) II 272, 274-276.
[4] BGE/RO 93 (1967) I 378, 381.
[5] BGE/RO 53 (1927) II 25, 31; 71 (1945) II 272; 81 (1955) II 455, 459-461.
[6] BGE/RO 72 (1946) II 67, 76 *et seq.*
[7] *Cf.*, *e. g.*, the decisions referred to in W. Robert Pfund, Verrechnungssteuer, § 3.15 (Basel, 1971).
[8] BGE/RO 75 (1949) I 340, 352.
[9] BGE/RO 83 (1957) II 312, 330; *cf. also* BGE/RO 101 (1975) II 293, 297.
[10] Compare BGE/RO 75 (1949) II 340, 354 and BGE/RO 100 (1974) II 159, 165 (concerning the holding of trademarks by a group member company not itself exercising an enterprise activity); and BGE/RO 86 (1960) II 270, 279 *et seq.* with BGE/RO 105 (1979) II 49, 52 (concerning the possibility of one group company using its trademark rights against the products of another company of the same group).
[11] BGE/RO 100 (1974) II 224, 227, and precedents cited therein.

D. Treatment of a Group as an Entity

It is interesting to observe from the development of the practice of the courts that there has even apparently been a tendency backwards, in so far as applying a unit treatment properly speaking to groups as a whole is concerned. Earlier the Federal Court favoured such a treatment in the tax field,[12] but later withdrew completely from an entity treatment in this respect.[13] The only decision in the area of private law which grants such treatment is also rather remote in time; it dates back to 1946 and held that a participation by an affiliate in its parent company was illegal in the same way as if the parent company itself were to hold it.[14] This decision, however, is not open to a wide interpretation, since it also carefully turns on the specific facts showing a particular degree of influence in the parent company. In any case it had no follow-ups.

IV. Scholarly opinions

A. Development

The preoccupation of legal research with the subject of company groups started as early as 1927, contemporaneously with the evolution in Germany. This first period was marked by the publication of a series of monographs dealing with the subject[15] and reached its climax when, in 1943, the Swiss Association of Lawyers *(Schweizerischer Juristenverein)* placed the topic of corporate groups on the agenda for its assembly of that year, and extended written reports were prepared and presented by two distinguished legal scholars and practitioners, G. Capitaine and W. von Steiger.[16] These efforts of legal literature focused on the question whether under *existing* law a group of companies should be treated as a unit or whether it should rather be legally segmented into its several formal parts. The lines of thought closely followed those of the German literature of the time, such as the publications of Friedländer, Flechtheim and Kronstein or, on the economic level, of Passow or Klug.[17] The majority favoured a treatment of the

[12] BGE/RO 46 (1920) I 175, and precedents cited therein.

[13] BGE/RO 59 (1933) I 272.

[14] BGE/RO 72 (1946) II 275.

[15] O. Härdy, Die Holding Company nach dem Schweizerischen Obligationenrecht, Abhandlungen zum Schweizerischen Recht, Vol. 33 (Bern, 1928); E. Naegeli, Die Doppelgesellschaft als rechtliche Organisationsform der Kartelle, Konzerne und andern Unternehmenszusammenschlüsse nach deutschem und schweizerischem Recht, Vol. I Rechtssoziologischer Teil (Zürich, 1935); R. W. Joss, Konzernrechtsfragen im deutschen und schweizerischen Recht (Diss., Zürich, 1936); P. Frankenberg, Die konzernmäßige Abhängigkeit (Diss., Zürich, 1937); E. Tobler, Die Haftungsverhältnisse in verbundenen Unternehmen (Diss., Bern, 1948).

[16] G. Capitaine, *Le Statut des sociétés holdings en Suisse, rapport à la Société suisse des juristes,* 62 Revue de Droit Suisse [RDS/ZSR] 1a-194a (1943); W. von Steiger, *Die Rechtsverhältnisse der Holdinggesellschaften in der Schweiz, Referat zum Schweizerischen Juristentag,* 62 RDS/ZSR 195a-337a (1943).

[17] For references to these and a survey of the current German situation, *see* V. Emmerich

group, tending to follow the doctrine which in Switzerland was called the "modified entity theory", according to which it should depend on the nature of the legal rule in question in the particular case whether it is to be attached to the group as a whole or to its segments.

After a period of silence following World War II, at the beginning of the 1970's a new generation of legal writing on company groups grew up. This recent research is characterized by the fact that it uniformly concludes by asking for new legislation on the matter and is not content with suggestions on the basis of applying the existing law.[18] The only link between these two periods is the remarkable work of Caflisch on the degree of legally tolerable dependence of one company on another.[19] The Swiss Association of Lawyers once more made the subject a part of its deliberations in the 1973 Assembly and was supplied on this occasion with a report by Louis Dallèves.[20] The particular importance attributed today to the problem in this country is strikingly shown by the fact that the Association has yet again put it on its agenda (for the Assembly of 1980) this time, as in 1943, as the sole item apart from a subject of public law. Reports were prepared for this occasion by Roland Ruedin and the present writer.[21] All these reports also come to the conclusion that new legislation is necessary.

It may be typical of the Swiss tendency to closely observe foreign developments that several books are devoted to a thorough comparison with the situation in specific areas abroad. Generally speaking, all authors are of course strongly inspired by the German *Aktiengesetz* of 1965 and the writings thereon. But in addition there is the work of Oesch specifically dealing with a comparison

& J. SONNENSCHEIN, KONZERNRECHT, 21 *et seq.* (Munich, 2d ed., 1977). *See also* H. Wiedemann, *The German Experience with the Law of Affiliated Enterprises, supra* this volume, at pp. 21 *et seq.*

18 G. Woernle, Die organähnliche Haftung des machtausübenden Hauptaktionärs gegenüber Gläubigern der abhängigen Aktiengesellschaft (Diss., Lausanne, 1970); A. PETITPIERRE-SAUVAIN, DROIT DES SOCIÉTÉS ET GROUPES DE SOCIÉTÉS, RESPONSABILITÉ DE L'ACTIONNAIRE DOMINANT – RETRAIT DES ACTIONNAIRES MINORITAIRES, ETUDES SUISSES DE DROIT EUROPÉEN, Vol. 7 (Geneva, 1972); M. Zweifel, Holdinggesellschaften und Konzern (Diss., Zürich, 1973); K. Tappolet, Schranken konzernmäßiger Abhängigkeit im schweizerischen Aktienrecht (Diss., Zürich, 1973); M. Plüss, Der Schutz der freien Aktionäre im Konzern (Diss., St. Gall, 1977); R. OESCH, DIE HOLDINGBESTEUERUNG IN DER SCHWEIZ (Zürich, 1976); R. TSCHÄNI, FUNKTIONSWANDEL DES GESELLSCHAFTSRECHTS, SCHWEIZER BEITRÄGE ZUM EUROPARECHT, Vol. 22 (Bern, 1978); P. O. GEHRIGER, FAKTISCHE ORGANE IM GESELLSCHAFTSRECHT, SCHWEIZER SCHRIFTEN ZUM HANDELS- UND WIRTSCHAFTSRECHT, Vol. 34 (Zürich, 1979); M. Albers, Haftungsverhältnisse im Konzern (Diss., Zürich, 1980); B. Slongo, Der Begriff der einheitlichen Leitung als Bestandteil des Konzernbegriffes (Diss., Zürich, 1980).

19 S. Caflisch, Die Bedeutung und die Grenzen der rechtlichen Selbständigkeit der abhängigen Gesellschaft im Recht der Aktiengesellschaft (Diss., Zürich, 1961).

20 L. Dallèves, *Problèmes de droit privé relatifs à la coopération et à la concentration des entreprises, rapport à la Société suisse de juristes,* 92 RDS/ZSR part II 559-685 (1973).

21 R. Ruedin, *Vers un droit des groupes?* 99 RDS/ZSR part II 151-272 (1980); J. N. Druey, *Aufgaben eines Konzernrechts,* 99 RDS/ZSR part II 277-387 (1980).

of the Swiss to the American law,[22] and that of Hoehener making the same comparison with British law[23] and of v. Graffenried dealing with the projects of the European Communities.[24]

B. The Basis of Law Reform Claims

The grounds which lead the legal writers to their opinion that new legislation is necessary are essentially the same as formulated in other countries. We may distinguish a systematic and an interest-protective approach. The former line of thought, which is very broadly shared, starts from the observation that the legal provisions on corporations as contained in the Code of Obligations promulgated in 1936 treat the company as an interest center. This means that each corporation is seen as running an enterprise of its own and being in this sense an independent action system on the market. The company integrated in a group deviates from this profile, because it serves interests beyond itself.[25]

The law, therefore, is considered to contain a lacuna with respect to groups, which can produce disadvantages on various sides, be it to the shareholders, creditors or to the group direction itself. This is seen to be true, although groups were already well known at the time the actual law was shaped, as is evidenced by the provisions cited under § II above.

As to a more detailed analysis of the interests involved, the Swiss doctrine follows common international streams. The interests usually identified as needing most protection are those of the independent shareholders in a dependent company not tied to the group, as well as those of the creditors of such a company. The interest of the creditors is sometimes seen as being of less importance in practice because: (1) they are usually only interested in the conservation of the substance and not in the increase of net worth; (2) they are preferred in coverage when compared with the shareholders; (3) strong provisions protect the share capital, in particular sec. 725 of the Code of Obligations providing that in case liabilities exceed assets the bankruptcy court has to be notified; (4) in case of bankruptcy, the creditors have a claim against other companies of the group unduly favoured by any transfers, theoretically without a backward limit in time.[26]

22 F. P. Oesch, Der Minderheitenschutz im Konzern nach schweizerischem und amerikanischem Recht (Diss., Bern, 1971).

23 M. A. Hoehener, Der Konzern im englischen Recht, Rechtsvergleichende Untersuchung unter Beizug des deutschen Rechts im Hinblick auf ein schweizerisches Konzernrecht de lege ferenda (Diss., Bern, 1976).

24 A. von Graffenried, Über die Notwendigkeit einer Konzerngesetzgebung (Diss., Bern, 1976).

25 *E. g.* Zwischenbericht, *infra* note 32, at p. 192-195; P. Forstmoser & A. Meier-Hayoz, Aktienrecht, p. 298 (Bern, 1976); Dallèves, *supra* note 20, at p. 683 *et seq.*; Petitpierre-Sauvain, *supra* note 18, at p. 20-29; Zweifel, *supra* note 18, at p. 165-176; v. Graffenried, *supra* note 24, at p. 88 and 127-130; Tschäni, *supra* note 18, at p. 89; Plüss, *supra* note 18, at p. 107-110.

26 Dallèves, *supra* note 20, at p. 683 *et seq.*; *cf. also* A. Hirsch, 92 RDS/ZSR part II 1047 *et seq.* (1973).

The problem of outside shareholders, on the other hand, is accentuated by the lack of effective minority protection in Swiss Company Law. If this sort of rule, however, were to be strengthened, the functioning of the group as such would be endangered. Therefore, the general tendency is more towards granting the outside shareholders a right to be refunded or to have an exchange of shares against those of the parent company.[27]

Special interest has been attracted by the particular problem of mutual shareholding. Under existing law this is generally not considered as being abusive per se,[28] but de lege ferenda severe restrictions have been proposed, similar to those of the French *Réglementation,* i. e. prohibition of any shareholding in a company which in turn holds at least 10% of the other companies.[29]

V. The Political Situation

A. Official Action

Whereas the legislation in the 1930's deliberately decided not to introduce any legal rules to regulate the life of company groups, thinking that abuses have not frequently shown up,[30] an initiative to introduce such a law was taken in 1973, when Professor Arnold Koller in his capacity as Deputy to the National Assembly asked for new legislation on the subject.[31] Only one year earlier, a commission of experts set up by the Swiss Government had come to the conclusion that legislative action on company groups was badly needed, although not urgently.[32] The initiative of Koller was welcomed and attentive examination was envisaged.[33] However, it was preferred first to complete another phase of revision of corporate law, namely of those issues which the Commission had considered should be given priority in the reform time-table, such as the disclosure of hidden reserves, the introduction of nonvoting participation rights *(Partizipationsscheine)* and of authorized capital, and others. The proposals of the Commission are at this time subject to examination by a second expert commission, headed by Professor von Greyerz, which apparently has also added to its agenda possible legislation on groups. It seems that a step

[27] *See* in particular, *e. g.* the report of Ruedin, *supra* note 21.

[28] *E. g.* A. Siegwart, in KOMMENTAR ZUM SCHWEIZERISCHEN ZIVILGESETZBUCH, Vol. V 5a, Einl. vor Art. 620 OR note 181 *et seq.* (Zürich, 1945); Steiger and Capitaine, *supra* note 16, at p. 319a *et seq.*, and 58a-60a respectively; F. v. STEIGER, DAS RECHT DER AKTIENGESELLSCHAFT IN DER SCHWEIZ, p. 156 (4th ed., 1970).

[29] L. DALLÈVES, PARTICIPATIONS RÉCIPROQUES, p. 34 *et seq.* (Geneva, 1970); *cf. also* J. A. ZULAUF, DIE WECHSELSEITIGE BETEILIGUNG, p. 101 *et seq.* (St. Gall, 1974); F. VISCHER & F. RAPP, NEUORDNUNG DES AKTIENRECHTS, p. 240-242 (Bern, 1968).

[30] *Cf.* Siegwart, *supra* note 28, at note 159.

[31] Motion A. Koller, Federal Counsellor, 26 June, 1973 STENBULL NATIONALRAT p. 889 *et seq.*

[32] ZWISCHENBERICHT ZUM VORSCHLAG FÜR EINE TEILREVISION DES AKTIENRECHTS, p. 192 (Bern, 1972).

[33] K. Furgler, Federal Counsellor, 26 June, 1973 STENBULL NATIONALRAT p. 891.

forward in this direction can be expected particularly with respect to consolidated accounts.

B. The Political Climate

Although the scholarly works rarely fail to claim that a law on groups of companies is also in the interest of the groups themselves, there is no doubt that the representatives of the major groups are strongly opposed to any change in the actual legal situation. This is illustrated by some opinions expressed in the discussions at the meeting of the Swiss Association of Lawyers in 1973 and 1980.[34] The problem, in these circles, is treated as being somewhat "academic", a mere matter of theory, since, as was also remarked in the Commission Report of 1972,[35] abuses are seldom observed.

This will certainly be a strong argument in the political debates on the subject which can be expected to come up in this decade.

No great interest has been manifested up to now by the political parties. There could one day be a split between right and left on this issue (against or for a law on groups respectively), but for the time being the subject has had the good luck to manage to remain outside such a confrontation and to conserve its "academic" character in this positive sense.

[34] *Cf.* 92 RDS/ZSR (1973) part II 1021-1061 and 99 RDS/ZSR (1980) part II *in fine*.
[35] *Supra* note 32.

Résumé:

Le droit des groupes de sociétés en Suisse

Sauf quelques clauses de détail, la législation suisse ne connaît pas le droit des groupes de sociétés dans le sens de règles s'adressant spécifiquement aux groupes. De même, la jurisprudence maintient une ligne conservatrice (aujourd'hui même plus qu'autrefois); mises à part quelques rares exceptions, elle s'attache au traitement formel de chacune des sociétés comme une unité séparée. D'autre part, la doctrine a depuis longtemps demandé un traitement unitaire du groupe entier allant bien plus loin. Tous les écrits à ce sujet publiés au cours de la dernière décennie – et ils sont nombreux – aboutissent à la demande de nouvelle législation sur les groupes, surtout pour protéger les actionnaires extérieurs et les créanciers dans les sociétés affiliées.

Tandis qu'une commission d'experts qui s'était penchée sur la réforme du droit des sociétés avait renoncé en 1972, après considération du problème, d'inclure un droit des groupes dans ses propositions, il faut croire qu'une nouvelle commission, dont le rapport est attendu vers la fin de 1981, pourrait présenter certaines suggestions importantes de ce genre, surtout concernant les comptes consolidés. En outre, il est bien possible qu'une troisième commission d'experts ayant le futur droit des groupes comme tâche centrale soit instituée.

Groups in Scandinavian Company Law

KNUT RODHE
Stockholm

I. Introduction

The Scandinavian countries – Denmark, Finland, Norway and Sweden – have all renewed their Companies Acts in the 1970's. The new Acts are the result of a cooperation between legislative committees working during the 1960's.

The Scandinavian legislative cooperation – which has been going on now for about 100 years – has produced a series of Acts in the field of commercial law, for example on formation of contracts, on sale of goods, on negotiable instruments, etc. The cooperation has been so successful that the Acts mentioned are to a great extent identical. This achievement is largely due to the fact that the legislative topics were on the whole politically uncontroversial.

Not so with the company law. Many issues are controversial, partly because of differences between business usages, partly because of differences in political ideology. As a consequence, the drafts produced by the four national company law committees were not as uniform as one could have hoped. Certainly, the drafts were built on a common structure and presented a great many identical provisions. But there were numerous differences, in part on important points. Unfortunately, the Governmental revisions of the drafts increased the differences. One reason was that Denmark at that time had decided to join the EEC and had to take into consideration the ideas prevailing in the work on harmonization of EEC company laws. Another reason was that the Swedish Cabinet Minister in charge was more interested in reaching political results than in maintaining Scandinavian unity. It would, however, be unfair to characterize the cooperation on company legislation as a failure; it can still be said that a considerable degree of uniformity has been reached.

The cooperation has resulted in Companies Acts being enacted in Denmark 1973,[1] in Sweden 1975,[2] in Norway 1977[3] and in Finland 1978.[4]

[1] The Danish Companies Act 1973 and the Danish Private Companies Act 1973 have been translated into English by the Ministry of Commerce (now the Ministry of Industry) (Copenhagen); and into English and German by A/S REVISIONS- OCH FORVALTNINGSINSTITUTTET (H. A. Anderson Boulevard 2, DK 1553, Copenhagen V.). For a German translation of the Danish Companies Act *see* DAS DÄNISCHE GESETZ ÜBER AKTIENGESELLSCHAFTEN VOM 13. JUNI (Frankfurt, Metzner, 1976).

[2] For an English translation of the Swedish Act *see* FEDERATION OF SWEDISH INDUSTRIES,

II. Scope of Provisions on Company Groups

The Scandinavian Companies Acts do not contain an elaborate system of provisions on company groups corresponding to the German provisions introduced by the Aktiengesetz 1965. Their approach has been much more cautious and the provisions cover only parts of the field.

The main interest of the legislation has been to promote the establishment of consolidated accounts and, from that point of departure, to prevent parent companies from paying dividends that are not justified by the economic results of the group as a whole.

Outside this field other provisions on groups do exist, but they are spread throughout the Acts and aim only at solving one problem here and one problem there.

Before entering into a discussion on the Scandinavian provisions on company groups I must point out that among the Scandinavian countries only Denmark has an equivalent to the private company (GmbH, SARL, etc.). The Danish public company is called "Aktieselskab" (A/S), the private company "Anpartsselskab" (ApS).[5] The other three countries have only one legal company form: Swedish "Aktiebolag" (AB),[6] Norwegian "Aksjeselskap" (A/S),[7] Finnish "Osakeyhtiö" (OY),[8] which is used both by the biggest companies and by the one-man company with a minimum share capital (in Finland 15,000 FMK; in Norway 50,000 NOK; in Sweden 50,000 SEK). In the following text I will for

THE SWEDISH COMPANIES ACT 1975 (WITH EXCERPTS FROM THE ACCOUNTING ACT 1976) (Stockholm, 1976) (with Cumulative Supplement of June 1978). The Swedish Accounting Act 1976 was published *in toto* one year later. *See* THE FEDERATION OF SWEDISH INDUSTRIES, THE SWEDISH ACCOUNTING ACT 1976 (Stockholm, 1977). The English translation of the provisions of the Swedish Companies Act relevant to the discussion in this article are reproduced, *infra* Annex II.3., pp. 320 *et seq.*

[3] For an English translation of the Norwegian Act *see* FEDERATION OF NORWEGIAN INDUSTRIES, THE NORWEGIAN COMPANIES ACT 1977 (Oslo, 1978).

[4] The Finnish Act has been published in English by Price Waterhouse & Co. (London).

[5] For a presentation of Danish Company Law, *see* for public companies: B. GRAESVAENGE, V. LARSEN & A. ROELSEN, AKTIESELSKABLOVEN AF 1973 (Copenhagen, 1973); for private companies, *id.*, ANPARTSSELSKABSLOVEN AF 1973 (Copenhagen, 1974). *See also* G. Carsten, *Das dänische GmbH-Recht und die deutsche GmbH-Rechtsreform*, 1974 GMBH-RUNDSCHAU 283 *et seq.*

[6] For a presentation of Swedish Company Law, *see* K. RODHE, AKTIEBOLAGSRÄTT. ENLIGT 1975 ÅRS AKTIEBOLAGSLAG (Stockholm, 9th ed., 1978); G. KEDNER & C. M. ROOS, AKTIEBOLAGSLAGEN MED KOMMENTARER, Part I (Stockholm, 1977) and Part II (Stockholm, 1979). *See also* G. Carsten, *Neue Entwicklungen im schwedischen Aktienrecht*, DIE AKTIENGESELLSCHAFT 1978, 8 *et seq.*

[7] For a presentation of Norwegian Company Law *see* J. SKÅRE, LOV OM AKSJESELSKAPER. MED KOMMENTARER (Oslo, 2d ed., 1977). *See also*, W. Steiniger, *Das norwegische Aktienrecht*, DIE AKTIENGESELLSCHAFT 1978, 189 *et seq.*

[8] For a presentation of Finnish Company Law *see* P. KOSKI & C. G. SCHULTÉN, UUSI OSAKEYHTIÖLAKI, Part I (Espoo, 1978); Part II (Tampere, 1979).

this legal form use the word "company" without any addition. Only when the two Danish legal forms have different provisions will I specify "public company" and "private company".

III. Group Definitions

A. Legal Provisions

The Scandinavian Acts have nothing like the series of definitions contained in Secs. 15-19 of the German *Aktiengesetz*. There are two group definitions, one primary and one secondary. In both definitions the *possibility of exerting a controlling influence* is the relevant point. The existence or non-existence of a centralized management is not relevant. Thus, the definitions correspond to Sec. 17 of the German *Aktiengesetz ("Abhängige und herrschende Unternehmen")*. But the terminology used is derived from the German *"Konzern"* (*Aktiengesetz* Sec. 18), namely "koncern" (Danish, Swedish) and "konsern" (Norway).

The primary definition (Swedish Act Ch. 1 Sec. 2, para. 1) focuses on the voting majority. The Swedish text reads:

> Where a company is holder of such a number of shares or parts of a Swedish or a foreign legal person that the holding represents more than half of the votes of the shares or the parts, the company is a parent company and the legal person a subsidiary. Where a subsidiary holds or where a parent company holds jointly with one or several subsidiaries or where several subsidiaries jointly hold such number of shares or parts of a legal person as mentioned above, that legal person is also a subsidiary of the parent company.

The secondary definition (Ch. 1 Sec. 2, para. 2) takes into account that control is not always based on a voting majority. The text of the Swedish Act reads:

> Where a company has otherwise, by virtue of its holding of shares or parts, or by virtue of agreement, a decisive influence over a legal person and a considerable share in its results, the company is a parent company and the legal person a subsidiary.

Finally, para. 3 adds:

> A parent company and its subsidiaries, taken as a whole, constitute a group.

B. Some Commentaries on the Definitions

1. *"Company"*

"A company" means a company regulated by the Swedish Companies Act. Thus, the top of a group is always a Swedish company limited by shares. On the other hand, a subsidiary can be any type of legal person, Swedish or foreign. One could say that the definition is closed upwards, but open downwards. The main interest of the legislator has, as I have already said, been to regulate the consolidated accounts and the paying of dividends in a parent company, and from this point of departure it has seemed natural that the parent company must be subject to the legislator's power. But the Swedish legislator, like the Danish and the Finnish, seems to have overlooked the possibility that other problems relating to company groups might have called for a definition that would have been open upwards and closed downwards, or open in both directions. Only the Norwegian legislator has taken this point of view into account: in Sec. 2, para. 4, it enumerated certain sections of the Act, where "parent company" shall include also a foreign company limited by shares or a foreign private company; and other sections, where "subsidiary" shall not include a foreign legal person.

The Danish legislation deviates from the pattern described. The Act on public companies has a definition according to which only Danish public or private companies count as subsidiaries, and the Act on private companies has the same definition.

2. *"Decisive Influence"*

It should be noted, that the secondary definition requires both that the parent company have a decisive influence on the subsidiary and that it have a considerable share in its profits. When the text states that a company can "otherwise", e. g. without having a majority of votes, have a decisive influence "by virtue of its holding of shares or parts", it is aimed at those cases where a company has a "working majority" in another company, the other shares of which are widely dispersed. How much a "considerable share" in another legal person's profits shall be deemed to be, nobody really knows. It is my impression that the Swedish business community and Swedish auditors in the past have paid little attention to this secondary group definition, which has, notwithstanding, been a provision in Swedish company law since 1948. Perhaps this will now change, as the Act of 1975 has made the publication of consolidated accounts compulsory, which it was not under the previous Act.

3. *Subsidiaries Held by Two Parents with 50% Each*

One more problem has arisen in Sweden. In the explanatory part of the Bill of 1975, the Cabinet Minister somewhat rashly declared, that if each of two companies possessed 50% of the shares and 50% of the voting power in a third company, this would constitute two groups, the third company being a subsidiary of each group. In such a case a resolution of the general meeting of the third company cannot be taken without the common consent of the two first-mentioned companies, unless by ballot. The Minister's point seems to have been that the words "decisive influence" in the secondary definition could apply also when one company cannot impose its will on another company but at least can prevent anybody else from doing so. This declaration was vehemently opposed by the Swedish Association of Authorized Public Accountants. A lengthy discussion arose, and at last the Government had to yield. A Bill has now been presented to the Swedish Parliament, proposing that the word "alone" be inserted into the secondary definition before the words "a decisive influence".

4. *Groups and Sub-Groups*

If A is a parent company and B its subsidiary, and if B is a parent company and C its subsidiary, then we have two groups, one consisting of A, B and C, another – the sub-group – consisting of B and C. Even sub-groups are groups within the meaning of the Act, and the provisions of the Act on groups apply also to a sub-group.

IV. Consolidated Accounts

According to the Swedish Act Ch. 11 Sec. 10, a parent company shall for each financial year prepare – in addition to its annual report – consolidated accounts consisting of a consolidated profit and loss statement and a consolidated balance sheet. Details on the consolidated accounts are given in Ch. 11 Sec. 11.

The consolidated accounts shall be examined by the auditors, who shall prepare a separate report on the group. At the annual meeting of the parent company shall be presented

(1) the annual report of the parent company,
(2) the auditors' report on this company,
(3) the consolidated accounts of the group,
(4) the auditors' report on the group.

At this general meeting resolutions shall be passed in respect of the adoption of the profit and loss statement and the balance sheet of the parent company and of the adoption of the profit and loss statement and the balance sheet of the group.

No later than one month after the profit and loss statements and the balance sheets of the parent company and of the group have been adopted, copies of these documents and of the auditors' reports shall be sent to the registration authority, where they become accessible to the public.

The Finnish and Norwegian Acts have the same provisions, with slight variations.

The Danish Act is less demanding. The company can choose between preparing consolidated accounts, consisting only of a balance sheet, or – in special circumstances – preparing only a group report containing certain information on the group. A financially small private company may give the registration authority only summary information on the company and its subsidiaries.

V. Distribution of Dividends

According to the Swedish Act Ch. 12 Sec. 2, dividends to the shareholders of a parent company may not exceed the amount which according to the adopted balance sheets of the parent company *and of the group* has been reported as the company's *and the group's* non-restricted equity capital.

In other words, there are two limits for the dividends to the shareholders of the parent company: the amount of this company's nonrestricted equity capital, and the amount of the group's non-restricted equity capital.

Furthermore, there is also another restriction on dividends: the so-called "general rule of prudence". From the same section we learn that dividends may not be distributed to such an extent that, in view of the parent company's *or the group's* consolidation needs, cash needs or financial position in other respects, the distribution would be contrary to good business practice.

Now, if we look at the four Scandinavian Acts, the picture is a little complicated:

The Swedish Act has, as I have just said, two group-related restrictions: the dividend may not exceed the group's non-restricted equity capital, and the general rule of prudence must be observed, as applied to the group.

The Finnish Act has no general rule of prudence, but the dividend may not exceed the group's non-restricted equity capital.

The Norwegian Act, on the other hand, does not limit the dividend to the group's non-restricted equity capital but relies only on the general rule of prudence, as applied to the group.

In Denmark, finally, where a group balance sheet is not compulsory and no general rule of prudence exists, a special rule of prudence imposes upon parent companies the duty to take into consideration the group's economic position when deciding on dividends.

VI. Transfers between Companies Belonging to the Same Group

Its is a very widely spread practice in Sweden for a parent company in the year-end closure books to make transfers between the companies in the group, in order to increase the result in one company and to decrease the result in another company. The purpose of such transfers is twofold: to help the weak parts of the group and to minimize the total tax burden on the group as a whole.

Group transfers are tacitly accepted by the Swedish Companies Act. They are subject to many provisions in tax law, where the problem is to what extent a transfer shall be deductible in the transferring company's income-tax return.

It must nevertheless be observed that company law principles may set limits to the use of group transfers. Business practice has, unfortunately, paid very little attention to this problem. Business managers and tax advisers have been content to find that a transfer was "permitted", thereby meaning that it was deductible for tax purposes, and they have seldom observed that they ought to have asked also if the transfer was permitted in company law.

The company law problem concerns transfers from a subsidiary to its parent company. Such a transfer must be characterized as a dividend distribution and it must be subject to the limits applying ordinarily to distribution of dividends. More precisely, the permissibility of the transfer must be tested in the following way: if the transfer had not been made and the same amount consequently had been added to the net profit of the year, could it then have been distributed as a dividend? If this profit should have been diminished by a loss brought forward from the year before, the answer must be no. Today, the insight that such limits must be set to the use of group transfers is spreading in the business community.

A further condition is that the subsidiary must be wholly-owned.

What I have said here concerns Swedish law; I am not able to report on our neighbours' views on this problem.

VII. Cash Loans to Shareholders and Directors

The Swedish Act has in Ch. 12 Sec. 7 very far-reaching provisions that prohibit cash loans by a company to its shareholders and directors and their relatives. The purpose of these provisions is mainly to prevent tax evasion and tax fraud. If the company belongs to a group, shareholders and directors of other companies belonging to the same group are also included. On the other hand, loans between companies belonging to the same group are excluded. This means particularly that a subsidiary may lend money to its parent company.

But here we meet a rather surprising consequence of the rigid group definition analyzed at the beginning of this paper. As I have said, the top of a group as defined by the Act must be a Swedish company. Consequently, if a Swedish company is the subsidiary of a foreign parent company, the shareholders and directors of the parent company do not belong to the circle of black-listed persons. On the other hand, the Swedish subsidiary may not give cash loans to its foreign parent (although such loans, thanks to another exception, may be given in the ordinary course of business).

Evidently, it would have been more adequate to use in these provisions a group definition that is open both downwards and upwards. The Norwegian Act takes a step in that direction insofar as its (not so far-reaching) provisions prohibiting cash loans to shareholders and directors include also the shareholders and directors of a foreign parent company in the circle of black-listed persons. But the general exception for loans to other companies belonging to the same group is not extended to foreign companies. The Danish and Finnish Acts follow the Swedish pattern, except that the prohibitions are not so far-reaching.

VIII. Acquisition of a Parent Company's Shares by a Subsidiary

All the Scandinavian Acts prohibit, with varying exceptions, a company from acquiring its own shares. The same prohibitions apply to a subsidiary's acquisition of shares in the parent company. The Norwegian Act also prohibits a Norwegian subsidiary from acquiring shares in its foreign parent company. The Swedish Act adds that if a company becomes a subsidiary and at that moment owns shares in the parent company, it must dispose of those shares as soon as they can be sold without a loss and not later than two years after entering the group, unless an exemption is granted by a public authority (the Board of Commerce).

All the Acts prescribe that shares owned by the company itself or by a subsidiary cannot be represented at the general meeting.

IX. Protection of the Minority Shareholders of a Subsidiary

The Scandinavian Companies Acts have elaborate systems for minority protection, but there are few rules specifically designed to protect the minority shareholders of a subsidiary. One important provision, to be found in all the Acts, gives a minority shareholder of a subsidiary the option to require that the parent company purchase his shares. The condition is that the parent company must own more than nine-tenths of the total number of shares and these shares must represent more than nine-tenths of the votes. In this situation also the parent company has an option to purchase the minority shares.[9] Nearly always the initiative for a redemption of minority shares comes from the parent company.

X. Protection of the Creditors of a Subsidiary

The Scandinavian Acts have no special rules aiming at the protection of the creditors of a subsidiary. But the general rules on creditor protection are so strict that on the whole no need has been felt for provisions of the German type. It should also be noted that bankruptcy law provisions – to a great extent common to the four countries – on setting aside preferential transfers and on recapturing property will in most cases keep a solvent parent company from stripping a subsidiary in the face of its impending break-down, especially as the "critical period" before the application for a declaration of bankruptcy, which is usually three months, is prolonged to two years *inter alia* when the opposite party is a parent company.

XI. Right of a Parent Company to Acquire Minority Shares in a Subsidiary

All the Scandinavian Acts give a parent company an option to purchase the remaining shares in a subsidiary, on condition that the parent company owns more than nine-tenths of the total number of shares and these shares represent more than nine-tenths of the votes.[10]

The Swedish Act, which is the most exhaustive on this point, prescribes that the parent company shall, if an agreement with all minority shareholders cannot be reached, ask the Court to appoint an administrator, who shall represent absent shareholders in the dispute. In such cases, the parent company can acquire 100% of the shares, even if some shareholders remain unknown.

A dispute shall be submitted to arbitration. The purchase price shall be the "real value" of the shares, without any deduction for their character of minority shares. But if the parent company has acquired the larger portion of its shares through an offer directed to a substantial number of persons, the purchase price shall be the same as the consideration contained in the offer, unless there are special reasons for a different price. This last-mentioned rule, which aims at avoiding the often heavy costs of a valuation of the assets of the subsidiary, is, however, only to be found in the Swedish Act.

According to the Norwegian Act, a foreign parent company may also invoke the purchase option.

[9] *See infra* § XI.

[10] *See, e. g.*, the Swedish Companies Act, Ch. 14. Secs. 9-13.

XII. Right of a Parent Company to Give Instructions to the Board and the Officers of a Subsidiary

In the Scandinavian countries there has been hardly any discussion of the legal aspects of the decision-making process in groups, and the Companies Acts do not touch upon the problem. Business practice is highly diversified: sometimes we find subsidiaries which enjoy a great deal of independence in the daily course of business, in other cases we find subsidiaries which are so absorbed by the parent company that it is difficult to tell where the parent company ends and the subsidiary begins. In neither case, however, do the managers of the parent company have any feeling that there might be any legal limits preventing them from giving instructions to the board and the officers of the subsidiary, which are disadvantageous to the subsidiary but serve the interests of the group. I can add, that I have never heard of a Swedish parent company concluding a contract of the German type[11] with its subsidiary.

The rising power of employees may bring a change. If the subsidiary has employee directors,[12] such directors may not accept to act as dummies. Some years ago one could read in the newspapers how the trade unions of an important and rather independently governed subsidiary of one of Sweden's biggest industrial groups protested when the parent company's management wanted to transfer a surplus from this prosperous subsidiary to help other not so successful sister companies in the group. A more general observation is that the Swedish trade unions nowadays are really troubled with the problem of how they should handle their relations with the different levels of a company group, taking into consideration the very far-reaching right of negotiation that an Act of 1976 on the "joint regulation of working life" has bestowed upon them.

XIII. Employee Representation on the Boards of Group Companies[13]

A Swedish Act of 1976 gives the trade unions the right to send two representatives with two deputies to the board of a company, provided that the company has at least 25 employees. If a company is the parent company of a group, the employees of the whole group shall be taken into consideration when determining if and how the Act shall be applied. Thus, if the trade unions so choose, there may be an employee representation on the board of the parent company and on the board of every subsidiary that has at least 25 employees. And if there

[11] For a discussion of the German practice, *see* H. Wiedemann, *The German Experience with the Law of Affiliated Enterprises*, *supra* this volume, pp. 21 *et seq.*, esp. at pp. 33 *et seq.*

[12] *See infra* § XIII.

[13] For an extensive discussion of employee representation and labour problems in relation to multinational groups, including comparisons with the Swedish system, *see* P. L. Davies, *Labour Law and Multinational Groups of Companies*, *infra* this volume, pp. 208 *et seq.*

are sub-groups, the boards of the parent companies of the sub-groups may have representatives of the sub-groups' employees.

The Norwegian Companies Act in Ch. 8 Sec. 18 has provisions on employee representation in a "supervisory council" and on the board. Here, also, the employees of the whole group may be taken into consideration when the rules are applied to a parent company.

XIV. Groups where the Parent is Not a Company Limited by Shares

We have seen that the Swedish Companies Act only regulates groups where the parent company is a Swedish company limited by shares. In December 1980 two Bills were adopted by the Swedish Parliament, introducing rules for groups where the parent is not a company limited by shares.

One of the new Acts amends the Act of 1951 on Co-operative Societies, providing that such a society shall prepare consolidated accounts, if it is the parent of a group. The group definition is copied from the definition in the Companies Act.

The other Bill introduced an "Act on Annual Reports of Certain Enterprises". The Act contains, *inter alia,* provisions on consolidated accounts in enterprises which are not companies limited by shares and not co-operative societies. The Act begins with a group definition, also copied from the definition in the Companies Act, aiming at groups where the parent is a trading partnership *(offene Handelsgesellschaft, société en nom collectif)*. It continues by saying that the provisions shall apply to groups of which the parent, whether a private individual or a legal person, is not a company limited by shares or a co-operative society or a foundation, if the parent is under a duty to prepare annual accounts pursuant to the Accounting Act. If a group so defined has during the financial year had an average number of employees of at least ten, the parent enterprise shall also prepare consolidated accounts.

Résumé:
Les groupes de sociétés dans les droits sur les sociétés scandinaves

Le rapport donne une vue d'ensemble des règles juridiques relatives aux groupes de sociétés en droit scandinave, c'est-à-dire dans le droit des sociétés danois, finlandais, norvégien et suédois. Ces règles sont contenues dans les lois sur les sociétés de 1973, 1978, 1977 et 1975 respectivement, lesquelles étaient le résultat d'une coopération entre les comités législatifs dans les quatre pays. Les règles sur les groupes sont dans une large mesure similaires; le rapport vise les dispositions suédoises et souligne les variations opérées à partir de ce modèle. L'intérêt principal de ces textes a été de promouvoir l'établissement de comptes consolidés et, à partir de ce point, d'éviter que les sociétés-mères ne payent de dividendes non justifiés par le résultat économique du groupe pris comme entité.

Dans les définitions de groupe, la possibilité d'exercer une influence contrôlant est un point pertinent. Une société-mère devra préparer, outre son rapport annuel, des comptes consolidés constitués par un rapport consolidé des profits et des pertes et un compte d'exercice consolidé. Les dividendes des actionnaires d'une société-mère ne doivent pas excéder le montant qui, d'après les comptes d'exercice de la société-mère et du groupe, a été présenté comme le fonds de réserve non-restreint de la société et du groupe. Des transferts entre des sociétés appartenant au même groupe sont admis, mais les transferts d'une filiale à sa société-mère sont soumis aux limites habituellement appliquées à la distribution des dividendes. Des dispositions existent sur les prêts accordés aux actionnaires et aux dirigeants d'une autre société du groupe. Les règles interdisant à une société d'acquérir ses propres parts s'appliquent également à l'acquisition de parts de la société-mère par la société-filiale. Une société-mère a l'option d'acquérir les parts restantes dans une filiale à condition que la société-mère possède plus de 9/10èmes du nombre total des parts et que ces parts représentent plus de 9/10èmes des votes. Les textes de loi ne parlent pas du droit pour une société-mère de donner des instructions au conseil d'administration et aux dirigeants d'une filiale.

Lorsque la loi suédoise sur la représentation des salariés dans les conseils d'administration des sociétés est appliquée à une société-mère, les salariés de tout le groupe doivent être pris en considération. En décembre 1980, le Parlement suédois a approuvé deux textes de lois sur les groupes lorsque la société-mère n'est pas une société anonyme.

Chapter/Chapitre III

Groups of Companies in the Law of the European Communities

Les groupes de sociétés dans le droit des Communautés Européennes

Examen critique des projets européens en matière de groupes de sociétés (le point de vue français)*

Yves Guyon
Paris

1. De prime abord le juriste français se sent mal à l'aise face aux projets européens qui tendent à coordonner les législations nationales en matière de groupes de sociétés. En effet, il a l'impression d'une accumulation de difficultés.

D'une part, les divers projets européens étudiés par la Commission de Bruxelles s'imbriquent les uns dans les autres selon des schémas complexes. Leur progression est irrégulière car elle dépend plus des contingences politiques que des nécessités logiques. Même si l'essentiel figure dans la proposition de neuvième directive – il faut aussi se référer à de multiples autres textes, car le droit des groupes est au cœur de presque toutes les questions qui intéressent le droit des sociétés et même celui de la concurrence et de la concentration.[1] La matière est donc foisonnante et mouvante. Elle est faite plus d'avenir que de droit positif, étant donné notamment que les quatres directives en vigueur ne concernent qu'indirectement les groupes.

D'autre part, la démarche intellectuelle suivie par les autorités bruxelloises paraît aux juristes français exagérément dogmatique. Or, en matière de groupe, les Français adoptent une position plus empirique que cartésienne. La majorité d'entre eux se borne à constater l'opposition entre le fait et le droit puisque le groupe est habituellement défini comme un ensemble de sociétés juridiquement indépendantes les unes des autres mais soumises en fait à une unité de décision économique.[2] Certes, quelques uns d'entre eux se demandent encore si le groupe constitue ou non une personne morale ou, ce qui revient au même, une unité

* Le présent rapport n'a pas pour objet de présenter un commentaire complet des projets européens en matière de groupes de sociétés. Il tend plus simplement à livrer les impressions et les réactions, nécessairement assez subjectives, d'un juriste français non spécialiste du droit européen face aux aspects principaux de ces diverses propositions.

[1] C. Bolze, Groupes de sociétés et droit de la concurrence dans la Communauté économique européenne (thèse, Nancy, 1979).

[2] M. Germain, Société dominante et société dominée en droit français et allemand (thèse, Nancy, 1974); voir aussi G. Keutgen, Le droit des groupes de sociétés dans la CEE (Bruxelles, 1973).

patrimoniale indépendante.[3] Mais, ces controverses paraissent insolubles ou dépassées. Le droit positif continue d'affirmer nettement le principe de l'indépendance des sociétés du groupe. Il en tire notamment les conséquences tant à l'égard des sociétés membres du groupe que des associés et des tiers.[4] Mais, il admet aussi de nombreux palliatifs à ce principe, notamment les extensions de passif, la théorie de l'unité d'entreprise utilisée en droit social[5] et la nécessité de renforcer la protection des actionnaires minoritaires ou hors groupes.[6]

Certes des efforts de réflexion systématique et de méthodologie ont été accomplis récemment. Ils permettent de mieux connaître et de mieux comprendre ce que sont les groupes en *droit français.*[7] Ils ont abouti notamment au dépôt par un député, Monsieur *Cousté,* de plusieurs propositions de lois.[8] De même, un projet de loi émanant du gouvernement prévoit l'obligation pour les sociétés cotées de publier des comptes consolidés.[9]

Nul ne conteste donc l'importance pratique du droit européen des groupes. Les statistiques montrent que pratiquement toutes les opérations européennes de concentration ont pris la forme de participation en capital ou de constitution de filiales communes et non d'absorptions.[10] Les groupes européens existent et leur influence sur les économies internes est sans doute déterminante.

2. Mais, ces projets n'ont pas soulevé beaucoup d'enthousiasme.

Les difficultés économiques du moment incitent plus à se préoccuper des entreprises en situation compromise que des entreprises saines. Le droit des groupes n'est donc plus envisagé pour lui-même, mais seulement en tant qu'un moyen parmi d'autres soit de prévenir les difficultés en améliorant l'information, soit d'accroître les garanties des créanciers en leur offrant un recours contre la société du groupe la plus solvable. Cette manière d'envisager les choses est évidemment peu constructive et risque même d'être déformante.

Plus fondamentalement, les juristes français sont accoutumés à se passer d'une réglementation d'ensemble. Ils ont l'impression que les abus les plus manifestes ont été corrigés par des interventions ponctuelles des pouvoirs publics ou par la

[3] R. Contin et H. Hovasse, *L'autonomie patrimoniale des sociétés, réflexion sur la finalité d'une organisation juridique des groupes,* D. 1971, 197.

[4] Y. Guyon, Droit des affaires, n° 613 (Paris, 1980).

[5] B. Oppetit, *Groupes de sociétés et droit du travail,* Rev. soc. 1973, 69.

[6] R. Rodière, *La protection des minorités dans les groupes de sociétés,* Rev. soc. 1970, 243. D. Schmidt, Les droits de la minorité dans les sociétés anonymes, n° 213 (Paris, 1970).

[7] CREDA, Les groupes de sociétés, une politique législative (Paris, 1975). B. Oppetit et A. Sayag, *Méthodologie d'un droit des groupes de société,* Rev, soc. 1973, 577.

[8] V. notamment proposition à l'Assemblée nationale n° 522 sur les groupes de sociétés et la protection des actionnaires, du personnel et des tiers du 28 juin 1978, "*Proposition Cousté*", reproduite, *infra,* annexe II.2, pp. 296-319. Pour le commentaire d'une précédente proposition du même député, v. J. Paillusseau, *Faut-il en France un droit des groupes de sociétés?* J. C. P. 1971, I, 2041 bis.

[9] Projet de loi (Assemblée nationale) n° 236 du 17 mai 1978, art. 43.

[10] Septieme rapport de la Commission de la C.E.E. sur la politique de concurrence, p. 227 (Bruxelles, 1978).

jurisprudence. Ils reprochent aux projets européens de mettre sur pied des mécanismes lourds et sans doute inefficaces face à des groupements souples, multiformes et insaisissables. L'exposé des motifs du projet Cousté se fait l'écho de ces critiques et de ces réticences. Il remarque notamment que la mise en oeuvre du statut allemand des groupes — qui inspire les projets européens — n'a pas donné entière satisfaction. Un lourd contentieux s'est formé depuis une dizaine d'années et l'on assiste à une fuite des groupes de droit vers les groupes de fait.[11]

3. Ce scepticisme d'ensemble à l'égard des projets européens est sans doute exagéré.

L'ampleur des difficultés à résoudre ne doit pas être une raison de refuser le combat, bien au contraire.

A y regarder de plus près, les projets européens ne sont pas aussi dogmatiques et irréalistes qu'on le croit trop souvent. Leurs auteurs constatent qu'une harmonisation des législations est souhaitable. Comme ils ne disposent que d'un seul modèle d'ensemble, le droit allemand, ils concluent que cette harmonisation se fera par alignement sur ce modèle. Mais elle ne sera ni immédiate ni totale.

Surtout elle ne sera pas absolument contraignante. En effet, le dispositif retenu repose sur deux techniques. La première est le développement de l'information, car les groupes sont d'autant plus dangereux qu'ils ont trop souvent un caractère occulte. Cette préoccupation est reçue avec faveur par les juristes français. Elle ne fait que transposer aux groupes une politique d'information appliquée par la loi du 14 juillet 1966 aux sociétés isolées et qui a connu un succès incontestable.

En revanche, le deuxième volet suscite d'avantage de réserves, puisqu'il tend à réglementer les groupes. Mais les projets laissent aux législations nationales une certaine faculté d'adaptation. Par conséquent, même si elle dérange les habitudes, la réglementation proposée paraît acceptable.

Telles sont les deux impressions ressenties par les non-spécialistes du droit européen. Il convient maintenant de les développer tour à tour.

I. Les projets européens et l'information sur les groupes de sociétés

4. Les projets européens et le droit français partent d'une même constatation: les groupes de sociétés ont trop souvent un caractère occulte, parce qu'ils sont des situations de fait, nécessairement plus difficiles à connaître que les situations de droit.

Ce manque d'information présente de multiples inconvénients. Il est dangereux pour les associés. Ignorant les liens de domination ou de dépendance qui unissent leur société à d'autres, ceux-ci risquent d'être plus facilement victimes d'abus de majorité que dans une société isoléee. A l'égard des tiers, le danger principal paraît inverse. Ceux-ci peuvent être abusés par l'unité apparente des sociétés du groupe et donc accepter de contracter avec une filiale peu solvable, croyant à tort que la société-mère est aussi engagée. Enfin, cette absence d'information ternit la réputation des groupes eux-mêmes, l'opinion publique

[11] Proposition Cousté, *supra*, note 8, exposé des motifs p. 4.

ayant tendance à présumer que tout ce qui n'est pas apparent est plus ou moins frauduleux.

Le meilleur moyen de pallier ces inconvénients est de transposer aux groupes les mesures de publicité et d'information applicables aux sociétés isolées. Les projets européens rejoignent donc les préoccupations du droit français lorsqu'ils organisent une information tant sur la constitution que sur le fonctionnement des groupes.

A. L'information sur la constitution des groupes

5. L'information sur la constitution des groupes doit se centraliser sur la société dont les actions font l'objet d'une acquisition suffisamment importante pour entrainer sinon immédiatement un lien de dépendance au moins une menace de perte d'indépendance.

L'avant-projet de neuvième directive prévoit essentiellement le mécanisme suivant. Celui qui acquiert plus de 10% du capital d'une société doit en avertir cette dernière (formalité dite de *notification*). Cette prise de participation fait l'objet d'abord d'une mesure d'information. Elle est portée à la connaissance des actionnaires, lors du rapport présenté par les dirigeants à l'occasion de la prochaine assemblée générale annuelle. Cette information est complétée par des mesures de publicité destinées à faire connaître aux tiers l'existence d'une participation ou d'un lien de dépendance.

6. Ce mécanisme présente *plusieurs avantages* par rapport à la réglementation française, encore très embryonnaire.[12]

Il permet d'informer à la fois les actionnaires et les tiers alors que le droit français se limite pour l'essentiel à l'information des seuls actionnaires lors du rapport qui leur est présenté sur les comptes de l'exercice au cours duquel la participation a été prise.[13]

Or, ici plus encore que dans d'autres domaines, il n'est pas justifié de prétendre distinguer une information réservée aux actionnaires d'une publicité destinée aux tiers. Les uns comme les autres ont intérêt à connaitre la prise de participation.

Le projet européen a également l'avantage du réalisme. Il s'efforce d'assimiler aux participations directes celles qui ont un caractère indirect et qui masquent une interposition de personnes. En effet, la qualité de l'information suppose que l'on connaisse la personne physique ou morale qui exercera en fait le pouvoir attaché aux titres acquis et non pas seulement l'identité de la filiale ou du prête-nom qui a réalisé l'opération. Au contraire la réglementation française reste pour l'essentiel une réglementation au premier degré. Seul le recours à la théorie de l'interposition de personnes permettrait aux tribunaux de rechercher, par delà la personne de l'acquéreur, celui qui est, en fait, le véritable instigateur de l'opération.

[12] H. Hémard, F. Terré & P. Mabilat, Sociétés commerciales, t. III, n° 580 (Paris, 1978).

[13] L. 24. 7. 1966, art. 358 al. 2; Décr. 23. 3. 1967, art. 251, al. 1.

Le réalisme se manifeste également dans la sanction du défaut de notification. L'acquéreur ne peut exercer aucun des droits attachés à ces actions tant qu'il n'a pas opéré la notification à la société émettrice. La méconnaissance de cette privation du droit de vote serait susceptible d'entrainer l'annulation des délibérations de l'assemblée. Cette sanction, assez insolite en droit des sociétés, montre toute l'importance que le droit européen attache au strict accomplissement de la notification. Au contraire, en droit français, le défaut de notification est seulement sanctionné par une amende correctionelle.[14]

Enfin, l'avant projet de directive présente un dernier mérite. Il prévoit que la publicité de la prise de participation doit être faite sans délai et donc avant que les dirigeants présentent leur rapport à l'assemblée. De ce point de vue le droit français présente une lacune regrettable car l'information sur les mouvements significatifs des capitaux n'est impérative qu'à l'occasion de l'assemblée générale. La C. O. B. incite cependant les sociétés cotées à rendre immédiatement publique l'identité de tout acquéreur de plus de 5% du capital, avec toutes les informations permettant de connaître le détenteur réel de la participation lorsque des holdings font écran entre lui et la société.[15] Il est en effet déplorable que les actionnaires apprennent par des rumeurs difficiles à contrôler les prises de participation dont leur société fait l'objet, notamment lorsqu'elles émanent d'investisseurs étrangers.

7. En revanche, *on regrettera* la relative étroitesse du domaine d'application de ces mesures de notification et de publicité. En effect, celles-ci ne paraissent s'imposer qu'en cas de prise ou de renforcement d'une participation au *capital* d'une société anonyme.

Les autres procédés d'affiliation ou de domination y échappent, qu'il s'agisse d'une communauté de dirigeants ou de relations d'intégration contractuelle. Or, la plupart des autres règles envisagées pour les groupes par les avant-projets tant de 7ème que de 9ème directive s'appliquent à toutes les entreprises ayant des dirigeants communs ainsi qu'à toutes celles qui sont susceptibles d'exercer, directement ou indirectement, une influence sur une autre.

Dès lors, on peut craindre qu'une publicité aussi partielle manque en partie son objet puisqu'elle laissera dans l'ombre des formes de relation plus diffuses, mais parfois aussi étroites et donc aussi dangereuses que des participations en capital. Bien plus, cette publicité ne serait-elle pas en elle-même dangereuse puisqu'elle pourrait laisser croire aux associés et aux tiers qu'ils sont parfaitement renseignés, alors qu'ils ne le sont pas. Il faudrait donc attirer l'attention des intéressés sur le fait que la publicité a été volontairement limitée aux relations qui peuvent être facilement découvertes. L'absence de publicité ne doit donc pas faire présumer que la société est indépendante.

Mais, ce n'est là que l'un des aspects d'une querelle plus vaste et quasiment insoluble: vaut-il mieux une information partielle que pas d'information du tout.

Si l'information sur la constitution des groupes est surtout nécessaire au

[14] L. 24. 7. 1966, art. 482.

[15] Rapport C. O. B. pour l'annéee 1978; J. O. Doc. Administ. 1979, 733.

niveau de la société dominée, celle qui porte sur le fonctionnement des groupes doit avoir un domaine plus large.

B. L'information sur le fonctionnement des groupes

8. En droit français l'information sur le fonctionnement des groupes est insuffisante.[16] Elle repose d'abord sur les dirigeants qui doivent à l'occasion de l'assemblée générale ordinaire annuelle, annexer au bilan un tableau sur la situation des filiales et des participations.[17]

Elle incombe aussi de manière plus indirecte au commissaire aux comptes puisque celui-ci jouit dans la société mère et dans les filiales des mêmes pouvoirs d'investigation que dans la société qu'il contrôle à titre principal.[18] Le juriste français n'est donc pas surpris de voir le projet européen s'édifier sur ces bases, en rejoignant d'ailleurs certaines des préoccupations les plus actuelles du législateur national.

1. Le rôle des dirigeants

9. Le rôle des dirigeants en matière d'information reste assez classique. Pour l'essentiel les projets européens transposent au groupe les techniques d'information pratiquées avec plus ou moins de succès au sein de chaque société envisagée isolément. L'art. 35 de l'avant-projet de neuvième directive prévoit donc d'abord que les dirigeants d'une société dépendante doivent présenter chaque année à l'assemblée générale ordinaire un rapport spécial. Celui-ci énumère les contrats que la société a pu conclure avec l'entreprise dominante, directement ou indirectement. De ce point de vue, le projet ne paraît pas apporter d'innovation quant au fond puisque ces contrats faisaient l'objet du rapport spécial des commissaires aux comptes car, dans presque tous les cas, ils avaient été conclus entre des sociétés ayant des dirigeants communs.[19] Mais le rapport spécial doit indiquer aussi si la société a pris ou s'est abstenu de prendre des mesures importantes, à l'instigation ou au profit d'intérêts qui lui sont étrangers. Il y a là des informations précieuses et jusqu'ici inédites pour les associés, car chacun sait que l'intérêt du groupe peut conduire à imposer à une filiale certains sacrifices ou l'acceptation de risques. Au regard des tribunaux français ces pratiques ne sont pas illicites lorsqu'elles n'excèdent pas les possibilités de la filiale et sont nécessaires à la poursuite d'une politique de groupe cohérente.[20] Mais il y a le plus grand avantage à ce qu'elles soient connues.

Les dirigeants auront aussi une autre obligation plus générale puisqu'elle intéresse à la fois la société dominante et la société dominée: celle d'établir des

[16] CREDA, *supra* note 7, p. 286 *et seq.*

[17] L. 24. 7. 1966, art. 357; Décr. 23. 3. 1966, art. 247. H. Hémard, F. Terré & P. Mabilat, *supra* note 12, n° 585.

[18] L. 24. 7. 1966, art. 229 al. 3; Y. Guyon & G. Coquereau, Le commissariat aux comptes, n° 105 (Paris, 1971).

[19] L. 24. 7. 1966, art. 101, al. 3.

[20] Paris 3 mai 1975, affaire "Agache-Willot", Le Bon Marché, G. P. 1976, 8, note A. P. S.; Rev. trim. dr. com. 1975, 123, note R. Houin.

comptes de groupe, dits encore comptes consolidés.[21] Ceux-ci constituent de loin la méthode d'information la plus efficace. Actuellement, en droit français, l'établissement de ces comptes est seulement facultatif.[22] Toutefois, la C. O. B. exige leur établissement avant de donner son visa préalable nécessaire à tout appel public à l'épargne ou à toute introduction en bourse.[23] L'art. 43 du projet de loi n° 236 entérinera cette pratique. Il prévoit que les sociétés cotées qui ont des filiales et des participations seront tenues d'annexer à leurs comptes un bilan et des comptes consolidés selon des modalités et méthodes déterminées par décret. Le renvoi à un décret peut être considéré comme une solution de facilité qui dispense le législateur français d'avoir à s'interroger, comme le fait la proposition de directive, sur les principes généraux qui gouvernent l'établissement des comptes de groupe, actuellement, le projet n° 974 sur la prévention des difficultés dans les entreprises. Les projets français et européens sont donc convergents sur ce point. On peut espérer leur aboutissement relativement rapide.

Très logiquement, la proposition de 7ème directive complète l'obligation d'établir des comptes consolidés par celle de leur donner, la même publicité qu'aux comptes des sociétés isolées.

2. *Le rôle des commissaires aux comptes*

10. Dans les groupes comme dans les sociétés isolées, les informations données par les dirigeants ne sont pleinement fiables que si elles sont contrôlées par un organe compétent et indépendant, le commissaire aux comptes. Les projets européens se heurtent donc au problème sur lequel le droit français a jusqu'ici échappé, l'organisation d'un contrôle des comptes de groupe.[24] Toutes les solutions qu'ils préconisent ne sont pas cependant nouvelles.

Les projets commencent par systématiser et renforcer certaines solutions qui existent, au moins dans leur principe, en droit interne français.

Ainsi, l'avant-projet de 9ème directive prévoit des incompatibilités entre l'exercice des fonctions de commissaire aux comptes d'une société et des liens trop étroits avec des entreprises du même groupe. Cette règle s'impose, même si sa formulation technique est souvent difficile, car un contrôle digne de ce nom suppose une indépendance du contrôleur. Des incompatibilités de ce type existent d'ailleurs déjà en droit français.[25] D'ailleurs, même si elles ne résultaient pas expressément d'un texte légal, l'art. 225 permettrait de récuser le commissaire nouvellement désigné en se fondant sur des présomptions sérieuses de manque d'indépendance. Par conséquent en matière d'indépendance du commissaire par rapport au groupe, le droit européen innove peu.

De même l'extension des pouvoirs d'investigation du commissaire aux

[21] Proposition de septième directive, J.O.C.E. C 14/2 du 17 janvier 1979.

[22] Décr. 23. 3. 1967, art. 248.

[23] Bull. C. O. B. n° 22, déc. 1970.

[24] D. Lange, Le commissaire aux comptes et le phénomène des groupes de sociétés (thèse, Tours, 1979).

[25] L. 24. 7. 1966, art. 220-3.

comptes en fonction dans une société aux entreprises du même groupe est déjà réalisée partiellement par le droit français.[26] Mais le projet européen est plus ambitieux puisqu'il étend le pouvoir d'investigation à toutes les sociétés dominées ou dominantes alors que le droit français se limite à la société mère et aux filiales directes, ce qui est trop restrictif. En outre, l'harmonisation est ici particulièrement utile car une difficulté peut se présenter actuellement lorsque les sièges des sociétés du groupe sont situés dans des États différents. En effet, d'une manière générale, une société est régie par la loi du lieu de son siège.[27] Or le commissaire qui contrôle les comptes de la société située en France tire jusq'ici ses pouvoirs de la loi française inapplicable à l'étranger, même dans les États membres des Communautés européennes. Donc, les dirigeants des sociétés situées à l'étranger, mère ou filiales de la société française, peuvent lui refuser de consulter leurs comptes, sauf disposition contraire de la loi locale.[28] Ces résistances peuvent d'ailleurs ne pas provenir du mauvais vouloir, assez improbable, des dirigeants locaux mais leur être imposées par la loi locale qui leur interdirait de communiquer les comptes à des tiers.

11. Mais l'innovation la plus remarquable est sans doute l'instauration par la proposition de 7ème directive d'un contrôle des comptes de groupe à l'article 23. Ce contrôle vient se superposer à celui qui, le cas échéant, a été exercé par chaque commissaire en fonction dans l'une des sociétés du groupe. Il conserve cependant un caractère individuel. C'est un commissaire, choisi parmi les membres de la profession, qui examine les comptes consolidés. La proposition de directive n'en dit pas davantage, ce qui est regrettable à bien des égards.

D'abord il ne semble pas que le contrôle des comptes consolidés, s'accompagne d'une obligation faite au commissaire d'en certifier la régularité et la sincérité. Sans doute a-t-on estimé que telle obligation aurait mis à la charge du commissaire une responsabilité démesurée. Pourtant l'expérience française incite au scepticisme quant à l'efficacité d'un contrôle qui n'est pas suivi d'une certification. En effet, ce système avait été pratiqué en France jusqu'à la mise en application de la loi du 24 juillet 1966. Il offrait peu de garanties aux actionnaires et aux tiers, car seul l'engagement personnel du commissaire, résultant de la certification, confère aux comptes une fiabilité suffisante.[29]

Ensuite les projets ne précisent pas exactement ce qu'il convient de contrôler. Or, ici encore, les doctrines et les pratiques ne sont pas fixées. Pourtant, il serait déraisonnable d'imposer au commissaire de groupe les mêmes diligences qu'au commissaire en fonction dans une société isolée. Mieux vaut prévoir des missions non pas répétitives, mais complémentaires. Le commissaire de groupe devrait donc d'abord apprécier la sincérité des données de base, ce qui peut d'ailleurs être difficile lorsque les comptes d'une filiale n'ont pas été contrôlés par un commissaire aux comptes. Ensuite le commissaire du groupe examinerait la

[26] L. 24. 7. 1966, art. 229.
[27] C. C. art. 1837.
[28] Bull. cons. nat. com. aux comptes 1974, 192.
[29] E. du Pontavice, *Le commissaire aux comptes et la certification*, Rev. soc. 1976, 257.

régularité des opérations de consolidation, ce qui supposerait un contrôle de l'imputation des valeurs consolidées.[30]

Enfin, on peut se demander s'il est opportun, comme le laisse entendre le projet, que le commissaire chargé de contrôler les comptes du groupe soit rattaché uniquement à la société dominante. N'aurait-il pas été plus logique d'essayer d'en faire un commissaire commun? Ou, solution analogue, n'aurait-il pas été possible de prévoir un contrôle des comptes du groupe exercé collégialement par les commissaires en fonction dans les sociétés diverses. Ce collège aurait aussi eu compétence pour certifier la régularité et la sincérité des comptes consolidés.

En tout cas, malgré ses insuffisances, le projet européen a au moins le mérite d'exister. Il pose le principe d'un contrôle des comptes consolidés, domaine dans lequel le droit français n'a jusqu'ici rien prévu.

12. Par conséquent, s'agissant de l'information sur des groupes de sociétés, l'impression du juriste français est, dans l'ensemble, plutôt favorable aux projets européens. Ceux-ci vont dans le même sens que les préoccupations actuelles du législateur interne. Ils faciliteront sa tâche car, compte tenu du caractère souvent international des groupes de sociétés, une information purement interne serait partielle et à la limite de l'inutile. En revanche, l'impression est plus réservée à propos du deuxième volet des projets européens, la réglementation des groupes de sociétés.

II. Les projets européens et la réglementation des groupes de sociétés

13. Les projets européens de réglementation des groupes commencent par reprendre certaines dispositions qui figurent déjà dans le droit français, où elles donnent de bons résultats. Ainsi, on y retrouve la prohibition des participations réciproques[31] et les précautions particulières destinées à garantir l'équilibre des contrats conclus entre des sociétés ayant des dirigeants communs.[32] Ces points ne méritent pas de commentaires.

Mais les projets européens vont plus loin. Ils visent à instaurer le statut d'ensemble des groupes, que le droit français ignore absolument. Or, le principe même de l'opportunité d'une réglementation a été critiqué, de manière souvent acerbe.[33] On a notamment reproché à ces projets leur caractère à la fois trop rigide, trop dogmatique, et trop général, qui risquerait de défavoriser les sociétés établies dans les Communautés européennes par rapport à leurs concurrents américains, japonais ou canadiens.

Ces griefs ne sont pas dépourvus de fondement, car les projets cherchent à réglementer tous les groupes c'est-à-dire non seulement ceux qui ont un caractère apparent, mais aussi ceux qui ne constituent que de simples situations de fait.

[30] D. Lange, *supra* note 24, p. 136 *et seq.*

[31] L. 24. 7. 1966, art. 358.

[32] *Id.* art. 101.

[33] R. Rodière, *Reflexions sur les avant-projets d'une directive de la Commission des Communautés Européeennes concernant les groupes de sociétés*, D. 1977, 136.

A. Les "groupes de droit"

14. La réglementation des groupes dits "groupes de droit" est celle qui devrait entraîner le moins de difficultés, au moins dans son principe. En effet des relations suivies, apparentes et en quelque sorte institutionnalisées entre sociétés ne permettent pas, sans artifice, de maintenir celles-ci dans l'état de splendide isolement qui est encore le leur dans la plupart des droits internes. Il faut néanmoins savoir jusqu'où doit aller la réglementation. En effet si les membres ont constitué un groupe, c'est précisément afin d'avoir plusieurs sociétés juridiquement indépendantes et non pas un seul ensemble intégré, de dimension plus importante. On priverait donc le groupe de son intérêt et de son originalité si on le transformait en une super-société, réunissant non plus des filiales autonomes, mais de simples succursales. Il faut donc doser l'autonomie et la dépendance, en dotant le groupe d'une structure plus fédéraliste que centralisée.

1. La constitution des "groupes de droit"

15. Les projets commencent par décrire les mécanismes qui permettent de constituer les groupes de droit ou de constater officiellement leur existence. Mais, ils le font en employant une méthodologie et une terminologie déroutantes pour les juristes français, qui ne sont pas certains d'en comprendre tous les mystères.

Le groupe peut d'abord résulter d'un *accord bi-latéral.* Il s'agit du contrat de domination, par lequel une société jusque-là indépendante se place librement sous la direction d'une autre entreprise.[34] Ce contrat doit être approuvé par l'organe de surveillance et par l'assemblée générale extraordinaire des actionnaires de la société dépendante. A cet effet, un rapport de l'organe de direction porte à leur connaissance les motifs et les conséquences probables de cette affiliation. Les projets prévoyent également des contrats de coordination par lesquels des sociétés jusque-là indépendantes décident d'un commun accord de se placer sous une direction unique, sans que l'une devienne dépendante de l'autre. Ils autorisent enfin les contrats de transferts de bénéfices ou de location gérance qui traduisent, dans un domaine limité, la domination qu'une société exercera sur une autre.

Ces contrats inspirent une certaine méfiance, car ils aboutissent à des asservissements difficilement acceptables même s'agissant de rapports entre personnes morales. Certes, on fait remarquer que les relations de domination existent et qu'il vaut donc mieux les réglementer que les ignorer. Mais, ce faisant, on risque d'en généraliser l'emploi et surtout de donner l'impression d'avaliser les bouleversements qu'elles apportent au droit classique des sociétés. Pourtant, la proposition de loi Cousté s'engage dans une voie analogue. Elle prévoit l'instauration en droit français d'un contrat dit d'affiliation, qui doit être approuvé par les assemblées générales des sociétés intéressées. Mais, cette proposition n'a pas reçu un accueil favorable, faute probablement d'avoir

[34] Avant-projet 9ème directive, art. 40.

organisé un contrôle judiciaire suffisant du contenu et de l'exécution du contrat d'affiliation.[35]

16. Le groupe peut aussi prendre naissance à l'*initiative de la société dominante*. Par conséquent, lorsqu'une entreprise a acquis, directement ou indirectement, au moins 90% du capital d'une société, elle peut au lieu de conclure un contrat de domination, faire à l'organe de la société une déclaration unilatérale qui emporte constitution du groupe. Cette hypothèse est relativement familière aux juristes français qui s'interrogent aussi pour savoir s'il est opportun de tirer les conséquences juridiques d'une absence d'autonomie qui existe déjà dans les faits. La réponse qu'ils y apportent est variable. Tantôt, l'absence d'autonomie est acceptée. Ainsi, le droit français reconnaît, à côté de la procédure normale d'O. P. A., une procédure simplifiéee dite "offre de ramassage" applicable lorsque la société initiatrice détient déjà au moins les 2/3 des actions de la société objet de l'offre.[36] Tantôt, au contraire l'absence d'autonomie est ignorée. Ainsi, l'absorption par une société mère de la filiale dont elle possède la quasi totalité des titres demeure soumise au droit commun des fusions, même si la C. O. B. déplore cette lourdeur.[37]

17. Enfin, les projets mentionnent ce qu'ils dénommèrent assez curieusement les *groupes organiques*. Il s'agit de l'hypothèse où l'initiative provient de la société dominée. En effet, le contrat de domination n'est satisfaisant que s'il est conclu entre des sociétés indépendantes au moment des négociations préalables. Sinon, il risque de consacrer des injustices en faisant prévaloir l'intérêt de la société dominante. Une société qui est en fait une société dominée doit donc pouvoir déclencher un mécanisme qui fera reconnaître officiellement cette dépendance, sans l'obliger à se mettre en situation d'infériorité en négociant un contrat avec la société dominante. Le projet met sur pied un mécanisme reposant sur une publicité effectuée en principe par les dirigeants de la société dépendante, avec possibilité pour les actionnaires ou les créanciers d'en demander l'application par voie judiciaire. Le mécanisme semble complété par un recours judiciaire ouvert à la société prétendue dominante, qui contesterait la publicité effectuée unilatéralement par la société qui se dit dominée. Mais, ce recours est organisé de manière passablement ambigue, alors pourtant que son existence paraît fondamentale.

Quelle que soit l'origine du groupe de droit, les conséquences qui vont en résulter seront sensiblement les mêmes.

2. *Le régime légal des "groupes de droit"*

18. L'économie du droit européen des groupes repose apparemment sur un compromis. La perte d'indépendance de la société est officialisée et acceptée dans toutes ses conséquences. Mais, elle a pour contre-partie une protection spécifique

[35] CREDA, *supra* note 7, p. 247.

[36] Règlement de la compagnie des agents de change, art. 199-4 *et seq*. F. Malan, *La procédure simplifiée d'OPA*, J. C. P. 1972, I, 2484.

[37] Rapport pour l'année 1978, J. O. Doc. Administ. 1979, 737.

des actionnaires et des créanciers. Le juriste français est assez choqué par ces conséquences, qui lui paraissent à bien des égards excessives.

La perte d'autonomie de la société dépendante est officiellement reconnue et acceptée. Le droit européen a donc le mérite du réalisme diront les uns, ou le défaut du cynisme, diront les autres.

Cette perte d'indépendance se manifeste notamment par le fait que les "dirigeants" de la société dominée – si l'on peut encore employer ce terme – sont tenus de suivre les *instructions de la société mère*. Si ces instructions concernent des actes soumis à l'approbation du conseil de surveillance, celui-ci ne peut s'y opposer qu'une fois. Puis, si la société-mère réitère sa demande, le conseil doit s'incliner. Bref, la société dominée devient une sorte de cadre vide. Ses organes sont désormais privés des compétences qui leur appartiennent normalement. Notamment, il n'y a plus à proprement parler d'organe délibératif. Mais la toute puissance de la société mère ne doit pas aboutir à son immixtion directe et désordonnée dans la société dépendante. Les ordres sont donc donnés aux dirigeants de la société dépendante et non directement au personnel de celle-ci. Cette précision, qui figure dans l'art. 23 de la proposition Cousté, pourrait être mentionnée plus clairement dans les projets européens.

Cet asservissement de la société dominée choque les juristes français qui s'étaient posé des questions analogues à propos notamment des filiales communes.[38] En effet, ici aussi on rencontre des protocoles, le plus souvent extra-statutaires, qui tendent à faire de la filiale un simple organe d'exécution des décisions prises en commun par les sociétés dominantes. Appellé à se prononcer sur la licéité de ces protocoles, le tribunal de commerce de Paris a donné une réponse nuancée.[39] Certains infléchissements sont valables, notamment la convention prévoyant une répartition égalitaire des sièges d'administrateurs. D'autres ne le sont pas. Ainsi les actionnaires de la filiale commune ne peuvent valablement décider de confier la direction de celle-ci à un arbitre, qui aurait plus de pouvoirs que le président du conseil d'administration.

Or, le droit européen admet un bouleversement des principes beaucoup plus radical puisque les actionnaires de la société dominée abdiquent leur souveraineté. A la limite, la société dominée n'est plus véritablement une filiale mais une simple succursale, un démembrement de la société dominante. Des conséquences aussi importantes supposent des contre-parties.

19. Les premières mesures de sauvegarde tendent à assurer la *protection des associés minoritaires* de la société dominée, c'est-à-dire ceux qui n'acceptent pas l'entrée dans le groupe. Les projets européens s'inspirent directement des art. 304 et 305 de l'Aktiengesetz allemand de 1965. En France, les mêmes techniques sont reprises par les art. 13 et s. de la proposition de loi Cousté.

[38] V. notamment les rapports présentés au colloque organisé par le doyen R. Houin sur: Les filiales communes, moyen de collaboration entre sociétés et groupes de sociétés (Paris, 1975).

[39] Trib. com. Paris 1 août 1974, Rev. soc. 1974, 685, note B. Oppetit; G. P. 1974, 525; Rev. trim. dr. com. 1975, 130, note R. Houin.

Les actionnaires doivent se voir offrir un choix entre un droit de retrait et une annuité compensatoire.

A bien des égards, le droit de retrait paraît constituer la meilleure des protections. Si le prix de rachat des titres est correct, l'associé opposé à l'entrée de la société dans le groupe ne subit pas véritablement de préjudice. D'ailleurs, le droit français a fait récemment du droit de retrait le recours suprême des minoritaires dans des cas assez nombreux.[40] Tantôt, cette faculté existe de plein droit, comme notamment dans les groupements d'intérêt économique[41] et les sociétés civiles professionelles.[42] Tantôt, elle est subordonnée à une autorisation judiciaire, à défaut d'accord de tous les autres associés comme dans les sociétés civiles de droit commun.[43] Enfin, dans les sociétés cotées en bourse, l'obligation faite à l'acquéreur d'un bloc de contrôle d'acheter au même cours, pendant 15 jours, toutes les actions qui lui sont proposées aboutit à un droit de retrait indirect et temporaire.[44] On remarquera toutefois que le retrait est, si l'on peut employer l'expression, d'inspiration "totalitariste". A l'époque de l'individualisme triomphant, les bouleversements du pacte social qui ne recueillaient pas l'unanimité étaient impossibles. Mieux, même l'associé dissident avait parfois la faculté de provoquer unilatéralement la dissolution de la société, lorsque celle-ci déviait de son but initial.[45] Ces dispositions avaient sans doute l'inconvénient de sacrifier la durée de la société à la mauvaise volonté d'un associé. Le droit de retrait présente les avantages et les inconvénients inverses. Il fait triompher l'intérêt collectif, mais il est dans son essence assez dur, puisqu'il revient à abandonner les hésitants ou les dissidents.

L'indemnité compensatoire a un effet moins radical et sauvegarde donc mieux l'avenir. Elle doit être d'un montant au moins égal à celui qui, compte tenu des résultats antérieurs de la société et de ses perspectives d'avenir, pourrait probablement être distribué comme dividende moyen pour chaque action. L'idée n'est pas absolument étrangère aux juristes français. Notamment, une loi du 13 juillet 1978 a instauré les actions à dividende prioritaire, dont l'inspiration est, par certains côtés, la même.[46] L'actionnaire monnaie ici son indépendance, là son droit de vote contre les avantages pécuniaires, car le dividende est souvent la seule chose qui l'intéresse vraiment. Mais la loi française prévoit une sanction au cas où le dividende prioritaire n'est pas intégralement versé pendant trois exercises: l'actionnaire retrouve son droit de vote.[47] Au contraire, les projets

[40] C. Lapoyade-Deschamps, *La liberté de se retirer d'une société*, D. 1978, 123.

[41] Ord. 23. 9. 1967, art. 7 al. 2; M. Boitard, *Les négociations de blocs de titres*, J. C. P. 1974, I, 2666; C. Gavalda, *La réglementation de la cession des blocs de titres*, Rev. soc. 1977, 395.

[42] L. 29. 10. 1966, art. 18.

[43] C. C. art. 1869.

[44] Règlement de la compagnie des agents de change, art. 201 *et seq.*

[45] C. C. art. 1869 ancien.

[46] L. 24. 7. 1966, art. 269-3; *cf.* C. Jauffret-Spinosi, *Les actions à dividende prioritaire sans droit de vote*, Rev. soc. 1979, 25.

[47] L. 24. 7. 1966, art. 269-3.

européens ne paraissent pas garantir de manière spécifique le paiement régulier de l'indemnité compensatrice.

Ils prévoient toutefois une mesure de sauvegarde définitive, mais qui ne joue qu'"à postériori". A l'expiration du groupe, la société dominée peut demander à la société dominante de compenser toute diminution des éléments d'actifs qu'elle aurait subie. L'intention est excellente. Sa réalisation risque cependant d'être difficile car elle suppose d'abord une évaluation indiscutable du patrimoine de la société dominée au moment où l'affiliation commence et au moment où elle finit. De plus, et surtout, la société dominante ne répond que des diminutions d'actif dues à son fait et non de celles qui proviendraient de causes antérieures. La preuve de ce lien de causalité sera particulièrement épineuse.

20. Il faut aussi *protéger les créanciers* de la société dépendante. Pour eux, la constitution du groupe équivaut à une cession de dette, opérée sans leur consentement au mépris de la théorie générale des obligations. Ils n'ont plus en face d'eux que le reflet de leur débiteur initial, reflet souvent amoindri car les rapports de domination peuvent vider la société de sa substance.

Les projets européens apportent à cette question une réponse de principe simple: la société dominante répond des obligations qui incombent à la société dominée. Cette garantie du passif a un domaine général. Elle s'applique non seulement aux dettes nées pendant l'affiliation, ce qui est logique, mais aussi à celles contractées antérieurement. En effet, il fallait protéger les créanciers antérieurs contre le risque de diminution voire de disparition de l'actif de la société débitrice.

Toutefois, cette prise en charge du passif n'équivaut pas à une cession de dette, car le créancier ne peut s'adresser à la société dominante qu'après avoir mis la société affiliée en demeure de payer. Mais, une simple mise en demeure suffit. Le créancier n'a pas à discuter les biens de la société affiliée. En principe, son recours peut donc s'exercer rapidement. Il court cependant un risque car la société dominante peut dégager sa responsabilité en prouvant que l'inexécution par la société affiliée de ses obligations est due à des causes ne résultant pas d'une influence qu'elle a exercé ou qu'elle s'est abstenue d'exercer. Justifiée dans son principe, cette restriction est la porte ouverte à toutes les manœuvres dilatoires, car toute appréciation d'un lien de causalité est sujette à discussions.

Le juriste français éprouve donc quelque scepticisme à l'égard de cette garantie, à la fois trop générale et trop rigide. Ses préférences iraient à un système inspiré de la protection des créanciers par le droit français en cas de fusion.[48] Pourquoi, par exemple, ne pas donner aux créanciers un droit d'opposition. Un tribunal apprécierait alors si la perte d'indépendance est de nature à compromettre la sécurité des créanciers actuels. Dans l'affirmative, il ordonnerait la constitution de garanties. Quant aux dettes contractées au cours de l'existence du groupe, ne serait-il pas préférable de prévoir une véritable solidarité entre la société dominante et la société dominée, quitte à tempérer les effets exégérés de celle-ci par des recours récursoires en contribution définitive au passif.

[48] L. 24. 7. 1966, art. 381; Décr. 23. 3. 1967, art. 261; R. Roblot, Droit commercial, t. I, n° 1594 (Paris, 10ème éd., 1980).

En tous cas, les difficultés économiques actuelles donnent à ce problème une grande importance. La situation incertaine et trop souvent médiocre des créanciers d'une filiale doit être clarifiée et améliorée aussi rapidement que possible.[49]

Cette réglementation des groupes de droit serait illusoire si elle ne se complétait pas par des dispositions applicables aux groupes de fait.

B. Les "groupes de fait"

21. Les "groupes de fait" sont ceux qui n'ont donné lieu à aucune notification. Ils existent néanmoins, de manière plus ou moins occulte. Une société exerce un pouvoir effectif sur une autre et l'oblige à avoir avec elle un comportement unique sur le marché.

Pour être efficace la réglementation des groupes de fait doit être extensive afin de s'appliquer à tous les cas de domination. Elle doit aussi être contraignante, afin d'inciter les sociétés à se placer spontanément sous le régime des groupes de droit, qui permet seul de méconnaître les intérêts de la société dépendante.

On laissera de côté ici une difficulté préalable, parce qu'elle n'est pas propre au droit européen. Il s'agit de la définition même du groupe de fait. Des études récentes ont montré que ni la détention par la société mère d'une part du capital de sa filiale, ni le concept d'unité de direction ne résistaient à une analyse réaliste d'une pratique infiniment nuancée et multiforme. Le groupe de fait est existence avant d'être essence, ce qui ne facilite pas sa réglementation.[50]

Les projets européens sont donc peut-être des édifices construits sur le sable. Mais leur architecture demeure classique puisqu'on y retrouve les deux constantes du droit des groupes: la protection des actionnaires et celles des créanciers.

1. La protection des actionnaires

22. La protection des actionnaires a sa source dans un *principe général:* en dehors des formes de groupes reconnues par le droit, il est interdit de gérer une société dépendante autrement que dans l'intérêt de celle-ci. Par conséquent, l'entreprise qui exerce une domination de fait est responsable de tout dommage résultant de ses fautes de gestion (ce qui n'est pas très original) et surtout d'actes qui ne sont pas conformes à l'intérêt de la société dépendante. Le critère de l'intérêt social, par opposition à l'intérêt de groupe, retrouve donc ici toute son efficacité.

La *mise en œuvre* de ce principe général se traduit par les mesures suivantes, qui sont assez disparates.

D'abord, si la société dominante, tenue à notification de sa prise de participation, s'est abstenue de le faire, elle est privée de l'exercice de son droit de vote.[51] Cette sanction a été qualifiée de féroce par un auteur.[52] Elle est séduisante dans

[49] Archambault, De la responsabilité des sociétés mères à l'égard des sociétés qu'elles contrôlent, Conférence générale des tribunaux de commerce (Lyon, 1976); J.-P. Sortais, *A propos de certaines questions de responsabilité suscitées par les groupes de sociétés*, Rev. de jurispr. com. 1977, 85.

[50] B. Oppetit et A. Sayag, *supra* note 7; CREDA, *supra* note 7.

[51] V. *supra* note 5.

[52] R. Rodière, *supra* note 33.

son principe puisque, si elle s'applique, elle empêchera la constitution de groupe de fait reposant directement sur des participations en capital. Mais, elle laissera le champs libre à toutes les autres formes de domination.

Ensuite, les actionnaires peuvent demander en justice la désignation d'un ou plusieurs contrôleurs spéciaux, chargés de vérifier si la société a subi un préjudice en raison de son appartenance à un groupe de fait. Cette mesure d'information rappelle aux juristes français l'expertise de minorité instaurée par l'art. 226 de la loi du 24 juillet 1966. Elle est excellente dans son principe, car les mécanismes normaux d'information, y compris l'intervention des commissaires aux comptes, ne permettent pas toujours de déceler les abus commis par l'intermédiaire de sociétés interposées. Reste à souhaiter que son application donne lieu à une jurisprudence moins restrictive que celle intervenue en France à propos de l'expertise de minorité.[53] Reste aussi à espérer que les pouvoirs de contrôleur spécial seront suffisants pour lui permettre de débrouiller, dans un délai raisonnable, l'écheveau complexe des procédés de domination et de mesurer le préjudice qui en résulte.

23. Enfin et surtout la protection des actionnaires hors groupe est assurée par des mesures judiciaires. Les projets européens prévoient qu'à la demande de tout intéressé, prouvant que la société dominée a subi un dommage du fait de la société dominante, le tribunal peut ordonner l'une des mesures suivantes.

Premièrement, le tribunal peut suspendre un ou plusieurs membres de l'organe de direction ou de surveillance de la société dominée. On regrettera que cette intervention judiciaire demeure négative et que le tribunal ne puisse pas désigner un administrateur provisoire, en attendant le retour à une situation normale. De ce point de vue, le droit européen serait donc plutôt en régression par rapport à la jurisprudence française. En effet, les tribunaux se reconnaissent le pouvoir prétorien de désigner un administrateur provisoire en cas d'abus de majorité. Cependant, ils ne semblent pas donner à cette mesure un contenu spécifique lorsque l'abus est commis au sein d'un groupe.[54] De plus, ils jugent que la désignation d'un administrateur provisoire est une mesure grave, qui ne peut être ordonnée qu'en cas de crise menaçant l'existence même de la société, ce qui est restrictif.[55] Sans aller jusqu'à instaurer un gouvernement des sociétés par les juges, on pourrait souhaiter que le droit européen et le droit français s'épaulent mutuellement pour mieux faire face à une situation de crise.

En second lieu, le tribunal peut interdire la poursuite de l'exécution des conventions préjudiciables à la société dominée de fait ou ordonner le retrait des mesures dommageables, sans qu'il soit porté atteinte aux droits acquis de bonne foi par des tiers. Compte tenu de cette restriction, il est probable que le retrait

[53] L. Boy, *Réflexions sur le sort de l'expertise de minorité*, D. 1980, 79; Y. Guyon, *L'expertise de minorité*, Jurisclasseur des sociétés, Fasc. 134 D.

[54] Paris 12 mai 1965, J. C. P. 1965, II, 14274 bis, note P. Nepveu; Trib. com. Toulouse 24 mai 1972, D. 1973, 196, note D. Schmidt.

[55] Trib. com. Seine 9 mai 1969, J. C. P. 1969, II, 16063, note Y. Guyon; Rev. trim. dr. com. 1969, 1024, note R. Houin.

demeurera exceptionnel, car il aura presque toujours un caractère rétroactif générateur de troubles dans les relations d'affaires.

La dernière mesure consiste à provoquer judiciairement l'obligation de rachat des actions des minoritaires, dans les mêmes conditions que si un contrat de domination avait été conclu.

Ces mesures sont dissuasives, puisqu'elles retirent tout intérêt à se cantonner dans la situation de groupe de fait. Mais, l'imagination des dirigeants peu scrupuleux leur permettra sans doute de mettre sur pied des mécanismes de domination si habilement dissimulés que les actionnaires, même aidés par un contrôleur spécial, ne parviendront pas à en prouver l'existence, en raison notamment de recours à de nombreuses sociétés interposées et établies de préférence à l'étranger. Par exemple le contrôle pourrait être exercé par plusieurs sociétés, apparemment indépendantes les unes des autres, mais ne constituant finalement que les organes d'exécution d'un holding unique. Le droit des groupes de fait risque donc soit de conduire à des mesures inquisitoriales, soit de demeurer un vœu pieux.

2. *La protection des créanciers*

24. La protection des tiers devrait entrainer moins de difficultés. En effet, contrairement aux actionnaires, les tiers se fient uniquement aux apparences. La question de la preuve est donc simplifiée.

Ou bien le groupe de fait n'a aucune apparence. Le tiers ne subit pas de préjudice en voyant son recours limité à la société avec laquelle il avait traité, ignorant que celle-ci appartenait à un groupe. Le seul cas douteux serait celui où, après le contrat, l'actif de la société serait transféré à l'entreprise dominante, de telle manière que le gage du créancier serait diminué ou anéanti. Mais le droit commun des obligations, et plus spécialement l'action paulienne, suffirait sans doute à pallier cet inconvénient.

Ou bien le groupe, quoique de fait, est apparent. On ne rencontre alors aucune difficulté pour prouver son existence. La seule question qui se pose est de savoir si le créancier de la société dominée de fait bénéficiera d'un recours contre la société dominante.

En ce domaine, les européens sont assez laconiques. Ils se bornent à prévoir que les créanciers qui n'ont pu être payés par la société dominée disposent d'une action contre la société dominante. Mais, c'est une action en responsabilité et non en extension de passif. Elle suppose donc la preuve que le non-paiement a été causé par des actes de gestion, décidés à l'initiative de la société dominante et contraires à l'intérêt de la société affiliée. Cette preuve sera difficile à rapporter et facilitera les manœuvres dilatoires de la société dominante, alors qu'en matière de paiement la rapidité des recours est essentielle. Il est donc probable, qu'au moins en droit français, la protection des créanciers continuera d'être assurée par les règles propres aux procédures de réglement judiciaire ou de liquidation des biens. Tantôt la société dominante sera considérée comme dirigeant de fait de la société dépendante, et comme telle susceptible d'être condamnée à combler tout ou partie de son passif.[56] Tantôt, si la filiale a perdu son autonomie patrimoniale, le

[56] L. 13. 7. 1967, art. 99. V. nos obs. au Jurisclasseur des sociétés, fasc. 193-3 bis.

tribunal pourra aller jusqu'à ordonner une procédure de liquidation commune.[57]

La protection des créanciers paraît donc être assurée plus efficacement par le droit commun que par le droit spécial des groupes de sociétés.

III. Conclusions

25. En définitive, il semble qu'on puisse adresser deux griefs principaux aux projets européens, toute question de méthodologie mise à part.

Par certains côtés, ces projets sont trop étroits. On regrettera notamment que la situation des salariés n'y ait pas été envisagée de manière plus systématique. Certes, la matière sera sans doute traitée par d'autres directives. Pourtant, l'expérience française montre qu'elle est difficile et génératrice de conflits tant en ce qui concerne les droits individuels[58] que la représentation[59] des salariés du groupe. A ne pas l'avoir envisagée, on aboutit nécessairement à une construction imparfaite et qui sera mal acceptée.

Par d'autres côtés, les projets paraissent trop larges ou mal centrés. Notamment la protection des créanciers et celle des associés minoritaires semble y tenir une place trop importante, alors que ces questions se posent tout autant dans les sociétés isolées.

La véritable question, mais qui dépasse les attributions d'une réunion d'experts gouvernementaux, est de donner aux groupes de sociétés une structure appropriée. Celle-ci ne saurait prendre la forme d'une personne morale, car un groupe doté d'une telle organisation ne serait plus vraiment un groupe. La solution consisterait peut-être à déterminer le degré d'indépendance et de subordination de chaque société du groupe, un peu comme le fait le droit public dans les Etats fédéraux. Mais, et c'est là qu'apparaît le caractère diabolique des groupes, en s'engageant sur cette voie ne risque-t-on pas de retomber sur la distinction classique, bien que jugée aujourd'hui peu satisfaisante, entre la personnalité interne et la personnalité externe?

Quoiqu'il en soit, un trés sensible allégement de l'avant-projet de 9ème directive doit être envisagé.

Note bibliographique:

Proposition d'une neuvième directive tendant à coordonner les législations nationales relatives aux liens entre entreprises et en particulier aux groupes, Doc XI/215/77-f; la publication d'une version modifiée est expectée. V. par exemple R. Sinay, *Vers un droit européen des groupes de sociétés*, Gaz. pal. 1967. i. doct. 70; R. Sinay, *Le droit des groupes dans le projet de statut des sociétés anonymes européennes*, Gaz. pal. 1968. i. doct. 118;

[57] V. par ex. Cass. com. 3 oct. 1978, Bull. civ. IV, n° 209 p. 177; Paris 18 janv. 1977, Rev. soc. 1978, 522, note J.-P. Sortais.

[58] I. Vacarie, *Groupes de sociétés et relations individuelles de travail*, Droit social 1975, 23; B. Oppetit, *Groupe de sociétés et droit du travail*, Rev. soc. 1973, 69.

[59] M. Despax, *Groupe de sociétés et institutions représentatives du personnel*, J. C. P. 1972, I, 2465; G. Cherrier-Thormann, L'expression du droit syndical dans les groupes de sociétés (thèse, Paris, 1980).

H. G. Koppensteiner, *Das Konzernrecht des EWG-Verordnungsentwurfs über eine europäische Aktiengesellschaft aus kollisionsrechtlicher Sicht*, AWD 1970, 433; W. F. Bayer, *Europäische Vertragskonzerne und europäisches Gesellschaftsrecht*, FESTSCHRIFT FÜR GESSLER (München, 1971); M. Lutter, *Vers un Konzern contractuel européen*, REV. TRIM. DR. COM. 1972, 1; K. Gleichmann, *Überlegungen zur Gestaltung eines Konzernrechts in den Europäischen Gemeinschaften*, FESTSCHRIFT FÜR SANDERS p. 449 (Deventer, 1972); G. Keutgen, *Vers un droit européen des groupes de sociétés*, REV. INT. BELGE 1972, 121; G. KEUTGEN, LE DROIT DES GROUPES DE SOCIÉTÉS DANS LA CEE (Bruxelles, 1973); R. Goerdeler, *Überlegungen zum europäischen Konzernrecht*, ZGR 1973, 389; U. Immenga et D. Klocke, *Konzernkollisionsrecht*, ZSR 1973, 27; M. Lutter, *Il gruppo di imprese (Konzern) nel diritto tedesco et nel futuro diritto europeo*, RIV. SOC. 1974, 1; H. Würdinger, *Die Konzernregelung im Statut der "Societas Europaea" und die Harmonisierung der nationalen Rechte in den Europäischen Gemeinschaften*, EuR 1974, 25; G. Minergini, *I gruppi di società nella Comunità Europea, Problemi di diritto societario*, RIV. INT. SC. ECON. 1974, 1130; C. ALQUIER, LA NOTION DE GROUPE EUROPÉEN DE SOCIÉTÉS (Montpellier, 1976); P. Derom, *The EEC Approach to Groups of Companies*, 1976 VA. J. INT. L. 565; U. Immenga, *Konzernverfassung ipso facto oder durch Vertrag?* EuR 1978, 242; W. Schilling, *Bemerkungen zum Europäischen Konzernrecht*, ZGR 1978, 415; U. Immenga, *Möglichkeiten der Konzernrechtsvergleichung*, FESTSCHRIFT FÜR FISCHER p. 297 (Berlin, New York, 1979); OCDE, RESPONSABILITÉ DES SOCIÉTÉS-MÈRES DU FAIT DE LEURS FILIALES (Paris, 1980); U. Immenga, *Company-Systems and Affiliation*, in INTERNATIONAL ENCYCLOPEDIA OF COMPARATIVE LAW ch. 7, vol. XIII (Tübingen, sous presse).

Summary:

A Critical Appraisal of the European Proposals for Harmonization in the Field of Groups of Companies: the French Point of View

This report examines in a deliberately critical manner the various European proposals in the field of groups of companies. It concentrates principally on the draft proposal of the Ninth Directive, which received a qualified welcome from French lawyers.

There is no doubt that the European proposals have positive aspects. In particular, they will assure that better information concerning groups of companies be made available, whereas in the current state of affairs group activities are only too often concealed. The introduction of measures imposing publicity requirements which apply both on the formation of groups (notification) and to the operation of a group are, therefore, to be welcomed with pleasure. The proposal for the Seventh Directive especially fills a lacuna by providing that groups of companies must establish consolidated group accounts, to be audited by authorized auditors. Shareholders and creditors will benefit from a global view of the financial position of the whole group.

On the other hand, the European proposals are much less satisfactory in so far as they attempt to regulate groups of companies. The legal rules to be applied to groups have been inspired by German law. They are based essentially upon the idea of contracts of control, which permit the parent company to use a subsidiary to further its own interests. In return for the loss of independence, non-group shareholders of the subsidiary find themselves offered the choice either of a right to sell out their interest or to receive an annual indemnity. As far as the creditors of the controlled company are concerned, they can press their claims against the dominating company. If the control is exercised outside a de jure group, the parent company is responsible for all the damages which result from its mismanagement and also from any acts which were not in conformity with the interests of the controlled company. These various mechanisms are not in themselves bad; however the method adopted to implement them is unnecessarily complex and the results at which they are aimed are already partially achieved through the case-law.

It can only be hoped therefore that the draft proposal for the Ninth Directive will be appreciably simplified.

Group Accounts under the Proposed Seventh EEC Directive:* A Practitioner's View

Welf Müller
Frankfurt a. M.

I. Introduction

A. The Different Interests Involved

A discussion on group accounts within a colloquium on multinational corporations in European corporate and antitrust laws must take into consideration that accounting, and specifically group accounting, is only one aspect and moreover a very specific aspect of the phenomenon of a group. It seeks to raise the question as to what information concerning its financial position a group should make available to the various interested parties.

The parties interested in group accounts are not only the shareholders and the supervisory body of the dominant undertaking but also inter alia, the present and future shareholders of all the group companies, together with their managerial and supervisory bodies, creditors (including suppliers), customers and employees. Over and above all these specific interested parties, the group accounts are also addressed to the general public with its various spheres of interest, such as competitors, the business and financial press, investment analysts etc. There is no doubt that the interest for the kind of information requested varies among the various users of group accounts and even the readiness and capability of the users to understand the type of information presented in group accounts differs considerably. A discussion of this matter must therefore consider both sides: The obligation of a group to disclose its financial position in an understandable form; and the needs and capabilities of the users.

The relationship between the value of the information provided for the users of the group accounts, and the amount of work required to produce such accounts is an important factor which must be borne in mind in drawing up regulations for group accounts. It makes little sense to make disclosure of group accounts mandatory if this gives information of real value only to a small number

* This paper is based on the negotiations concerning the seventh EEC Directive as of the end of May 1980. Developments subsequent to this date have not been taken into consideration.

of specialists, because the information is not understandable for other parties interested in the group.

B. Striking the Right Balance

Accounting, and specifically group accounting, has developed into a very complex matter and for an outsider – and most interested parties are outsiders in these matters – it is very difficult to understand. Generally speaking, the rules to be followed must strike a balance between three points of view: 1)The group accounts must present a true and fair view of the situation of the group; 2) they must be understandable for all interested parties; and, 3) last but not least, the work required to produce the group accounts must be commensurate to the benefits derived from them.

C. The Need for Group Accounts

The necessity for group accounts arises from the indisputable fact that the annual accounts of a single company which is a member of a group are less meaningful than the accounts of an independent company. This is indicated quite clearly in the *Explanatory Memorandum to the Proposal for a Seventh Directive:*

> The basic characteristic of such groups is that the management of the companies belonging to them is coordinated in such a way that they are managed on a central and unified basis by the dominant company or companies in the interest of the group as a whole.[1]

The true economic and financial position of an individual company belonging to a group can only be assessed against the background of the overall position of the group. This applies both to the assessment of the overall performance of a single group company as well as to the assessment of individual items in its balance sheet, for example, the value of assets transferred within the group and accounts receivable from other group companies. Experience has shown that the collapse of the dominant company or of a substantially material company within the group will endanger the existence of all the other companies in the group.

D. The Development of Group Accounts

This state of affairs has given rise to the development of group accounts. However, the nature and intensity of this development has been different in the various countries within and outside the EEC. Within the EEC there are at present statutory regulations relating to the preparation of group accounts in a number of countries such as Belgium, Denmark, France, Germany, Great Britain, Ireland, and to a certain extent also the Netherlands. On the other hand, there are no such statutory regulations in Italy and Luxembourg.

Group accounts are the result of the combination of the accounts of the individual companies in the group in order to produce a uniform consolidated set of accounts. However, even within a single country this can give rise to problems

[1] 1976 Bulletin of the E. C., Supplement 9/76 p. 19-32, at 19.

where, for example, as in Germany, different accounting principles apply to the various legal forms of undertakings. This problem becomes considerably greater when foreign undertakings are included in the consolidation since their accounts may have been drawn up in accordance with quite different principles. The consolidation of accounts under these circumstances would be more likely to produce a confusing conglomeration of differing accounting and valuation procedures rather than a reliable presentation of meaningful information. Again to take Germany as an example, this has been the reason why compulsory consolidation has hitherto been restricted to domestic group companies. In principle we have here a similar problem to that which Prof. Lindencrona mentioned in his contribution about unitary taxation.[2] This system might work only if there were to be a worldwide harmonization of the rules and principles of how to compute the results of a business. But we are far from such a consensus. Within the EEC, however, these difficulties will, to a large extent, be resolved, because the adoption of the Fourth Directive[3] and the changes in national laws to conform with that Directive will result in a harmonization of accounting principles throughout the EEC. While the co-ordination measures will only apply to the types of companies specified in the Fourth Directive,[4] it may nevertheless be expected that the accounting and valuation principles provided in the Directive will also influence the accounting standards for other types of undertakings. Thus the way has been prepared for group accounts within the EEC on the basis of the presentation and valuation rules contained in the Fourth Directive. This then is the course which has been followed in the Proposal for a Seventh Directive[5] which, both for the presentation of the group accounts and

[2] G. Lindencrona, *What is Wrong with Unitary Taxation?*, *infra* this volume, at pp. 230 *et seq.*

[3] Directive 78/660/EEC, Fourth Council Directive of 25 July 1978 based on Article 54 (3) (g) of the Treaty on the Annual Accounts of Certain Types of Companies. O. J. E. C., Vol. 21, L 222 p. 11 (1978). *See generally*, ERNST & WHINNEY, THE FOURTH DIRECTIVE: ITS EFFECTS ON THE ANNUAL ACCOUNTS OF COMPANIES IN THE EUROPEAN ECONOMIC COMMUNITY (London, 1979). For an extensive general discussion of accounting law reform in Germany and the E. E. C., *see* M. BIERICH, W. BUSSE VON COLBE, G. LASSMANN & M. LUTTER, eds., RECHNUNGSLEGUNG NACH NEUEM RECHT, Special Issue no. 2 of 1980 ZGR; N. WENTLAND, DIE KONZERNBILANZ ALS BILANZ DER WIRTSCHAFTLICHEN EINHEIT KONZERN; GRUNDLAGEN DER KONZERNRECHNUNGSLEGUNG UNTER BERÜCKSICHTIGUNG DER VORSCHRIFTEN DES AKTIENSGESETZES UND DER VORSTELLUNGEN EINER 7. EG-RICHTLINIE (Frankfurt, 1979). For the general comparative law basis, *see* D. Vagts, *Law and Accounting in Business Associations*, in INTERNATIONAL ENCYCLOPEDIA OF COMPARATIVE LAW, Ch. 12a, vol. XIII (Tübingen, 1972).

[4] Cf. Art. I.

[5] References throughout are to the Commission's Amended Proposal for a Seventh Directive Pursuant to Art. 54 (3) (g) of the EEC Treaty Concerning Group Accounts, submitted by the Commission to the Council on 14 December 1978, O. J. E. C., Vol. 22, C 14 p. 2 (1979) [hereinafter "The Draft Directive"]. Reference should also be made to the Opinion on the proposal for a Seventh Directive, O. J. E. C., Vol. 20, C 75 p. 5 (1977); and to GROUP ACCOUNTS: PROPOSAL FOR A SEVENTH DIRECTIVE, 1976 BULLETIN OF THE EUROPEAN COMMUNITIES, SUPPLEMENT 9/76. Also, *see* generally, ACCOUNTANTS

for the valuation of the items included therein, will conform with the relevant provisions of the Fourth Directive.[6]

E. The Reasons for Group Accounts

The aims of the proposal for a Seventh Directive are set out very aptly in the *Explanatory Memorandum,*[7] as follows:

(1) to ensure that consolidated accounts are laid down with regard to the information to be supplied in such accounts in order to provide certain minimum standards for the protection of shareholders, employees and third parties in all the Member States, thus making it easier for the companies to exercise their right of establishment;
(2) to enable a common market of undertakings to be established;
(3) to provide the right conditions to enable a European capital market to function;
(4) to avoid a situation where various legal requirements relating to the way in which accounts are presented distort competition between companies within the Community.

One can only endorse these aims. While it is true that a number of large groups, both within and outside the EEC, publish group accounts either on a statutory or a voluntary basis, there are as yet no standards of comparability at least on an international level.

II. Definition of a Group in the Draft Seventh Directive

A. Central and Unified Management

Under the original draft of a Seventh Directive the group (i. e. a group based on the relationship of dependency) was defined in Art. 3 as follows:

> For the purposes of this Directive, a dominant undertaking and one or more undertakings dependent on it shall constitute a group if the dominant undertaking exercises in practice its dominant influence to the effect that all such undertakings are managed on a central and unified basis by the dominant undertaking.[8]

This definition is based on the concept of the *group as an economic unit* which, detached from the legally independent member-companies, forms a superior

International Study Group, Consolidated Financial Statements (1973); Kommission Rechnungswesen im Verband der Hochschullehrer für Betriebswirtschaft e. V.: *Vorschläge zur endgültigen Fassung der 7. und 8. EG-Richtlinie,* 1979 Die Betriebswirtschaft 497; K. Küting, *Zur Problematik des Art. 18 der 7. EG-Richtlinie,* 1980 Der Betrieb 5; E. Müller, *Zum geänderten Entwurf einer 7. EG-Richtlinie über den Konzernabschluß,* 1980 Der Betrieb 265; W. Schaffer, *7. EG-Richtlinie (Konzernrichtlinie) im Vergleich zu den Vorschriften im Aktiengesetz und anderen international diskutierten Normen,* 1980 Der Betrieb 889 and 941.

6 *See* Art. 11 (1), 15 (a), Draft Directive.

7 *Supra* note 1, at p. 19.

8 O. J. E. C., Vol. 22, C 14 p. 5 (1979).

quasi-legal entity.[9] It is clear that, for the creation of such an economic and quasi-legal unit, mere dependency is not sufficient but must be accompanied by a further characteristic, namely central and unified management. This concept is, for example, found in the German Corporation Law.[10]

B. Dominance and Dependency

On the other hand, there is a concept which regards the group, at least for the purpose of consolidation, as principally a system of majority-owned subsidiary companies or, in other words, a system based on dominance and dependency. This concept is, as far as I am aware, the basis of Anglo-Saxon point of view. This view has also evidently been adopted by the latest version of the draft of the Seventh Directive which in Art. 3 defines a group as follows.

> For the purposes of this Directive, a dominant undertaking and one or more undertakings dependent on it shall constitute a group.[11]

Thus, at least for the purpose of consolidated group accounts, the fine distinction between dominant influence (resulting in a relationship of dependence) and management on a central and unified basis (resulting in a group) has been given up, and a group is now completely identified with the concept of dominance and dependency.

C. Evaluation of the Change in Concept

I, personally, consider that this change in the draft Directive is a sensible one as far as group accounts are concerned, even if I am not in agreement with certain opinions which have been expressed in the relevant literature on this subject.[12] I should like to emphasize the proviso "as far as group accounts are concerned", and expressly leave open the question of whether or not the yardstick of management on a central and unified basis is indispensable in other areas of company law, co-determination and the law of competition.

From my own practical experience, I know only too well the difficulties which can arise in establishing whether central and unified management does or does not exist. These difficulties are often practically impossible to resolve in the time available. The accounts of single companies and consolidated group accounts must, to a large extent, be prepared on the basis of formalized data or conventions, otherwise the preparing company and the auditor will have to deal with very difficult questions of law – both as regards establishing the relevant facts and as regards the legal interpretation thereof. As I have already indicated,

9 The "entity concept" which must be clearly distinguished from the "entity doctrine" discussed in D. Prentice, *Groups of Companies: the English Experience*, *supra* this volume at pp. 99 *et seq.*

10 Sec. 18 AktG 1965. *See* H. Wiedemann, *The German Experience with the Law of Affiliated Enterprises*, *supra* this volume pp. 21 et seq., esp. at § I.B.2. (a).

11 *Supra* note 8, at p. 5.

12 *See* Müller, *supra* note 5, p. 265 *et seq.*

such problems would almost always also have to be resolved under the pressure of time because, unfortunately, the time available for the preparation of annual accounts is always too short. I think that everyone who has been confronted with these matters in practice will confirm how difficult it is to draw the line in this respect. The problem is that, from the viewpoint of a preparer of company accounts, a practical and easy to handle definition of central and unified management is just not available. Moreover, it may be said that as a rule a relationship of dependence gives the dominant company control over the dependent company. This should be sufficient for the purposes of consolidation even if "control" and "central and unified management" are defined differently.

D. Dependency: An Irrefutable or a Refutable Presumption?

The fact that the draft Directive is basically acceptable does not exclude the possibility that the global statement in Art. 3, under which a relationship of dependence automatically results in a group, should be somewhat refined. The provisions in the draft Directive concerning dependency make the presumption of dependency *irrefutable* in certain circumstances.[13] Since these circumstances may sometimes overlap, it is possible under the present draft Directive that dependence on more than one undertaking may arise. Some examples are:

(1) A owns the majority of C's subscribed capital.
B owns the majority of the voting rights in C;

(2) A owns the majority of the voting rights in C.
B can, by reason of special rights, appoint more than half of the members of C's supervisory body;

(3) A owns the majority of C's subscribed capital.
B has entered into a control agreement *(Beherrschungsvertrag)* with C.

I could give further examples. It is doubtful whether such a state of affairs, arising from an irrefutable presumption of dependency, was really intended. The authors of the draft Directive have, evidently, also had similar thoughts on this matter and, by means of a further irrefutable presumption, have excluded the irrefutable presumption of dependency, where severe, long-term restrictions prevent an undertaking from exercising its rights as to the assets or management of another undertaking.

In this connection, the German method of a *refutable* presumption of dependency seems to me to be more practical. In any event, it should not be possible for a company to be regarded as belonging to more than one group by reason of a presumption of dependency.[14]

[13] Art. 2, Draft Directive. Contrast the position in, *e. g.*, German law where such a presumption may be refuted. *See* generally, H. Wiedemann, *supra* note 10.

[14] For a discussion of the possibility of proportional consolidation in such case *see infra* § IV. B.

E. Horizontal and Vertical Groups

Besides the group based on the relationship of dependency (vertical group) the draft Directive also recognizes horizontal groups and requires them to draw up group accounts.[15] In the case of such a group there is no interrelationship of dependence between the companies but it suffices if they "act over the long term, as regards their assets or their management in a concerted manner and in a common interest". In contrast to the vertical group, here the criterion of unified management, in whatever form, is indispensable for the definition of the group.

Here too, the draft Directive makes irrefutable presumptions and counter-presumptions. So far horizontal groups have been very seldom encountered in practice. This, in my opinion, was because there were no relevant statutory regulations or because the relationships between the companies concerned were not transparent. In practice one does in fact come across groupings of not inconsiderable importance where the companies therein are bound together merely by a common shareholder or by common administrative, managerial or supervisory bodies. In other cases, the relationship may be based on contracts between the parties. The requirement to consolidate the accounts of such horizontal groups is justified and is to be welcomed.

III. Types of Companies Required to Prepare Group Accounts

A. The Limited Liability Company Restriction

The draft Directive[16] requires that group accounts be drawn up only if one of the undertakings in the group is a limited liability company. This may be either the dominant undertaking of the group or any dependent group undertaking or a member of a so-called horizontal group.

B. Shortcomings of Such a Restriction

As was stated in the *Explanatory Memorandum*,

> The purpose of this Directive in requiring group accounts to be drawn up is to protect the interest linked with limited liability companies.[17]

This may be convincing to the extent that one regards the shareholders as the parties interested in the group accounts, since, as a rule, their interests are in need of greater protection than in the case of other types of commercial enterprises. This is particularly so when the shares are traded anonymously on the capital market. If, however, one thinks of other interested parties, for example, creditors, employees or the general public, either in the narrow or wider sense, the concept is not quite so evident. This concept is also contained in German

[15] Art. 4, Draft Directive.
[16] Art. 6, Draft Directive.
[17] *Supra* note 1, at p. 23.

Corporation Law.[18] However, with the coming into force of the Disclosure Law on 15 August 1969,[19] Germany established accounting and disclosure requirements, including group accounts, for all enterprises of major size regardless of their legal form. The criteria are: (1) Balance sheet total more than DM 150 million (2) Turnover more than DM 250 million (3) Employees more than 5,000. Two of the three criteria must be met by the enterprise in order for it to be subject to the Disclosure Law.

Making the consolidation requirement conditional upon the legal form of the enterprises, or of an enterprise, in the group can lead to purely fortuitous results. For example, a group consisting principally of partnerships must draw up and publish group accounts if only one single group undertaking in any of the EEC Member States has the form of a limited liability company. If this dependent undertaking were to change its legal form (which in such a case would be advisable), or if the relationship of dependence was terminated, there would no longer be any compulsion to prepare group accounts.

IV. World-Wide Group Accounts

A. The Principle

According to the draft Directive, the annual accounts of all the group undertakings must be included in the consolidated group accounts regardless of where their registered offices are situated.[20] The resulting consolidation thus represents world-wide group accounts. For the purpose of giving a complete true and fair view of the assets, liabilities, financial position and results of the group this is to be welcomed. Naturally, the preparation of such world-wide group accounts gives rise to a number of practical difficulites of which I will mention only a few.

B. Problems

The individual companies included in a multinational group draw up their annual accounts in accordance with the various local national accounting regulations and principles. Before consolidation, the form of presentation and, above all, the method of valuation of the items in the individual companies' accounts must be made to conform to the Fourth EEC Directive and to the procedures applied by the dominant group undertaking.[21] For this purpose it is usually necessary for the group companies to draw up a second set of accounts purely for consolidation purposes. This requires considerable organization, time and expense, for numerous reasons. For instance, the translation of foreign currencies is a particularly difficult problem which has to be resolved. I cannot go into this complicated question here, but I note that the draft Directive does not make any

[18] Sec. 329 AktG/Sec. 28 EG AktG.
[19] Publizitätsgesetz 1969.
[20] Art. 6 (2), Draft Directive.
[21] Art. 15, Draft Directive.

mention of this matter. In addition, obtaining the necessary information for the consolidation can give rise to difficulties. Here the draft Directive has a disarmingly pragmatic solution: in Art. 2 (5) b it provides that the power to exercise a dominant influence shall be considered excluded where

> insurmountable difficulties prevent the information necessary for drawing up the group accounts in accordance with this Directive from being obtained.

All of these difficulties can, however, be resolved in practice and must be considered as a price worth paying for the considerably more meaningful presention of the group's position. Accordingly, at least in Germany, more and more of the larger companies are already producing world-wide consolidated accounts on a voluntary basis.

V. Exemption from Group Accounts

The preparation of group accounts is an expensive exercise, especially if the consolidation includes all group companies on a world-wide basis. Smaller companies, which might well operate internationally, cannot be expected to incur the heavy expense involved. In such a case the interests of disclosure of information must give way to the fully justified interest of such a smaller undertaking not to have to maintain an accounting department which is excessive for its real needs. The draft Directive has recognized this situation, but has set the minimum levels for exemption much too low. According to Art. 6 (1) (a) and Art. 8 (a) (which have not yet been finally agreed to), the Member States may grant exemption from the requirement to draw up group accounts if the limits of two of the three criteria defined in Art. 11 of the Fourth EEC Directive are not exceeded at group level. These criteria are:

(1) Balance sheet total: 1,000,000 EUA[22]
(2) Net turnover: 2,000,000 EUA
(3) Average number of employees during the year: 50

One wonders which small undertakings the draft Directive had in mind when setting these limits. The accounting requirements can hardly be met with one or two book-keepers. Moreover, there is also the obligation to publish a group annual report and to have the group accounts examined by an independent auditor.[23] In this case, the draft Directive has, in my opinion, failed completely to establish a reasonable relationship between the work and expense involved and the value of the information disclosed. In this connection, it is interesting to note that the Group of Experts on International Standards of Accounting and Reporting commissioned by the United Nations Organization, which is in other respects much more radical, has recommended that group accounts should only be required from undertakings of the following size:

[22] In autumn 1980, 1,000,000 EUA = approx. DM 2,850,000 = approx. U.S. $ 1,582,000.

[23] Art. 23, Draft Directive.

(1) Total assets: more than US$ 50 million
(2) Net turnover: more than US$ 100 million
(3) Employees: more than 2,500

The limits set by the German Disclosure Law are in the same region. The reasonable limit is probably somewhere between these figures and the criteria provided in the draft Directive.

VI. Sub-Group Accounts

A. The Requirement of Sub-Group Consolidated Accounts

A very controversial subject contained in the draft Directive is the obligation to draw up sub-group consolidated accounts. The current version of the draft Directive[24] provides that each dependent group undertaking through which other group undertakings are dominated, regardless of where the registered office of the dominating undertaking is situated, must draw up sub-group

Table 1
Group Structure

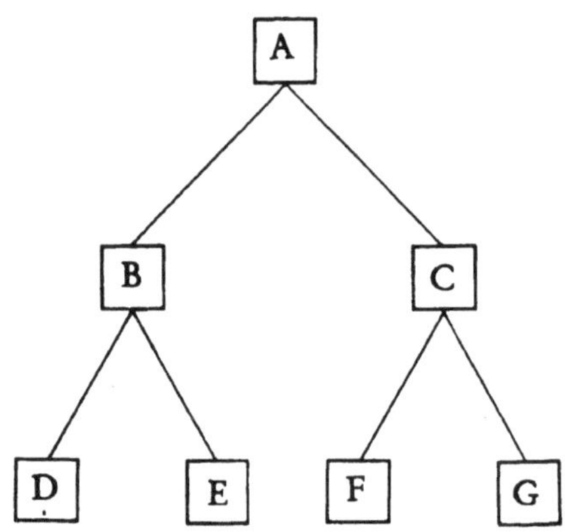

Table 2
Geographical Allocation

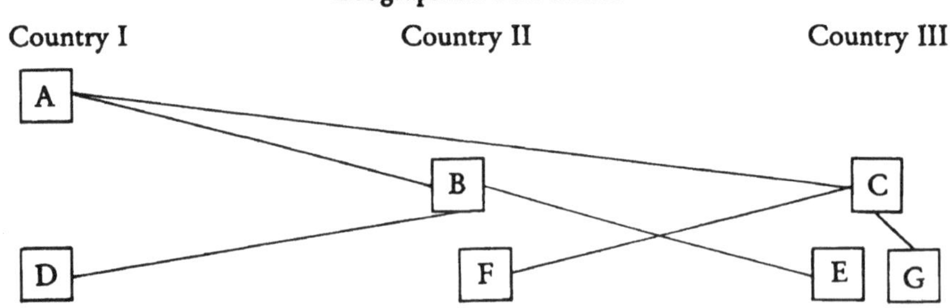

[24] Art. 6a (1), Draft Directive.

In case of such a group structure (table 1) and such a geographical allocation (table 2) the following sets of annual accounts will be necessary:

Table 3
Annual Accounts of the Group

	Differing methods of valuation			Differing translation of currencies	
Accounts in accordance with	National law/Local currency (individual company accounts)	Uniform valuation principles for sub-group accounts	Uniform valuation principles for the whole group	Currency for sub-group	Currency for whole group
Company	Accounts I	Accounts II	Accounts III		
A	x				
B	x		x		x
C	x		x		x
D	x	x	x	x	x
E	x	x	x	x	x
F	x	x	x	x	x
G	x	x	x	x	x

consolidated accounts. This means group accounts at practically every level of the group. Here one must ask whether too much disclosure of information is being required, and moreover, of information which is not of great importance but which will cause the undertaking a considerable amount of additional work and expense. E. Müller[25] has given an example of the various sets of accounts which would be necessary under this provision in the case of a group comprising the group companies A-G which is demonstrated in Tables 1, 2 and 3.

B. Secondary or Primary Function of Sub-Group Accounts

It cannot be denied that, as in the case of the annual accounts of the individual group companies, the sub-group consolidated accounts can also only give an incomplete picture, since a true impression of the sub-group's position cannot be obtained if it is divorced from the whole group. In recognition of this fact, German law only requires subgroup accounts where the dominant entity does not prepare group accounts which include the dependent entity.[26] This shows clearly the subsidiary nature of the sub-group accounts. The provision in the draft Directive is based on a completely different philosophy which does not regard the sub-group accounts as a subsidiary but rather as a primary obligation of the dependent group members. In the *Explanatory Memorandum* the following statement is made:

[25] Müller, *supra* note 5, at 265-266.
[26] Sec. 330 AktG; Sec. 11 (3) PublG.

The Commission considers that sub-group accounts play a useful part in supplementing the information already given in the group accounts and add to the protection of the various parties having an interest in dependent group companies required to draw up such accounts. The shareholders and creditors of such companies obtain a better view of their company's position, since in place of a mere reference to the book value of their holdings, a complete rundown is given of the situation and activities of that part of the group in which they are particularly concerned. Obviously, this provides no more than supplementary information in addition to that given in the company's annual accounts and the group accounts. Moreover, this information cannot be evaluated without these other two documents. The situation might arise, for example, where the sub-group accounts showed a profit while the group accounts showed a loss. Both sets of information are important for shareholders in dependent group companies.[27]

I will not deny that there are arguments to justify sub-group accounts to a certain extent. I think, however, that it is not so much the shareholders (since the majority of the group companies are wholly owned) but rather other interested parties such as creditors, employees and their organizations who would be very much interested in these segment accounts, particularly when the whole group accounts are available for comparison purposes. There is no doubt that this would enable interesting conclusions to be drawn and controls to be effected. However, one must be careful because the part of the whole group which is not consolidated in the sub-group accounts is treated as an outside third party which means, for example, that intercompany profits will not be eliminated.

C. Exemption from Sub-Group Accounting Requirement

However, the example which I have demonstrated seems to warrant the question whether the necessary expense is justified by the very limited additional information provided by the sub-group accounts. The draft Directive takes this point into consideration and provides that Member States may grant exemption from the obligation to draw up sub-group accounts, where the following conditions are fulfilled:

(1) the annual accounts of the undertakings forming the sub-group are consolidated in the whole group accounts;

(2) the group consolidated accounts and annual report are published together with the auditors' report;

(3) Shareholders holding at least 90% of the shares in each of the limited liability companies forming part of the sub-group have declared their agreement to the exemption (first solution)

or

Shareholders holding at least 10% of the shares in each of the limited liability companies forming part of the sub-group have not objected to the exemption (second solution);

(4) Creditors of any limited liability company forming part of the group have not objected to the exemption;

(5) the number of employees of the sub-group does not exceed 250.

[27] *Supra* note 1, at p. 24.

The situation here is similar to that relating to the criteria for the exemption from whole group accounts; the conditions for exemption more or less ensure that in practice an exemption will hardly be possible. For example, how can the consent of all the creditors of each of the limited companies in the subgroup be obtained? In my opinion, it would be preferable either to emphasize the subsidiary character of sub-group accounts or perhaps to combine this with a joint liability on the part of the group's dominant company, or to make sub-group accounts obligatory if certain size criteria are exceeded in the sub-group. Such size criteria must, however, be fixed considerably above those provided in the draft Directive (somewhere in the region of the limits set by the German Disclosure Law). Only then would I regard the additional work and expense required of the companies to be acceptable. In considering the work involved, it must be remembered that the sub-group accounts will always be drawn up in a currency different to that of the whole group accounts, namely in the currency of each country in which the registered office of the dominant company of each sub-group is situated. For the whole group accounts, or even in sub-group accounts at a higher level, the items in the accounts of the companies included in the sub-group must again be translated into another currency and must also possibly be revalued in accordance with other valuation rules.[28] A really frightening task![29]

D. Sub-Group Accounts of EEC Subsidiaries of Non-EEC Parents

Where the dominant undertaking of the group is domiciled outside the EEC and there are, within the EEC, several dependent undertakings on the same level in relation to the dominant undertaking of the group, then each of these dependent

Table 4

Group Structure and Geographical Allocation

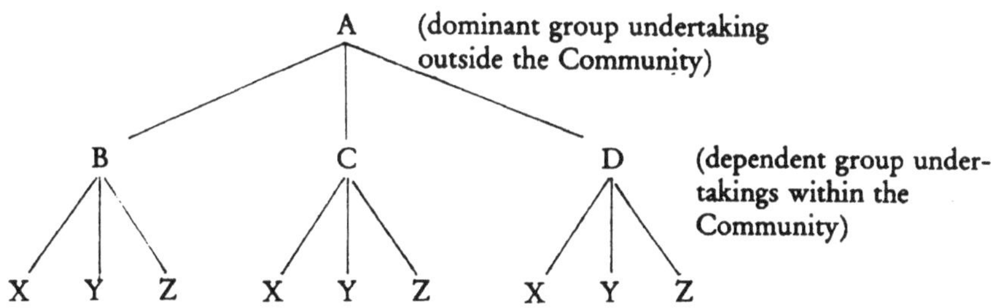

[28] Art. 15 (c), Draft Directive.

[29] There seems to be more flexibility in the recent discussion by the European Commission. The Commission now seems to be prepared to exempt the group's subsidiaries from providing sub-group accounts if the parent company presents consolidated accounts that are deemed to be comparable to the provisions of EEC legislation. Probably there would be no difficulty for American or Swedish parent companies to satisfy this concept of comparability. However, difficulties might possibly arise for Swiss parent companies.

undertakings must draw up sub-group accounts which include all the dependent (same level) undertakings. In other words, they must prepare horizontal sub-group accounts. This situation is best presented by the following example (see table 4):

Under the provisions of Art. 6 (a) of the draft Directive,[30] B, C and D must draw up sub-group accounts; each of these sub-groups will include the relevant subsidiaries X, Y and Z. In addition to this, however, they must under Art. 6 (b) also prepare another set of subgroup accounts, i. e. B will consolidate C and D, including subsidiaries; C will consolidate B and D, including subsidiaries; and D will consolidate B and C, including susidiaries. This obviously exaggerated disclosure obligation would lead to six sets of group accounts in the example I have given. However, this exaggeration is recognized by the draft Directive which provides that it will suffice if only one of the undertakings B, C or D prepares sub-group accounts which include the other two plus subsidiaries. In this case, in my opinion, it would be consistent to require that these sub-group accounts also be published by the other group companies of the same level. I could not, however, find any such requirement in the draft Directive.[31] One is only surprised that, as opposed to the earlier versions, the current version of the draft Directive contains no provision for exemption from these horizontal sub-group accounts. In this respect the horizontal group provisions of the draft Directive are more stringent than the requirements for vertical group accounts. In my opinion, exemption should always be granted from such horizontal group accounts, which are only of limited significance, where the company heading the whole group voluntarily publishes group accounts which largely comply with the provisions of the Fourth and Seventh EEC Directives. Furthermore, the draft Directive or the national legislators should consider how the undertakings concerned are to obtain the necessary information concerning the various sister companies and their subsidiaries, since they have no right to demand such information. The preparation of the sub-group accounts will in many cases only be possible with the cooperation of the company heading the whole group. This company is, however, not subject to the jurisdiction of an EEC Member State.

E. The Case of Horizontal Groups

On the other hand it seems logical for the draft Directive to make it compulsory for a horizontal group to draw up group accounts.[32] Doubts have also been expressed in this respect, namely that it would be very difficult to obtain the necessary data where the undertakings are (by definition) independent of each other. As opposed to the previous example which I have just described, I do not think that these objections are justified, because in a horizontal group there will be a permanent flow of information between the undertakings for accounting

[30] Described *supra* § 3.
[31] Perhaps Art. 24 might have this result.
[32] Art. 7, Draft Directive.

purposes. It is sufficient if at least one of the undertakings on the same level draws up group accounts. However, in my opinion, the draft Directive should again in this case make it clear that each of these undertakings must publish the group accounts.

VII. Consolidation Methods and the Treatment of Minority Interests

A. Methods of Consolidation

Naturally, I cannot go into the details of the technical and accounting problems which arise in connection with the preparation of the consolidated group accounts. I should like, however, to draw attention to some of these problems.

Consolidation is basically the combination of the assets and liabilities of the group companies in a consolidated balance sheet. The book values of the dominant group undertaking's holdings in the capital of the dependent group undertakings are replaced by the corresponding percentage of the capital of the undertakings in question including reserves, results and results brought forward. Intercompany debtors and creditors within the group are set off against each other and intercompany profits and losses arising from transactions within the group are eliminated. The draft Directive has adopted the so-called *"Anglo-Saxon" method of consolidation.* Under this method the book value of the dominant group undertaking's holding in a subsidiary is set off against the corresponding percentage of the subsidiary's capital and reserves (= net assets) as they stood at the time of the acquisition of the holding. In Germany in particular this will mean a change in the consolidation procedure. Hitherto this set-off of the book value of the holding against the corresponding percentage of the subsidiary's capital and reserves has been made each year at the date of the group accounts. Under this method the changes in the subsidiary's reserves during its group membership will disappear into the consolidation differences and will not be shown under the group reserves in the group accounts. The "Anglo-Saxon" method provided in the draft Directive is clearly to be preferred because of the fuller information which it gives on the group results.

Differences arising from the set-off of the book value of the holding and the corresponding percentage of the subsidiary's capital and reserves shall be entered, *as far as possible* (per the latest version of the draft Directive), directly against the relevant items in the group consolidated balance sheet. This is illustrated by the following example:

Acquisition of 100% of the shares in A at cost	1,000,000
Capital and reserves (= net assets) of A	600,000
Difference	400,000
Secret reserves (= undervalued assets) in A	200,000
Goodwill	200,000

The relevant individual tangible assets of A will be written up by 200,000 in the consolidated balance sheet. In practice, this means that a valuation must be carried out of the undertaking to be consolidated with all the problems connected therewith. This can be accepted so long as the draft Directive's proviso "*as far as possible*" remains in force.

Where consolidation differences cannot be entered wholly or in part against the various items in the group consolidated balance sheet and are shown as such as a separate item on the assets side, the amount shall be treated as goodwill[33] and shall be written off in the group accounts within five years. The Member States can, however, permit a longer period for the write-off. In my opinion, it would be desirable for the Member States to do this. Particularly in the case of the acquisition of an undertaking with high earnings, the consolidation difference (goodwill) can be considerable. A compulsory write-off over five years could have a material effect on the group results and could even lead to a loss being reported although the aquisition was a good one for the group to make.

B. Full or Proportional Consolidation

The assets and liabilities and the income and expenditure of the group undertakings included in the group accounts shall be *incorporated in full* in the consolidated group accounts not merely in proportion to the holdings in the companies concerned.[34] This is in keeping with the concept that the group is an "economic entity". The shares held by persons outside the group in the capital and reserves and the results of dependent group undertakings shall be shown as separate items in the group consolidated accounts. There are, therefore, two classes of proprietary interest in the economic entity of the group namely, the majority or dominant interest and the minority interest. Although this concept is not consistently followed in all respects – for example, there is no new valuation of the reserves and goodwill attributable to the minority shareholders – it forms the basis for most of the rules for the consolidation of the group companies.

C. The Case of Joint Ventures

An exception to this concept is the provision in Art. 18 of the draft Directive which permits consolidation on a proportional basis in the case of a joint venture, i. e. of an undertaking managed jointly with one or more other undertakings which do not form part of the group.

Using this method, asset and liability items and income and expenditure items contained in the annual accounts of an undertaking managed jointly are incorporated into the group accounts on a *pro rata basis* according to the percentage of the capital held by the group.

The argument used against this method of consolidation, particularly in Germany where it is at present not permitted, is that it contradicts the single unit theory. The legal construction of a joint venture is such that, as a rule, having

[33] Art. 16, Draft Directive; Art. 37, Fourth Directive, *supra* note 3.

[34] Art. 12 (2), 13, Draft Directive.

regard to the influence exercised by the participants in the undertaking and the sharing of the resulting profits, a pro rata allocation clearly reflects the actual circumstances. For the purpose of presenting a true and fair view of the group's assets, liabilities, financial position and results, exclusion of the share in the joint venture would be just as wrong as a full consolidation. It should not be overlooked that a considerable volume of business is transacted by means of joint ventures, and in this connection one need only think of the consortia which are formed for the purpose of carrying out many major projects. Incidentally, the draft Directive makes no reference to the question of whether a joint venture is a group undertaking or not.

D. So-Called Associated Enterprises

A basic change, at least for Germany, is the treatment in the group accounts of the so-called associated undertaking. This means an undertaking over which another undertaking exercises, directly or indirectly, a significant influence. An undertaking is presumed to be associated with another undertaking where the latter undertaking holds, directly or indirectly, 20% or more of the capital of the former undertaking or of the votes attaching to the shares issued by that undertaking.[35] It should be noted, however, that an associated undertaking is not a group undertaking.

The draft Directive provides[36] that associated undertakings should be valued by the equity method for the purpose of inclusion in the group consolidated balance sheet. This method of valuation is in effect a "mini-consolidation". The associated undertakings are shown as investment holdings under a separate heading in the group consolidated balance sheet. The amount of any differences existing when such holdings were acquired between their purchase price and the corresponding percentage of the capital and reserves (– net assets) of such associated undertakings, shall be shown separately in the group consolidated balance sheet or in the notes to the accounts. The process is essentially the same as the full consolidation procedure, and for the purpose of valuing the holdings in the associated undertakings the "consolidation difference" will be dealt with in the same way. This means that, where appropriate, the value of the holding must be reduced by the amount of the difference.[37] In order to be able to analyse the composition of the "consolidation difference" an insight into the accounting records of the associated undertaking will be necessary. The purchase price of holdings in the capital of an associated company must be increased or reduced in the group consolidated balance sheet by a proportion, corresponding to the percentage of the capital held, of the profit or loss accruing to the associated undertaking irrespective of whether the associated undertaking is to distribute its profits or not. However, where the associated undertaking distributes dividends to the group undertaking, the book value of the holding in the group consolidated balance sheet must be reduced accordingly.

[35] Art. 1, Draft Directive.

[36] Art. 17, Draft Directive.

[37] In an extreme case within five years, Art. 17, Draft Directive.

Profits and losses arising from transactions with the associated undertaking must be eliminated in full. In my opinion, this elimination of intercompany profits and losses is inconsistent. Associated undertakings are not a part of the "economic unit" and transactions with them should therefore be treated as transactions with third parties; at the most there should only be a proportional elimination. In general, however, I think that the valuation of associated undertakings by the equity method is acceptable in practice, since it contributes to the objective that the group accounts should give a true and fair view of the group's assets, liabilities, financial position and results.

The question which remains, however, is whether and how the group will be able to obtain the necessary information in order to apply the equity method of valuation, when it only owns between 20% and 50% of the associated undertaking. But this problem will also be resolved in practice by the simple argument that where the necessary information cannot be obtained the presumption of significant influence is rebutted;[38] and the holding should not therefore be valued by the equity method.

VIII. Conclusion

I have only been able to select a few of the problems arising from the proposed Seventh EEC Directive. I have not dealt with the difficult questions relating to valuation or to the notes to the accounts, or to the audit and publication of the group accounts. I have excluded these matters because they are, at least in part, also relevant to the annual accounts of individual companies and the problems connected therewith are already known.

One last remark: From the viewpoint of the parties most interested in the forthcoming regulations who are principally the undertakings which will be required to prepare group accounts, but also the readers of such accounts, it would be very desirable for the Seventh Directive to come into force as soon as possible. The regulations relating to group accounts could then, as far as possible, be incorporated into the national legislations together with the regulations of the Fourth Directive relating to the annual accounts of individual undertakings. The two areas of accounting are so closely tied to each other that they should, from the outset, be dealt with simultaneously.

[38] Art. 1 (1), Draft Directive.

Résumé:

La comptabilité des groupes et la proposition d'une septième directive du point de vue de la pratique

Le droit comptable et la pratique seront influencés et transformés au cours des prochaines années par différentes Directives du Conseil des Communautés Européennes, en particulier la quatrième Directive, déjà en vigueur, ainsi que la septième. Cette dernière réalisera une harmonisation de la comptabilité des groupes à l'intérieur de la CEE. De plus la septième Directive, à des degrés divers selon les différents États-Membres de la CEE, exigera des entreprises commerciales qu'elles prennent plus en considération les problèmes de comptabilité des groupes. Cette contribution traite de questions telles que: la définition d'un groupe dans l'optique de la comptabilité des groupes, les types de société concernés, les exonérations pour les comptes des groupes, le problème de la comptabilité des sous-groupes, les méthodes de consolidation et de traitement des intérêts minoritaires.

Chapter/Chapitre IV

Multinational Groups of Companies: Banks, Labour, Taxes

Les Groupes de sociétés multinationaux: banques, travail, fisc

La surveillance administrative d'un groupe multinational: L'exemple des banques multinationales

ALAIN HIRSCH
Genève

I. Introduction

1. Nous examinerons ici la surveillance des banques multinationales non dans une perspective de droit bancaire, mais pour illustrer certains problèmes généraux posés par les sociétés multinationales. En effet, la surveillance des banques a pour but essentiel la protection des déposants. La surveillance des banques multinationales est donc confrontée aux problèmes posés par la protection des créanciers dans les sociétés multinationales. D'autre part, l'exemple des banques dépasse le cadre du droit privé et relève en partie du droit administratif économique, puisque la protection des déposants est généralement assurée par un système de surveillance administrative, visant à prévenir les dommages plutôt qu'à les réparer. Or, les sociétés multinationales, vu leur importance économique, sont parfois soumises à une certaine surveillance administrative, notamment lorsqu'elles font appel au public pour se financer.

2. Du fait que les banques multinationales sont soumises à la surveillance de plusieurs autorités nationales différentes, les conflits de compétence s'ajoutent aux conflits de lois. En matière administrative, ces conflits de compétence sont bien plus difficiles à règler qu'en matière judiciaire, car l'autorité administrative est traditionellement territoriale. En outre, la coopération internationale des autorités administratives nationales est encore aujourd'hui embryonnaire dans tous les domaines (par exemple, en matière fiscale, en droit de la concurrence, etc.). En effet, ces autorités sont souvent chargées de poursuivre des buts d'intérêt national, qui peuvent être différents, voire même contradictoires.

En matière bancaire, la coopération internationale des autorités de surveillance ne fait que commencer depuis quelques années.[1] Néanmoins, elle semble avoir des perspectives intéressantes, car les autorités compétentes comprennent de plus en plus qu'en l'absence d'une coopération internationale, la surveillance des banques multinationales est illusoire. Cette expérience est déjà d'un très grand prix pour l'étude générale des sociétés multinationales.

[1] En particulier dans le cadre du *"groupe de contact"* créé à cet effet en 1974 par le *"Groupe des dix"* à Bâle, portant traditionnellement le nom de son président: *"Blunden Committee"*, puis *"Cooke Committee"*.

3. Nous nous limiterons ici aux problèmes posés par la surveillance classique des banques *("prudential supervision")*, visant à empêcher les déconfitures bancaires, dans l'intérêt des créanciers; nous n'aborderons pas les réglementations bancaires inspirées par la politique monétaire nationale ou internationale.

Nous examinerons tout d'abord les problèmes posés par les banques ayant certaines activités à l'étranger, notamment par l'intermédiaire de succursales, *("branches")*, c'est-à-dire d'établissements sans personnalité juridique. Nous examinerons ensuite, et de manière plus approfondie, le cas plus délicat et plus fréquent des banques exerçant leurs activités à l'étranger par l'intermédiaire de filiales *("subsidiaries")*; nous partirons de l'idée qu'il s'agit de filiales à 100% ou en tout cas de filiales manifestement contrôlées par la banque-mère. Nous ne ferons qu'une brève allusion pour terminer au cas spécial des filiales communes *("joint ventures")*, c'est-à-dire des filiales ayant deux ou plusieurs banques-mères.

Il convient de souligner que ce sujet est encore très nouveau. Il n'y a donc pratiquement encore aucune doctrine publiée à ce sujet et les seuls articles disponibles émanent de personnalités responsables de la surveillance des banques.[2]

II. Activités bancaires à l'étranger

A. Activités à l'étranger sans succursale

4. Une banque peut avoir des activités occasionnelles ou régulières à l'étranger, sans y avoir installé un établissement. Ainsi, elle peut consentir des prêts à l'étranger ou y acquérir des participations. Elle peut recevoir (ou même solliciter) des fonds provenant de clients étrangers. Elle peut offrir ses services pour des opérations à l'étranger ou intéressant des clients étrangers: achat et vente de titres ou autres valeurs, accréditifs ou autres formes de garantie, etc.

Toutes ces opérations "étrangères" font partie intégrante de l'activité de la banque. Elles relèvent donc normalement de l'autorité de surveillance du siège de la banque, exactement comme s'il s'agissait d'opérations purement "nationales".

[2] *Cf.* G. Blunden, *International Cooperation in Banking Supervision*, BANK OF ENGLAND QUARTERLY BULLETIN 17/3 (Septembre, 1977); U. H. Schneider, *Bankenaufsicht im Konzern*, WM 1978, 1249; I. L. Bähre, *Bankenaufsicht – international?*, DEUTSCHE BANK, BEITRÄGE ZU WIRTSCHAFTS- UND WÄHRUNGSFRAGEN 1978/16; B. Müller, *Die Internationalisierung der Banken als aufsichtsrechtliches Problem*, SCHWEIZERISCHE AKTIENGESELLSCHAFT 1979, p. 1; M. Schneider, *Internationale Aspekte der Bankenaufsicht*, in WIRTSCHAFTSPRÜFUNG UND WIRTSCHAFTSRECHT, BEITRÄGE ZUM 75JÄHRIGEN BESTEHEN DER TREUHANDVEREINIGUNG (Stuttgart, 1980); International Faculty for Corporate and Capital Market Law, *Regulation of Multinational Banking Institutions, Geneva Symposium*, 3 JOURNAL OF COMPARATIVE CORPORATE LAW AND SECURITIES REGULATION 49 (1981); Conference on the Internationalization of the Capital Markets, New York, 19.-21. 3. 1981; les documents de la conférence (396 pp.) sont disponibles, chez l'American Law Institute, 4025 Chestnut Street, Philadelphia, Pa. 19104 U.S.A.

La surveillance de l'autorité du siège peut cependant se heurter à des difficultés pratiques. En effet, il n'est pas toujours facile à l'autorité de contrôler des opérations étrangères, effectuées dans un contexte économique et juridique qu'elle connaît mal. Parfois, certains contrôles devraient être faits à l'étranger, où l'autorité ne dispose d'aucune compétence officielle, son intervention pouvant même se heurter à une interdiction du droit public étranger.[3]

5. D'autre part, comment ces opérations sont-elles considérées par l'Etat du lieu où elles sont exercées? En pratique, s'il s'agit d'activités occasionelles, l'Etat local ne les soumet pas à des mesures de surveillance particulières. Toutefois, si ces activités deviennent importantes, la constitution d'une succursale devient parfois indispensable. Certains pays exigent même la constitution d'une succursale pour pouvoir exercer certaines activités,[4] par exemple pour pouvoir solliciter des dépôts de fonds.

B. Succursales à l'étranger

6. Economiquement, la succursale est un établissement relativement indépendant, dont l'activité peut ressembler à celle d'une banque locale. Juridiquement, au contraire, la succursale n'est qu'une partie de la société qui l'a créée: elle n'a aucune indépendance juridique. Ses actifs appartiennent juridiquement à la société; ses créanciers sont juridiquement créanciers de la société.

Relevons cependant qu'en cas d'insolvabilité, le problème se complique parfois. En effet, certaines législations connaissent une procédure spéciale de faillite pour les succursales dépendant des sociétés étrangères. Ces faillites ne portent que sur les actifs de la succursale et seuls les créanciers de la succursale peuvent y participer. Une telle procédure revient donc, en cas d'insolvabilité, à conférer une certaine indépendance juridique à la succursale.

7. En matière bancaire, les activités des succursales étrangères sont donc juridiquement imputables à la banque dont elles dépendent. Chaque législation sur les banques s'applique donc intégralement aux succursales étrangères des banques nationales, qui sont surveillées par l'autorité administrative nationale comme s'il s'agissait de succursales établies dans le pays.

8. L'Etat du lieu où la succursale est établie prétend toutefois aussi la réglementer. Les législations bancaires s'appliquent en principe aux succursales des banques étrangères établies sur le territoire national, même si les règles sont parfois différentes de celles applicables aux banques nationales.[5]

[3] En outre, la coopération de l'autorité bancaire étrangère se heurte parfois à l'obstacle juridique du secret de fonction. Certaines lois autorisent maintenant expressément la coopération internationale des autorités de surveillance bancaire (par exemple en Belgique, art. 40 de l'arrêté royal de 1935, modifié par la loi du 30 juin 1975. *Cf.* aussi art. 12 de la directive "banques" CEE du 12 décembre 1977, J.O.C.E. 1977 L 322/30.)

[4] Cette exigence peut sembler contraire au principe de la libre prestation des services dans la Communauté européenne. Il faut cependant reconnaître que la prestation de services, en matière bancaire, est souvent liée à un mouvement de capitaux; or la liberté des mouvements de capitaux est encore loin d'être réalisée au sein du marché commun.

[5] *Cf.*, par exemple, en Suisse, art. 2 al. 2 de la loi sur les banques (RS 952.02) et

Du point de vue de la protection des créanciers, la surveillance séparée d'une succursale bancaire est cependant illusoire, dès lors qu'une grande partie de ses actifs est généralement située à l'étranger. Or, en cas d'insolvabilité, c'est pratiquement la loi du pays de situation qui décidera si ces actifs doivent être remis au pays de la succursale ou au pays de la banque principale. Par conséquent, les législations bancaires devraient, en bonne logique, imposer que les actifs de la succursale restent intégralement situés sur le territoire national, ce qui serait évidemment excessif. Seule la Belgique connaît une réglementation de ce genre (les actifs situés en Belgique devant être au moins équivalents aux passifs "belges").[6]

Si la plupart des législations prétendent néanmoins s'appliquer aux succursales des banques étrangères, quitte à prévoir certaines exceptions, c'est probablement parce que le législateur ne veut pas admettre son impuissance dans ce domaine. C'est aussi, et peut-être surtout, dans un but d'égalité de concurrence, pour garantir aux banques nationales que les banques étrangères ne peuvent par leur faire localement concurrence en étant soumises à des règles moins strictes.

9. Ainsi, dans la plupart des cas, la succursale d'une banque étrangère est soumise cumulativement à deux lois et à deux autorités: celle où elle exerce son activité et celle du pays où la banque a son siège. Cette situation peut créer des complications importantes pour la succursale en la soumettant toujours à la règle la plus stricte de deux législations, voire en la soumettant à des exigences contradictoires. Des conflits peuvent même se produire entre les autorités nationales chargées de surveiller les banques. Nous examinerons ces problèmes plus bas, car ils se posent de la même manière dans le cas des filiales étrangères.

Contentons-nous de relever ici que, s'agissant de succursales, on tend aujourd'hui à admettre qu'il serait théoriquement préférable de les soumettre au contrôle unique de l'autorité de surveillance du siège de la banque. Seule la Grande Bretagne a appliqué jusqu'ici ce principe en pratique. Les Etats membres du marché commun ont décidé de l'établir progressivement entre eux,[7] mais au prix d'une harmonisation préalable des législations bancaires nationales, éliminant ainsi les problèmes d'inégalité de concurrence; cette harmonisation devrait prendre encore un bon nombre d'années.

III. Filiales bancaires à l'étranger

A. La filiale: banque juridiquement indépendante

10. Une société filiale reste formellement une société juridiquement indépendante. Elle a son propre patrimoine et ses propres créanciers, qui ne se confondent pas avec le patrimoine ou les créanciers de la société-mère ou du groupe tout

ordonnance de la Commission fédérale des banques du 14 septembre 1973 (RS 952.III).

[6] Art. 10 de l'arrêté royal de 1935 (modifié par le loi de 1935). Quelques États américains ont adopté des règles analogues.

[7] Première directive "banques" CEE du 12 décembre 1977, en vigueur depuis l'année 1980, publiée au J.O.C.E. 1977 L 322/30.

entier. En principe, si la filiale devient insolvable, ses créanciers n'ont pas de droit contre les autres sociétés du groupe.

Par conséquent, la filiale d'une banque est d'abord considérée comme une banque indépendante. Elle est intégralement soumise au droit bancaire de son siège et elle est surveillée par l'autorité compétente de son siège. Ce principe semble incontesté et même incontestable.

Nous allons en revanche examiner deux problèmes très délicats: dans quelle mesure l'autorité de surveillance du siège de la banque-mère peut-elle étendre ses préoccupations aux filiales bancaires à l'étranger? Dans quelle mesure l'autorité de surveillance de la filiale peut-elle, à son tour, étendre ses préoccupations à la banque-mère, voire aux autres filiales?

B. L'autorité responsable de la banque-mère et le groupe multinational

11. Traditionnellement, la législation sur les banques n'est pas applicable aux filiales étrangères d'une banque nationale. Ces filiales se reflètent simplement dans le bilan de la banque-mère, sous la forme d'une participation, éventuellement d'une avance. L'autorité bancaire de la banque-mère doit donc simplement s'assurer (tâche bien limitée, même si elle n'est pas toujours aisée) que ces valeurs au bilan ne sont pas trop élevées.

12. Cependant, depuis quelques années, les autorités bancaires ont compris que cette approche était insuffisante, parfois même illusoire. En effet, les banques multinationales sont pratiquement gérées comme une seule entreprise, même lorsqu'elles développent leurs activités étrangères par l'intermédiaire de filiales. D'ailleurs, le choix de constituer une filiale ou une succursale dans un pays déterminé est souvent dicté par le hasard des lois locales plus que par les réalités économiques. En matière bancaire, le crédit du groupe est manifestement lié à celui de chaque filiale. Souvent, la filiale porte même le nom de la banque mère; sinon, elle se réfère d'une autre manière au groupe bancaire dont elle fait partie. Les déposants n'accordent guère d'importance à "leur" filiale, mais au groupe bancaire dont elle dépend.

Ainsi, une banque multinationale ne peut guère songer, sauf cas tout à fait exceptionnel, à laisser l'une de ses filiales tomber en faillite, ou même connaître des difficultés de paiement. Si une filiale connaît des difficultés, la banque-mère doit la soutenir économiquement, qu'elle le veuille ou non, dans son propre intérêt. Economiquement, une filiale bancaire ne se distingue donc guère d'une succursale.

13. Face à cette situation, les autorités bancaires doivent admettre que le crédit (et finalement la solvabilité) de la banque-mère est lié à celui de son groupe. Elles sont donc amenées à étendre leur surveillance, dans une mesure variable, aux filiales étrangères des banques qu'elles surveillent, par exemple:

(1) en demandant à la banque-mère d'établir un bilan consolidé, en principe conformément à sa loi nationale (notamment en matière de provisions pour risques, etc.)[8];

(2) en faisant contrôler ce bilan comme le bilan ordinaire de la banque-mère[8], ce qui peut entraîner des conflits délicats de compétence avec l'Etat de la filiale, selon le mode de contrôle employé;

(3) en exigeant que, sur la base de ce bilan consolidé, le groupe dans son ensemble dispose de fonds propres suffisants, conformément à la loi de la banque-mère;[8] en revanche, on admet que les règles sur la liquidité ne sont en principe pas applicables à l'ensemble du groupe;
(4) en exigeant que les règles prévues par la loi de la banque-mère pour protéger les créanciers (par exemple répartition des risques, crédits à des dirigeants ou à des actionnaires, etc.) soient également respectées pour l'ensemble du groupe;
(5) en exigeant même parfois (mais encore très rarement aujourd'hui, semble-t-il) que les filiales étrangères respectent dans leur organisation et leurs activités certaines règles prévues par la législation de la banque-mère, par exemple sur l'organisation de la banque, sur les qualifications des dirigeants, sur l'interdiction d'effectuer certaines opérations "non bancaires", etc.;
(6) en soumettant les filiales au système d'assurance des dépôts, obligatoire pour la banque-mère.

14. Cette évolution n'en est aujourd'hui qu'à ses débuts et les difficultés qu'elle soulèvera ne sont donc pas encore apparentes. Mais on voit déjà qu'elle impose le respect simultané de deux lois bancaires pour chaque filiale d'une banque multinationale. Comme nous l'avons vu ci-dessus (ch. 9) pour les succursales, cette solution implique la discussion avec deux autorités administratives, dont les vues peuvent être fort différentes, voire même divergentes ou franchement contradictoires.

En outre, cette évolution comporte aussi le risque de conflits de lois et de compétence entre les Etats concernés.[9] Même si l'Etat de la filiale accepte en

[8] Ainsi par exemple en Suisse, déjà dès 1978 conformément à une circulaire de la Commission fédérale des banques du 17 mai 1978 (Rapport de gestion pour 1978, p. 12), et plus clairement dès 1981 en vertu d'une modification du 1er décembre de l'ordonnance d'exécution de la loi sur les banques (art. 12 al. 2 et art. 44 litt. b).

[9] Dans le rapport de gestion pour 1978 de la Commission fédérale des banques (Suisse), on lit ce qui suit:

La surveillance des banques dans le domaine international

Dans le rapport annuel de 1977, nous avons souligné que les activités internationales croissantes des banques, par l'intermédiaire de leurs filiales et de leurs succursales à l'étranger, mettaient les autorités de surveillance de tous les pays devant des problèmes difficiles; ceux-ci ne pourront être résolus, pendant longtemps encore, que de manière pragmatique.

Il faut également placer dans ce contexte les demandes de renseignements des autorités de surveillance étrangères sur *les modalités selon lesquelles une filiale ou une succursale en Suisse peuvent être contrôlées par la banque mère étrangère et son autorité de surveillance.* Pour répondre à ces questions, la Commissions des banques s'est fondée sur les principes suivants:

– *Une succursale* en Suisse s'intègre juridiquement dans la banque étrangère. Elle fait partie de cette banque et, par conséquent, le secret bancaire qui protège les clients n'est pas opposable aux organes de la banque étrangère. Celle-ci peut diriger et contrôler sa succursale en Suisse selon ses propres prescriptions. Elle peut également charger ses propres inspecteurs du contrôle de la succursale et ceux-ci ont aussi accès à tous les dossiers.

principe l'intervention de l'autorité bancaire étrangère, il peut assortir son accord de certaines conditions; par exemple, en exigeant que les informations ainsi recueillies par l'Etat étranger soient exclusivement utilisées dans des buts de surveillance bancaire et de protection des créanciers: à l'exclusion de toute autre mesure de politique économique, monétaire, fiscale, anti-cartellaire, ou même à l'exclusion de toute procédure pénale.

Il apparaît ainsi que la surveillance des banques multinationales se situe dans un contexte général de politique juridique, où les traditions nationales s'affrontent.

C. L'autorité responsable de la filiale et le groupe bancaire multinational

15. En principe, l'autorité bancaire locale surveille une filiale d'une banque multinationale comme s'il s'agissait d'une banque nationale indépendante. Le fait qu'un groupe bancaire multinational soit géré comme une unité économique doit certes impliquer des compétences accrues pour l'autorité de la banque-mère, non pour celles des succursales ou des filiales. Une solution contraire serait absurde, un groupe multinational ne pouvant pas être soumis à une série de lois différentes, ni être surveillé par une série d'autorités nationales diverses.

16. Ce principe souffre toutefois certaines exceptions, dans des cas particuliers.

Tout d'abord, au moment où une filiale est constituée, l'autorité nationale qui lui donne l'autorisation nécessaire peut à juste titre s'enquérir de la situation financière du groupe bancaire dans son ensemble, comme elle peut s'informer

Comme la succursale est soumise au droit suisse, elle est néanmoins tenue de respecter les prescriptions suisses. Les organes de la banque, et notamment les inspecteurs du service de revision interne étranger, ont le devoir d'exercer leurs activités qui se rapportent à la succursale en Suisse en respectant l'ordre juridique suisse. Des informations et des déclarations aux autorités de surveillance étrangères ne sont autorisées que dans la mesure où il est certain que ces renseigenements ne serviront qu'à des buts de surveillance. Pour éviter des abus et des risques aucune information sur des créanciers ou des débiteurs déterminés ne peut être transmise sans motifs impérieux de surveillance. L'autorité de surveillance étrangère ne peut en aucun cas opérer des contrôles directs dans la succursale.

Les *filiales* sont des personnes juridiques indépendantes et sont totalement soumises au droit suisse. Les actionnaires sont des tiers et le secret bancaire doit être respecté à leur égard. Cependant, dans la mesure où une banque est le principal actionnaire, celle-ci doit être à même de contrôler l'activité de sa filiale en Suisse. Le conseil d'administration de la filiale en Suisse peut donc communiquer aux organes de la banque étrangère les informations nécessaires au contrôle de l'entreprise dans son ensemble. Il peut aussi charger l'institution de revision suisse de communiquer directement certaines informations aux reviseurs de la banque mère étrangère. Il est normal également que le service de revision interne de la banque étrangère fasse les contrôles nécessaires pour établir un bilan consolidé et pour veiller à l'application des règlements du groupe bancaire. Les informations que la banque mère étrangère a reçues à ce titre ne peuvent être transmises à son autorité de surveillance qu'aux mêmes conditions que celles prévues plus haut pour les succursales.

plus généralement sur la personne et la situation économique des fondateurs d'une nouvelle banque.

D'autre part, lorsqu'une banque est la filiale d'une entreprise étrangère non bancaire, l'autorité qui la surveille ne peut alors plus compter sur la surveillance du groupe multinational par l'autorité du siège de la société mère. Il est alors normal que cette autorité demande régulièrement certaines informations sur le groupe, pour vérifier notamment si la banque est gérée de manière indépendante ou si elle est utilisée pour financer les autres sociétés du groupe. Ajoutons que si une entreprise non bancaire a ainsi plusieurs filiales bancaires dans des pays différents, une telle pratique implique la coopération des diverses autorités bancaires concernées.

17. Abstraction faite de ces exceptions, se pose un problème général et plus délicat. Il arrive qu'un groupe bancaire soit dominé par une banque ayant son siège dans un pays n'ayant institué qu'une surveillance insuffisante, ou du moins très inférieure à celle existant au siège de certaines filiales. Il est surtout possible que, dans le pays de la banque-mère l'autorité se borne à surveiller celle-ci, sans étendre sa surveillance au groupe multinational dans son ensemble. Il arrive enfin parfois que certaines filiales prennent une importance considérable dans l'ensemble du groupe, pouvant même atteindre celle de la banque-mère. Dans ces cas, on comprend que l'autorité bancaire d'une filiale se préoccupe de la situation d'ensemble du groupe bancaire multinational. Il serait cependant excessif que, dans un tel cas, les autorités de *chaque* filiale prétendent régir le groupe dans son ensemble. Si une filiale est nettement plus importante que les autres, il serait logique que son autorité assume les fonctions de "chef de file". Sinon, une coopération des diverses autorités nationales semble indispensable.

18. Les États-Unis ont adopté, dans ce domaine, une politique plus ambitieuse. En effet, en novembre 1980,[10] le "*Federal Reserve Board*" a décidé d'obliger les filiales américaines (et naturellement aussi les succursales américaines) des banques étrangères à fournir des informations assez précises sur le groupe bancaire international dont elle dépendent.

Tout d'abord, les filiales américaines doivent fournir trimestriellement des indications détaillées sur les opérations qu'elles ont conclues avec une autre banque (ou société non bancaire) de leur groupe (formule Y-8 f). Ce genre d'information est certainement nécessaire pour le contrôle efficace de la filiale aux Etats-Unis et n'appelle aucune critique.

D'autre part, les filiales américaines doivent fournir annuellement un rapport sur les résultats financiers globaux de leur groupe international (et notamment sur les activités non bancaires que ce groupe exerce aux Etats-Unis) (formule Y-7). En principe, les indications contenues dans ce rapport sont accessibles au public, sauf dérogation accordée dans des cas particuliers par le "*Federal Reserve Board*".

Enfin et surtout, les filiales américaines doivent remettre chaque anée un "rapport confidentiel" sur les opérations de leur groupe international (formule

[10] Lors du colloque de Florence, nous avions commenté les projets de 1979. Ce paragraphe a été mis au point ultérierement, sur la base des textes définitifs.

2.068). Ce rapport doit contenir de nombreuses indications qui ne sont généralement pas publiques, comme les résultats annuels réels (sans constitution ou dissolution de réserves latentes), le détail des pertes sur débiteurs et des pertes sur titres, etc. Malgré son caractère "confidentiel", ce rapport sera entout cas à la disposition des autres autorités américaines chargées de surveiller les banques; en outre, il n'est pas exclu que d'autres autorités américaines puissent en prendre connaissance.

Il est préoccupant de constater la tendance ainsi adoptée par les autorités américaines, qui prétendent ainsi commencer à surveiller globalement les groupes bancaires multinationaux ayant simplement un établissement aux États-Unis. On peut comprendre les raisons qui ont inspiré cette nouvelle exigence, notamment lorsque les filiales bancaires aux États-Unis sont importantes, ou lorsqu'elles dépendent d'un groupe bancaire international qui n'est pas convenablement surveillé par l'autorité responsable de la banque-mère. Dans les autres cas, une telle politique est difficilement acceptable par les autres pays; elle pourrait donc porter un coup sérieux à la coopération internationale des autorités de surveillance, qui commence seulement à s'esquisser. En outre, si d'autres pays adoptaient des pratiques analogues, ce serait le désordre dans la surveillance des banques multinationales. Il faudra donc suivre de près l'application de cette nouvelle réglementation américaine et les modifications qu'elle subira probablement au cours des prochaines années.

D. Filiale bancaire commune

19. Dans ce domaine, aujourd'hui encore inexploré, nous serons particulièrement bref.

Il arrive que deux ou plusieurs banques constituent ensemble une filiale commune à l'étranger. Bien entendu, ces filiales communes ne peuvent pas être assimilées à des succursales, puisqu'elles dépendent de plusieurs groupes bancaires différents. Il n'en reste pas moins que parfois leur crédit est pratiquement lié à celui d'un ou de plusieurs de ces groupes bancaires.

Si une filiale commune devient importante, les autorités bancaires chargées de surveiller les banques-mères souhaiteront obtenir au moins certaines informations sur cette filiale. Dès lors qu'en pratique seulement deux ou trois banques mères sont impliquées, une coopération entre l'autorité de la filiale commune d'une part, les autorités des banques-mères d'autre part, ne devrait pas être trop difficile.

IV. Conclusions

20. Il apparaît aujourd'hui clairement que la surveillance des banques multinationales ne peut pas être convenablement effectuée si chaque autorité nationale se borne à surveiller exclusivement les banques ayant leur siège sur son territoire. Une surveillance globale du groupe bancaire multinational est indispensable.

Pour des raisons évidentes, la surveillance globale d'une banque multinationale doit être en principe assurée par l'autorité compétente pour la banque-mère.

Cette autorité doit pouvoir compter sur la coopération des autorités étrangères chargées de surveiller les filiales, qui doivent à leur tour lui faire confiance.

Cette perspective n'est évidemment possible que si les législations bancaires et l'efficacité pratique de la surveillance sont relativement comparables. Dans les cas où la banque-mère est surveillée de manière insuffisante, d'autres méthodes, plus délicates, doivent être envisagées.

Ces perspectives commencent seulement à être appliquées depuis quelques années, très progressivement. Il sera intéressant d'examiner l'évolution de la coopération internationale des autorités de surveillance au cours des prochaines années, et les difficultés auxquelles elle se heurtera.

Dans le secteur bancaire, la réalité économique des groupes multinationaux est particulièrement frappante. C'est pourquoi le droit ne peut déjà plus l'ignorer. L'unité des groupes industriels ou commerciaux est moins évidente, plus nuancée. L'exemple des banques multinationales est néanmoins intéressant sur un plan plus général.

Summary:

Administrative Control of Multinational Groups: the Example of Multinational Banks

It is clear today that it is not possible effectively to control multinational banks if each national authority is limited to controlling only those banks which have their seat within the national territorial limits. A global supervision of multinational groups of banks is necessary.

For obvious reasons, the world-wide supervision of multinational banks should in principle be assured by the authority in charge of the supervision of the parent bank. This authority should be able to count upon the cooperation of the foreign authorities in charge of supervising the subsidiaries, and, in turn, the latter should have full confidence in the former authority.

Such an approach is certainly not possible unless the banking laws and their practical effect in the various countries involved are relatively similar. Where the parent bank is not sufficiently controlled, other, more delicate, methods would have to be devised.

These views have only begun to emerge in the last few years and have evolved very gradually. It will be interesting to examine the evolution of the international cooperation amongst the controlling authorities over the next few years and to observe the difficulties which they will encounter.

In the banking sector, the economic reality of multinational groups is particularly striking. That is why it is impossible for the law to ignore the phenomenon any longer. The unity of industrial or commercial groups is less evident, more open to nuance, but the case of multinational banks is nevertheless also of interest in a more general perspective.

Labour Law and Multinational Groups of Companies

PAUL L. DAVIES
Oxford

I. Introduction[1]

The 1970's has been a decade which has seen much discussion of and concern expressed about the labour law and labour relations aspects of multinational groups of companies, i. e., typically companies which, incorporated and functioning in one (home) country, operate also through subsidiary companies in one or more other countries. Thus, in the U. K., whereas the evidence of the trade unions to the Royal Commission on Trade Unions and Employers' Association of 1965-1968 made hardly any reference to multinational companies, by 1970 the Trade Union Congress had carried out a special review of the topic, and the activities of multinational companies and ways of controlling them have now become a standard element in the annual reports of the General Council of the T. U. C. to the meetings of the affiliated unions. Evidence of the interest in this topic on the part of trade union movements in other western European countries and in North America could easily be provided. In a general way the interest of national trade union movements in this area is not surprising. It has been pointed out, for example, that there are only four governments in the Western World with national budgets greater than the turnover of General Motors, and that over a quarter of U. K. "exports" are intra-corporate transactions and that one in ten workers in Scotland (an area of high unemployment) is employed by an American multinational.[2] Although it might be argued that the U. K. is in a special position vis-à-vis investment by foreign multinationals because it has been the second largest destination (after Canada) for direct investment by U. S. companies,[3] which make the preponderant – although declining – share of all direct investments by multinational companies, nevertheless it seems likely that at least the smaller European countries (e. g. Belgium and the Netherlands) have an equal dependence upon foreign multinationals; and all European governments in a time of economic recession appear extremely anxious to encourage such investment in their countries.

[1] This paper is written from a Western European and, to a lesser extent, North American perspective. It does not touch on the important topic of multinational companies and developing countries or the important issues raised by the "North-South" dialogue.

[2] K. W. Wedderburn, *Industrial Relations* in H. R. HAHLO, J. G. SMITH WRIGHT, eds., NATIONALISM AND THE MULTINATIONAL ENTERPRISE 244-5 (Leiden, 1973).

[3] On the significance of American investment in the U. K. economy, *see* generally J. H. Dunning, The Role of American Investment in the British Economy, P. E. P. No. 507 (London, 1969).

Trade union movements in countries which are the potential bases for investment by foreign multinational companies tend to be both sensible of the advantages that such investment may bring (especially in creating or maintaining employment) and acutely aware of the dependence of such benefits upon decisions taken outside the country. This has led them both to identify multinational companies as raising a distinct set of issues for trade unions and to be especially sensitive to any adverse consequences of foreign multinationals' actions. In particular, two, rather separate groups of criticisms are often levelled by trade unions against foreign multinational companies: first, that their employment and industrial relations policies ignore, even flout, national customs, practices and even legal requirements; second, that multinational companies have a greater ability than purely nationally based companies to weaken the bargaining power of workers and trade unions.[4] On the other hand, the concern of trade union movements in the home countries of multinationals (which, with growing direct investment by European companies in the U. S., are increasingly likely to be also the recipients of foreign direct investment) is primarily that investment abroad should not reduce the job opportunities available in the home country. In order to set the background for a discussion of the legal issues involved it seems appropriate to attempt to evaluate the strength of these three sets of criticisms.

II. Adaption to National Industrial Relations Systems

Although much research has been carried out on the labour relations activities of multinational companies, the results have provided us with only fragmentary understanding, no doubt in part because of the cost of carrying out a comprehensive, cross-national investigation. The most reliable work appears to be that carried out by the International Labour Office (I. L. O.) in the mid-1970's.[5] Contrary to some earlier research findings, the I. L. O. research concluded that "for the most part multinational plants operating in Western European countries have adapted, or had to adapt, to host country labour practices", though the I. L. O. also pointed out that in all countries studied there were to be found exceptions, which seem "at least as important to unions as does the general, over-all assimilation of these companies."[6] The I. L. O. research also suggested that the levels of adaption were not uniform across countries and that,

[4] *See* D. Kujawa, *The Labour Relations of United States Multinationals Abroad: Comparative and Prospective Views*, 4 LABOUR AND SOCIETY 3 (1979), which contains a very useful summary of research findings on which I have drawn heavily.

[5] This research is usefully summarised by A. Gladstone, *Multinational Enterprises, Social Policy and the I. L. O.*, 10 BULL. OF COMPARATIVE LABOUR RELATIONS 54-59 (1979).

[6] I. L. O., MULTINATIONALS IN WESTERN EUROPE: THE INDUSTRIAL RELATIONS EXPERIENCE, p. 64 (Geneva, 1975). *See also* PILOT STUDY ON RELATIONS BETWEEN MANAGEMENT OF TRANSNATIONAL ENTERPRISES AND EMPLOYEE REPRESENTATIVES IN E. C. COUNTRIES, p. 62 (report submitted to the Commission of the European Communities, Brussels, 1977).

for example, greater conformity with national practices in Germany, as opposed to the U. K., could be explained by "the manner in which so much of the substance and structure of labour-management relations is prescribed by law in [Germany] as compared to more voluntaristic systems like that in the U. K."[7] Both these latter points seem apposite to experience in the U. K. with the recognition by multinationals of trade unions for the purposes of collective bargaining. Thus, the sometimes violent disputes at *Roberts-Arundel* in Stockport and *Fine Tubes* at Plymouth in the early 1970's were seen by trade unions as casting doubt on the willingness of all multinationals to recognise trade unions, though such violent recognition disputes are in fact uncommon and, when they have occurred, have sometimes involved British companies (e. g. *Grunwick*). But there are a small number of British subsidiaries of foreign based multinationals (e. g. *I. B. M.*, *Kodak* und *Michelin*) which have adopted an explicit, non-recognition policy, although they are companies of a size and type where it would be very unusual (but not illegal) for a British company not to recognize a trade union. There may also be variations by type of industrial technology, length of time in the "host" country, and home country of the multinational, but all are variations within a general pattern of assimilation.

The I. L. O. research also tended to devalue the opposite assertion about multinationals' employment practices that is sometimes made, viz. that, far from not living up to national norms, they tend to exceed them, especially in relation to wages and working conditions. Although on an economy-wide basis multinationals' wage-rates seemed to exceed those for national companies by anything from 5 to 22 per cent, comparisons made on an industry basis tended to cause this advantage to be reduced or even to disappear, because the multinationals were located in the higher paying industries. The research also suggested that in relation to working conditions "multinationals adapt rather closely to the practices of the countries where they operate."[8]

Adaption by foreign multinationals to national practices does not, of course, imply that they must forgo attempts to bring about reform from within the national system, as, for example, with productivity bargaining in the U. K. This was an innovation of the 1960's which was introduced by the subsidiaries of certain U. S. companies (notably in the oil refining industry), which was taken up by a number of British companies, and which received the endorsement and encouragement of the Royal Commission on Trade Unions and Employers' Associations, although it was not a development welcomed by all sections of the trade union movement.

[7] The research attributed greater assimilation of multinationals to national practices in Sweden, not to the legal framework, but to the "great strength of union and management federations and the structure of their joint relations." I. L. O., *op. cit.*, *supra*, note 6, at p. 65.

[8] I. L. O., WAGES AND WORKING CONDITIONS IN MULTINATIONAL ENTERPRISES p. 50 (Geneva, 1976). *See now* also J. H. Dunning and E. Morgan, *Employee Compensation in U. S. Multinationals and Indigenous Firms: An Exploratory Micro/Macro Analysis*, 18 BRITISH JOURNAL OF INDUSTRIAL RELATIONS 179 (1980).

III. Multinational Companies and the Bargaining Power of Trade Unions and Workers

It is sometimes argued that labour relations is a subject which is generally the responsibility of the management of subsidiaries of multinational companies, so that, from the point of view of bargaining the union and the workers should find themselves in no different position when negotiating with a multinational subsidiary than with a purely nationally based company. As a matter of fact, it is unclear whether labour relations responsibility is generally decentralized in this way – an extensive empirical study would probably discover a variety of patterns – and there seems to be agreement that even in decentralized systems the parent company would have to be consulted on important issues, such as a long strike or a major reform of industrial relations arrangements. More important, there may be a range of non-industrial relations issues in which the union has a clear interest (notably investment decisions)[9] and which are overwhelmingly likely to be reserved for central decision-making by the parent of the group. Thus, in a number of ways the national trade unions and workers' associations may find themselves without direct access to the locus of decision-making on the matters in which they are interested.

Other considerations go more directly to the bargaining power of employers, notably their ability to withstand strike, and other industrial action taken against them by a national labour movement. In part, it is simply that an even fully effective strike in one country will close down only part of the multinational's operations whilst the continuing operations in other countries will provide financial resources to the group that will enable it to hold out longer than would a national company. The force of this argument would be weakened, even reversed, where production in the various countries is integrated, for then, in fact, a national trade union would have additional leverage in its bargaining. Although there is evidence of growing production integration in the automobile industry, one authority has concluded that in general "production integration at any significant level does not exist" and that "the 'external financial resources' threat to unions at an individual subsidiary . . . is likely to be quite realistic."[10]

A related consideration is the extent of the potential for multinational companies to transfer production from a struck plant to subsidiaries in another country so as to enable market commitments in the country of the strike to be met. An extension of this point would be for a multinational to switch production, not merely during the strike, but on a permanent basis, so as to avoid labour relations problems in the first country. The I. L. O. research found several examples of production switching during strikes,[11] though the technical

[9] Professor O. Kahn-Freund has pointed out "the gradual, but now complete, collapse of the old distinction between 'social' and 'economic' purposes of working class and especially trade union action" in O. Kahn-Freund, *Industrial Democracy*, 6 Industrial Law Journal 65, 73.

[10] Kujawa, *op. cit., supra*, note 4, at p. 6-7.

[11] I. L. O., *op. cit., supra*, note 6, at p. 24-25.

feasibility of this obviously varies from industry to industry and, indeed, within groups from time to time according to whether foreign subsidiaries have spare capacity. The threat, at least, to switch production on a permanent basis is certainly made by multinational companies from time to time, not usually in the sense of threatening to close down existing facilities (though this has happened) but in the sense of threatening to locate new investment elsewhere, if a particular strike is not settled quickly or if an improvement is not made in the general industrial relations record. Certainly, the *Ford Motor Co.* gave as one of its reasons for locating new car assembly facilities in Spain rather than the U. K. the unsatisfactory production record of its British plants.[12] In general, although that company's share of car sales in the U. K. has increased significantly, its assembly facilities in Britain have not been similarly expanded, and *Ford* at times has been the largest importer of cars into the country. No doubt labour relations matters are only one factor in investment decisions, but at least it can be said that the threat of permanent production switching is seen by trade unions as a real one.

IV. Job Losses in the Home Country

This is perceived as a problem by the union movements in the home countries of multinationals, and in particular has been a matter of concern to North American unions (and more recently to European labour movements with regard, for example, to the decision by *Volkswagen* to invest in production facilities in the U. S. A. or, in Britain, with regard to increased investment by *I. C. I.* in production facilities in other European countries). It is, however, an area in which it is virtually impossible to come to firm conclusions about whether such investment does reduce the total number of job opportunities in the home country or alter the type of job that is available there,[13] but it is clear that this is a matter in respect of which trade unions would want to bring their influence to bear.

It might seem a fair summary of the above to say that it is less the failure of subsidiaries of multinationals to adapt to national practices (though such adaption is not uniform or complete) as the ability of multinationals to undermine the bargaining position of national trade unions that raises the most pressing problems for national labour movements. To put it another way, it is less the foreign ownership and management of the subsidiary that gives rise to problems as the membership by the subsidiary of an international group of companies. Thus, also, "home" multinational groups may pose as many problems for trade union movements as foreign-based groups. Unfortunately, of the two problems the second is the more difficult to solve, whether it be through

[12] *See* J. P. Dubois, *Multinational Enterprises and Collective Bargaining at International Level*, 11 COMMON MARKET LAW REVIEW 141 at 146 (1974).

[13] The relevant research is summarised in I. L. O., THE IMPACT OF MULTINATIONAL ENTERPRISES ON EMPLOYMENT AND TRAINING, p. 20-24 (Geneva, 1976).

social action by trade unions or through legislative action by governments, because the international nature of the group of companies cannot be easily encompassed by purely national social or legislative actions. Within western European labour law and labour relations systems there are two main methods of bringing worker influence to bear upon employers' decisions that concern employees: the method of collective bargaining and the method of institutionalised representation within the company (whether through works councils or through employee representation at board level). It is proposed to examine in turn the application of these methods to multinational groups of companies. We shall then turn to the role of international organisation in this field.

V. Collective Bargaining

We have already noted the difficulties national trade union movements may experience in securing access to levels of decision-making which exist above the national subsidiary and in exerting effective bargaining strength against part only of an international group of companies. An obvious solution to the problem might be thought to be international collective bargaining. It is intended therefore to look, first, at the international organisation of trade unions and, second, at the record of international industrial action.

A. The International Organisation of Trade Unions[14]

After the cold-war splits of the 1940's there are three organisations for the affiliation of national trade union centres on a world-wide basis. The majority of Western trade union centres belong to the International Confederation of Free Trade Unions (I. C. F. T. U.), but for very different reasons neither the A. F. L. – C. I. O. (U. S. A.) nor the C. G. I. L. (Italy) and the C. G. T. (France) are affiliated, the last mentioned being a member of the largely communist World Federation of Trade Unions and the C. G. I. .L. sending observers to its meetings. The I. C. F. T. U. operates mainly as a lobbyist at intergovernmental level, and far more important for international collective bargaining are the international trade union secretariats (ITS), to which individual national trade unions (rather than trade union centres) affiliate and which are organized on an industrial basis. There are seventeen ITS and half a dozen analogous organisations in the air transport and radio, television and entertainment industries.[15] They vary considerably in size, strength and activity, but the most active have been the International Metalworkers' Federation (I. M. F.), the International Federation of Chemical, Energy and General Workers' Unions (I. C. E. F.), the

[14] Among voluminous literature on this topic *see* H. R. Northrup & R. L. Rowan, Multinational Collective Bargaining Attempts: the Record, the Case and the Prospects, Ch. 1. (Philadelphia, 1979); W. Kendall, The Labour Movement in Europe, Ch. 10 (London, 1975); and C. Wilms-Wright, Transnational Corporations: A Strategy for Control, Fabian Research Series No. 334 (London, 1977).

[15] *See* Northrup and Rowan, *op. cit., supra*, note 14, at p. 15-21.

International Union of Food and Allied Workers (I. U. F.) and the International Transport Workers' Federation (I. T. F.). More recently there have developed European regional organisations, notably the European Confederation of Trade Unions (E. C. T. U), an organisation of trade union centres (including C. G. I. L. but not the C. G. T.). The E. C. T. U. has itself created industry committees (to which national unions affiliate), of which the most important is the European Metalworkers' Federation (E. M. F.). The relationship between these industry committees and the ITS is unclear. Some ITS have created "company councils" for particular multinational companies and there are sometimes unofficial contacts between plant-level worker representatives in particular companies e. g. the British and German Ford plants.

B. International Industrial Action

A recent exhaustive survey, addressed to the question of how extensive multinational collective bargaining was, concluded that the only multinational collective agreements were to be found in the rather special circumstances of the European recording, radio and television industries.[16] The absence of multinational agreements came perhaps as no surprise to most academic writers in the field, for it has long been accepted that the difficulty in different national circumstances of formulating common claims would render such bargaining problematic. However, the authors were also unimpressed by the evidence of successful coordinated bargaining with multinational companies, i. e. of instances where it was suggested that ITS had coordinated the separate bargaining activities of their national affiliates so as to achieve maximum impact upon a particular multinational company.[17] Their main positive findings were that there could be documented "several cases of information exchange between multinational corporations and multinational union groups and a very few instances of regular multinational union-management consultation."[18]

It is also possible to document instances of solidarity or sympathy action taken by workers employed by a multinational in one country in support of industrial action embarked upon by the employees of the multinational in another country in connection with collective negotiations in that other country. Indeed, it is possible to compile a relatively long catalogue of such instances[19] and it has to be said that the practice of international industrial action to date has consisted overwhelmingly in sympathy action of this type. It is an obvious tactic for national unions to wish to invoke to counter transfers of production, but it is

[16] *Ibid.* p. 533. See also P. A. Miscimarra, *The Entertainment Industry: Inroads in Multinational Collective Bargaining*, 19 British Journal of Industrial Relations 49 (1981).

[17] The classic example is that of St. Gobain, *but see* Northrup and Rowan, *op. cit., supra*, note 14, at p. 156-166, where perhaps it may be said that the authors' evidence is less conclusive than they appear to think.

[18] *Ibid.*, p. 533.

[19] *Ibid.*, *passim*.

not clear how effective sympathy action is in preventing such transfers or how often requests for sympathy action are not met for one reason or another.

Standing somewhat in between, on the one hand, multinational collective bargaining and, on the other, sympathy action is the long-standing campaign of the I. T. F. against flags of convenience. The I. T. F. acting through its national affiliates, has since 1948 at least attempted to secure that the crews of flags-of-convenience ships are paid at a certain minimum level.[20] Flags-of-convenience ships are now defined as ships registered in a country other than the one in which there resides the beneficial ownership of the company owning the ship. Typically, the ship is registered in country A, the beneficial ownership of the company owning the ship is in country B, and the crew are nationals of either country A or a third country C.[21] The current policy of the I. T. F. is that the crew should be remunerated on the I. T. F. scale (said to be the median of the rates negotiated by national trade unions in Western European countries) or that the ship should be registered in the country of beneficial ownership. If the ship-owner agrees to the former course of action he will enter into an agreement with the I. T. F. Although these are not agreements, usually, with multinational companies, they are (dating from 1950) perhaps the first agreements signed between an employer and an ITS and they now constitute a considerable corpus of joint regulation (perhaps in excess of 1000 agreements by 1979). The I. T. F. has also developed an executive structure for securing compliance with its policies through the appointment in eighteen key ports of I. T. F. inspectors, who are usually also officials of the relevant national affiliate. Perhaps the most important feature of I. T. F. activity from the point of view of this paper is, however, that it has given rise to a considerable amount of litigation in a number of countries (notably England, where the I. T. F. has its headquarters, Sweden, Norway, Denmark, Germany, Holland and the U. S. A.) and this litigation provides an important case-study of the impact of varying legal régimes upon the extent and effectiveness of international sympathy action and internationally coordinated industrial action.

VI. The Legality of International Solidarity Action

The almost complete lack at present of multinational collective bargaining and the relative infrequency of international solidarity action has been explained by a number of factors: the reflection at international level of the ideological divisions among certain national trade union movements (e. g. in France and Italy); different traditions of industrial relations in different countries, even within otherwise relatively homogeneous economic groupings (e. g. the E. E. C.);

[20] *Ibid.* Ch. XVII.

[21] *See, e. g.*, N. W. L. Ltd. v. Woods [1979] I. C. R. 867 (H. L.), an important recent British House of Lords judgment involving a ship registered in Hong Kong, owned by Swedish interests and employing a Hong Kong crew; or Star Sea Transport Corporation v. Slater [1979] 1 Lloyd's Rep. 26 (C. A.), where the ship flew the Liberian flag, had an Indian crew and was managed by British agents.

national rivalries between trade union movements; the unwillingness of national trade union leaders to cede power to international federations, but also the legal obstacles created by divergent systems of labour law which, like industrial relations systems, reflect very closely the social and cultural identities of nation states (unlike, for example, systems of company law, which display a remarkable uniformity across capitalist countries). Certainly in respect of international solidarity action the legal obstacles loom large, and it is proposed to investigate how far national systems of labour law have accommodated themselves to the problems raised by such action.

A. Restrictions on International Solidarity Action

It must be said at once that in most Western European countries the legal status of sympathy action (even within a purely national context) is often in doubt and so statements in this paper about the national legal position must be taken in that light. It seems possible to classify the actual and potential responses of national legal systems to international sympathy action into three categories. First, the fact that the action has an international dimension may be seen as a reason for *withdrawing* from the workers taking the action the protection of national laws that might otherwise be available to them. This approach, which is, of course, inimical to the development of international solidarity action, derives from notions of the comity of nations and the purely territorial applicability of national labour laws. Thus, in a series of cases the U. S. Supreme Court has held[22] that usually the National Labor Relations Act (N. L. R. A.) will not apply to disputes between foreign ship owners and U. S. unions even when the ship is berthed in a U. S. port, because the economic activities of the foreign ship-owner do not "affect commerce between states", as the federal law requires. This leaves such disputes to be regulated by state law, and in the *Windward Shipping* and *American Radio* cases[23] the Supreme Court upheld the enjoining by state courts of peaceful picketing by six maritime unions of foreign registered ships whose crews were not remunerated at I. T. F. rates, even though such peaceful picketing was probably protected under the N. L. R. A. Northrup and Rowan comment that: "This has ended, at least for the present time, effective support by American longshore and shipping unions for I. T. F. boycotts of flags or crews of convenience."[24] It may well be that these cases fall short of depriving employees in all international solidarity actions of the protection of the N. L. R. A., but they are illustrative of the unexpected difficulties that the

[22] Benz v. Compania Naviera Hidalgo 352 U. S. 889 (1957); McColloch v. Sociedad Nacional de Marineros 372 U. S. 10 (1963); Incres Steamship Co. v. International Maritime Workers 372 U. S. 24 (1963); Windward Shipping (London) Ltd. v. American Radio Association 415 U. S. 164 (1974); American Radio Association v. Mobil Steamship Association 419 U. S. 215 (1974); *cf.* International Longshoremen, Local 1416 v. Ariadne Shipping Co. 397 U. S. 195 (1970).

[23] *Supra* note 22.

[24] *op. cit., supra*, note 14, at p. 484.

international element can give rise to. Further, in an admittedly much criticised case, a German court has held[25] that German workers who refused to handle work transferred from struck British plants were deprived of the benefit of the guarantees enshrined in the Federal Republic's Constitution because the original strike took place abroad. Since the Constitution could apply only to the national territory the rights which it recognizes could not be exercised in support of a strike in another country. This seems to be a view of quite general application to international solidarity action.

B. The Application of National Rules

The second possible type of response of a legal system to international solidarity action, and the one most commonly found in practice, is for the national system to apply the same rules to such action as are applied to national solidarity action. This may be a matter of express policy, as in the U. K., where the legal protections of strikers depend crucially upon their actions being characterised as taken "in contemplation or furtherance of a trade dispute." As a result of an amendment in 1976 the Trade Union and Labour Relations Act 1974 (T. U. L. R. A.) now provides that: "There is a trade dispute for the purposes of this Act even though it relates to matters occuring outside Great Britain."[26] This guarantees international solidarity action no lesser, though equally no greater, legal protection than national solidarity action. Between 1974 and 1976 the Act treated a foreign dispute as a trade dispute only if the terms and conditions of employment of the workers taking the solidarity action in the U. K. stood to be affected by its outcome, a rule which would have placed greater restrictions upon international than upon national solidarity action, where no such requirement is imposed.[27] Before 1974 there was no express rule in English law on international solidarity action and, not so much as a matter of policy but as a matter of unconcern, probably the same rules applied as for national action. This last position seems to be the stance of most Western European legal systems.[28]

Thus, a full answer to the question of the legal status of international solidarity action would require an examination of many national labour law systems, in particular an examination of how far in each country sympathy action is regarded as compatible with the "peace obligation" in collective agreements and how far it is regarded as giving rise to tortious (delictual) liability quite apart

[25] Arbeitsgericht Wuppertal, 24 November 1959.

[26] S. 29 (3) T. U. L. R. A. 1974.

[27] Indeed until 1980 the national solidarity action did not need even to be objectively capable of aiding the primary strikers, provided that those taking the secondary action honestly thought it would do so: Express Newspapers Ltd. v. McShane [1980] I. C. R. 42 (H. L.). The Employment Act 1980, s. 17 requires that the secondary action be reasonably capable of achieving its object, but this still falls short of a requirement that the terms and conditions of employment of those taking the secondary action be likely to be affected by the outcome of the dispute.

[28] A. Pankert, *Some Legal Problems of Workers' International Solidarity*, 116 International Labour Review 67 (1977).

from its contractual status. Such a task is far beyond the scope of this paper. Nevertheless, a few remarks on the topic may be offered. In addition to the generalisation that in all Western European countries some doubt surrounds the legal status of sympathy action, one may offer the generalisation that the approaches of each system to the problem are often very different from one another and, as often as not, so are the practical effects of the conclusions arrived at. This, as the experience of the I. T. F. indicates, makes the coordination of sympathy action in a number of different countries, a difficult, and perhaps impossible, matter. This is not to say that some national systems do not adopt a liberal attitude towards sympathy action. Thus, in Sweden, where, at least until recently, the law has recognised only limited bases for the tortious liability of strikers (whether sympathetic or otherwise), the question has turned upon the extent of the peace obligation imposed by what is now S. 41 of the Joint Regulation Act 1976 and Ch. III of the Basic Agreement concluded between the central employers and trade union federations.[29] But this peace obligation is not absolute. In general, provided the primary strikers are free to take industrial action, sympathy action by other workers in support of them will not be a breach of the peace obligation imposed by S. 41 on the secondary employees, provided the latter do not aim to bring about any alteration of the agreement that binds them.[30] Chapter III of the Basic Agreement increases the restrictions upon sympathetic action, but contains a wide definition of non-neutrals, who are not protected by the Chapter, and makes an exception in relation to disputes about the making of collective agreements; and, in any case, it confers a right of action only upon the employer of the secondary employees, the party to the agreement, and not upon the primary employer.

The U. K. was also until recently a liberal system as far as sympathy and secondary action is concerned. Here the debate has turned not so much upon the peace obligation – since collective agreements are not in any case usually legally binding – but upon the scope of strikers' tortious liabilities. Unlike in Sweden, the English common law of tort is essentially hostile to any "right to strike" and only because of statutory immunities granted to strikers against these common law liabilities is the "right to strike" effectuated.[31] Until recently, however, these immunities were widely drafted and protected all those acting "in contemplation or furtherance of a trade dispute",[32] irrespective of whether the trade dispute was one between themselves and their own employer or not.[33] In other words the U. K. law adopted the extremely liberal position of not in principle distinguish-

[29] In this section I have drawn heavily on F. Schmidt, Law and Industrial Relations in Sweden, p. 167-190 (Stockholm, 1977).

[30] And provided, rather curiously, that the sympathy action is temporary. *See* the famous Dagsposten case (A. D. 1945:62).

[31] For an important general discussion of the English position, *see* K. W. Wedderburn, *Industrial Relations and the Courts*, 9 Industrial Law Journal 65 (1980).

[32] Trade unions as such are even more widely protected from actions in tort. *See* T. U. L. R. A. 1974, S. 14.

[33] *See* N. W. L. Ltd. v. Woods [1979] I. C. R. 867; Express Newspapers Ltd. v. McShane [1980] I. C. R. 42; Duport Steels Ltd. v. Sirs [1980] I. R. L. R. 112 (all H. L.).

ing between primary and secondary action at all as far as its legality was concerned. The Employment Act 1980, s. 17 now restricts the immunities for secondary action (other than picketing where more rigorous measures are to be taken) largely to secondary action taken by employees of an employer who is a direct supplier to or customer of the primary employer.

By contrast German law has developed tortious restrictions upon the freedom to take industrial action that are far reaching. Under the theory of social adequacy, which requires in particular that the dispute be terminable by the conclusion of a collective agreement and that all chances of arriving at a peaceful settlement be exhausted before the strike is resorted to, the right to engage in sympathy action has been much restricted, if not eliminated entirely.[34] On a number of occasions German workers have refused to engage in international solidarity action on the grounds that it would be unlawful under German law.[35] More generally, after a survey of the history of I. T. F. boycotts, Northrup and Rowan[36] concluded that in the efforts of the I. T. F. to secure that national affiliates take part in coordinated campaigns to "black" or boycott flags-of-convenience vessels within national jurisdictions, the relative receptiveness of the legal systems of each country to such action has been a factor second only to the willingness of affiliated unions to adopt the I. T. F. policy in ensuring the success or failure of the campaigns. In particular, the I. T. F., has secured extensive blacking of flags-of-convenience vessels in the U. K.,[37] Sweden,[38] and

[34] *See, e. g.*, T. Ramm, *The Restriction of the Freedom to Strike in the Federal Republic of Germany*, in O. KAHN-FREUND, ed., LABOUR RELATIONS AND THE LAW – A COMPARATIVE STUDY, p. 207 (London, 1965).

[35] WILMS-WRIGHT, *op. cit., supra*, note 14.

[36] *Op. cit., supra*, note 14, at p. 512. Of course, I. T. F. coordinated boycotts are not pure examples of international solidarity action, but rather are examples of coordinated national sympathy action taking place simultaneously in a number of countries, but this difference is not relevant for the point in the text.

[37] NORTHRUP AND ROWAN, *op. cit., supra*, note 14, at p. 503 describe the I. T. F.'s legal victory in the case of Camellia Tanker S. A. Ltd. v. I. T. F. [1976] I. C. R. 274 (C. A.) as giving the I. T. F. campaign "a substantial boost" and its subsequent victory in N. W. L. Ltd. v. Woods [1979] I. C. R. 867 (H. L.) (which overruled a case in which an I. T. F. inspector had been enjoined from organising blacking of a ship in the U. K.: Star Sea Transport Corporation v. Slater [1979] 1 Lloyd's Rep. 26 (C. A.)) as indicating "the difficulty that shipowners will continue to face in Britain in an effort to obtain injunctions against I. T. F. action" (*id.* p. 506). *But cf.* the text accompanying note 32 *supra*. The N. W. L. decision has been applied subsequently by the Court of Appeal in Universe Tankships Inc. of Monrovia v. I. T. F., [1981] I. C. R. 129. A recent British Government consultative document, CMND. 8128, TRADE UNION IMMUNITIES, at p. 53–54 (H. M. S. O., London, 1981) discusses whether British law should not be amended so as to permit the blacking of international shipping in British ports only where there is a dispute between members of the crew and their employer. The arguments in favour of such a change include the statements that at present it is "much easier to pursue a campaign of blacking in British ports than in any other Western European ports" and that "foreign ships coming to Great Britain [are] particularly vulnerable to the campaign by the I. T. F. against the use of 'flags of convenience'", so

Finland, but has been relatively unsuccessful in the U. S.,[39] the Netherlands,[40] Denmark,[41] and Germany.

Even in the most liberal legal systems, however, the application of national rules to international solidarity action can cause difficulties if it is a requirement of the legality of the sympathy action that the primary action also be legal, as indeed will usually be the case.[42] Is the legality of the primary action to be judged according to the law of the country where it is taking place or according to the law of the place of the secondary action? S. 29 (3) of the U. K. T. U. L. R. A. 1974 seems to apply the latter rule, i. e. the U. K. definition of a "trade dispute" must be applied to the foreign facts to see if they fall within it. In Sweden, in a case[43] involving sympathetic action by Swedish stevedores in blacking Danish ships in support of striking Danish stevedores and seamen, the Labour Court, on the other hand, required the legality of the primary strike to be judged according to Danish law. Although the Labour Law Committee proposed to reverse this decision (which has been criticised by commentators), the Joint Regulation Act did not expressly do so. Either solution has its disadvantages, but the U. K. solution at least avoids apparently similar pieces of sympathy action being treated differently in the same country and avoids also questions arising about the acceptability of foreign strike law to the national courts. The I. C. F. T. U. has come out in favour of applying the law of the country of the secondary action.[44]

that British international trade suffers because only high-cost shipping is safe in U. K. ports.

[38] Evidently in 1975 110 ships were stopped in Sweden: NORTHRUP AND ROWAN, *Op. cit., supra*, note 14, at p. 495.

[39] That is, after the decisions in the Windward Shipping and American Radio cases (see text accompanying note 22 *supra*). Before that U. S. unions enthusiastically supported I. T. F. policy. *See* NORTHRUP AND ROWAN, *op. cit., supra*, note 14, at p. 481 and 484.

[40] Especially after the restrictive *Hoge Raad* decision of 1960 (N. J. 1960, nr. 84).

[41] *See* Industrial Court Case No. 7745 (1976) which NORTHRUP AND ROWAN (*op. cit. supra*, note 14, at p. 499) describe as causing the failure of the Scandinavian Transport Workers' Federations' boycott of 1976 in Denmark and they comment that "it seems likely that the court's decision has restrained any significant union participation in future regional boycotts."

[42] Pankert, *op. cit., supra*, note 28, at p. 71. An analogous problem which has arisen in the English courts – the I. T. F. has its headquarters in London – concerns the Federation's liability in England for torts committed by it outside the jurisdiction. The rule in English law is that the acts committed outside the jurisdiction must be tortious not only in the place where the act was committed but also, if it had been committed in England, under English law, if a defendant within the jurisdiction is to be held liable for them in an English court. English courts have sometimes ignored these requirements. *See* Hanseatic Ship Management Ltd. v. I. T. F. [1974] I. C. R. 112 (criticised by Freedland 3 INDUSTRIAL LAW JOURNAL 56 (1974) and Camellia Tanker S. A. v. I. T. F. [1976] I. C. R. 274 (C. A.) (criticised by Lord Diplock in N. W. L. Ltd. v. Woods [1979] I. C. R. 867, 873).

[43] A. D. 1961: 30.

[44] I. C. F. T. U., *Charter of Trade Union Demands for the Legislative Controls of*

C. The Encouragement of International Solidarity Action

The third possible response of a legal system would be to give international solidarity action especially favourable legal treatment, i. e. treatment more favourable than that accorded to national sympathy action. It seems unlikely that anything more than isolated examples of this approach can be found. However, it seems that in Swedish law the requirement in S. 45 of the Joint Regulation Act that seven days' notice of industrial action be given was qualified by the phrase "provided no valid obstacle exists" precisely in order to allow stevedores to take action without such notice against ships flying flags-of-convenience which would otherwise be able to load or unload and leave port within the seven-day period. Although the approach of granting especially favourable treatment to international solidarity action would no doubt be opposed by multinational companies on the grounds that it infringes the principle of "national treatment",[45] if multinational companies were thought to be in an especially powerful position vis-à-vis national trade unions, such a policy could be defended as merely redressing the balance. The I. C. F. T. U.[46] has proposed that "trade unions which have not the right to take sympathy measures in favour of workers in a subsidiary of a multinational company should be given that right", apparently irrespective of whether this would introduce into national law a divergence between national and international solidarity action. And the Group of Eminent Persons which reported to the Economic and Social Council of the United Nations in 1974 urged national governments to adopt a liberal rather than a restrictive approach to expressions of international solidarity by national labour movements.

Given the competition among Western European countries for investment by multinational companies and, indeed, their desire to protect the position of their "own" multinational companies, it is unlikely that such measures will be introduced on a wide scale. More modestly, Jacobs[47] has developed an interesting argument for harmonisation within the E. E. C. of national strike laws as far as sympathy action (whether national or international) is concerned. Taking the right of workers to engage in international solidarity action as the true counterpart of the free movement of capital (rather than the free movement of individual workers),[48] he proposes harmonisation towards the more liberal national systems. Beside adoption of the principle that international solidarity action should not be regarded as less lawful than national action merely on the ground that it has an international scope, and suggesting a solution to the problem of the correct law by which to judge the legality of the primary action,

Multinational Companies, Appendix II, 7 Bull. of Comparative Labour Relations 431 (1976).

[45] *See infra* section VIII.

[46] *See supra*, note 44.

[47] A. Jacobs, *Towards Community Action on Strike Law*, 15 Common Market Law Review 133 (1978).

[48] An argument originally developed by K. W. Wedderburn, *Multinational Enterprise and National Law*, 1 Industrial Law Journal 16 (1972).

his proposals concentrate on the link that should exist between the primary and the secondary action. In fact, it seems possible to view this link in three ways: from the point of view of the relations between the primary and secondary employers (as with systems like those of the U. S. and the U. K. between 1971 and 1974 which declare secondary action unlawful in general but not in respect of secondary employers who have allied themselves with the primary employer); from the point of view of the interests of the secondary employees (as with the now-repealed qualification to S. 29 (3) of the 1974 Act in the U. K.); and from the point of view of the likely impact of the secondary action in aiding the primary employees (as with the 1980 Act in the U. K.[49] or as is evidently the case in Germany[50]). Jacobs proposes that a sufficiently close connection should always be assumed between subsidiaries of the same multinational group. This would take the "ally" doctrine further than it has been developed in most systems e. g. the U. S. (where in the absence of "struck work" being contracted out to the secondary employer common management and some integration of operations seem to be required) or Sweden, and would contradict the position adopted in the U. K. between 1971 and 1974, when the legislature expressly provided that the relationship of parent and subsidiary or of common ownership did not take the secondary employer, outside the area of neutrality.[51] In all other cases Jacobs proposes a link based upon the impact of the industrial action in helping the primary employees, and specifically the adoption of the German test. Although these proposals mark a start towards a solution, they do not really achieve much in the way of reform where the national legal system extensively restricts primary industrial action and the legality of the primary action is a sine qua non for the legality of the secondary action.

VII. Institutional Representation

The second main way of protecting employee interests vis-à-vis employers in Western European labour law systems is through institutional mechanisms, namely works councils and, at least where the employer is incorporated, through representation of the employees at board level.[52] Again, it seems possible to categorise the application by national legal systems of these provisions to multinational groups of companies in three broad ways.

A. Special Restrictions upon Institutional Mechanisms in Multinational Groups

Some systems impose special restrictions upon the application of institutional representation mechanisms to multinational groups. The best example of this is

[49] *See supra*, note 27.

[50] W. Gitter, *Probleme des Arbeitskampfes in supranationaler, internationaler und international-privatrechtlicher Sicht*, [1971] Zeitschrift für Arbeitsrecht 130 at 150.

[51] Industrial Relations Act 1971, S. 98.

[52] Works councils are a very widespread institution (though they are not found in the U. K.) whereas employee representation at board level is somewhat less common.

the rules on board-level representation in Dutch law. The basic rule of Dutch law in respect of groups of companies is that subsidiaries shall not be subject to employee representation (even if otherwise qualified for it) provided the holding company is subject to the system.[53] The purpose of the rule is to preserve coherence in group decision-making, though it does so only at the cost of denying employee influence over decisions which have been delegated to subsidiaries.[54] However, in the case of a multinational group where the parent company is a Dutch company and the majority of the group's employees work abroad, the holding company is exempted from employee representation. In a national group this would mean that employee representation should be introduced at the level of the Dutch subsidiaries. This is indeed the case with the multinational group, but, even here, the coherence of group decision-making is preserved by empowering the parent (which has no employee representation) to appoint the managing board of the subsidiary and to adopt its accounts.[55] The argument for exempting the holding company is, apparently, that it would be inappropriate for Dutch employees to influence supervisory board decisions by the holding company where these employees are a minority of all employees employed in the group. Finally, where a Dutch company is a subsidiary of a foreign holding company, which is necessarily not subject to the Dutch law of employee representation, employee representation is required at the subsidiary level, but, again, only in the modified way indicated for Dutch groups having the majority of the employees abroad.[56] This preserves coherence of decision-making in the multinational group, but only at the expense of employee influence at subsidiary level and at holding company level.

The Dutch are unusual in imposing express restrictions upon their employee representation provisions in favour of multinational groups, an approach which no doubt reflects the particular exposure of that economy to investment by foreign multinationals and to the success of the Dutch-based multinational groups. However, in other systems the presence of an international dimension can render the application of national provisions problematic. Thus, in France there is a requirement for companies above a certain size to have works councils, where appropriate both at establishment and at enterprise level. Suppose a foreign company operates in France through several unincorporated branches. At each branch a *comité d'établissement* may have to be created, but it was argued that no *comité d'entreprise* could be required, because French law requires the *comité d'entreprise* to meet at the *siège social* of the company, which would be outside France: "*une loi de statut territorial ne saurait comporter d'effet en dehors du territoire national*".[57] In the *Compagnie des wagons-lits*

[53] Commercial Code, art. 52 (c) 3 (a).
[54] *Cf.* the more flexible instrument of the "binding instruction" in S. 308 of the German Aktiengesetz (1965), which is not incompatible with employee representation on the supervisory board of the subsidiary.
[55] Commercial Code, arts. 51 (c) (3) (b) and 52 (e) (1).
[56] Commercial Code, art. 52 (e) (1).
[57] A. Rouast, *La loi sur les comités d'entreprises et les sociétiés étrangères,* (1947) DROIT

case[58] the *Conseil d'État* overruled this view and required the foreign company to create in France a *comité d'entreprise* in its principal place of activity in France to deal with its French activities. The decision has given rise to a lively debate about the theory of private international law by which this decision might be justified (*"la doctrine des lois d'application immédiate"*).

B. The Application of National Rules

The normal approach of national legal systems is simply to apply in an unamended way the national laws to companies within the jurisdiction. It seems that no country except Holland exempts "its" multinational companies from the full application of the worker-representation laws, nor is it usual to exempt the subsidiaries of foreign multinational groups. It may be, of course, that some of the older institutional representation laws do not take account of the existence of groups of companies at all (whether national or multinational), as, for example, with the absence of any requirement in French law for a *comité* at group level. Once, however, the economic significance of groups is recognised, the adaption of the representation mechanisms to group structures is largely a technical matter, although difficulties do arise in securing coherent group decision-making and effective employee representation. It seems possible to achieve satisfactory results without adopting the extreme Dutch approach of removing employee representation from the boards of subsidiaries.[59]

The application of national laws in an unamended way implies, however, that they cannot be applied to subsidiaries outside the jurisdiction of "home" multinationals, nor to the parent companies of foreign multinationals. It is one thing to reject the existence of such subsidiaries or parent companies as a reason for not applying national law to companies within the jurisdiction, but it seems that no country has attempted to extend the reach of its laws on participation to companies incorporated elsewhere. This may be a severe limitation upon even the most advanced national laws on participation. Thus, in relation to German law one authority has recently remarked that multinational companies have decisively changed the rules of the game and that neither the works council nor the board-level representation provisions of German law come near to embracing decisions taken by parent companies outside Germany.[60] But after consider-

SOCIAL 67, quoted in B. GOLDMAN AND P. FRANCESCAKIS, eds., L'ENTREPRISE MULTINATIONALE FACE AU DROIT, p. 316 (Paris, 1977) (on which this section is heavily based).

58 Conseil d'Etat, 29 June 1973.

59 *See* CMND. 6706, REPORT OF THE COMMITTEE OF INQUIRY ON INDUSTRIAL DEMOCRACY (the Bullock Committee), (U. K.) at p. 130-142 (H. M. S. O., London, 1977); COMMISSION OF THE EUROPEAN COMMUNITIES, EMPLOYEE PARTICIPATION AND COMPANY STRUCTURE, p. 103-106 (Brussels, 1975).

60 "Die 'Spielregeln' haben sich damit entschieden geändert – dies gilt erst recht für Betriebsverfassung und Unternehmensmitbestimmung, die angesichts ausländischer Entscheidungszentren völlig versagen", W. Däubler, Arbeitsbeziehungen und Recht in der Bundesrepublik – Eine Skizze. Other German writers might take a less pessimistic view.

ing arguments that foreign multinational groups be treated more severely than national groups, the Bullock Committee in the U. K. concluded that such a course of action "would be seen as an attempt to impose through the medium of national law an element of control over multinationals, which by their nature can only effectively be controlled by international means. It would not act as a control, therefore, but merely as a deterrent to potential investors in the U. K."[61]

It is perhaps not surprising that a critical comment upon the impact of multinational groups on national forms of institutional representation should come from Germany, because it is in that country that these forms of representation are furthest developed, notably by the requirement that a range of decisions be jointly agreed between employer and works council.[62] At this point the parallels between institutional representation and collective bargaining are at their closest, and the inability of both national collective bargaining and national "codetermination" to impose the principle of joint agreement upon decisions taken outside the country is a common one. But institutional representation may have much more modest goals than joint agreement, e. g. consultation, the right to make representations or mere disclosure of information. With regard to this last it is possible to avoid the limitations of the national jurisdiction by requiring a subsidiary within the jurisdiction to provide information about the activities of the multinational group as a whole. Several European countries have such provisions in their works councils laws, usually as part of a general requirement that subsidiaries provide information about the groups of which they are part. It has now been proposed by the European Commission that there should be EEC legislation on disclosure of information to employee representatives specifically by multinational groups, although it is unclear at the time of writing what the final shape of these proposals will be.[63] It is possible, of course, to graft disclosure (and even consultation) provisions onto institutional representation and collective bargaining systems alike and thus to some extent to bridge the gap between them.[64]

As far as institutional representation is concerned, an alternative way forward would be the elaboration of such representation within international corporate bodies. As, however, experience with the European Company shows, even

[61] CMND. 6706, *supra*, note 59, at p. 147. The Committee was, however, concerned to see that multinational groups within the U. K. should be under equivalent control as national groups (pp. 144-150).

[62] *See e. g.* Betriebsverfassungsgesetz 1971, ss. 87, 91, 99, 102, 112.

[63] A Draft Directive has in fact now been adopted by the Commission and was formally submitted to the Council on 24th October 1980. *See* Commission Proposal for a Council Directive on procedures for informing and consulting the employees of undertakings with complex structures, in particular transnational undertakings, O. J. E. C., Vol. 23, C 297 p. 3 (1980). The proposal is still, however, far from being accepted by the Council. *See, e. g.*, The Financial Times, 3 Oct. 1980 p. 2.

[64] *See, e. g.*, Council Directives 75/129 on collective redundancies, O. J. E. C., Vol. 18, L 48 p. 29 (1975); or 77/187 on transfers of undertakings, O. J. E. C., Vol. 20, L 61 p. 26 (1977).

within a relatively homogeneous area agreement among different nations as to the appropriate form of transnational instrument may not be easy to secure, and it is precisely the employee representation provisions, especially those operating at board level, that have caused so many disagreements. Nevertheless, from a technical point of view the solutions seems rather easy. Thus, the present European Company (E. C.) proposals envisage,[65] where the E. C. operates in two or more community countries via unincorporated branches, a European Works Council at enterprises level[66] and where the E. C. operates through incorporated subsidiaries a Group Works Council.

VIII. International Guidelines

We have already noted the feebleness of international collective bargaining and the difficulties that have arisen in creating transnational corporate bodies within the framework of which employees might be represented institutionally. It is perhaps for these reasons that at this moment most attention seems to be focused upon guidelines issued by international bodies as ways of controlling multinational groups of companies. In 1976 the O. E. C. D. adopted its *Declaration and Decisions on Guidelines for Multinational Enterprises, National Treatment, International Investment and Consultation Procedures*, which were reaffirmed (with minor amendments) in 1979.[67] In 1977 the I. L. O. adopted a *Declaration of Principles Concerning Multinational Enterprises and Social Policy* and the U. N. Commission on Transnational Corporations is also working towards a set of guidelines.[68] It is proposed to concentrate here on the O. E. C. D. Guidelines, which seem likely to be the most influential.[69]

The O. E. C. D. is an organisation of 24 countries, embracing all the industrial Western countries and Japan, in which countries some three quarters of total foreign direct investment is located. Although an inter-governmental organisation, the O. E. C. D. can operate as, in effect, a tripartite body, through consultations with the two independent, representative organisations connected with it: the Business and Industry Advisory Committee (B. I. A. C.) and the Trade Union Advisory Committee (T. U. A. C.). The 1976 Declaration reflected these tripartite interests and is not purely an instrument of control over multinationals. Thus, governments in the Declaration commit themselves to certain restrictions on the competition *inter se* for multinational investment and they also commit themselves, in favour of multinational companies, to the

[65] 1975 Bull. of the European Communities, Supplement 4/75, Arts. 100 and 130.

[66] *Cf.* the *Wagon-Lits* case discussed above, note 58 and accompanying text.

[67] O. E. C. D., International Investment and Multinational Enterprises (Paris, 1979).

[68] These three sets of guidelines are all of general application to multinationals. An important specific set of guidelines is the E. E. C. Code of Conduct for companies operating in South Africa.

[69] R. Blanpain, 10 Bull. of Comparative Labour Relations at p. 25 (1979). *See* now the set of papers in N. Horn, ed., Legal Problems of Codes of Conduct For Multinational Enterprises (Deventer, 1980).

principle of "national treatment", i. e. treatment of foreign firms not less favourable than that of domestic enterprises. For present purposes the main interest resides, however, in the Guidelines for Multinational Enterprises.

These state the following general principles. Multinationals should:

(a) respect their employees' right to be represented by trade unions and other bona fide organisations of employees, and negotiate with the employee organisations (either individually or through employers' associations) with a view to reaching agreement on employment conditions, including provisions for dealing with disputes over the interpretation of the agreements;
(b) provide information and facilities to employees' representatives necessary for the negotiation of meaningful collective agreements, including information on the performance of the entity or, where appropriate, the enterprise as a whole;
(c) observe employment and industrial relations standards not less favourable than those observed by comparable employers in the host country;
(d) utilise, train and upgrade members of the local labour force to the greatest extent practicable, in co-operation with employees' representatives and with relevant government authorities where appropriate;
(e) provide reasonable notice to employees' representatives and to appropriate government authorities in case of closure involving collective lay-offs or dismissals, or other changes in operation that may have major effects, and help mitigate the adverse effects;
(f) follow employment policies, including hiring, discharge, promotion, pay and training, without discrimination, except where selectivity is in accord with government policies to promote equal employment opportunities;
(g) not threaten to transfer all or part of an operating unit to another country in an effort to hinder the right to organise or to influence unfairly bona fide negotiations with employee representatives (bona fide negotiations may include labour disputes as part of the negotiation process, depending upon law and practice in the country concerned); and
(h) enable authorised employees' representatives to negotiate on labour-management relations issues with management representatives who are authorised to take decisions on the matters under negotiation.

In 1979 point (g) was amended so as to embrace also the transfer of employees from one subsidiary to another.

It is right to be rather sceptical about the efficacity of international guidelines. The O. E. C. D. Guidelines are clearly very generally phrased and do not easily provide solutions to concrete problems. They also have only the status of recommendations, although they no doubt carry considerable moral weight. Nevertheless, the interesting point is that the O. E. C. D. has developed a partly judicial and partly political mechanism for considering the application of these guidelines in specific cases. This occurs through the Committee on International Investment and Multinational Enterprises (I. M. E.), a committee of the O. E. C. D. staffed by senior civil servants of the member governments. This committee is specifically forbidden to reach conclusions on particular cases, but it may consider general problems raised by the Guidelines. The *Badger* case[70]

[70] R. Blanpain, The Badger Case and the O. E. C. D. Guidelines for Multinational Enterprises (Deventer, 1977).

(1977) shows how use can be made of this procedure by astute and determined parties. The case concerned the Belgian subsidiary of a U. S. company, which went into liquidation without having sufficient assets to meet the severance claims of its employees. The problem was whether under the guidelines the parent company was obliged to discharge these obligations of the subsidiary. The Belgian government took up the case of the employees and succeeded in securing a debate within the I. M. E. on the general principle of the responsibility of foreign parents for their wholly owned subsidiaries. Although the I. M. E. reached no conclusions on the particular case, the members of the committee had been briefed by the Belgian government and unions and undoubtedly had the particular case in mind when discussing the general principles. Equally, the Belgian government and unions were able to use the general conclusions of the Committee as to when the Guidelines imposed responsibility upon the parent for the debts of its subsidiary in subsequent negotiations with the Badger company, which resulted in the parent supplementing the subsidiary's assets, though probably not to the extent originally claimed.

The utilisation of the Guidelines and the I. M. E. Committee in this way so soon after the adoption of the Guidelines established a procedure that has subsequently been utilised (by mid-1978) once more by a government and some twenty times by the T. U. A. C.[71] In the 1979 review of the Guidelines the position of the I. M. E. was strengthened. Although it still does not have power to consider individual cases, the Council of the O. E. C. D. accepted that the I. M. E. has responsibilities for the classification of the general principles and that it should be the responsibility of the Committee to respond at all appropriate times to requests for clarification.

IX. Conclusion

There is a strange contrast between the great significance of multinational groups of companies for national labour movements and the relative feebleness of the international responses of these movements to international accumulations of capital. Should such social responses by labour movements develop, there will clearly be a range of legal problems that national labour law systems will have to face (only some of which have been touched upon in this paper). Until that time, however, national labour law systems may be able to get by with surprisingly little explicit considerations of these problems.

[71] T. W. Vogelaar, 10 Bull. of Comparative Labour Relations 72 (1979).

Résumé:

Le droit du travail et les groupes de sociétés multinationaux

Cet article propose différentes réflexions de droit comparé, d'un point de vue de l'Europe occidentale, sur les implications des groupes de sociétés multinationaux sur les relations employeurs-salariés nationales et les systèmes de droit du travail. Nous avons au début une recherche de la preuve empirique pour et contre les critiques les plus fréquentes sur les sociétés multinationales, à savoir leur manquement à se conformer aux pratiques nationales, leur capacité à miner le pouvoir des syndicats nationaux et leur influence sur l'emploi dans le pays d'origine. La conclusion est qu'il y a certaines preuves que la seconde critique est valable. Puis nous avons une étude des tentatives qui ont été faites par les syndicats nationaux et transnationaux pour contrebalancer leurs faiblesses en établissant des conventions collectives multinationales. Nous voyons que peu de progrès ont été réalisés dans ce domaine, mais une action solidaire internationale, restreinte mais en voie de développement, peut être enregistrée. Les problèmes juridiques relatifs à l'action solidaire internationale sont étudiés de manière assez détaillée, ainsi que des propositions pour une harmonisation et une réforme qui récemment ont été faites. L'article enfin se consacre à deux autres méthodes de neutralisation des faiblesses des syndicats qui ont été proposées: la représentation institutionelle des salariés au sein des groupes multinationaux et l'établissement de codes de conduite internationaux, en particulier par l'OCDE. La mise en œuvre de ces derniers codes est brièvement analysée.

What is Wrong with Unitary Taxation?

Gustaf Lindencrona*
Stockholm

I. Unitary Taxation of Multinationals: the California Scheme

In the study of taxation of multinational enterprises (hereinafter referred to as MNEs), no question has recently attracted such vivid interest as the attempt by the State of California to extend application of the so-called "unitary" or "global" method of taxation to foreign, i. e., non-U. S. MNEs.[1] According to the unitary method of transactional allocation of profits, there is an overall division of the profits of an enterprise among the various countries in which the enterprise operates.[2] California currently applies this method to U. S. MNEs operating within its jurisdiction but, until recently, has exempted non-U. S. MNEs from the practice. The California allocation formula is based upon a percentage calculation of three types of business income: sales, property, and payroll. The California portion of each factor is then compared to the global portion, which results in a figure (ratio) that is used for apportioning global income attributable to California.[3]

The California method of unitary taxation of MNEs is in complete breach of internationally accepted principles of income taxation.[4] According to these

* The author wishes to acknowledge the valuable help of David Burman, J. D., Los Angeles.

1 This interest primarily surrounds the re-negotiation of the U. S./U. K. tax convention.

2 S. S. Surrey, *Reflections on the Allocation of Income and Expenses Among National Tax Jurisdictions*, 10 Law & Policy in International Business 409 at 415 (1978). For a description of the global method formula allocation, *see* C. S. Shoup, *Taxation of Multinational Corporations*, in Technical Papers: Taxation, The Impact of Multinational Corporations on Development and International Relations, U. N. Doc. ST/ESA/11, 34 (U. N. Dept. of Economic and Social Affairs, New York, 1974).

3 For a description of formula allocation in state taxation in the U. S., *see* C. E. McLure, *State Income Taxation of Multi-state Corporations in the U. S. A.*, in Technical Papers, *supra* note 2.

4 Transactional allocation of income of MNEs has developed in most Western countries around the concept of the "arm's length" principle. The notion is best expressed and its precepts 'codified' in OECD, Transfer Pricing and Multinational Enterprises, Report of the Committee on Fiscal Affairs (adopted by the Council on 16 May 1979) (Paris, 1979); *see* generally, Surrey, *supra* note 2; W. Kumpf, *General Principles for the Determination of Arm's Length Prices in International Groups*, 1976 Intertax 359;

principles, the taxable income attributable to each subsidiary of an MNE is calculated on the basis of the arm's length principle: thus, if the parent company is domiciled in one country and a subsidiary in another, all transactions between the two are expected to be conducted as if they were independent parties dealing at arm's length. For tax purposes they are treated as separate entities and taxed accordingly. In practice, rules have been promulgated governing the allocation and apportionment of income and deductions among the members of a MNE.

II. The Effects of the California Scheme and U. S. Federal-States Relations

The Commerce Clause[5] and the Due Process Clause[6] of the United States Constitution place restrictions on the power of individual states to tax the income of companies engaged in interstate activities. Thus for state tax purposes, income derived from interstate activities must be apportioned among the different states where business is conducted.

It is deplorable that the individual states, despite their many attempts to agree on a uniform system of profit allocation among themselves, have been unable to do so. Since the states are tax sovereign, in principle they share some of the same problems as independent sovereign countries. Indeed it can be said that on the international level there has been greater success in resolving the issue of transactional, as well as jurisdictional, allocation of income, than there has been progress within the United States. This development is primarily due to the acceptance of the OECD's Draft and Model Conventions, in particular Article 9 of the 1963 and 1977 Model Conventions.[7] In the United States, there has not been the same cooperation. Some states apply the arm's length principle, the same principle as is used in international taxation. Other states, such as California, apportion business income according to the unitary or global

C. T. Ebenroth, Die verdeckten Vermögenszuwendungen im transnationalen Unternehmen (Bielefeld, 1979). For examples of national legislation, *see* (U. S.) Internal Revenue Code, § 482 and Treasury Reg., § 1.482; (Germany) Foreign Taxation Act, § 1 and Income Tax Act, § 8; (Italy) Presidential Decree n. 597 (1973), arts. 3, 53 & 56; (France) Code Général des Impôts, arts. 57, 155 A & 238 A.

5 U. S. Constitution, art. I, § 8, cl. 3. The Commerce Clause requires that a state's taxation of interstate business must be fairly apportioned to the commerce carried on within the taxing state. Western Livestock v. Bureau of Revenue, 303 U. S. 250, 82 L. Ed. 823 (1938).

6 U. S. Const., Amend. 14. The Due Process Clause places two restrictions on a state's power to tax income generated by the activities of an interstate business. First, no tax may be imposed unless there is some minimal connection between those activities and the taxing state: Nat'l Bellas Hess Inc. v. Dept. of Revenue, 386 U. S. 753, 18 L. Ed. 2d 505 (1967). Second, the income attributed by the State for tax purposes must be rationally related to value connected with the taxing state: Norfolk & Western R'ly Co. v. Missouri State Tax Commissioner, 390 U. S. 317, 19 L. Ed. 2d 1201 (1968).

7 OECD, Draft Double Taxation Convention on Income and Capital (Paris, 1963 and 1977).

method. It is worth noting that the policy of the California State Franchise Tax Board is to *require* apportionment of business income by formula, not only to permit it.[8]

Different opinions have certainly been expressed both within and without the United States on the various methods practised by the individual states in order to establish a fair tax base for state tax purposes. The question became the focus of international attention when California recently extended its unitary method to non-U. S. MNEs and required accounting information from these companies on a world-wide basis in order to properly calculate their taxable income in California. This extension of the unitary method was not the result of new legislation, but rather the result of a change in policy by the California tax authorities. Since it was a gradual change, it is difficult to pinpoint its exact beginning – however, it began generally in the mid-1970's. The California example has spread along the Pacific and Oregon and Alaska have passed legislation enabling similar methods to be used.[9]

Technically, only companies that are engaged in business in California are subject to California income and franchise tax. Under the California philosophy, however, a parent and its subsidiaries (whether or not located in California) are treated as one "unit" (thus the name "unitary method") in order to determine the correct tax base for California state tax purposes. Two or more entities are considered to be conducting a "unitary business" if they are controlled by the same interests. Control has been interpreted to mean direct or indirect ownership of 50% or more of the outstanding voting stock.[10] Originally, criteria other than control were also used to determine unity of operation of affiliated companies. With the passage of time, the control test has come to be regarded as the basic criterion.[11] The effect on a non-U. S. MNE is that if one of its subsidiaries, which is more than 50% foreign controlled, is doing business in California, all operations of the parent (wherever located) are considered as a unit in order to establish the correct tax base in California. The separate corporate identity of the members of an MNE are thus completely ignored for California state tax purposes.[12] The corporate taxpayer in California is required to file a Combined Report along with its tax return which shows how unitary business income was determined and apportioned.[13] This means that the world-wide income of an MNE doing business in California through a branch or subsidiary must be calculated according to California rules.[14] California state tax

[8] E. J. Peterson and F. I. Walsh, *The Impact of the California Unitary Business Concept on the Taxation of Multinational Corporations*, 1978 INTERTAX 107.

[9] ICC, THE POTENTIALLY DANGEROUS EFFECT UPON INTERNATIONAL COMMERCE OF THE "GLOBAL" OR "UNITARY" BASIS OF ASSESSMENT, Doc. No. 180/195, Or. Rev., p. 3.

[10] CALIFORNIA STATE FRANCHISE TAX BOARD, GUIDE FOR CORPORATIONS FILING A COMBINED REPORT, FTB 1001 (3-78) p. 4 (1979).

[11] ICC, *supra*, note 9, at 3.

[12] FRANCHISE TAX BOARD GUIDE, *supra* note 10, at 3.

[13] *Id.* at 3.

[14] *Id.* at 4.

is then computed pursuant to the three factor formula. For each factor a ratio is established, e. g., sales in California over global sales. The average percentage of the three factors is calculated and multiplied by the amount of unitary business income to be apportioned. The product represents income taxable in California.[15]

I will not discuss in this paper the constitutionality of the California unitary taxation method, as I regard it mainly as of U. S. internal character. Two recent U. S. Supreme Court cases on the subject are, however, worthy of comment. In *Moorman Manufacturing Co. v. Bair*,[16] the Court held that an Iowa single-factor sales formula did not violate the Due Process Clause of the 14th Amendment, as resulting in extraterritorial taxation by a state within the United States. However, in *Japan Line Ltd. v. County of Los Angeles*,[17] it was held that California's imposition of its non-discriminatory tax on shipping containers violated the Commerce Clause since the tax resulted in the multiple taxation of instrumentalities of international commerce and prevented the United States from "speaking with one voice" in regulating foreign trade. Thus, when applied internally by and among the individual states, the unitary method appears to be sanctioned by the Constitution. Whether the method is impermissible with respect to state taxation of non-U. S. MNEs cannot definitely be concluded from reading the opinion in the *Japan Line* case, since it dealt with an ad valorem property tax and not an income tax. Ostensibly, the extraterritorial application of the unitary method does prevent the United States from "speaking with one voice" in international affairs.

In the U. S. Senate, the question of unitary taxation has been mixed with the question of States' rights.[18] When the U. S./U. K. Treaty came up for renegotiation, it was agreed that the Treaty should include a clause preventing states from applying the unitary basis to profits of companies within a U. K. group in so far as they were operating outside the U. S. The Senate Foreign Relations Committee recommended adoption of the Treaty. During the Senate vote, however, the Treaty did not attract the two-thirds majority necessary for approval. The Senators voting against ratification stated that they did not want to infringe upon the states' power of taxation. In the U. K., the House of Commons accepted the Treaty without an effective anti-unitary clause (Section 9 (4)), while condemning the unitary basis of assessment.[19]

[15] *Id.* at 7.

[16] 437 U. S. 267, 57 L. Ed. 2d 197 (1978).

[17] 437 U. S. 267, 60 L. Ed. 2d 336 (1979).

[18] The concept of "states' rights" emerged during the time of independence of the colonies, and is commonly referred to as the conflict between the states and the federal government with regard to what extent they may infringe upon each others powers. *See* generally, for a discussion of this concept, E. I. Michelman, *States' Rights and States' Roles: Permutations of "Sovereignty" in National League of Cities v. Usery*, 86 YALE L. J. 1165 (1977).

[19] ICC, *supra* note 9, at 4. Article 9 (4) remains but applies now only to the Federal Government and is thus without importance.

The opinion in the United States on unitary taxation is, at least in respect of foreign relations, divided. Bills have been introduced in Congress to forbid unitary assessment of income tax. In California, there is pending a bill to abolish unitary taxation of non-U. S. MNEs. It was passed by the State Assembly[20] and is now before the State Senate. The bill does not, however, condemn the unitary method as contrary to generally accepted principles of international taxation, but rather simply takes the position that foreign investment in California is dwindling because foreign MNEs fear being taxed in California on a unitary basis.

III. The International Reaction

A. International Chamber of Commerce

The reaction of the international legal community to the California system of taxing MNEs on a unitary basis has been strong. The International Chamber of Commerce (ICC), which represents the business community of the world, has adopted the following resolution:

> The ICC views with concern the inevitability that an increase in cases in which profits taxes are levied by political sub-divisions unencumbered by treaty obligations, will result in mounting double taxation of profits (which tax treaties set out to avoid). This is particularly so if the basis of assessment in any such political sub-division is not entirely consistent with that of the country itself and extends to operations carried on outside the country. This problem has manifested itself in an acute form in connection with the attempts of the State of California to impose the "global" or "unitary" form of assessment based on income of companies involved in international operations outside the U. S.
>
> The dangers of double taxation and the administrative problems arising from the taxation policy of California, and other political sub-divisons, have undoubtedly deterred would-be investors from making investments which would otherwise have been undertaken. This approach, if it should spread, could easily become a most important threat to international trade since international operations would inevitably be confronted with a real danger of multiple taxation of the same profits and unacceptable administrative burdens. The dangers were also recognized by the Council of the OECD in rejecting the so-called "global" method in its recent report on Transfer Pricing (*Transfer Pricing and Multinational Enterprises*. OECD, Paris, July 1979, pp. 14-15).
>
> The ICC reconfirms its view that, as a general rule, tax should be based on a fair measure of income as computed by reference to the amount which could be expected to arise between independent parties dealing at arm's length. This rule has universal application. The ICC therefore recommends that, in all cases where the taxation policies of political subdivisions extend to non-domestic operations, all possible measures should be taken to ensure that the terms of an agreement or treaty dealing with taxation on income should bind all authorities having jurisdiction within the boundaries of each contracting State. This recommendation is in accordance with the OECD model taxation Convention 1977 (Art. 2) and a considerable number of international friendship, trade and shipping treaties.

[20] Under the condition, however, that California taxes are not reduced by the Jarvis II popular referendum proposals for California tax code reforms.

B. OECD

The Organization for Economic Co-operation and Development (OECD), which represents the governments of Western Europe, Australia, Canada, Japan, New Zealand and the United States, has recently published a report prepared by the Committee on Fiscal Affairs entitled *Transfer Pricing and Multinational Enterprises.*[21] The report makes the following strong comment:

> Proposals for radical reformulations of the approach to intra-group transfer pricing which would move away from the arm's length approach towards so-called global or direct methods of profit allocation, or towards fixing transfer prices by reference to predetermined formulae for allocating profits between affiliates, are not endorsed in this report. The use of such alternatives to the arm's length principle is incompatible in fact with Articles 7 and 9 of the OECD Model Double Taxation Convention. Such methods would necessarily be arbitrary, tending to disregard market conditions as well as the particular circumstances of the individual enterprises and tending to ignore the management's own allocation of resources, thus producing an allocation of profits which may bear no sound relationship to the economic facts and inherently running the risk of allocating profits to an entity which is in truth making losses (or possibly the contrary). A number of such methods are sometimes advocated, allocating profits in some cases in proportion to the respective costs of the associated enterprises, sometimes in proportion to their respective turnovers or to their respective labour forces, or by some formula taking account of several such criteria. They are all however to some degree arbitrary. For example, it does not follow that profit is uniformly related to cost at all stages in an integrated production and marketing process. Indeed the problem of allocating costs could well be no easier than in using the cost plus method to arrive at an arm's length price. Nor does it follow that labour costs are the same for the same labour in different countries, or that profits are necessarily related to any simple combination of such factors. To allocate profits by such methods in a way which reduced the arbitrariness of the results to a negligible degree would necessitate a complex analysis of the different functions of the various associated enterprises and a sophisticated weighing up of the different risks and profit opportunities in the various different stages of manufacturing, transportation, marketing and so on. Nor would the information necessary for such an assessment be readily available or, in many cases, available at all. The need would be for full information about the total activities of the whole MNE. While the widest range of such information may be available to the tax authorities in the country of the parent company in a group even those tax authorities will be limited to some extent in the information which they can compile. The tax authorities of the country in which a subsidiary is situated will on the other hand be in no position to acquire even this amount of information without imposing on the MNE itself a possibly intolerable administrative burden, or a similar burden on the tax authorities of the parent company's country if they seek to get the information by way of exchange of information provisions under double taxation agreements. Nor can it be generally assumed that the tax authorities of the country of the subsidiary should in any case be entitled to quite such a wide range of information about the group's worldwide activities. In practice moreover the information may simply not be available to those authorities. Even if the information were available, however, the varied activities of any MNE and the varied circumstances and situations in which they are carried on must make it impracticable for the tax authorities of the country in which one

[21] OECD, *supra* note 4. For a critical response to the "report" *see* Business and Industry Advisory Committee, BIAC's Response to the OECD's Report on Transfer Pricing and Multinational Enterprises, (Annex) 29 Oct. 1979.

subsidiary is situated to judge in any satisfactory manner the profitability of any of the other parts of the group situated elsewhere. Moreover, problems would still arise in the comparison of figures produced in different countries by different accounting methods and different legal requirements. Another major disadvantage of any attempt to use such global methods of profit allocation as an alternative to the arm's length principle is that their unco-ordinated use by the tax authorities of several countries would involve the danger that, overall, the MNE affected would suffer double taxation of its profits. This is not to say, however, that in seeking to arrive at the arm's length price in a range of transactions, some regard to the total profits of the relevant MNE may not be helpful, as a check on the assessment of the arm's length price or in specific bilateral situations where other methods give rise to serious difficulties and the two countries concerned are able to adopt a common approach and the necessary information can be made available.[22]

C. International Fiscal Association

During the general debate at the 1979 Congress of the International Fiscal Association (IFA), a certain passage in a proposed resolution (on another subject) was deleted specifically because it might be interpreted as acceptance in principal of unitary taxation.

IV. What is Wrong with Unitary Taxation?

For one unfamiliar with the economics of international taxation, it may be easy to find the idea of unitary taxation appealing. Would it not be a progressive step to tax an MNE and all its subsidiaries and branches uniformly, and thus avoid the problems of finding an uncontrolled market price for transfers between affiliated companies? Would this not ensure that MNEs are taxed fairly and that each country receives its due share of tax?

Despite the growing economic importance of California, the taxation in that state alone is no reason for international concern. The situation in California is of interest only because of the potential that unitary taxation of MNEs might be adopted by other states, as well as by other countries that are not bound by treaty obligations. If the system in California were non-malignant, curiosity into its nature might be purely academic – after all, California, in itself, is a place where one has learned to expect the unusual. But the threat of infection is quite real and thus necessitates prudent observation, careful diagnosis and appropriate counter-measures. The following discussion is based on the assumption that the system might spread to other countries.

A. Unitary as Distinguished from Uniform Taxation

Unitary taxation is not uniform taxation. Under the unitary tax system, an MNE doing business in California through a branch or subsidiary is required to disclose financial information on its world-wide operations according to U. S. accounting standards. This may be difficult because the foreign groups' financial

[22] OECD, *supra* note 4, at 14.

statements are based on foreign accounting standards.[23] Quite naturally, the tax laws of sovereign countries are not alike. The differences might sometimes be considerable. Even within the European Coummunities, efforts to achieve tax harmonization with regard to the computation of business income have not been successful. Should the California system be adopted by other states, and by other countries, this would lead us away from a goal of uniformity. It would mean that the MNEs would be forced to compute their world-wide profits according to the accounting standards of the different countries applying a unitary system in which it was doing business.

Unitary taxation is suitable only in either of two situations: (1) If the world-wide profits of MNEs are calculated according to the rules of *one* country. This situs must be the country of residence of the parent. (2) If the tax laws of all countries in the world are made uniform. Such unification is certainly a goal worthy of international cooperation. It is evident, however, that this goal is distant. Even a step such as taxing the world-wide income of a MNE in the country of the parent is in breach with current principles of international taxation if the same income is later allocated by formula pursuant to a unitary system. All existing double taxation treaties would have to be renegotiated. Much can be said for and against such a system of taxation. I will demur from that discussion in this context. It is important to note, however, that this is not what the unitary system implies. The unitary system means that every country in which a branch or subsidiary of a MNE operates will tax, on a world-wide basis, the income of the group according to its own rules.

B. Double Taxation

The impetus for cooperation in the field of international taxation has been the desire to avoid international double taxation, the result when the same income is taxed in more than one country. With the tax rates now in effect in many countries, double taxation can be financially disastrous. Double taxation is avoided mainly through double taxation conventions, or tax treaties. Tax treaties have acquired a growing degree of uniformity due to the successful work of the OECD which has influenced the development of treaties through its Model Conventions of 1963 and 1977. The rules for the avoidance of double taxation have thus become much more uniform.

It is apparent, however, that the unitary system will lead to increased double taxation. The California tax authorities apply the unitary method regardless of whether the tax due will be higher or lower than the amount calculated under the arm's length method.[24] Since all countries of the world, as well as the political sub-divisions of the United States, are tax sovereign, they each might invent different formulas for income apportionment. Different formulas would invari-

[23] M. Burge, *The 1975 U. K. Treaty as a Concrete Example of How Some Problems Can Be Handled*, in N. Y. U. INTERNATIONAL INSTITUTE ON TAX AND BUSINESS PLANNING, 1977 TAX TREATIES AND COMPETENT AUTHORITY (New York, 1978).

[24] Petersen and Walsh, *supra* note 8, at 109.

ably result in double taxation. This result is all the more likely as every country seeks a formula which, on the average, is most favourable to that country. A country with high property values, such as a country dependent on mining, would attribute greater importance to property than sales if all production is sold abroad. It is, of course, possible that the increased tax burden resulting from a more widespread use of unitary taxation principles can be avoided through double taxation conventions. This would require renegotiation of all existing treaties. In addition, it is difficult to find the principles necessary for the avoidance of double taxation given the unitary system. There appears to be no possibility other than agreeing upon a uniform formula for the apportionment of income. Still, this would not be enough. So long as different methods for the computation of income are used in various countries, the *amount* of world-wide income to be apportioned would vary according to the accounting standards applied. Whether this is regarded as double taxation is a matter of definition. It is not likely that the parties to a convention, however, would be inclined to accept such a result.

The current situation under the application of the arm's length principle is quite different. Each country retains the right to apply its own rules for the levying of tax on specific types of income according to the treaty. Under this system, the provisions are used only for the computation of profits that are to be taxed in that country. Under the unitary system, the internal rules of each country are used for the computation of the world-wide profits of the entire MNE. If the Contracting States try to avoid this problem by agreeing on uniform rules for the computation of world-wide group profits, we would be moving in the direction of a global uniform system. Only in this case would the problem of double taxation be resolved. Double taxation can thus be avoided only when the tax law of the country where the parent is resident is used or when the tax laws are uniform.

C. Taxable Income and Actual Profits

Under the arm's length principle, income is apportioned according to the productive activities giving rise to that income in a particular country. This principle is easy to grasp and is widely accepted.[25] The use of an apportionment system of the California type does not produce the same result – taxable income might be very different from the actual profits produced in the taxing country. There is, therefore, no necessary relationship between the profits actually earned by the enterprise in that jurisdiction and the base upon which it is taxed.[26] If sales are unprofitable – due to price regulations or other reasons – high sales are no indication of high profits; sales values are increased by high sales tax; high payroll costs could as well be a sign of low profitability as of high profitability; in some developing countries property costs are low and profits are large.[27] Thus

[25] *See* generally, *supra* note 4.

[26] M. Gammie, *The Anglo-American Double Taxation Treaty: End of the Road at Last?* TAXATION, March 29, 1979 at 418.

[27] ICC, *supra* note 9, at 5.

local factors which affect the margin of profit are accorded no consideration.

There are other problems, too. Exchange fluctuations can increase or decrease the world-wide income of an MNE and the income allotted to each country without any change in profits. Exchange controls may make big profits of minor value to owners abroad.[28] In short, acceptance of the unitary system results in a system of taxation that bears no rational relationship to actual earnings.

D. Consequences for Minority Shareholders

Minority shareholders present a special problem in a tax system of the California type. As mentioned, an MNE is taxed as a "unit" if it owns more than 50% of the outstanding voting stock of a subsidiary. This means that there may exist a rather large number of minority shareholders, which is not an uncommon situation. When the arm's length principle is applied, the minority shareholders of a subsidiary of an MNE will bear taxes on the profits of the subsidiary. In a system of unitary taxation, minority shareholders of a subsidiary must bear taxes that are based on the world-wide income of the MNE in which they may own no shares.[29] In other words, buying shares in a subsidiary, from a tax point of view, is almost the equivalent to buying shares in the controlling company. From a civil law point of view, however, the difference is as great as before. Unitary taxation thus means a widening gap between corporate law and tax law.

E. Tax Sovereignty of Political Sub-Divisions of a State

A special problem with the unitary tax system in California stems from the fact that California is a political sub-division of the United States. As mentioned, the Constitution of the United States permits the states a certain degree of tax sovereignty.[30] They are thus entitled to levy taxes in the same way as the federal government. Foreign relations are, however, in the exclusive hands of the federal government. United States tax treaties cover only federal taxes, not state and municipal taxes.[31] The states are prohibited from entering into treaties with foreign governments.[32] This means that if an individual state levies a tax directly or indirectly on foreign income, no treaty remedy is specifically provided. The states could, however, be bound by the terms of a treaty as the supreme law of the land if they are covered by it.[33] From a technical tax point of view such methods as unitary taxation pose special problems for the United States in respect of foreign relations.

[28] *Id.*

[29] *Id.* at 6.

[30] *Supra* notes 5 and 6.

[31] H. J. Ault & P. R. McDaniel, Introduction to U. S. Inter-Taxation, at 153 (Deventer, 1977).

[32] U. S. Const., art. I, § 10, cl. 1.

[33] Kolovrat v. Oregon, 366 U. S. 187, 6 L. Ed. 2d 218 (1961).

V. Is the Arm's Length Method Infallible?

The basic philosophy behind the internationally accepted arm's length principle for transfer pricing in MNEs, is that the "comparable uncontrolled price" is correct from a tax point of view. Independent parties doing business in a free market look out for their own interests and try to get the best price. The market price is subject to less artificial manipulation and expresses a reasonable compromise between buyer and seller. The problem with transfer pricing between affiliated companies is, however, that it may be impossible to determine a comparable uncontrolled price. Determining the price of goods appears to present less difficulties than doing so for services, technology or royalties, for example. However, where a large MNE is vertically integrated, it may purchase all the production of a semi-finished product from one of its subsidiaries, a product being neither produced nor sold elsewhere. The MNE may in turn sell the finished product to another member of the group. Therefore, there exists no market outside that particular MNE, in which to determine a comparable uncontrolled market price.

The difficulty in finding a correct price has led the United States to issue detailed regulations under Internal Revenue Code § 482 on the application of the arm's length principle. The Federal Republic of Germany and the United Kingdom, although having basic statutes on the subject,[34] are still formulating their own rules. The OECD report deals extensively with the problem of finding generally agreed practices in determining transfer prices for tax purposes on the basis of the arm's length principle. For goods, the comparable uncontrolled price method, the resale price method and the cost plus method are recommended. I will not discuss here the advantages and disadvantages of these methods. It is clear that great difficulties exist in finding a reasonable price for tax purposes.[35] If the transfer price used by an MNE in dealing with an affiliate abroad is not acceptable, the tax consequences can be severe. Many tax treaties contain a provision similar to Article 9 of the 1963 OECD Model Double Taxation Convention, which does not foresee any adjustment of taxable income of the company in the other state. A reallocation of profits due to the fact that a price was not at arm's length will thus inevitably lead to double taxation. A solution could possibly be found by a mutual agreement between the Contracting States, but it is by no means certain. The OECD 1977 Model Double Taxation Convention does include in paragraph 2 of Article 9 a provision requesting the Contracting State that made the initial adjustment to "make an appropriate adjustment to the amount of tax charged therein on those profits". Unfortunately, several countries have reserved their position on this paragraph.

The arm's length principle thus does have severe problems of its own. To a

[34] For Germany, *see supra* note 4; United Kingdom, Income and Corporation Taxes Act 1970, s. 485.

[35] For a recent example, *see* T. Nielsen, *The Arm's Length Test: A Rule of Law – or an Excuse for Arbitrary Taxation?*, 1979 INTERTAX 296 (on Denmark and the Oil Companies).

certain extent it is possible to overcome them. First of all it should be remembered that corporate tax rates do not differ much in the Western industrialized countries (roughly around 50%). The MNEs that operate principally in these countries thus have no real interest in shifting profits from one country to another by manipulating prices. The large MNEs have a business interest in avoiding distortions in transfer prices as these prices are the only method by which the parent can receive any real information on the activities of its subsidiaries. Apart from public relations considerations, it is probably a better idea for the MNEs to do some careful tax planning, e. g., using holding companies in tax haven jurisdictions to hold shares, intellectual property rights or other assets. A recent Scandinavian study shows, however, that such measures are scarcely employed by large MNEs with subsidiaries in Scandinavia.[36]

Controversies between tax administrations can be avoided to a certain degree by finding better internationally accepted methods for computing an arm's length price. The OECD report is an important step in this direction. If, however, a transfer price is not accepted by one tax administration, it is extremely important that a method exists by which double taxation is avoided.

The proposal by the Commission of the European Communities for a council directive on the elimination of double taxation in connection with the adjustment of transfers of profits between associated enterprises *(arbitration procedure)*[37] would, if adopted in one form or another, be an important step forward. It makes it mandatory for the members of the EC to eliminate double taxation due to the adjustment of transfer prices between affiliated companies, and it establishes an arbitration procedure which could be set in motion if a solution of the double taxation problem is not found by other means.[38]

VI. The Future

Evidently, the arm's length principle has its shortcomings. They are not by far, however, as many or as severe as the shortcomings of the unitary tax system. They can be overcome to a certain extent. It is acknowledged that the basic deficiency remains – the difficulty in finding an uncontrolled market price in a world in which international trade between members of MNEs is growing at a rapid pace. This deficiency could be overcome by taxing the whole group in the country where the parent company is resident, and then dividing by some formula the taxable profits among the countries in which the MNE conducts business. It is evident that this step cannot be taken until there exists world-wide

[36] LODIN, INTERNATIONAL ENTERPRISES AND TAXATION. SOME PRELIMINARY RESULTS OF AN EMPIRICAL STUDY CONCERNING INTERNATIONAL ENTERPRISES (The Nordic Council for Tax Research, 1979). *See also* 1979 INTERTAX 311.

[37] O. J. E. C., Vol. 19, C 301 p. 4-7 (1976).

[38] For further details *see* G. Lindencrona and N. Mattson, Arbitration in Taxation (to be published), where the authors examine the possibility of using arbitration on an even wider scale to resolve tax problems that cannot be resolved by conventional means, by the inclusion of an appropriate provision in double taxation conventions.

confidence among countries and a high degree of uniformity in corporate tax laws.

Whatever solution the future holds for the taxation of MNEs, it must be based upon sound economic principles and international confidence. A solution can only be achieved through international cooperation – not by unilateral action. In the meanwhile, in practice the arm's length method seems to be the best available for transfer pricing among MNEs.

Résumé:
Les défauts d'un système unitaire de l'imposition des entreprises multinationales

Dans l'étude de l'imposition des entreprises multinationales, aucun problème n'a récemment soulevé un intérêt aussi vif que les efforts de l'État de Californie pour élargir l'application de ce qui est appelé la méthode d'imposition "unitaire" ou "globale" aux entreprises multinationales étrangères, c'est-à-dire non-américaines. Dès qu'une société exerce une activité commerciale en Californie, toutes les sociétés du groupe, qu'elles soient ou non établies en Californie, sont traitées comme une "unité" afin de déterminer l'assiette de l'impôt correcte en Californie. Cela signifie que le revenu mondial d'une entreprise multinationale ayant une activité commerciale en Californie au moyen d'une branche ou d'une filiale, doit être calculé selon les dispositions californiennes. L'impôt d'État californien est calculé conformément à une formule en trois volets: ventes, patrimoine et bilan comptable en Californie en relation avec les ventes, le patrimoine et le bilan comptable globaux.

La méthode californienne est une rupture complète avec le principe internationalement accepté de l'imposition des groupes, la méthode "arm's length" (redressement en cas d'un transfert indirect de bénéfices entre les membres du groupe). La réaction internationale a été très forte, car on craignait que l'exemple californien ne soit suivi par d'autres États fédéraux ainsi que par d'autres pays non liés par des traités.

Le systeme californien présente les désavantages suivants: tout d'abord l'imposition unitaire n'est pas une imposition uniforme. Le système unitaire signifie que chaque pays dans lequel une branche ou une filiale d'une entreprise multinationale a une activité imposera sur une assiette mondiale le revenu du groupe et cela selon ses propres règles. Les difficultés administratives pour les entreprises multinationales et les administrations fiscales seront considérables. En second lieu, comme chaque pays cherchera une formule qui lui soit le plus souvent favorable, le système conduira à une double imposition. En troisième lieu, il n'existe aucune relation entre les profits réellement réalisés par une entreprise sur un territoire déterminé et la base sur laquelle elle sera imposée. Quatrièmement, les actionnaires minoritaires d'une filiale doivent supporter les impôts calculés sur le revenu mondial du groupe alors qu'ils ne possèdent pas de parts dans la société-mère. Cinquièmement la Californie, une subdivision politique des États-Unis, applique des principes, d'imposition internationale incompatibles avec les principes appliqués par les États-Unis.

La méthode "arm's length" n'est pas sans défauts. Des réformes doivent cependant être entreprises non par une action unilatérale, mais à travers la coopération internationale.

Annex/Annexe I

Discussion Report / Résumé de la discussion

Colloquium on Multinational Corporations in European Corporate and Antitrust Laws, 28-31 May 1980 at the European University Institute in Florence*
(Volume II: Groups of Companies in European Laws)

RAIMUND T. RAITH
Ann Arbor

Chapter I: Horizontal Groups and Joint Ventures: the Practical Experience

I. Horizontal Groups and Joint Ventures in Europe: Concepts and Realities

REPORTER: Dr. W. F. BAYER

The first report relating to corporate law aspects of multinational corporations was presented by Dr. *Bayer*, who described the situation of horizontal groups and joint ventures from a practitioner's point of view.

Horizontal groups are a mainly European phenomenon and their peculiarity is that they have a bi-national structure, mostly on the basis of a 50/50 equity capital distribution. The reasons for the setting up of many horizontal groups can be traced to the creation of a European Common Market, some national groups, even those with foreign affiliates, fearing that their existing structure would not suffice to cope with the new requirements of a common market. Some companies thought it more efficient to enter into a bi-national tie with another firm rather than to establish their own facilities in a foreign country where the production and market conditions were to a great extent unknown.

The problems encountered by such groups were manifold. In the beginning there was a great deal of ignorance on both sides concerning the legal and factual order of the other country. But the principal problem resided in the substantial divergences existing amongst the tax and labour law applied within the different

* This Discussion Report is prepared as a supplement to the National and European Community Reports published in this volume. Utilizing the wealth of comment offered at the Colloquium it tries to highlight those features which seemed most interesting and enlightening in relation to the different reports.

European countries, which was in part the result of the different employment and restructuring policies of national governments. When these structures were first introduced it was greatly hoped that the EEC would harmonize the relevant laws, but over the last twenty years there seems to have been more disintegration than integration in this field.

At present, horizontal groups are undergoing a phase of important changes: some have already separated, such as *Kléber-Semperit* or *Fokker-VFW;* some have undergone important restructuring, as in the case of *Agfa-Gevaert* or *Dunlop-Pirelli,* where the original distribution of the equity capital has been considerably altered. Only smaller sized groups operating in rather specialized areas seem to be really successful, as for example the *Polygram* group. In conclusion, it can be said that horizontal groups have proved in general to be much less successful than traditionally structured multinational enterprises and since 1974/75 few new bi-national horizontal groups have been established. The main reason for the relative failure of this type of structure is to be found in the lack of harmonization in the fields of labour, tax and accounting law, on which this kind of group depends to a much higher degree than the traditional multinational group.

This rather pessimistic view was not shared by all. Interestingly enough Professor *Hopt* could give the latest newspaper financial news to the audience, where the establishment of a new horizontal group between *St. Gobain* of France and *Olivetti* of Italy was announced. Subsequently Professor *Hirsch,* in contrast to *Bayer's* rather pessimistic outlook, underlined that the "mini horizontal" type of group does have a very positive perspective, and that, therefore, the subject of horizontal groups, particularly in a European law context, could still be of some interest.

Professor *Champaud* mentioned the lack of strategic considerations – as opposed to purely political and technical considerations – which seems more frequently to have underlain the creation of horizontal groups, as the principal reason for their failure. But at the same time, he pointed out that new forms of horizontal groups are emerging, for instance, in the domain of cooperation between enterprises of industrialized countries on the one side and of third world countries on the other, where the host country's national law frequently requires a 50% participation in the equity capital by a domestic partner; in the field of common distribution companies, where the horizontal group structure is used to reduce individual costs for the system; and in order to limit the risks of entering new markets. *Champaud* believes that these latter forms of horizontal groups have a positive future.

Professor *Dunning* answering Professor *Jacquemin's* question on the probable future structures of multinational undertakings, pointed out that there will be a considerable spectrum, ranging from 100% participation with a very centralized decision-making policy on one side, to purely contractual ventures on the other side. It will depend largely, first, upon the field of activity; second, on the intended place of business; and third, upon the country from which the investors come. It seems that there is a learning process in progress, and that management have learnt that it is no longer necessary to hold 51% of the equity capital in order to control a company: even a 2% shareholding if combined with some other means of influence can equally confer control.

Bayer drew attention to the national origins of the investor as a factor in determining the legal structure which a group will take; thus it seems that U. S. based undertakings are generally much more eager to obtain control than investors based in smaller countries. On the whole, however, he did not agree that there exists a tendency towards decentralization, although the pattern may change.

Chapter II: Groups of Companies in Major European Laws

I. The German Experience with the Law of Affiliated Enterprises

REPORTER: PROFESSOR H. WIEDEMANN

Professor *Wiedemann* referring to the German Law concerning groups, pointed out that the basic idea of German law is to establish rules of conduct for a dominating enterprise in relation to the management of a controlled, and therefore dependent, enterprise. The law starts from the assumption that there exists a certain equilibrium among the shareholders and, therefore, ideally both the basic decisions and the conduct of management are oriented around a common company interest. The interests of creditors and employees are thereby simultaneously protected in an indirect manner. This harmony is endangered if one shareholder, or a coherent group thereof, holds a majority, and in particular if this majority shareholder is itself a commercial enterprise operating in a field which is related to the field in which the dominated enterprise is active. The main aim of German Law is to protect the parties relevant under company law of the dependent company, without making changes in the dominant enterprise, looking at the structures which already exist rather than at the process of formation.

According to a survey in 1971, there existed at that time 287 contracts of control; but in recent years this figure seems to have decreased considerably, the reason for this development being, probably, the corporation tax reform of 1977 (corporation tax traditionally being the most important incentive for the formation of a combine).

German law distinguishes between contractual combines and de facto combines. The weakness of the system becomes evident when, for example, one looks at the enterprise contracts (which are only contracts in form but not in substance), since the terms of the contracts are not freely negotiated but dictated by the dominant partner at a time when the relationship of dominance is already in existence. Upon the conclusion of a contract of control or for the transfer of profits, the outside shareholders of the dependent company have a right either to adequate compensation or to withdraw from the company in return for a grant of the dominant enterprise's shares, but it has to be kept in mind that compensation and indemnity claims involve a great deal of risks for the outside shareholders. Furthermore the dominant enterprise has an obligation to indemnify every annual deficit of the dependent corporation.

The second alternative is the de facto combine and in this case the law prohibits the dominant enterprise from prejudicing the dependent company. If the dependent company should suffer any damage from a transaction executed upon the orders of the dominating enterprise, this latter will be liable for the damage; in practice, however, it has turned out to be extremly difficult to prove such damage.

The present law thus does not protect sufficiently the legally approved interests of outside shareholders, creditors and employees. In the last report of the Commission on Enterprise Law a new proposal for the reform of the relevant sections of the German Stock Corporation Law has been proposed, but as extensive other parts of the Law would have to be changed as well, the chances of this reform being realized seem to be very small.

II. Groups of Companies in French Law

Reporter: Professor R. Houin

Professor *Houin* presented the French law on combined enterprises, observing that in France also there exists a strong tendency towards concentration, but that no such tax incentives as, for example, can be found in Germany exist.

There is no definition of a group, the law merely defines a "filiale" as a company which is owned by more than 50% by another; and a "participation" as a 10-50% shareholding; the existence of a real dependency is not important. If these requirements are fulfilled, there is a duty to inform the shareholders, a limitation concerning the possibility of cross-participations and an incompatibility for auditors to serve for both companies at the same time.

Of interest also is the fact that it is illegal under French law for a subsidiary to be 100% owned by another company, but it is obvious that within a group it is not difficult to comply with this rule.

Concerning the acquisition of stocks a fundamental distinction has to be made between stocks quoted on the stock exchange and those which are not quoted. Whereas the latter are not governed by any special rules, the former are subject to a large number of restrictions, e. g., the shares can only be sold via a registered broker, who will only approve a price which is in the area of the average stock exchange quotation. Since 1970 increasingly strict rules have been introduced covering public offers and transfers of control creating quantities of stocks. In order to avoid the situation in which the equity capital of a company exists only on paper, it is forbidden that more than 10% of a cross-participation be held, but this rule can be relatively easily circumvented through circular participations.

A parent company is normally not liable for losses incurred by a subsidiary; this rule will only be departed from in cases of confusion of funds or fraud.

Champaud intervened at this stage to draw attention to the fact that the accumulation of power at the top of such groups often results in difficulties for management to really control such monsters. Therefore, he proposes very strict rules of responsibility to apply to those parent companies which exercise a very centralized decision-making role, thus giving them an incentive to decentralize their power structure in order not to be under such strict rules of responsibility. His second point concerned the vigorous resistance shown by French industry against a Law of groups. A Law of groups will be introduced at some time or another, because it is a historical fact that legal vacua will be filled; it may be filled upon pressure from labour unions, from social law or from tax law. This phenomenon should be explained now to the captains of big French industry in order to achieve a reasonable solution as soon as possible. In fact, a Parliamentary initiative has been made (by Mr. *Cousté*), proposing the adoption of a revised Law on groups, but unfortunately this proposal is remarkably timid.

III. Groups of Companies and the Belgian Experience

Reporter: Professor P. Van Ommeslaghe

Professor *van Ommeslaghe* explained that in Belgium almost all industrial and even commercial companies are affiliated enterprises in one form or another. Concerning the method of affiliation, there is the particularity that contracts between shareholders (e. g., on the distribution of seats in the supervisory board) are a very frequent and effective phenomenon, even if these contracts are legally not binding. The Law makes no reference to groups and all companies are regarded as if they were independent units.

The "*Commission Bancaire*" merits particular attention since it plays a very important role in the economic life of Belgium. It was created in 1935 by a Royal Decree, and has its own legal personality; it consists of ten members and a permanent staff of about fifteen persons. The Commission is not a tribunal, but it has always, very successfully, tried to persuade the parties by recommendations. In various fields it has developed a law praeter legem, thus anticipating the response to problems of modern business. The Commission has particular powers to supervise holding companies, namely in obtaining information and in checking and asking for further information. The Commission will allow neither a company to acquire its own shares, nor the acquisition of shares in the parent company by dependent enterprises. It has introduced a policy that in take-over transactions all shareholders have to be treated equally, and it has assumed particular supervisory duties in the process of a public acquisition offer – remarkably the supervision starts in this case already during the formation phase.

Another interesting development has emerged in the important commercial tribunals, such as the one in Brussels, where a sort of information service (so-called "*service de dépistage*") was established in order to examine the financial situation of companies which seem to be in a weak situation. The tribunals can then ask a parent company to give guarantees for their subsidiaries which seem to be in financial difficulties, to transfer credits into equity capital and the like. It seems as if this approach works well.

Upon Professor *Hirsch's* question on the practical proceedings in gathering information if the relevant company is the subsidiary of a foreign parent company, it became clear that the power of the *Commission Bancaire* ends at the national boundaries, but that in practice the required information will be provided by the Belgian subsidiary itself or by the auditors. *Hirsch* also mentioned the problem of the extension of bankruptcy to a foreign parent company and *Van Ommeslaghe* cited a case in which the Belgian branch of a British parent company was manifestly under-capitalized; the Belgian court declared the branch bankrupt and ruled at the same time that the debts of the branch were at the charge of the parent company. Eventually the British parent in collaboration with some affiliated companies in the group outside Belgium accepted to assume responsibility for the bankrupt branch.

IV. Groups of Companies: the English Experience

Reporter: Dr. D. D. Prentice

Next Dr. *Prentice* explained the English attitude towards groups. English law does not give any definition of a group. The principle of limited liability is upheld also within groups, but, as Lord Denning indicated recently, there is a slight tendency to look at groups as an economic entity.

With regard to creditor protection there exists no liability of a parent company towards creditors of a subsidiary if the latter becomes insolvent. The City Code on Take-overs has adopted an attitude of suspicion towards partial bids because they can create a situation where the remaining shareholders will become a powerless minority, therefore such an operation has to be approved by the remaining shareholders of the target company. If someone acquires in concert with another person more than 30% of the voting shares in a company, he has to make a mandatory bid to acquire the shares of the remaining shareholders as well; this is to prevent shareholders from ending up in an unwanted minority position, by providing all shareholders with an equal opportunity to sell.

Under English law there exists a strong majority rule, which renders minority shareholders vulnerable to oppressive majority action. As a result the courts have formulated the rule that shareholders in effecting an alteration to the corporate constitution must act bona fide for the benefit of the company as a whole. The company can enter into arrangements with its shareholders or creditors if two conditions are fulfilled: first, three-fourths of each class of shareholders or creditors must approve the arrangement; and, second, the court must give its consent.

In the subsequent discussion *Prentice* added another aspect of minority protection: as groups are normally of some importance for the national economy as a whole, their behaviour is often commented on by the very good English financial press, thus any minority oppression would be commented on immediately. He then underlined further the diversity of interests which minority shareholders may have; many of them are very powerful financial institutions and in such cases majority shareholders will be very careful towards them and will often inform them beforehand about their intentions or even ask them for their consent in advance. *Jacquemin* added that it is a general phenomenon to find financial institutions as shareholders, and it is not very clear whether they exercise real power in a company or whether they confine themselves to a control in terms of liquidity maintenance and the like. *Prentice* mentioned a survey on voting patterns in large British companies showing that these institutions do not exercise their voting rights; therefore, it seems as if they get in and out of investment on purely financial terms and do not intend to exercise ownership functions.

V. Company Groups in Swiss Law

Reporter: Professor J. N. Druey

Professor *Druey* stated that in Switzerland about 70% of all companies belong to a group and that they are almost exclusively based upon majority shareholding; domination and transfer of profit contracts are entirely unknown. The courts recognize groups only in very special circumstances; in general it can be said, that there is a tendency backward in the courts, towards looking at the individual company rather than the economic entity.

Scholarly discussions on this topic started as early as 1927 and two reports presented at the 1980 meeting of the Swiss Association of Lawyers came to the conclusion that new legislation in the field of groups is necessary. There are some projects under way in this direction, but it seems that there will be no action in the near future. The Swiss economic world is strongly opposed to any legislative regulation of groups and therefore the whole affair is more or less deemed to be of academic nature.

Professor *Ruedin* was less pessimistic than Druey on this point, but stressed that a distinction has to be made between the various reform proposals and projects. First, it seems quite probable that the Working Group engaged on investigating this issue will put forward proposals concerning a general regulation for groups: the common direction of groups would become explicitly legalized; the right of the dominating company to buy the remaining shares in a subsidiary, and certain information requirements making it easier to become aware of groups, would also be introduced. A second problem, however, is whether such a project would be adopted by Parliament, and on this point there was much less optimism, in particular because the pre-project of 1975 had been severely criticized as being too far-reaching. But the mere existence of a working group and of a draft proposal may give rise to some hope that in the course of time such proposals will be received more warmly.

Houin wanted to know whether the Swiss dispositions on the abuse of legal personality can also be applied in cases of abuse of majority power, e. g., in cases where assets and profits are transferred from a dependent company to a holding or other affiliated company. *Druey* replied that in fact transfers of this kind of considerable importance are executed every day, but this happens under the responsibility of the board of directors of the dependent company who will be responsible for resulting detriments caused to the company. *Hirsch* added to

Houin's remark that in Switzerland most abuses are committed in individual companies with few shareholders, e. g., by contracts which favour some dominant shareholders with excessive remunerations and the like; there are very few court decisions on this topic, simply because the minority shareholders rarely get any information about these practices.

Hirsch also expressed some reservations about a really effective law of groups; the possibility of a company being able to instruct another in which it has no obvious controlling interests or without its apparently exercising its controlling power must always be kept prominently in mind, and in this respect a comparison with European Community Law is instructive. If we take the famous *Dye Stuffs* case (where it was relatively easy to prove that there were agreements) as an example, we can be sure that today the parties would certainly act much more prudently in organizing their affairs and probably reach the same factual result whilst keeping within the letter of the law; it seems that if important legal consequences are attached to the common direction of a group, then companies will try everything in order to make it impossible or very difficult to prove that such a common direction exists.

Van Ommeslaghe agreed with Hirsch that the notion of instruction is really at the centre of the definition of a group. In his practical experience there are always cases in which such instructions are given directly from the dominant to the dependent company without having gone through the decision-making process of the latter. Given the factual difficulties in spotting groups, he thinks that a contractual solution which would legalize such proceedings, prudently drafted so as not to deter, could be an interesting alternative.

The problem of the distinction between the interest of the individual subsidiary and the interest of the group as a whole gave rise to an interesting discussion between *Houin* and *Druey*, with the latter acknowledging that there may be a conflict between these two interests, even if in general every member of the group has its specific function within the group and, therefore, the individual operation of each subsidiary can be justified by the particular role which this subsidiary plays within the group; and he underlined that a possible law of groups should not only look at the distinct interests of each individual group member, but also at the interest of the group as a whole.

Hopt wondered in this context why in a country like Switzerland, which is well known for its tradition of tolerance, there is so little concern about minorities and outsiders. Professor *Forstmoser* speculating on this topic gave three possible reasons: first, the historical experience of the necessity of compromising; second, the existence of a kind of personal control, because Swiss businessmen know each other quite well; and third, the classic nature of the Swiss legal system which dates to the 19th century. *Hirsch* expressed additionally the Swiss feeling that the overall interest is somewhat more important than the individual interest and that therefore, the minority should give in to the majority. *Hopt* underlined in this context that apparently in smaller countries this kind of "personal control" functions effectively.

VI. Groups in Scandinavian Company Law

Reporter: Professor K. Rodhe

A very close cooperation among the four Scandinavian countries emerged from Professor *Rodhe's* report on the Scandinavian approach towards groups. Between 1973 and 1978 all the Scandinavian countries passed new Company Acts.

The important point in their laws of groups is the possibility to exercise a controlling influence, the existence of a central management being of no importance. There exists a primary definition, which is that the parent company holds more than 50% of the voting shares; and a secondary definition, which requires a considerable shareholding and a decisive influence on the subsidiary.

The Swedish Law is addressed only to the situation where a Swedish stock-company is the holding company, whereas the dependent companies can also be foreign and have any kind of legal form. The law prescribes that such a group must establish consolidated accounts and a separate report on the group. There exist certain restrictions concerning the distribution of dividends to the shareholders of the holding. Capital transfers within the group are generally accepted – from the point of company law – but have to be regarded as dividend distributions. A company is not permitted to buy its own shares, nor can a subsidiary buy shares in the holding company. If the parent company owns more than 90% of the voting shares it also has a right to acquire the remaining shares in the subsidiary. In the analogous situation the minority shareholders may ask the parent company to buy their shares.

If a dependent company has more than twenty-five employees, the trade union may send two representatives to its Board of Directors and also is entitled to representation on the Board of the parent company, therefore the holding company will encounter increasing difficulties when giving orders to a subsidiary which may be to the detriment of the latter and its employees. Upon *Hopt's* question on the organisational structure of the Swedish trade unions, *Rodhe* explained that there exist two different organisations, with regional subdivisions and a "club" in every enterprise. The great problem they have to face is that very often the interest of one club is entirely opposed to the interest of another club and thus it is very difficult to find a common policy.

In this context *Houin* expressed some doubts whether it would be wise to regulate the decision-making procedures for all kinds of groups equally because for example in the case of 100% subsidiaries the problem of minority protection no longer exists. *Van Ommeslaghe* added that the project for an EEC directive in fact introduces very simplified procedures for 100% owned subsidiaries. *Hirsch* drew attention to the problem of the protection of third parties who are in contractual relationships with companies belonging to a group and here, again, there exist the alternatives of either looking at every company as an independent unit, or looking at the group as an entity, which has tremendous repercussions on contractual relationships.

Chapter III: Groups of Companies in the Law of the European Communities

I. A Critical Appraisal of the European Proposals for Harmonization in the Field of Groups of Companies: the French Point of View

Reporter: Professor Y. Guyon

Professor *Guyon* presented in his report a critique of the proposed law of groups of the EEC from the French perspective. Even if the proposed Ninth Directive is at the centre of the problem, there are too many other texts which have to be taken into consideration. The EEC approach seems, from a French point of view, to be too dogmatic and the intention of the project to cover the entire field causes some scepticism. The additional duties to provide information which are stipulated in the EEC project are welcome, and, in fact, this desire to make the relationships public represents the same starting point as in French law. The proposed duty of notification in the case of an enterprise acquiring more than 10% in another company is a better alternative than the existing French solution. The EEC propsal is very realistic, both in its information requirements, which will enable anyone to reach the persons who are really exercising the power (the French law is much more limited in this respect), and in its sanctions, which will prevent a buyer who has not complied with the information requirements from exercising his voting rights.

The attempt to standardize group accounting is also very welcome, particularly for cases in which part of the group is situated outside France. On the other hand, the proposal to establish a general group statute seems to create an over-centralized structure; a more "federal" structure would seem to be more reasonable, particularly in order not to prejudice European groups vis-à-vis American or Japanese groups.

The proposal to make the parent company responsible for all debts of its subsidiaries is too general a rule. In addition the proposals for the regulation of de facto groups seem to lack the flexibility needed to meet the requirements of the multitude of different forms in which such domination may occur in practice. Another criticism can be made about the lack of a systematic regulation of the employee's situation.

Van Ommeslaghe, who has been involved for many years in the elaboration of EEC directives, explained the unsurmountable obstacles which exist in finding doctrinally sound solutions within an EEC context because of the enormous differences which are to be found in the nine legal systems.

The only way to come to practicable results is to define, first, the problem and then to look to see whether the solutions offered in the national laws are satisfactory; eventually solutions have to be found suitable to influence a factual situation, abstracting entirely any dogmatic consideration. Following these ideas it has been realized that groups exist and that they create problems in relation to creditor and shareholder protection. The perhaps very simple answer is to say, rule one, that existing groups can legalize their practices by adhering to a certain pattern; and, rule two, that if they do not freely adhere to such a pattern there will be a number of remedies available to protect creditors and shareholders.

Champaud underlined in this context once more the various forms in which minorities may occur. There are the kind of shareholders who do not even know in which company they own shares, because they have charged their bank with selling and buying. For this category it is essential to have a right to information, and the possibility of entering and of withdrawing from a company on the basis of such information. The second group consists of those who would like to be in the majority but, being a minority, and lacking an appropriate organisational system, they cannot assure a majority in the shareholders' meeting; their problems seem to be more or less well resolved in the different laws. There remains, as a last category, the group of the controlling shareholders. It may seem astonishing to mention them, but if minorities are to be given certain rights for protection, it must be ensured that these rights are used for protection only, and not in order to squeeze the majority.

Guyon underlined once again the importance of the right to withdraw from a company and not only in the context of groups but also of individual companies; if such a right could be exercised under objectively acceptable conditions, the problem of shareholder protection would be resolved to a great extent.

II. Group Accounts under the Proposed Seventh EEC Directive: A Practitioner's View

REPORTER: DR. W. MÜLLER

Dr. *Müller* presented some impressions on the proposed Seventh Directive of the EEC; he stressed particularly that it is very important when establishing rules for group accounts to always keep in mind the relationship between the value of the additional information provided by such rules and the additional amount of work and cost involved in drawing up such accounts.

The need for group accounts undoubtedly exists, because the annual accounts of a single company which is a member of a group are less meaningful than the accounts of an independent enterprise, and, as experience has shown, the collapse of the parent company or another substantial part of the group will endanger the existence of all the companies in the group. The Fourth EEC Directive will lead to a certain harmonization in the field of accounting principles and, therefore, constitute a sort of foundation for the Seventh Directive.

The definition of a group in the proposal is based on dependency and central management (entity concept), but the draft covers not only vertical groups but also horizontal groups, even where there exists no inter-relationship of dependence between the companies.

According to the draft the annual accounts of all group undertakings must be included in the consolidated group account regardless of where their registered office may be situated (principle of world wide group accounts). In this respect, the problem of different accounting principles will still survive to a certain extent into the future in respect of those parts of the group which are situated outside the EEC. The exemption rules, on the basis of minimum thresholds, are much too low, and it seems it would have been much wiser to have adopted minimum threshold levels such as those stipulated in the U. N. proposal or in German law.

The draft directive also introduces the obligation to draw up sub-group consolidated accounts. Keeping in mind the initial efficiency consideration, it must be said that the additional work and expense of such sub-group accounts are often in no reasonable relationship with the additional information they can provide.

In general *Müller* welcomed the proposed Seventh Directive and wished it to come into force as soon as possible. *Hirsch* expressed some doubts whether it really makes sense to establish consolidated accounts for conglomerate groups, but *Müller* did not entirely agree with this approach, underlining that it could at least make sense in order to see the overall financial situation of the whole group. Concerning *Hirsch's* criticism about sub-group balance sheets in the case when the dominant company is domiciled outside the EEC and has only a few subsidiaries within the EEC, *Müller* agreed that all the criticisms concerning sub-group accounts in general, are of course true in this case, but in order to see whether this kind of balance sheet makes sense or not it is necessary to look carefully at every individual situation. *Houin* and *van Ommeslaghe* expressed their conviction that even in cases of conglomerate groups consolidated accounts are highly useful. Upon *Houin's* question *Müller* explained the tremendous time pressure under which group accounts have to be established; the time for their preparation being the same as for the accounts of an individual company, which means in practice a period of four to five months at the maximum.

Chapter IV: Multinational Groups of Companies: Banks, Labour, Taxes

I. Administrative Control of Multinational Groups: the Example of Multinational Banks

REPORTER: PROFESSOR A. HIRSCH

Professor *Hirsch* demonstrated how multinational groups can be administratively supervised by referring to multinational banks. The general tendency in this field is that the law looks rather at the legal entity than at the economic entity. Therefore it seems wise to start by distinguishing the different legal types of foreign activities; a branch, for instance, is entirely dependent on the parent company and without its own legal personality: its fate is entirely dependent on the well-being of the whole group. Some legislation, however, has adopted a special procedure for the winding-up of a branch. Traditionally the supervision of branches is assured by the authorities of the country in which the parent company has its seat; but, as the Belgian example (where the equity capital actually situated in Belgium must at least equal the liabilities of the branch) illustrates, a branch may find itself in a situation of a more or less cumulative supervision. De lege ferenda a branch should be exclusively under the supervision of the authorities of the parent bank; so far only the UK applies this principle entirely. A subsidiary, which has its own legal personality, will in principle be regarded by the host state as if it were a national bank and, therefore, be entirely under the supervision of the host country's authorities.

In the case of banks the risk that a parent will allow its branch or subsidiary to fail is very limited, because the winding up of one of these would cause enormous detriment to the whole group and therefore the parent acts in its own interest by supporting its dependent companies. This is one of the reasons why the national authorities of the parent bank try to extend their supervision also to foreign subsidiaries. A question which can become very important when the parent bank in country A suffers because the subsidiary in country B is doing badly, is whether it is for the authorities of country A or of B or a concerted action of A and B together to assure an appropriate supervision. In the major banking countries there is a general understanding that the state of the seat of the parent bank has a certain responsibility for the entire group. Traditionally the authorities of the country in which the subsidiary is located have no means to go beyond their own territory; there are only few exceptions to this rule, e. g. at the time of formation of the subsidiary, when the host country may ask for information on the whole group.

In case of joint subsidiaries where both parent banks are domiciled in different countries, the problem gets an additional dimension.

Hirsch explained upon *Jacquemin's* question that in principle multinational banks are more or less in an equal position as regards competition, because a Swiss branch of a foreign establishment will offer more or less the same services as a Swiss bank with foreign establishments.

On *Jacquemin's* second question on how to assure the compliance of multinational banks with national monetary policies, the answer is in principle the same as on the competition issue, but here indeed multinational banks, particularly when dealing with other multinational enterprises, have a variety of possibilites to circumvent national restrictions.

Mr. *Raith* asked whether the supervision of foreign establishments could be improved by putting them under stricter rules than national banks. *Hirsch* quoted in this context the case of insurance companies, where indeed this solution is generally accepted, but the situation in international banking is totally different: multinational banks are a truly international affair and the host countries accept this, also in the interest of their own economies.

Upon *Rodhe's* question on how welcome a Swedish government inspector would be in Switzerland in order to inspect the subsidiary of a Swedish parent bank, *Hirsch* repeated that Switzerland acknowledges the presumption that the national authorities of the parent bank have a certain responsibility for the whole group; but the question still remains of the means to ascertain this responsibility. Switzerland believes firmly in international administrative cooperation, but this does not mean that Switzerland encourages foreign officials to come to

Switzerland in order to do their business there; recent examples have made this absolutely clear. But this procedure is not necessary at all, because the foreign parent can send its own internal inspectors to its Swiss establishment, or they can have their Swiss subsidiary supervised by an auditing firm of their choice. The foreign authorities can ask for information or clarification and the Swiss bank authorities will answer these questions within the limits of Swiss law; however, if bank supervision serves totally different objectives, as in the case of the United States, this cannot work. Upon *Guyon's* question on the effects of President Carter's executive order in respect to Iranian assets, *Hirsch* explained that this problem has not really arisen in Switzerland, because Iran does not have important dollar assets in Switzerland.

II. Labour Law and Multinational Groups of Companies

Reporter: Dr. P. L. Davies

Dr. *Davies* talked about the labour law aspects of multinational groups of enterprises. He quoted an ILO research from which it appears that multinational enterprises adapt or have had to adapt to a very large extent to the host country's labour practices; but still there are some exceptions, such as *IBM*, *Kodak* and *Michelin* which in the United Kingdom have adopted a policy of non-recognition of trade unions.

When dealing with multinational companies national unions face the problem that their bargaining power is considerably reduced, because their possibilities of access to the remote decision making bodies are very limited. Also the efficacy of industrial action in confrontation with a multinational undertaking is much weaker, as this latter can transfer its activities from one country to another. The appropriate answer to these problems would be some sort of international collective bargaining, also on the unions' side; but given the very different structures of labour relations in the various countries, international collective bargaining is not at all well developed. The only extensive multinational collective agreements are to be found in the – quite peculiar – European recording, radio and television industries. In general the difficulties in formulating common claims are considerable. The ITF's campaign against flags of convenience is somewhat in between collective bargaining and sympathy action.

The central question concerning international industrial action is the question about the legality of solidarity action. Broadly speaking, there are three categories to be distinguished: first, such countries as the USA and Germany, where the international character renders the action illegal under national law; second, other countries like the UK, where the ordinary national rules are applied; and, thirdly there remains the possibility of actively encouraging international solidarity action, but it seems Sweden is the only country which has opted for this solution.

Another problem area is the institutional representation of employees in multinational groups. Dutch law for example adopted a system which imposes special restrictions upon the application of institutional representation requirements in the case of multinational groups. In other countries the national rules about employee representation are applied in the same way as if the multinational were a purely national company. In the UK, the ***Bullock Report*** clearly rejected the remaining alternative of imposing more severe rules of employee representation upon members of a multinational group, as they considered this a deterrent to potential foreign investment.

An interesting phenomenon is the increasing importance of international guidelines, such as the O.E.C.D. Guidelines of 1975. These guidelines are only recommendations, but they carry considerable moral weight. The O.E.C.D. Guidelines have the additional peculiarity of a partly judicial, partly political mechanism for determining their application (well illustrated in the famous *Badger* case).

Mr. *Opie* added that very often labour relations in British subsidiaries of multinational groups are much better than in their domestic competitors. But as in Britain 98% of the firms have not had a single strike during the last ten years and 2% have had all the strikes, it is very difficult to find a real trend on this question; for example *Ford* of the UK had considerable labour disputes, whereas *General Motors* of the UK had very few.

Upon *Jacquemin's* mentioning the importance of a right to information for the employees, not only about the situation of the individual company in which they are working, but also about the group as a whole, *Davies* asked if a works council can realize its right to information under Belgian law in respect of a foreign parent company. *Jacquemin* answered that indeed the right to information is not limited to the Belgian subsidiary under Belgian law but also comprises information about foreign parent or affiliated companies. *Bayer* added that in horizontal groups with a bi-national character there is a tendency for labour unions to get closer together over the state boundaries, thus establishing some kind of mutual understanding and some coordination.

III. What is Wrong with Unitary Taxation?

REPORTER: PROFESSOR G. LINDENCRONA

Professor *Lindencrona* highlighted some taxation problems connected with multinational groups. His starting point was the introduction of a peculiar system of unitary taxation by the state of California. This new System will also be applicable to foreign, non-US, multinational enterprises which do business in California. The idea is to establish the California tax share by using a three factor formula (sales, property and pay-roll) and then to apportion the world-wide figures on the basis of the California figures thus establishing the California tax share.

This procedure constitutes a complete breach with traditional internationally accepted principles of taxation. Traditionally, the so-called arm's length method is used, where the taxation of each group member is based upon its individual results as if it were an independent company using arm's length prices. The reaction of the international business community articulated by the International Chamber of Commerce was very negative. In its report on Transfer Pricing and Multinational Enterprises of 1979 the Council of the O. E. C. D. rejected very strongly the idea of unitary or global taxation.

The most prominent problem for a unitary system is the difficulty of obtaining the necessary information; it seems to be extremely difficult to force a foreign group member to provide the requested information and it seems to be practically impossible to check such information.

The minority of shareholders will find themselves in an awkward situation under a unitary system: under the traditional system they were taxed on the basis of the profits of the company in which they owned shares; under a unitary system they will be taxed on the basis of a part of the group's entire profits, thus being assessed as if they owned shares in the parent company.

It is true that there exist many problems with the arm's length method (e. g. how to establish the correct market price for intra-group transfers) but so far no better method has been found to replace it. De lege ferenda there could at some time in the future evolve a system in which the whole group would be taxed at the domicile of the parent company with a part of the amount thus levied being distributed to countries in which the group was active. This approach presupposes, of course, a great deal of world-wide confidence and a very high level of uniformity in company taxation.

Hirsch wondered whether California was already applying the unitary system to the great number of subsidiaries of foreign owned banks which do business in California, and stressed once again the enormous difficulties which the California authorities will meet when asking foreign parent companies to provide information. *Lindencrona* explained in reply that California first started to apply this system in the mid-1970's and is proceeding step by step.

General Concluding Remarks

Speaker: Professor K. Hopt

Professor *Hopt*, in summing up, mentioned the obvious similarity of problems confronting the various nations which of course is due to the similar stage of industrial and social development in western European countries. He underlined the general understanding that certain interests merit protection such as those of creditors and of minority shareholders and in this latter category it may even be necessary to differentiate between classes, whilst one must not forget the protection of the legitimate interests of the group as a whole. Faith in legislation differs a great deal from one country to another, ranging from very strong in Germany to very weak in the UK. Surprisingly, although theoretical considerations seem to play an important role in national discussions, their role fades considerably on the comparative level to the benefit of pragmatic considerations, and it is in some ways comforting to see that our laws have been influenced by each other to a considerable extent.

Annex/Annexe II

Relevant Legal Provisions/Textes des Lois

1. The Federal Republic of Germany/République Fédérale d' Allemagne

The German Stock Corporation Law of 1965: Connected Enterprises Sections 15-22, 291-338*

Book One
Stock Corporation (§§ 1-277)

First Part
General Provisions

[§§ 1-14 omitted]

§ 15
Connected enterprises

Connected enterprises are legally independent enterprises which in relation to each other constitute either enterprises held by a majority and enterprises holding the majority (§ 16), dependent and dominating enterprises (§ 17), combine enterprises (§ 18), mutually participating enterprises (§ 19), or parties to enterprise contracts (§§ 291, 292).[1]

§ 16
Enterprises held by a majority and enterprises holding the majority

(1) If the majority of the participations in a legally independent enterprise belongs to another enterprise or if another enterprise is entitled to the majority of the voting rights (holding the majority), then such enterprise constitutes an enterprise held by a majority, and the other enterprise is an enterprise holding it with a majority.

(2) For (ordinary) corporations[2] the portion of the participations which belongs to an enterprise is determined by the ratio which the aggregate nominal amount of the participations belonging to it bears to the nominal capital, and for

* With kind permission taken from: R. Mueller & E. G. Galbraith, eds. and trans., The German Stock Corporation Law and the German Law on the Accounting by Major Enterprises Other than Stock Corporations (bilingual edition with an Introduction) (Frankfurt am Main, Fritz Knapp Verlag, 2d ed., 1976).

[1] Sections referred to in this Law without further identification are sections of this Law.

[2] "Kapitalgesellschaften" or "(ordinary) corporations" comprise stock corporations (§ 1) associations limited by shares (§ 278) and associations with limited liability (see note to § 355).

mining corporations[3] by the ratio between the number of the mining shares. Participations held in its own enterprise shall be deducted, for (ordinary) corporations from the nominal capital, for mining corporations from the number of the mining shares. Participations in the enterprise belonging to another for the account of the enterprise are deemed to be equivalent to holding participations in its own enterprise.

(3) The portion of the voting rights to which an enterprise is entitled is determined by the ratio of the number of the voting rights which it may exercise from the participations belonging to it to the aggregate number of all voting rights. From the aggregate number of all voting rights there shall be deducted the voting rights from participations held in its own enterprise as well as from participations which are equivalent pursuant to para 2 sentence 3.

(4) In participations belonging to an enterprise there shall also be included participations belonging to an enterprise dependent on it or to another for the account of the enterprise or of an enterprise dependent on the latter and, if the owner of the enterprise is a single trader, also those participations which constitute other property of the owner.

§ 17
Dependent and dominating enterprises

(1) Dependent enterprises are legally independent enterprises on which another enterprise (dominating enterprise) is able to directly or indirectly exercise a dominating influence.

(2) It is presumed that an enterprise held by a majority is dependent on the enterprise holding the majority.

§ 18
Combine and combine enterprises

(1) If a dominating and one or more dependent enterprises are joined by the uniform direction of the dominating enterprise, then they constitute a combine; the individual enterprises are combine enterprises. Enterprises between which a contract of domination exists (§ 291) or if one of them is integrated into the other (§ 319) are to be considered as joined by a uniform direction. It is presumed that a dependent enterprise forms a combine with the dominating enterprise.

(2) If legally independent enterprises are joined by a uniform direction without the one enterprise being dependent on the other, then they also constitute a combine; the individual enterprises are combine enterprises.

§ 19
Mutually participating enterprises[4]

(1) Mutually participating enterprises are enterprises with a domestic domicile in the legal form of an (ordinary) corporation or a mining corporation which are

[3] As constituted subject to state law, e. g. in §§ 94-134 of the "Allgemeines Berggesetz", new version for Northrhine Westphalia of 1961 as amended.

[4] For transitory provisions see § 6 Introductory Law.

connected in such manner that each enterprise owns more than one fourth of the participations in the other enterprise. § 16 para 2 sentence 1, para 4 apply to the determination of whether or not an enterprise owns more than one fourth of the participations in the other enterprise.

(2) If one of the mutually participating enterprises holds a majority in the other enterprise or if one is able to directly or indirectly exercise a dominating influence on the other enterprise, then the one is to be considered as a dominating, the other as a dependent enterprise.

(3) If each of the mutually participating enterprises holds a majority in the other enterprise or if each is able to exercise a dominating influence directly or indirectly on the other enterprise, then both enterprises are to be considered as dominating and as dependent.

(4) § 328 is not to be applied to enterprises which constitue dominating or dependent enterprises pursuant to paras 2 and 3.

§ 20

Duty to inform

(1) As soon as an enterprise owns more than one fourth of the shares of a stock corporation with a domestic domicile it shall inform the association of this fact in writing without undue delay. § 16 para 2 sentence 1, para 4 apply to the determination of whether or not the enterprise owns more than one fourth of the shares.

(2) With respect to the duty to inform pursuant to para 1 there shall also be counted as shares belonging to the enterprise those shares

1. the transfer of ownership of which the enterprise, or an enterprise dependent on it, or another for the account of the enterprise or of an enterprise dependent on the latter, may demand;

2. which the enterprise, or an enterprise dependent on it, or another for the account of the enterprise or of an enterprise dependent on the latter, is obligated to take over.

(3) If the enterprise is an (ordinary) corporation or a mining corporation, then it shall also inform the association in writing without undue delay as soon as it owns more than one fourth of the shares, not including the shares pursuant to para 2.

(4) § 328 is not to be applied to enterprises which constitute dominating or dependent enterprises pursuant to paras 2 and 3.

(5) If the participation no longer exists in the amount creating the duty to inform pursuant to paras 1, 3 or 4, then the association shall be informed of this fact in writing without undue delay.

(6) The association shall publish the existence of a participation of which it has been informed pursuant to paras 1 or 4 in the association's journal[5] without undue delay; the enterprise to which the participation belongs shall be named therein. If the association is informed that the participation has ceased to exist in the amount creating the duty to inform pursuant to paras 1 or 4, then this fact shall also be published in the association's journal without undue delay.

[5] See § 25.

(7) Rights from shares which belong to an enterprise obligated to inform pursuant to paras 1 or 4 may not be exercised for the period in which the enterprise has failed to give the information neither by the enterprise itself, nor by an enterprise dependent on it, nor by another for the account of the enterprise or of an enterprise dependent on the latter.

§ 21
Duty of the association to inform

(1) As soon as the association owns more than one fourth of the participations in another (ordinary) corporation or mining corporation with domestic domicile it shall inform the enterprise in which the participation exists of this fact in writing without undue delay. § 16 para 2 sentence 1, para 4 apply accordingly to determine whether or not the association owns more than one fourth of the participations.

(2) As soon as the association holds the majority (§ 16 para 1) in another enterprise it shall inform the enterprise in which it holds the majority of this fact in writing without undue delay.

(3) If the participation no longer exists in the amount creating the duty to inform pursuant to paras 1 or 2, the association shall inform the other enterprise of this fact in writing without undue delay.

(4) Rights from participations which belong to an association obligated to inform pursuant to paras 1 or 2 may not be exercised for the period in which it has failed to give the information.

§ 22
Evidence of participations so communicated

An enterprise to which an information has been given pursuant to § 20 paras 1, 3 or 4, § 21 paras 1 or 2 may request at any time to be shown evidence of the existence of the participation.

Book Three
Connected Enterprises

First Part
Enterprise Contracts[6]

First Division
Kinds of Enterprise Contracts

§ 291
Contract of domination. Contract to transfer profits

(1) Enterprise contracts are contracts by which a stock corporation or an association limited by shares subjects the direction of its association to another

[6] For transitory provisions as to enterprise contracts concluded before January 1, 1966 see § 22 Introductory Law.

enterprise (contract of domination) or by which it obligates itself to transfer all its profits to another enterprise (contract to transfer profits). A contract by which a stock corporation or an association limited by shares undertakes to conduct its enterprise for the account of another enterprise is also considered as a contract to transfer all of the profit.

(2) If enterprises which are not dependent on each other submit themselves by contract to a uniform direction, without having one of them become therewith dependent on another of the contracting enterprises, then this contract does not constitute a contract of domination.

(3) Consideration from the association on the basis of a contract of domination or to transfer profits is not considered as a violation of §§ 57, 58 and 60.

§ 292
Other enterprise contracts

(1) In addition enterprise contracts are contracts by which a stock corporation or an association limited by shares

1. obligates itself to pool its profit or the profit of one or more of its establishments wholly or partly with the profit of other enterprises or of one or more establishments of other enterprises for the purpose of dividing a joint profit (profit pool),
2. obligates itself to transfer a part of its profit or the profit of one or more of its establishments wholly or partly to another (contract to transfer profits in part),
3. leases or otherwise leaves the business of its enterprise to another (shop leasing contract, business transfer contract).

(2) A contract for profit sharing with members of the board of management and of the supervisory board or with individual employees of the association as well as a stipulation of profit sharing in current business contracts or in license contracts does not constitute a contract to transfer profits in part.

(3) A shop leasing contract or a business transfer contract and the resolution by which the shareholders' meeting has consented to the contract are not void for the reason that the contract violates §§ 57, 58 and 60. Sentence 1 does not exclude the contesting of the resolution for this violation.

Second Division
Conclusion, Amendments and Termination of Enterprise Contracts

§ 293
Consent of the shareholders' meeting

(1) An enterprise contract only becomes effective with the consent of the shareholders' meeting. The resolution requires a majority which comprises at least three fourths of the share capital represented at the passing of the resolution. The articles of association may determine a greater capital majority and additional requirements. The provisions of the law and of the articles of

association regarding amendments of the articles of association are not to be applied to the resolution.

(2) A contract of domination or to transfer profits to which the other party is a stock corporation or an association limited by shares, only becomes effective if the shareholders' meeting of this association consents as well. Para 1 sentences 2 to 4 apply accordingly to the resolution.

(3) It is required that the contract be in writing. It is to be made available for inspection by the shareholders in the premises of the association as of the call of the shareholders' meeting which is to decide the consent. At his request a copy shall be given to every shareholder without undue delay. The contract shall be made available for inspection in the shareholders' meeting. It shall be explained by the board of management at the beginning of the proceedings. It shall be attached to the record as an exhibit.

(4) In the shareholders' meeting which decides the consent to a contract of domination or to transfer profits, information shall also be given to every shareholder on his request on all matters of the enterprise with which the contract shall be concluded which are material for the conclusion of the contract.

§ 294
Registration. Effectiveness

(1) The board of management of the association shall apply for entry into the trade register of the existence and the kind of the enterprise contract as well as of the name of the other party to the contract, in the case of contracts to transfer profits in part, also the agreement on the amount of the profit to be transferred. To the application there shall be attached the contract and in case it is only effective with the consent of the shareholders' meeting of the other party to the contract, the record of this resolution and its exhibits, in the original, an authorized record or an officially certified copy.

(2) The contract only becomes effective after its existence has been entered into the trade register of the domicile of the association.

§ 295
Amendments

(1) An enterprise contract may only be amended with the consent of the shareholders' meeting. §§ 293, 294 apply accordingly.

(2) The consent of the shareholders' meeting to an amendment in the provisions of the contract which provide for the obligation to compensate the outside shareholders of the association or to acquire their shares requires a special resolution of the outside shareholders to become effective. § 293 para 1 sentences 2 and 3 apply to the special resolution. Information shall also be given to every outside shareholder on his request in the meeting which decides the consent on all matters of the other party to the contract which are material to the amendment.

§ 296
Cancellation

(1) An enterprise contract may only be cancelled as of the end of the fiscal year or the otherwise contractually stipulated accounting period. A retroactive cancellation is not permitted. It is required that the cancellation be in writing.

(2) A contract which gives rise to an obligation to compensate outside shareholders or to acquire their shares can only be cancelled if the outside shareholders consent by special resolution. § 293 para 1 sentences 2 and 3, § 295 para 2 sentence 3 apply accordingly to the special resolution.

§ 297
Termination

(1) An enterprise contract may be terminated for cause without observing a notice period. Cause exists in particular if it can be foreseen that the other party to the contract will not be able to perform its obligations existing on the basis of the contract.

(2) The board of management of the association may only terminate without cause a contract which gives rise to an obligation to compensate the outside shareholders of the association or to acquire their shares if the outside shareholders consent by special resolution. § 293 para 1 sentences 2 and 3, § 295 para 2 sentence 3 apply accordingly to the special resolution.

(3) It is required that the termination notice be in writing.

§ 298
Application and registration

The board of management of the association shall apply without undue delay for the entry into the trade register of the termination of an enterprise contract, the reason and the date of the termination.

§ 299
Exclusion of directives

The association may not, on the basis of an enterprise contract, be directed to amend, maintain or terminate the contract.

Third Division
Securing the Association and the Creditors

§ 300
Legal reserve

The legal reserve shall be credited in place of the credit determined in § 150 para 2 no. 1,

1. if a contract to transfer profits exists, with a credit out of the profit for the year as results without the profit transfer and after deducting a loss carried forward

from the previous year, which is necessary to replenish the legal reserve evenly in the first five fiscal years which begin during the existence of the contract or after the execution of a capital increase, up to a tenth or a higher part of the share capital determined by the articles of association, at least however with the credit stated in no. 2;

2. if a contract to transfer profits in part exists, with a credit which would have to be credited to the legal reserve pursuant to § 150 para 2 no. 1 out of the profit for the year, as results without the profit transfer and after deducting a loss carried forward from the previous year;
3. if a contract of domination exists without the association being also obligated to transfer all its profit, with the credit required to replenish the legal reserve pursuant to no. 1, at least however with the credit stated in § 150 para 2 no. 1, or, if the association is obligated to transfer its profit in part, the credit stated in no. 2.

§ 301
Maximum amount of the profit transfer

Irrespective of agreements which have been made for the calculation of the profit to be transferred, an association may transfer as its maximum profit the profit for the year as results without the profit transfer and after deducting a loss carried forward from the previous year and the credit which is to be credited to the legal reserve pursuant to § 300. If credits were credited to free reserves during the term of the contract, then these credits may be taken from the free reserves and be transferred as profit.

§ 302
Assuming losses

(1) If a contract of domination or to transfer profits exists, then the other party to the contract must, to the extent it is not compensated by amounts withdrawn from the free reserves which were credited thereto during the term of the contract, compensate for every loss for the year which otherwise results during the term of the contract.

(2) If a dependent association has leased or has otherwise left the business of its enterprise to the dominating enterprise, then the dominating enterprise must compensate every loss for the year which otherwise results during the term of the contract, to the extent the stipulated consideration is not equal to an adequate compensation.

(3) The association may only waive or compromise a claim to compensate three years after the date at which the entry of the termination of the contract into the trade register is considered to be published pursuant to § 10 of the Commercial Code. This does not apply if the party obligated to compensate is insolvent and enters into a composition with its creditors to avert or remove bankruptcy proceedings. The waiver or composition is only effective if the outside shareholders consent by special resolution and a minority, the aggregate shares of which equal one tenth of the share capital represented at the passing of the resolution, does not object in the record of the meeting.

§ 303
Protection of creditors

(1) If a contract of domination or to transfer profits terminates, then the other party to the contract must render security to the creditors of the association for claims which were founded before the entry of the termination of the contract into the trade register is considered to be published pursuant to § 10 of the Commercial Code, provided they report to it for this purpose within six months after the publication of the registration. The creditors shall be advised of this right in the publication of the registration.

(2) The right to request security does not pertain to creditors who have a right in the case of bankruptcy proceedings to obtain preferred satisfaction from a fund which is established and supervised by the government for their protection pursuant to statutory provisions.

(3) The other party to the contract may guarantee the claim instead of rendering security. § 349 of the Commercial Code regarding the exclusion of the objection of first suing the debtor is not to be applied.

Fourth Division
Securing the Outside Shareholders in Contracts of Domination and to Transfer Profits

§ 304
Adequate compensation

(1) A contract to transfer profits must provide an adequate compensation for the outside shareholders by a recurring consideration in money related to the nominal amounts of the shares (compensation payment). Provided the association is not also obligated to transfer all its profit a contract of domination must guarantee to the outside shareholders, as adequate compensation, a specific annual dividend following the amount as determined for the compensation payment. The determination of an adequate compensation may only be dispensed with if the association has no outside shareholder at the date of the passing of the resolution on the contract by its shareholders' meeting.

(2) A compensation payment must be promised in the amount of at least the annual payment which foreseeably could be distributed as an average dividend to the individual share pursuant to the theretofore operating results of the association and its future income expectations, considering adequate depreciations and diminutions in value, however without the formation of free reserves. If the other party to the contract is a stock corporation or an association limited by shares, then a payment that may also be promised as compensation payment is the amount which is distributed as a dividend each time on the shares of the other association, having at least the respective nominal amount. The respective nominal amount is determined in accordance with the ratio by which, in case of a merger, shares of the other association would have to be granted in exchange for one share of the association.

(3) A contract which contrary to para 1 does not provide for compensation at all is void. The resolution by which the shareholders' meeting of the association has consented to the contract or to an amendment of the contract pursuant to § 295 para 2 cannot be contested on the basis of § 243 para 2 or by the fact that the compensation stipulated in the contract is inadequate. If the compensation stipulated in the contract is inadequate, then the court determined in § 306 shall upon motion determine the compensation contractually owed, it must thereby determine the compensation pursuant to para 2 sentence 2 if the contract provides for a compensation so calculated.

(4) Every outside shareholder is entitled to make the motion. The motion may only be made within two months from the date at which the entry of the existence or of an amendment of the contract pursuant to § 295 para 2 into the trade register is considered to be published pursuant to § 10 of the Commercial Code.

(5) If the court determines the compensation, then the other party to the contract may terminate the contract within two months after the decision is final, without observing a period of notice.

§ 305
Indemnity

(1) Apart from the obligation to compensate pursuant to § 304, a contract of domination or to transfer profits must contain the obligation of the other party to the contract to acquire the shares of an outside shareholder, at his request, for an adequate indemnity stipulated in the contract.

(2) As an indemnity the contract must provide

1. if the other party to the contract is a not dependent and not majority held stock corporation or association limited by shares with a domestic domicile, for the granting of its own shares of this association,
2. if the other party to the contract is a dependent or majority held stock corporation or association limited by shares and if the dominating enterprise is a stock corporation or association limited by shares with a domestic domicile, either for the granting of shares of the dominating or of the majority holding association or for an indemnity in cash,
3. in all other cases for an indemnity in cash.

(3) If shares of another association are granted as an indemnity, then the indemnity is to be considered as adequate if the shares are granted in accordance with the ratio by which shares of the other association would have to be granted in exchange for one share of the association in case of a merger, whereby residual amounts may be compensated by additional cash payments. The adequate compensation in cash must consider the association's financial position and its operating results at the date of the passing of the resolution on the contract by its shareholders' meeting.

(4) The obligation to acquire the shares may be subject to a time limit. The period terminates at the earliest two months after the date at which the entry of the existence of the contract into the trade register is considered to be published

pursuant to § 10 of the Commercial Code. If a motion has been made to let the court referred to in § 306 determine the compensation or the indemnity, then the period terminates, at the earliest two months after the date at which the decision on the last decided motion was published in the Federal Gazette.

(5) The resolution by which the shareholders' meeting of the association has consented to the contract or to an amendment of the contract pursuant to § 295 para 2 cannot be contested on the basis of the fact that the contract does not provide for an adequate indemnity. If the contract does not provide for an indemnity at all or for one which does not conform to paras 1 to 3, then the court referred to in § 306 shall upon motion determine the indemnity to be granted by the contract. It shall thereby in the cases of para 2 no. 2, if the contract provides for the granting of shares of the dominating or majority holding association, determine the ratio by which these shares are to be granted, and if the contract does not provide for the granting of shares of the dominating or majority holding association, an adequate indemnity in cash. § 304 paras 4 and 5 apply accordingly.

§ 306
Procedure

(1) The Landgericht in the district of the domicile of the association whose outside shareholders are entitled to the motion is competent. § 132 para 1 sentences 2 to 4 are to be applied.

(2) § 99 para 1, para 3 sentences 1, 2, 4 to 9, para 5 apply accordingly.

(3) The Landgericht shall publish the motion in the journal of the association whose outside shareholders are entitled to the motion. Outside shareholders may still make motions of their own within a period of two months after this publication. This right shall be indicated in the publication.

(4) The Landgericht shall hear the parties to the enterprise contract. It shall appoint a joint representative who enjoys the position of a legal representative to guard the rights of the outside shareholders who are not applicants pursuant to § 304 para 4 or § 305 para 5 or have made motions of their own pursuant to para 3 sentence 2. If a determination of an adequate compensation and the determination of an adequate indemnity has been applied for, then it shall appoint a joint representative for each motion. The appointment may be dispensed with if the rights of these outside shareholders are secured in another way. The Landgericht shall publish the appointment of the joint representative in the association's journal. The representative may claim from the association a refund for reasonable cash disbursements and for compensation for his services. The disbursements and the compensation are assessed by the Landgericht. At the request of the representative it may charge the association with the payment of advances. The judicial execution of the assessment follows the Code of Civil Procedure.

(5) The Landgericht shall serve its decision on the parties to the enterprise contract as well as on the applicants pursuant to § 304 para 4, § 305 para 5, on the outside shareholders who have made motions of their own pursuant to para 3 sentence 2 and if a joint representative is appointed, on him.

(6) The board of management of the association shall publish the final decision, without the reasons, in the association's journal.

(7) The Regulation of Court Costs applies to the costs of the proceedings. For proceedings of the first instance the double of the full fee is assessed. For proceedings of the second instance the same fee is assessed; this applies even if the appeal is successful. If the motion or the appeal is withdrawn before a decision has been rendered, then the fee is reduced by one half. The ligitation value shall be determined ex officio. It is determined pursuant to § 30 para 1 of the Regulation of the Court Costs. Advances on cost are not collected. The debtors for the costs are the parties to the enterprise contract. The costs may however be charged wholly or partly to another of the parties if this corresponds to equity.

§ 307
Termination of the contract to secure outside shareholders

If the association has no outside shareholder at the date of the passing of the resolution by its shareholders' meeting for a contract of domination or to transfer profits, then the contract terminates at the latest by the end of the fiscal year in which an outside shareholder participates.

Part Two
Power to Direct and Liability in Case of Dependence of Enterprises

First Division
Power to Direct and Liability if a Contract of Domination Exists

§ 308
Power to direct

(1) If a contract of domination exists, then the dominating enterprise has the right to give directives to the board of management of the association with regard to the direction of the association. Unless otherwise provided in the contract, directives which are disadvantageous for the association may also be given, if they serve the interests of the dominating enterprise or of the enterprises connected with it and the association in a combine.

(2) The board of management is obligated to follow the directives of the dominating enterprise. It has no right to refuse to follow a directive because it does not, in its opinion, serve the interests of the dominating enterprise or of the enterprises connected with it and the association in a combine, except when it obviously does not serve these interests.

(3) If the board of management is directed to enter into a transaction which may only be entered into with the consent of the supervisory board of the association and if this consent is not given within a reasonable period, then the board of management must communicate this fact to the dominating enterprise.

If the dominating enterprise repeats the directive after this communication, then the consent of the supervisory board is no longer required; if the dominating enterprise has a supervisory board, the directive may only be repeated with its consent.

§ 309

Liability of the legal representatives of the dominating enterprise

(1) If a contract of domination exists, then the legal representatives (the owner in the case of a single trader) of the dominating enterprise shall employ the diligence of an orderly and conscientious manager towards the association in giving directives to it.

(2) If they violate their duties, then they are jointly and severally liable to the association for the damage resulting therefrom. If it is contested whether or not they have employed the diligence of an orderly and conscientious manager, then the burden of proof is on them.

(3) The association may only waive or compromise the damage claims three years after the accrual of the claim and only if the outside shareholders consent by special resolution and unless a minority, the aggregate shares of which equal at least one tenth of the share capital represented at the passing of the resolution, objects in the record. The time limit does not apply if the person liable for the damage is insolvent and enters into composition with his creditors to avert or remove the bankruptcy proceedings.

(4) The damage claim of the association may also be asserted by every shareholder. The shareholder may however demand the compensation only for the association. In addition the damage claim may be asserted by the creditors of the association, to the extent they are unable to obtain satisfaction from it. The liability for damages towards the creditors is not excluded by a waiver or composition by the association. If bankruptcy proceedings have been instituted against the assets of the association, then as long as they continue, the receiver in bankruptcy exercises the right of the shareholders and the creditors to assert the damage claim of the association.

(5) The claims from these provisions are barred after five years.

§ 310

Liability of the members of the boards of the association

(1) The members of the board of management and of the supervisory board of the association are jointly and severally liable, apart from the persons liable for damage pursuant to § 309, if they have acted in violation of their duties. If it is contested whether or not they have employed the diligence of an orderly and conscientious manager, then the burden of proof is on them.

(2) The liability for damages is not excluded by the fact that the supervisory board has approved the action.

(3) No liability for damages by the members of the boards of the association exists if the damaging action rests upon a directive which was to be followed pursuant to § 308 para 2.

(4) § 309 paras 3 to 5 are to be applied.

Second Division
Liability in the Absence of a Contract of Domination

§ 311
Limits of the influence

(1) If no contract of domination exists, then a dominating enterprise may not use its influence to cause a dependent stock corporation or association limited by shares to take legal transactions disadvantageous to it or to take or omit measures to its disadvantage except when the disadvantages are compensated for.

(2) If the compensation does not in fact take place during the fiscal year, then it must be determined when and by which advantages the disadvantage shall be compensated for, at the latest at the end of the fiscal year in which the disadvantage was caused to the dependent association. The dependent association shall be granted a legal claim to the advantages determined as compensation.

§ 312
Report of the board of management on the relations with connected enterprises

(1) If no contract of domination exists, then the board of management of a dependent association shall within the first three months of the fiscal year prepare a report on the relations of the association with connected enterprises. The report shall list all legal transactions which the association has taken in the past fiscal year with the dominating enterprise or with an enterprise connected with it or caused by or in the interest of these enterprises, and all other measures which it has taken or omitted in the past fiscal year, caused by or in the interest of these enterprises. There shall be stated as to the legal transactions, the performance and the consideration, as to the measures, the reasons for the measure and its advantages and disadvantages for the association. As to a compensation for disadvantages, there shall be stated in detail how the compensation did in fact take place during the fiscal year or for which advantages the association has been granted a legal claim.

(2) The report shall accord with the principles of conscientious and faithful accounting.

(3) At the end of the report the board of management shall state whether or not pursuant to the circumstances which were known to it at the date on which the legal transaction was concluded or the measure taken or omitted, the association has received in each legal transaction an adequate compensation and was not put at a disadvantage by the fact that the measure was taken or omitted. If the association was put to a disadvantage, it shall also state whether or not the disadvantages were compensated for. The statement shall also be included in the report of the management.

§ 313
Examination by the auditors of the financial statements

(1) The report on the relations with connected enterprises shall be submitted to the auditors of the association simultaneously with the annual financial statements and the report of the management. They shall examine whether or not

1. the factual statements of the report are correct,
2. the consideration of the association for the legal transactions stated in the report was not inadequately high pursuant to the circumstances which were known at the date of their taking; to the extent this was the case, whether or not the disadvantages were compensated for,
3. the measures stated in the report must be judged, pursuant to the circumstances to be essentially different from the opinion of the board of management.

§ 165 applies accordingly.

(2) The auditors shall report on the result of the examination in writing. If they find while discharging their duties pursuant to para 1 and § 162 that the report on the relations with connected enterprises is incomplete, then they shall report this as well. The auditors shall sign their report and submit it to the board of management.

(3) If no objections are raised pursuant to the final result of the examination, then the auditors shall confirm this by the following attestation of the report on the relations with connected enterprises:

On the basis of my/our dutiful examination and judgment I/we confirm that

1. the factual statements of the report are correct,
2. the consideration of the association for the legal transactions stated in the report was not inadequately high or that disadvantages were compensated for,
3. the measures stated in the report must not be judged, pursuant to the circumstances to be essentially different from the opinion expressed by the board of management.

If the report does not list a legal transaction, then no. 2 of the attestation, if it does not list a measure, then no. 3 shall be omitted. If the auditors have found that in no legal transaction listed in the report was the consideration of the association inadequately high, then no. 2 of the attestation is to be limited to this confirmation.

(4) If objections are raised or if the auditors have found that the report on the relations with connected enterprises is incomplete, then they shall qualify or refuse the attestation. If the board of management itself has stated that the association was put to a disadvantage by certain legal transactions or measures without the disadvantages having been compensated for, then this shall be stated in the attestation and the attestation shall be limited to the remaining legal transactions or measures.

(5) The auditors shall sign the attestation by indicating the location and the date. The attestation shall also be included in the examination report.

§ 314
Examination by the supervisory board

(1) The board of management shall submit the report on the relations with connected enterprises and the report of the auditors to the supervisory board, together with the documents referred to in § 170. Every member of the supervisory board is entitled to take notice of the reports. The reports shall also on request be handed to every member of the supervisory board, to the extent the supervisory board has not decided otherwise.

(2) The supervisory board shall examine the report on the relations with connected enterprises and report on the results of its examination in its report to the shareholders' meeting (§ 171 para 2). In addition in this report it shall give an opinion on the result of the examination of the relations with connected enterprises by the auditors. An attestation given by the auditors shall be included in the report, a refusal of the attestation must be expressly indicated.

(3) At the end of the report the supervisory board shall state whether or not as a final result of its examination, objections must be raised against the statement of the board of management at the end of the report on the relations with connected enterprises.

(4) The auditors shall on request take part in the proceedings of the supervisory board regarding the report on the relations with connected enterprises.

§ 315
Special examination

Upon motion of a shareholder the court must appoint special auditors to examine the business relations of the association with the dominating enterprise or an enterprise connected with it, if

1. the auditors have qualified or refused the attestation of the report on the relations with connected enterprises,
2. the supervisory board has stated that objections are to be raised against the statement of the board of management in the end of the report on the relations with connected enterprises,
3. the board of management itself has stated that the association has been put to a disadvantage by certain legal transactions or measures without the disadvantages having been compensated for.

Against the decision an immediate appeal is permissible. If the shareholders' meeting has appointed special auditors to examine the identical facts, then every shareholder may make the motion pursuant to § 142 para 4.

§ 316
No report on relations with connected enterprises for the contract to transfer profits

§§ 312 to 315 do not apply if a contract to transfer profits exists between the dependent association and the dominating enterprise.

§ 317
Liability of the dominating enterprise and its legal representatives

(1) If a dominating enterprise causes a dependent association with which no contract of domination exists to take a legal transaction disadvantageous to it or to take or omit a measure to its disadvantage without in fact compensating for disadvantage until the end of the fiscal year nor granting a legal claim to the dependent association for an advantage determined as compensation, then it is liable to the association for the damage resulting therefrom. In addition it is liable for the damage resulting therefrom to the shareholders, to the extent they have suffered damage apart from the damage they have suffered by the association being damaged.

(2) The liability for damage does not arise if an orderly and conscientious manager of an independent association would also have taken the legal transaction or would have taken or omitted the measure.

(3) Apart from the dominating enterprise, the legal representatives of the enterprise who have caused the association to take the legal transaction or the measure are jointly and severally liable.

(4) § 309 paras 3 to 5 apply accordingly.

§ 318
Liability of the members of the boards of the association

(1) The members of the board of management of the association are jointly and severally liable, apart from the persons liable for damages pursuant to § 317, if they have omitted in violation of their duties to list in the report on the relations of the association with connected enterprises the disadvantageous legal transaction or the disadvantageous measure or to state that the association was put to a disadvantage by the legal transaction or the measure and that the disadvantage was not compensated for. If it is contested whether or not they have employed the diligence of an orderly and conscientious manager, then the burden of proof is on them.

(2) The members of the supervisory board of the association are jointly and severally liable, apart from the persons liable for damages pursuant to § 317, if they have violated their duty, with regard to the disadvantageous legal transaction or the disadvantageous measure, to examine the report on the relations with connected enterprises and to report to the shareholders' meeting the result of the examination (§ 314); para 1 sentence 2 applies accordingly.

(3) Liability for damages to the association and also to the shareholders does not arise if the action rests upon a legally valid resolution of the shareholders' meeting.

(4) § 309 paras 3 to 5 apply accordingly.

Part Three
Integrated Associations

§ 319
Integration

(1) The shareholders' meeting of a stock corporation may decide the integration of the association into another stock corporation with domestic domicile (main association), provided all shares of the association are held by the future main association. The provisions of the law and of the articles of association regarding amendments of the articles of association are not to be applied to the resolution.

(2) The resolution for the integration only becomes effective if the shareholders' meeting of the future main association consents. The resolution for the consent requires a majority which comprises at least three fourths of the share capital represented at the passing of the resolution. The articles of association may determine a greater capital majority and additional requirements. Para 1 sentence 2 is to be applied. On request every shareholder is also to be given information in the shareholders' meeting which decides the consent, on all matters of the association to be integrated which are material in connection with the integration.

(3) The board of management of the association to be integrated shall apply for the entry of the integration and of the name of the main association into the trade register. The board of management shall state in the application that the resolutions of the shareholders' meetings were not contested within the period allowed or that the contesting action was refused by final judgment. There shall be attached to the application the records of the shareholders' meetings and their exhibits, in an authorized record or an officially certified copy.

(4) The association is integrated into the main association with the entry of the integration into the trade register of the domicile of the association.

§ 320
Integration by majority resolution

(1) The shareholders' meeting of a stock corporation may also decide the integration of the association into another stock corporation with domestic domicile provided shares of the association in the aggregate nominal amount of ninety five per cent of the share capital are held by the future main association. Its own shares and shares which belong to another for the account of the association are to be deducted from the share capital. Paras 2 to 7 apply to the integration, apart from § 319 para 1 sentence 2, paras 2 to 4.

(2) The publication of the integration as a subject on the agenda is correct only, if

1. it contains the name and the domicile of the future main association,
2. a statement of the future main association is attached by which it offers its own shares to the retiring shareholders in exchange for their shares as an indemnity and in the case of para 5 sentence 3 an additional indemnity in cash.

Sentence 1 no. 2 also applies to the publication of the future main association.

(3) On request every shareholder is also to be given information, in the shareholders' meeting which decides the integration, on all matters on the future main association which are material in connection with the integration.

(4) All shares which are not held by the main association pass over to it with the entry of the integration into the trade register. If share certificates for these shares were issued, then until rendered to the main association they only certify to the claim to an indemnity.

(5) The retired shareholders have a claim to an adequate indemnity. As an indemnity they shall be granted the main association's own shares. If the main association is a dependent association, then the retired shareholders shall be granted, at their choice, the main association's own shares, or an adequate indemnity in cash. If shares of the main association are granted as an indemnity, then the indemnity is to be considered as adequate if the shares are granted in accordance with the ratio by which shares of the main association would have to be granted in exchange for one share of the association in case of a merger, whereby residual amounts may be compensated by additional cash payments. The adequate indemnity in cash must consider the association's financial position and its operating results at the date of the passing of the resolution for the integration by the shareholders' meeting. For the indemnity in cash as well as for additional cash payments, five per cent interest per annum shall be paid as of the publication of the registration of the integration; asserting an additional damage is not excluded.

(6) The resolution by which the shareholders' meeting of the integrated association has decided the integration of the association cannot be contested on the basis of § 243 para 2 or by the fact that the indemnity offered by the main association pursuant to para 2 no. 2 is inadequate. If the offered indemnity is inadequate, then upon motion the court determined in § 306 shall determine the adequate indemnity. The same applies if the main association has not or not properly offered an indemnity and a contesting action based thereupon has not been brought within the period allowed or has been withdrawn or refused by a final judgment.

(7) Every retired shareholder is entitled to the motion. The motion may only be made within two months after the date on which the entry of the integration into the trade register is considered to be published pursuant to § 10 of the Commercial Code. § 306 applies accordingly to the procedure.

§ 321
Protection of creditors

(1) To the extent they cannot demand satisfaction the creditors of the integrated association whose claims were founded before the entry of the integration into the trade register was published shall be rendered security provided they report for this purpose within six months after the publication. The creditors shall be advised of this right in the publication of the registration.

(2) The right to request security does not pertain to creditors who have a right in the case of bankruptcy proceedings to obtain preferred satisfaction from a fund which is established and supervised by the government for their protection pursuant to statutory provisions.

§ 322
Liability of the main association

(1) As of the integration, the main association is accountable to the creditors of the integrated association jointly and severally for this association's liabilities which were founded before this date. It is in the same way accountable for all liabilities of the integrated association which are founded after the integration. An agreement to the contrary is ineffective towards third persons.

(2) If a claim for a liability of the integrated association is asserted against the main association, then it may raise objections, which are not based on its own position, only to the extent they may be raised by the integrated association.

(3) The main association may refuse to satisfy the creditor as long as the integrated association has the right to contest the legal transaction on which the liability is based. The same right pertains to the main association as long as the creditor may satisfy himself by a setoff against a due claim of the integrated association.

(4) A judicial execution based on an executable document of debt directed against the integrated association cannot take place against the main association.

§ 323
Power of the main association to direct and liability of the members of the board of management

(1) The main association has the right to give directives to the board of management of the integrated association with regard to the direction of the association. § 308 para 2 sentence 1, para 3, §§ 309, 310 apply accordingly. §§ 311 to 318 are not to be applied.

(2) Consideration the integrated association pays to the main association is not considered as a violation of §§ 57, 58 and 60.

§ 324
Legal reserve. Transfer of profit. Assuming losses

(1) The legal provisions for the formation of a legal reserve, for its application and for credits of amounts to the legal reserve are not to be applied to integrated associations.

(2) §§ 293 to 296, 298 to 303 are not to be applied to a contract, between the integrated association and the main association, to transfer profits, a profit pool or a contract to transfer profits in part. It is required that the contract, its amendment and its cancellation be in writing. The maximum profit which may be transferred is accumulated earnings as they result without the transfer of the

profit. The contracts ends, at the latest, with the end of the fiscal year in which the integration ends.

(3) The main association is liable to compensate for any accumulated losses otherwise resulting to the integrated association, to the extent they exceed the amount of the disclosed reserves.

§ 325
No submission and publication of the annual financial statements

(1) § 177 regarding the duty to submit the annual financial statements and the report of the management to the trade register as well as to publish the annual financial statements, does not apply if the integrated association is included as of the closing date of its annual financial statements in consolidated financial statements or partially consolidated financial statements prepared by the main association.

(2) If the annual financial statements and the report of the management are not submitted to the trade register or if the annual financial statements are not published, then the board of management of the integrated association shall without undue delay after the shareholders' meeting for the annual financial statements of the main association (§ 337 para 2), submit to the trade register the consolidated financial statements or the partially consolidated financial statements with the attestation and the report of the management for the combine or partial combine. § 338 para 1 sentences 2 and 3 are to be applied. In addition the board of management shall submit to the trade register the publication of the consolidated financial statements or the partially consolidated financial statements.

(3) The court shall only examine whether or not the submitted consolidated financial statements or the partially consolidated financial statements accord with § 338 para 1 sentences 2 and 3 and whether or not the association is included in it pursuant to the report of the management for the combine or partial combine.

§ 326
Right of information of the shareholders of the main association

Every shareholder of the main association is to be given information on matters of the integrated association in the same measure as on matters of the main association.

§ 327
Termination of the integration

(1) The integration terminates

1. by resolution of the shareholders' meeting of the integrated association,
2. if the main association ceases to be a stock corporation with domestic domicile,
3. if all shares of the integrated association are no longer held by the main association,

4. by dissolution of the main association.

(2) If all shares of the integrated association are no longer held by the main association, then the main association shall communicate this to the integrated association in writing without undue delay.

(3) The board of management of the previously integrated association shall report the termination of the integration, its reason and its date, for entry into the trade register of the domicile of the association without undue delay.

(4) The claims against the former main association for liabilities of the previously integrated association are barred after five years from the date on which the entry of the termination of the integration into the trade register is considered to be published pursuant to § 10 of the Commercial Code, unless the claim against the previously integrated association is subject to a shorter statute of limitation. If the claim of the creditor becomes due only after the date on which the entry of the termination of the integration into the trade register is considered to be published, then the period of the limitation begins with the due date.

Part Four
Mutually Participating Enterprises[7]

§ 328
Limitation of rights

(1) If a stock corporation or an association limited by shares and another enterprise constitute mutually participating enterprises, then as soon as the existence of the mutual participation has become known to one enterprise or the other enterprise has made a communication to it pursuant to § 20 para 3 or § 21 para 1, rights from the participations of the other enterprise which belong to it may only be exercised in the maximum of one fourth of the aggregate participations of the other enterprise. This does not apply to the right to new shares from a capital increase from reserves. § 16 para 4 is to be applied.

(2) The limitation of para 1 does not apply if before it had received such a communication from the other enterprise and before the existence of the mutual participation has become known to it, the enterprise has made a communication on its own to the other enterprise pursuant to § 20 para 3 or § 21 para 1.

(3) If a stock corporation or an association limited by shares and another enterprise constitute mutually participating enterprises, then the enterprises shall communicate to each other the amount of their participation and every change in writing without undue delay.

[7] For transitory provisions as to an existing mutual participation see § 6 Introductory Law.

Part Five
Accounting of the Combine[8]

§ 329
Preparation of consolidated financial statements and reports of the management for the combine

(1) If the combine enterprises of a combine are under the uniform direction of a stock corporation or an association limited by shares with a domestic domicile (head association), then the board of management of the head association shall prepare as of the closing date of the annual financial statements of the head association, a consolidated balance sheet and a consolidated profit and loss statement (consolidated financial statements) as well as a report of the management for the combine. If the closing dates of the annual financial statements of the enterprises included in the consolidated financial statements deviate from each other, then the consolidated financial statements may also be prepared as of another closing date provided this serves the presentation of clear and well set out consolidated financial statements. The consolidated financial statements and the report of the management for the combine shall be prepared within the first five months after the closing date of the consolidated financial statements.

(2) The consolidated financial statements shall include every domestically domiciled combine enterprise in which the participations belonging to combine enterprises are more than one half. The inclusion may be dispensed with if because of the small significance of the combine enterprise the presentation of the financial position and of the operating results of the combine is not thereby impaired. It must be dispensed with if it would impair the value of the disclosures in the consolidated financial statements. Other combine enterprises may be included in the consolidated financial statements; they must be included if they have a domestic domicile and if their inclusion leads to a different judgment on the financial position and operating results of the combine.

§ 330
Preparation of partially consolidated financial statements and of reports of the management for partial combines

(1) If the combine enterprises of a combine are under the uniform direction of an enterprise with a domestic domicile (main establishment) which is not obligated to prepare consolidated financial statements pursuant to § 329 or to the Law for the Accounting by Certain Enterprises and Groups of Enterprises, but if the combine direction dominates, through one or more stock corporations or associations limited by shares with domestic domicile belonging to the combine, other combine enterprises, then the boards of management of the stock

[8] The provisions apply also to an association with limited liability or to a mining corporation (see note to § 16 (2)) if they belong to a combine as determined by § 28 Introductory Law.

corporations or associations limited by shares with domestic domicile which are closest to the combine direction shall each prepare partially consolidated financial statements and a report of the management for the partial combine; this does not apply if these stock corporations or associations limited by shares are to be included in partially consolidated statements pursuant to the Law for the Accounting of Certain Enterprises and Groups of Enterprises. §§ 329, 331 to 338 apply accordingly to the partially consolidated financial statements and to the report of the management for the partial combine. The preparation of partially consolidated financial statements and of reports of the management for partial combines may be dispensed with provided the combine direction accounts in such a way as a head association must account pursuant to §§ 329, 331 to 338.

(2) Para 1 sentences 1 and 2 apply accordingly if the combine direction has its domicile (main establishment) abroad. The preparation of partially consolidated financial statements and of reports of the management for partial combines may be dispensed with provided the combine direction publishes in the Federal Gazette consolidated financial statements which were prepared pursuant to the principles of §§ 331 to 333 and examined by Wirtschaftsprüfer.

§ 331
Consolidated balance sheet

(1) The consolidated balance sheet shall consolidate the balance sheets of the head association and of the other included enterprises prepared as of the closing date of the consolidated financial statements, pursuant to the following principles:

1. for the participations in the other included enterprises there shall be substituted the assets and liabilities, the special captions with reserves in part, provisions for accrued liabilities and for diminution in value and deferred charges included in the balance sheets of these enterprises at the values at which they are included in these balance sheets unless a lower value must be stated pursuant to para 2;
2. a "compensating caption for participations held by others" shall be shown separately for participations in the other included enterprises by partners outside of the combine, in the amount of their participations in the capital, the disclosed reserves and the profit and loss; the amount pertaining to the profit and to the loss shall be indicated separately;
3. if the values at which the participations in the other included enterprises are stated higher or lower than the amounts of capital and the disclosed reserves of the enterprises relating to the participations, then the amount of the difference shall be shown separately;
4. accounts receivable and liabilities between the enterprises included in the consolidated financial statements shall be omitted.

(2) Assets of an included enterprise existing at the closing date of the consolidated financial statements which constitute wholly or partly sales or services by other included enterprises if they

1. are destined for resale without or after treatment or processing, or
2. were not acquired in the course of the usual sales and service transactions

may be stated in the consolidated financial statements only up to the maximum value at which they could be stated in the enterprise's annual balance sheet prepared as of the same closing date, if the included enterprises would as a matter of law constitute a sole enterprise.

(3) The enterprises included in the consolidated financial statements shall have the same closing date for their financial statements. If the closing date of the annual financial statements of an included enterprise deviates from the closing date of the consolidated financial statements, then there shall be used as a basis financial statements which are prepared as of the closing date of the consolidated financial statements for the period covered by the consolidated financial statements. If a supervisory board is provided the financial statements require its consent.

(4) §§ 149, 151 paras 1 to 3, 5, § 152 para 1 sentence 1, paras 2, 3, 5, 7 to 9 are to be applied to the consolidated balance sheet to the extent its nature does not require a deviation. The inventories may be shown under one caption.

§ 332
Consolidated profit and loss statement

(1) The profit and loss statements of the head association and of the other included enterprises prepared as of the closing date of the consolidated financial statements shall be consolidated in the consolidated profit and loss statement pursuant to the following principles:

1. Against proceeds from turnover proceeds from sales and services between the enterprises included in the consolidated financial statements (proceeds from internal turnover) shall be shown separately from the proceeds from external turnover, except where they are set off against the pertaining costs of the recipients of the sales and services or are shown as changes in inventory or as other capitalized own performances;
2. other income from services between the enterprises included in the consolidated financial statements are to be set off against the pertaining costs of the recipients of the services.

(2) § 331 para 3 sentences 2 and 3 apply accordingly.

(3) §§ 149, 157 paras 1 and 2, § 158 paras 1 to 4 are to be applied to the consolidated profit and loss statement insofar as its nature does not require a deviation. The withdrawals from disclosed reserves and the transfer to disclosed reserves may each be shown under one caption. The profit pertaining to outside partners of the combine and the loss applicable to them shall be shown separately before the caption "consolidated profit / consolidated loss".

§ 333
Consolidated profit and loss statement in simplified form

(1) A simplified form may be used for the consolidated profit and loss statement if the income from sales and services between the enterprises included

in the consolidated financial statements are set off against the pertaining costs of the recipients of the sales and services or shown as changes in inventory or as other capitalized own performances.

(2) If the simplified form is used the following captions shall be shown separately in reducing balance form without prejudice to further classification unless the business purpose of the combine requires a different classification which must be equivalent:

1. proceeds from external turnover		....	
2. expense which need not be shown separately after set off against changes in inventory and own performances		....	....
			....
3. income from participations in enterprises not included in the consolidated financial statements		....	
4. income from the other financial assets		....	
5. other interest and similar income		....	
6. income from appreciation		....	
7. income from release of provisions for accrued liabilities		....	
8. other income		....	....
			....
9. depreciation and provisions for diminution in value of fixed assets and intangible assets		....	
10. depreciation and provisions for diminution in value of financial assets		....	
11. interest and similar expenses		....	
12. taxes			
a) on income, on yield and on net assets	....		
b) other[9]	....	....	
13. expenses resulting from the assumption of a loss of an enterprise not included in the consolidated financial statements		....	....
14. profit for the year / loss for the year			....

[9] For the equalization of burdens levy see § 16 (1) Introductory Law.

15. profit carried forward / loss carried forward from the previous year		....
		....
16. withdrawals from disclosed reserves		....
		....
17. transfers to disclosed reserves		....
		....
18. profit attributable to partners outside the combine	....	
19. loss attributable to partners outside the combine	....	....
20. consolidated profit / consolidated loss		....

(3) In the case of partially consolidated financial statements, profits to be transferred on the basis of a contract to transfer profits or to transfer profits in part to enterprises not included in the partially consolidated financial statements shall be shown separately before the caption "profit/loss for the year", and losses which are to be assumed by an enterprise not included in the consolidated financial statements shall be shown separately after the caption "other income".

(4) § 331 para 3 sentences 2 and 3 apply accordingly. § 157 para 2, § 158 paras 1 to 4 are to be applied.

§ 334
Report of the management for the combine

(1) The enterprises with domestic domicile belonging to the combine shall be listed individually in the report of the management for the combine. The enterprises with domestic domicile included in the consolidated financial statements are to be indicated. The inclusion of enterprises with domicile abroad shall be stated. Detailed reasons shall be given if enterprises with domestic domicile, in which the participation belonging to combine enterprises is more than one half, are not included in the consolidated financial statements. There shall be attached to the report of the management for the combine financial statements of these enterprises, prepared as of the closing date of the consolidated financial statements, to the extent they constitute stock corporations or associations limited by shares.

(2) In the report of the management for the combine there shall be set forth the course of the business and the situation of the combine and of the enterprises included in the consolidated financial statements. Events of special significance which have occurred after the closing date of the consolidated financial statements shall also be reported. If major losses have been incurred or are to be expected by combine enterprises which are not included in the consolidated financial statements, then this shall be stated.

(3) In addition the consolidated financial statements shall be explained in the report of the management for the combine. Therein shall also be discussed material deviations from the last consolidated financial statements. Every report of the management for the combine shall make statements on

1. the causes and the nature of differences in an amount shown pursuant to § 331 para 1 no. 3;
2. liabilities not evident from the consolidated financial statements, including the granting of security for liabilities of the enterprises included in the consolidated financial statements;
3. the legal and business relations with enterprises with a domestic domicile which do not belong to the combine but are connected with a combine enterprise, as well as on business events in these enterprises which may have material influence upon the situation of the combine.

(4) The report shall accord with the principles of conscientious and faithful accounting. The reporting may be dispensed with to the extent this is essential for the welfare of the Federal Republic of Germany or of one of its states. In the reporting pursuant to para 3 no. 2 and 3 details need not be stated to the extent it must be expected, in accordance with a reasonable business judgment, that by the statements considerable disadvantages would arise to the association or to a connected enterprise. If statements are not made on the basis of sentence 3, then this shall be indicated in the report of the management by reference to the required number that use has been made of the protective clause pursuant to sentence 3 for statements under this number.

§ 335
Submission of records

(1) All combine enterprises shall without undue delay submit to the head association their annual financial statements, reports of the management and if an examination of the annual financial statements was made, the examination reports as well as financial statements prepared as of the closing date of the consolidated financial statements, if the closing date of the annual financial statements differs from the closing date of the consolidated financial statements.

(2) The board of management of the head association may demand from every combine enterprise all explanations and evidence which the preparation of the consolidated financial statements and of the report of the management for the combine require.

§ 336
Examination of the consolidated financial statements

(1) The consolidated financial statements are to be examined by one or more expert auditors (auditors of the consolidated financial statements) by including the report of the management for the combine. Provided no other auditors are appointed, then those auditors are held to be auditors of the consolidated financial statements who were appointed for the examination of the annual

financial statements of the head association as of the closing date for which the consolidated financial statements are prepared. If the closing date of the consolidated financial statements deviates from the closing date of the annual financial statements of the head association, then provided no other auditors are appointed, those auditors are held to be appointed who were appointed for the examination of the next following annual financial statements of the head association after the closing date of the consolidated financial statements. §§ 163, 164 apply to the appointment of the other auditors.

(2) The examination of the consolidated financial statements shall include whether or not the provisions for the consolidated financial statements have been complied with. The report of the management for the combine shall be examined for whether or not § 334 paras 1, 3 and 4 have been complied with and whether or not the other statements in the report create a wrong impression of the situation of the combine and of the combine enterprises. § 169 applies accordingly.

(3) The auditors of the consolidated financial statements shall also examine for whether or not the financial statements of the enterprises included in the consolidated financial statements on which the consolidated financial statements are based are prepared in accordance with proper accounting principles. This does not apply to financial statements which were examined pursuant to §§ 162 to 168 or to other statutory provisions or, without a statutory obligation, pursuant to the principles of §§ 162, 164 to 167.

(4) The board of management of the head association shall submit to the auditors of the consolidated financial statements the consolidated financial statements and the report of the management for the combine, the annual financial statements, the reports of the management and the examination reports of all combine enterprises as well as the financial statements submitted to it pursuant to § 335 para 1. The auditors of the consolidated financial statements have the rights pursuant to § 165 to all combine enterprises, in addition the rights pursuant to § 165 paras 2 to 4 towards the auditors of the combine enterprises.

(5) The auditors of the consolidated financial statements shall report in writing on the results of the examination and sign the report. The report shall be submitted to the board of management of the head association.

(6) If no objections are raised on the basis of the final result of the examination, then the auditors of the consolidated financial statements shall confirm this by the following attestation of the consolidated financial statements:

> The consolidated financial statements and the report of the management for the combine accord with the legal provisions on the basis of my (our) dutiful examination.

If objections are raised, then the auditors of the consolidated financial statements shall qualify or refuse the attestation. The auditors of the consolidated financial statements shall sign the attestation by indicating the location and the date. The attestation shall also be included in the examination report.

(7) If the board of management of the head association changes the consoli-

dated financial statements or the report of the management for the combine after the submission of the examination report, then the auditors of the consolidated financial statements shall reexamine the consolidated financial statements and the report of the management for the combine to the extent the changes require it. An attestation already granted is ineffective.

(8) § 168 regarding the liability of the auditors applies accordingly.

§ 337
Submission of the consolidated financial statements and of the report of the management for the combine

(1) Without undue delay after receipt of the examination report of the auditors of the consolidated financial statements, the board of management of the head association shall submit the consolidated financial statements, the report of the management for the combine and the examination report to the supervisory board of the head association for information. Every member of the supervisory board is entitled to take notice of the submitted documents. The submitted documents shall also be handed on request to every member of the supervisory board to the extent the supervisory board has not decided otherwise.

(2) If the consolidated financial statements are prepared as of the closing date of the annual financial statements of the head association, then the consolidated financial statements and the report of the management for the combine shall be submitted to the shareholders' meeting which has to receive or to determine these annual financial statements. If the closing date of the consolidated financial statements deviates from the closing date of the annual financial statements of the head association, then the consolidated financial statements and the report of the management for the combine shall be submitted to the shareholders' meeting which shall receive or determine the next following annual financial statements after the closing date of the consolidated financial statements.

(3) § 175 para 2 applies to making available for inspection the consolidated financial statements and the report of the management for the combine and to giving copies, § 176 para 1 applies to the submission to the shareholders' meeting and to reporting by the board of management.

(4) The duty of the board of management of the head association to give information in the shareholders' meeting in which the consolidated financial statements and the report of the management for the combine are submitted extends also to the situation of the combine and of the enterprises included in the consolidated financial statements.

§ 338
Publication of the consolidated financial statements

(1) The board of management of the head association shall submit the consolidated financial statements with the attestation and the report of the management for the combine to the trade register of the domicile of the head association, without undue delay after the shareholders' meeting for the annual

financial statements (§ 337 para 2). The attestation attached to the submitted consolidated financial statements must be signed by the auditors of the consolidated financial statements. If the auditors of the consolidated financial statements have refused the attestation, then this must be stated on the submitted consolidated financial statements, this statement must be signed by the auditors of the consolidated financial statements.

(2) The board of management of the head association shall publish the consolidated financial statements, together with the annual financial statements, in the journal of the head association and submit the publication to the trade register of the domicile of the head association.

(3) The court shall examine whether or not the submitted consolidated financial statements accord with para 1, whether or not they have been published pursuant to para 2 and whether or not the publication accords with para 4. It need not examine for whether or not the consolidated financial statements and the report of the management for the combine accord with the legal provisions.

(4) § 178 para 1 no. 1 and 2, paras 2 and 3 apply accordingly to the publications and duplications of the consolidated financial statements and of the reports of the management for the combine.

2. France

Proposition de loi sur les groupes de sociétés et la protection des actionnaires, du personnel et des tiers (Proposition "Cousté", version 1978)

Exposé des Motifs

Mesdames, Messieurs,

Le droit français actuel des sociétés est fondé sur un postulat: celui de l'indépendance de la société.

Or la concentration des entreprises qui s'est développée depuis plus de dix ans pour faire face aux nécessités de la libre concurrence dans le cadre notamment de la Communauté économique européenne, a conduit à la constitution de groupes de sociétés plus ou moins importants.

Une incompatibilité fondamentale existe aujourd'hui entre le droit et les nécessités économiques et pratiques du fonctionnement des unités de production ou de prestation de services.

Si une société prend le contrôle d'une autre société, c'est peut-être pour empêcher une société concurrente de le faire, plus souvent pour acquérir de nouveaux actifs industriels et commerciaux (brevets, marques, réseau de distribution, personnel spécialisé, etc.), également pour mettre en place une organisation décentralisée avec une certaine autonomie de «divisions», selon la technique de management des grandes entreprises aux Etats-Unis.

Le phénomène d'organisation des entreprises sous forme de groupes de sociétés est général et en grande partie indépendant du processus d'intégration des entreprises. Si la démultiplication des formes sociales aboutit à des structures complexes, elle présente des qualités de souplesse qui font du groupe un instrument particulièrement adapté de la concentration des entreprises. La raison d'être de nombreuses filiales ne doit pas même être cherchée dans le recours aux procédés de la croissance externe. Si la constitution d'une filiale est la forme normale d'implantation à l'étranger, il n'en est pas de même sur le territoire national.

Le besoin apparaît pour les dirigeants d'entreprises à structure unitaire, lorsque celles-ci arrivent à un degré de complexité et d'importance élevé, de dissocier juridiquement certains départements ou certaines fonctions de l'entreprise. Cette dissociation offre d'importants avantages de souplesse et de clarté. A l'intérieur du groupe, chaque société constitue une unité de gestion maniable, les dirigeants en sont davantage responsables des résultats, la gestion financière ou par objectifs est plus facile à définir, et la division des risques en découle naturellement. Les avantages de la décentralisation juridique se manifestent plus encore en cas d'opérations communes, dans lesquelles il faut délimiter nettement les actifs et les activités mis en commun et les isoler du reste des entreprises en cause. La division juridique permet alors au groupe de collaborer avec des partenaires différents selon le niveau ou le domaine d'activité concerné. Et le régime du bénéfice consolidé a fait disparaître, au moins en partie, l'intérêt que présentait une structure unitaire pour la compensation entre bénéfices et pertes des différents départements.

Dans chaque cas, toutefois, la société dominante devra exercer et exercera dès lors un pouvoir dans la société contrôlée, soit directement, soit par le canal d'une société intermédiaire.

Au principe juridique d'indépendance des sociétés s'oppose donc le fait économique de la dépendance. Les membres des organes de direction, d'administration ou de surveillance de la société ont, dans notre droit, la mission fondamentale de se conduire selon les intérêts sociaux à l'exclusion de tous autres. L'accomplissement de cette mission suppose chez eux une indépendance absolue de décision. Or dans un groupe, les organes de la société contrôlée, tout comme le contrôle lui-même, obéissent à un intérêt différent, celui de la société dominante qui se confond avec l'intérêt du groupe. Ainsi l'anéantissement de l'indépendance par le contrôle se conjugue à l'anéantissement de l'intérêt social (initial) de la société contrôlée.

Il n'en reste pas moins que l'entrée d'une société isolée dans un groupe peut léser les intérêts des associés qui se trouvent en situation minoritaire et que la prise de participation dans un but de contrôle (et non de simple placement) crée un déséquilibre qu'aucune disposition légale ne permet de pallier.

L'urgente nécessité d'encourager la concentration sur le plan tant national qu'européen rend opportun l'examen des moyens de faciliter la constitution des groupes, tout en instituant la protection des intérêts minoritaires et du personnel des entreprises concernées par les mouvements de concentration.

*
**

Les dernières années ont montré que juristes et économistes avaient compris qu'il importait de ne plus retarder la solution de tels problèmes.

En rénovant son droit des sociétés anonymes par *l'Aktiengesetz* de 1965, la République fédérale allemande s'est la première dotée d'un droit complet des groupes. Celui-ci repose sur la notion économique de contrôle : article 17 de l'Aktg «les entreprises dépendantes sont des entreprises autonomes sur lesquelles une autre entreprise (l'entreprise dominante) peut exercer une influence directe ou indirecte». La loi distingue les groupes de fait et les groupes de droit. Le groupe de droit repose sur le pacte de domination qui est un contrat passé volontairement entre les deux sociétés et publié par elles au registre du commerce; le pacte rend licites les atteintes portées par l'entreprise dominante aux intérêts de l'entreprise dominée, et les actionnaires externes peuvent choisir de rester actionnaires moyennant une allocation compensatrice annuelle ou de se défaire de leurs actions dans le cadre d'un règlement terminal. Dans le groupe de fait, qui ne recourt pas au statut du droit précédent, les agissements préjudiciables aux actionnaires externes entraînent seulement le versement, pour chacun d'eux, d'une compensation. La mise en œuvre de ce statut des groupes n'a d'ailleurs pas donné entière satisfaction; un lourd contentieux s'est formé depuis sept à huit ans et on assiste à une fuite des groupes de droit vers les groupes de fait.

Dans son «Projet de règlement portant statut de la société anonyme européenne» soumis le 30 juin 1970 à l'examen du Conseil des Ministres, la Commission des Communautés européennes a, de son côté, inséré un statut des groupes qui occupe le titre VII. Le projet est très largement inspiré du projet Sanders, et reprend une grande partie du dispositif mis en place par la République fédérale allemande. Il est d'autant plus important d'en tenir compte que les dispositions qui sont contenues dans ce titre VII seront applicables, sans intervention du Parlement français, à toute entreprise dépendante qui aura son siège en France et à ses relations avec la société européenne dominante ainsi qu'aux relations entre une société européenne dépendante et l'entreprise dominante qui aura son siège en France (art. 224). Cependant les réticences demeurent sérieuses à l'égard de ce texte dans les milieux économiques européens; et l'union des industries de la communauté européenne, en déplorant que le statut envisagé propose des règles plus contraignantes même que celles existant dans n'importe laquelle des législations des Etats membres, a été jusqu'à s'interroger sur l'opportunité d'une réglementation en la matière.

Dans notre pays, la loi n° 66–357 du 24 juillet 1966 sur les sociétés commerciales contient plusieurs amorces d'un droit des groupes de sociétés, dans la mesure où elle reconnaît l'existence possible de liens entre sociétés juridiquement autonomes. Ces liens toutefois ne résultent toujours que de l'existence d'une participation dans le capital, ce qui ne représente qu'un des critères du contrôle. Au moment du vote de la loi en question, M. le Garde des Sceaux, ministre de la Justice, avait fait la promesse de mettre à l'étude l'établissement d'un droit français des groupes. Cet engagement n'a encore été concrétisé par aucun texte.

Mais le groupe U. D. R. de l'Assemblée national faisait déposer, sous les noms de M. Cousté et de quelques-uns de ses collègues et le n° 1055 le 19 février 1970, une proposition de loi en trente-six articles dont l'objet était de réglementer en droit français les groupes de sociétés et d'assurer la protection des actionnaires et du personnel. Ce texte a fait l'objet d'une large diffusion et a retenu l'attention des pouvoirs publics ainsi que des juristes et des milieux économiques. Dans une très importante lettre en date du 4 novembre 1970, adressée à M. Cousté et ensuite dans une déclaration faite le 8 juin 1971 au cours d'un dîner-débat organisé par le Conseil supérieur de l'Ordre des experts-comptables et des comptables agréés dans le cadre des «Mercredis de la comptabilité», M. René Pleven, garde des Sceaux, avait manifesté l'intérêt de la Chancellerie pour le sujet en question et l'orientation qu'il souhaitait voir prendre aux études qui se poursuivaient, dans le sens d'un contrat volontaire d'affiliation. Le Comité d'études du financement des entreprises (C. E. F. E.), dont les travaux sur les groupes de sociétés publiés à l'occasion du XXIIIe Congrès de l'Ordre des experts-comptables et des comptables agréés en 1968 ont largement contribué à éclairer le sujet, s'est livré à une vaste enquête sur l'accueil réservé à la proposition de loi 1055 et a recueilli les nombreuses observations formulées par les représentants des grandes entreprises, des groupes de sociétés et internationaux, des délégués du patronat, des juristes, etc. La Fondation nationale pour le droit de l'entreprise a tenu en 1971 à Montpellier et à Rennes des journées d'études sur le même sujet qui ont été très suivies et dont les débats et conclusions ont été publiés.

Pour sa part le groupe «Droit et financement des entreprises», dit groupe de prospective juridique appliquée, constitué dans le cadre de l'élaboration du VIe Plan, et présidé par M. Michel Vasseur, conseiller d'Etat, professeur à la Faculté de droit et des sciences économiques de Paris retenait comme un des thèmes principaux de réflexion la question des groupes de sociétés; le sous-groupe ad hoc animé par M. Stephen Gorlin, directeur des études financières à la société Rhône-Poulenc, renonçant à donner une définition juridique du groupe, s'efforçait de présenter diverses propositions qui permettraient d'assurer un meilleur fonctionnement des groupes et une meilleure protection des actionnaires minoritaires.

Enfin, conscient que la concentration de l'industrie française s'effectue au niveau des groupes, et que l'exploitation d'une branche ou d'une activité particulière d'une entreprise au moyen d'une ou plusieurs filiales est plus rationelle, le législateur fiscal a veillé à ce que le fonctionnement des groupes ne soit pas entravé sur le plan interne ni sur un plan international. La loi du 12 juillet 1965 et le décret du 11 septembre 1967 ont introduit à cet effet un système d'imposition dit du bénéfice mondial apportant une dérogation à la règle de territorialité, et un autre appelé du bénéfice consolidé autorisant les sociétés d'un groupe à faire abstraction de la notion de personnalité distincte de chacune et à constituer une masse globale de leurs résultats. Mais ces deux régimes étaient réservés à certains groupes français à vocation internationale et ne furent accordés qu'aux groupes disposant de filiales ou d'établissements à l'étranger. C'est seulement par l'article premier de la loi n° 71-1025 du 24 décembre 1971 que l'extension du régime du bénéfice consolidé a été acquise en faveur des groupes purement nationaux, sur agrément du ministre de l'Economie et des Finances, et pour les filiales constituées à l'occasion d'une concentration d'entreprise ou de la restructuration interne de groupe.

Ainsi le moment paraît-il venu de faire la synthèse des éléments disponibles, des études et observations formulées tant à propos du projet de statut d'une société anonyme européenne que de la proposition de loi n° 1055, et de proposer ainsi un droit cohérent des groupes de sociétés en France.

*
**

Tout comme la précédente proposition et comme le règlement de société anonyme européenne, la nouvelle proposition part du fait économique; l'état de dépendance d'une société par rapport à une autre, quelle que soit la source d'où naît le groupe, dès lors que la société dominante établit entre elle et la société dépendante l'unité de direction.

La différence est de conception quant à l'emprise du droit sur le fait ainsi défini.

Le législateur peut organiser un système de conséquences directes où le fait, sous la seule réserve de sa constatation indiscutable, entraîne inéluctablement l'application du statut des groupes. Il en est ainsi dans la proposition n° 1055.

Un autre système, celui de la nouvelle proposition, ne consacre le fait en droit que par la conclusion d'un «contrat d'affiliation». Le groupe ne sera légalement constitué qu'une fois le contrat passé entre la société dominante et la société dépendante. Alors seulement celle-ci de «dépendante» devient «affiliée».

A cette conception du groupe répondent les titres premier et second de la proposition.

Deux éléments de base définissent le groupe, le lien de dépendance et la direction unique.

Il faut entendre par sociétés dépendantes des sociétés juridiques autonomes sur lesquelles une autre société, qui est la société dominante, peut exercer une influence prédominante. A l'image de la proposition de loi n° 1055, la présente proposition a préféré, à la dénomination «société dépendante» qui pourrait être ressentie comme dépréciante, celle de «société affiliée». Il est clair que ces définitions sont d'interprétation restrictive et s'appliquent pour la mise en œuvre de la présente loi seule.

La dépendance peut se realiser par des moyens juridiques tirés le plus souvent du droit des sociétés: telle la participation (en quotité de capital détenu ou en droit de vote), ou le contrat (rappel des contrats interentreprises du droit allemand, *Organschaftsverträge*). Elle peut aussi revêtir une forme larvée, accords et conventions de coopération, concession, spécialisation, sous-traitance, qui ont en apparence un autre objet, mais aboutissent aussi certainement à la dépendance qu'un contrat de domination quand les partenaires ne sont pas libres et égaux. Elle peut enfin être fondée uniquement sur des éléments de fait: telle l'union personnelle résultant de l'identité des dirigeants.

L'article 4 de la présente proposition prévoit que le lien de dépendance entre deux sociétés est établi valablement entre elles par un contrat dit d'affiliation. Ainsi est respecté le principe de la liberté de constitution des groupes, sur lequel le groupe «Droit et financement de l'entreprise» du VIe Plan mettait l'accent, dans l'état actuel de notre système économique et politique. Toute reconnaissance de l'existence d'un groupe sans le consentement des sociétés en cause et sur déclaration faite par une juridiction, telle qu'elle était prévue dans la proposition de loi n° 1055, est écartée.

Cependant, pour tenir compte de la structure des groupes français et de la prépondérance des participations comme forme d'exercice du contrôle, une présomption de dépendance est établie chaque fois qu'une société dispose, dans une autre société, de plus de 50% des voix attachées à l'ensemble des titres émis (art. 2). Il s'agit d'une présomption non irréfragable. Encore est-elle exclue si les statuts de la société affiliée prévoient que certaines décisions de gestion des associés doivent être prises à une majorité supérieure au nombre de voix dont dispose, directement ou indirectement, la société dominante.

Quand cette présomption correspond à la réalité des faits, un contrat d'affiliation peut être proposé par la société dominante à la société dépendante, qui lui permettra d'obtenir de celle-ci l'obéissance à ses ordres de direction, et par conséquent de gérer les affaires de la seconde dans l'objectif d'une gestion rationelle du groupe et non dans le seul intérêt des propres actionnaires ou associés de cette société dépendante, qui ne coïncide pas toujours avec celui du groupe. Si une telle proposition n'est pas faite, la société-mère et sa filiale n'accéderont pas au statut de groupe de droit, et le groupe de fait constitué devra respecter les règles du droit actuel des sociétés, c'est-à-dire que seront interdites à la société dominante toutes opérations de nature à aller à l'encontre des intérêts des actionnaires minoritaires de la société dépendante.

La seconde condition d'existence du groupe est que la société dominante réunisse les sociétés qui dépendent d'elle sous une direction unique. Si le lien de dépendance conditionne le groupe et si celui-ci ne peut exister sans lui, il peut y avoir dépendance sans groupe si la direction unique manque. Aucune incertitude d'interprétation ne peut être envisagée; l'article 3 de la présente proposition définit clairement le groupe.

La notion de direction unique est liée à celle d'unité de décision; c'est celle qui s'exerce à travers les entités de droit multiples que sont les sociétés juridiquement autonomes soumises au contrôle. C'est de l'unité de direction qu'émaneront, tout au long de la vie du groupe, les directives qui en guideront la gestion et en assureront, en fonction de l'intérêt global, l'unité économique.

Il s'agit en fait de l'exercice du pouvoir de décision dont dispose la société dominante, quelle que soit la nature de ce pouvoir (financier, humain, etc.). Cet exercice n'est pas exclusif d'une très large décentralisation et n'implique pas obligatoirement l'existence d'une cellule unique de prise de décision. Il est clair par exemple qu'une société holding, qui assure les moyens de financement des projets d'investissements, même établis au niveau des sociétés affiliées, détient le pouvoir de décision et assure personnellement l'exercice de ce pouvoir puisqu' elle est dispensatrice des capitaux nécessaires. A plus forte raison en est-il de même d'une société dominante vis-à-vis de sociétés dépendantes entre lesquelles une communauté d'administrateurs a été réalisée, même s'il n'y a pas de participation de la première au capital des secondes. Le degré de hiérarchisation du groupe peut être très variable naturellement. Dans certains cas, la structure pyramidale se manifeste clairement, les dirigeants et les cadres de la société dominante planifient l'activité générale de la société-mère et des sociétés affiliées, qui se bornent à exécuter. Dans les petits groupes, il peut même s'agir simplement de services érigés en sociétés autonomes sans que celles-ci fonctionnent comme telles. Dans les grandes sociétés le degré de centralisation varie selon le domaine d'activité: il peut y avoir plusieurs niveaux de centralisation et ceux-ci varient selon les fonctions. Le plus souvent la planification à long terme, le financement, le développement sont dirigés d'une manière centralisée. Et l'administration du groupe tend souvent à être confiée à une holding spécialisée.

Une disposition consacrant le pouvoir de commandement est essentielle dans tout droit des groupes: tel est l'objet de l'article 27 de la présente proposition. Mais la toute-puissance du contrôle ne doit pas aboutir à son immixtion désordonnée dans la société dépendante: la société dominante ne doit jamais pouvoir s'adresser directement au personnel de la société dépendante (art. 28).

Bien qu'elle apparaisse ainsi toute-puissante, la société dominante est soumise à de nombreuses contraintes: juridiques, économiques, sociales. Or l'autonomie des dirigeants de la société dépendante qu'implique l'application des méthodes modernes de gestion, et le respect ou la crainte des actionnaires minoritaires risquent d'empêcher la société dominante d'appliquer la politique qu'elle désire mener. Il convient de l'autoriser clairement à déroger au droit actuel et à faire exécuter par la société dépendante certains actes qui autrement auraient constitué des détournements de biens sociaux ou des abus de droit: prestations ou livraisons de produits à prix coûtant ou même à perte, transfert d'actifs, glissement de bénéfice en vue du financement d'investissements ou d'équilibre de fonds de roulement: tels sont les objets des articles 30 et 31 de la présente proposition de loi. Quand de telles opérations sont de nature à porter préjudice à la société dépendante, plus particulièrement à ses actionnaires minoritaires, une contrepartie doit être offerte à ceux-ci, qui peut consister en garanties de dividendes et/ou indemnités compensatrices.

Des opérations seront ainsi légalisées dont la pratique, économiquement normale, voire nécessaire, ne peut, à défaut de droit des groupes, s'exercer que par des procédés occultes, en infraction souvent aux lois pénales aussi bien que commerciales. Il fallait dire clairement que, ces opérations devenant licites, aucune responsabilité ni pénale ni civile ne saurait plus désormais être encourue de leur chef. Cela est proclamé par l'article 33 de la proposition.

De fait la domination par les liens de groupe s'est jusqu'à ce jour située tout entière en marge du droit, vérité constamment méconnue autant qu'éprouvante par la menace des sanctions civiles et pénales qu'elle porte en elle. Nombre d'auteurs et praticiens ne se sont pas fait faute d'attirer là-dessus l'attention des tenants de l'absence de législation des groupes, avant que le discours du ministre de la Justice du 9 juin 1971, en les réitérant, ne donne une plus forte résonance à ces avertissements.

Comment les dirigeants des groupes ne seraient-ils pas sensibles aux avantages d'une gestion de groupe désormais affranchie de toute équivoque s'exerçant en pleine lumière et liberté? Autant qu'aux actionnaires externes, aux créanciers, au personnel des sociétés dépendantes, le droit des groupes leur ouvre à eux aussi l'accès à des garanties, celles de rectitude dans la légalité.

L'ensemble de ces dispositions répond, cette fois encore, au deuxième principe dégagé par le groupe «Droit et financement de l'entreprise» du VIe Plan, selon lequel c'est la majorité qui décide dans les sociétés de capitaux: la minorité doit s'incliner devant la volonté de la majorité, sous réserve que celle-ci ne lèse pas la minorité ou, si elle lui cause un préjudice, elle l'en indemnise.

Il est clair que la mise en œuvre de ces dispositions dans le cadre des contrats d'affiliation, notamment des transferts d'actifs et des prestations ou livraisons à prix coûtant et même à perte de la société affiliée à la société dominante (art. 30) est de nature à entraîner des conséquences fiscales graves. Les auteurs de la présente proposition de loi se sont refusés volontairement à prendre celles-ci en considération et à rechercher les solutions possibles en ce domaine, ne voulant en aucune façon aliéner l'indépendance du législateur fiscal et soucieux de laisser celui-ci dégager les solutions les plus équitables en même temps que les plus adéquates à la vie des groupes, dans le sens de l'évolution ci-dessus rappelée qui a abouti notamment aux dispositions de l'article premier de la loi de finances du 24 décembre 1971.

*
**

Dans un droit des groupes qui reconnaît la validité des opérations réalisées par la société dominante au profit de l'intérêt seul du groupe, la protection des actionnaires et associées minoritaires, dits externes, n'est pas le point le moins important.

La présente proposition confère aux intéressés, en cas de prise de contrôle de leur société, l'option entre deux solutions dont l'ensemble constitue le règlement terminal et qui doivent être portées à la connaissance des intéressés en même temps que le contrat d'affiliation:
- leur retrait de la société dépendante, soit par échange de leurs actions contre des titres de la société dominante, soit par versement d'une indemnité en espèces;
- leur maintien dans la société dépendante avec le bénéfice d'une allocation compensatrice annuelle.

L'offre du règlement terminal appartient à la société dominante et la proposition prévoit de laisser à celle-ci le choix entre les titres qu'elle doit offrir en échange des actions de la société dépendante. Il pourra s'agir ainsi d'actions ordinaires, mais aussi d'obligations convertibles en actions, ou même d'obligations simples (art. 15). La société dominante pourra pourvoir à ses besoins en ce domaine par une augmentation de capital ou un rachat d'actions en bourse: il est laissé au décret d'application de réglementer ce point (art. 17). Mais il est essentiel que les modalités d'échange des actions ou de calcul de l'indemnité en espèces soient à l'abri de toute contestation: c'est pourquoi le soin de les déterminer est laissé conjointement aux commissaires aux comptes des sociétés dominantes et affiliées (art. 8) dont le rapport doit être adressé à tous les intéressés.

La seconde branche de l'option offerte aux actionnaires et associés externes consiste dans le versement, à l'actionnaire qui refuse le règlement terminal et veut se maintenir dans la société dépendante tout en subissant les préjudices éventuels dus à l'exécution par celle-ci des ordres de direction de la société dominante, d'une allocation compensatrice annuelle. Cette allocation peut être calculée de deux façons:
- ou bien il s'agit d'une somme fixe, versée chaque année pour le même montant, qui sera établi au départ en tenant compte du rendement passé de la société affiliée et de ses perspectives futures. A l'opposition manifestée à cet égard contre la disposition analogue insérée à l'article 21 de la proposition de loi n° 1055, on peut répondre que le problème du calcul de cette allocation ne diffère pas tellement du problème de l'évaluation d'une société au moment de la fusion ou de la scission et que les commissaires aux comptes sont en mesure d'effectuer une telle évaluation, comme le font les commissaires aux apports;

- ou bien il s'agit d'une somme variable représentant une fraction des résultats du groupe. L'une des obligations du groupe est d'établir des comptes consolidés (art. 45) et de publier périodiquement, pour chaque société, l'état de ses participations. Il paraît donc possible de se fonder sur les résultats globaux du groupe pour déterminer, selon des procédures comptables faciles à appliquer et en partant de la parité établie entre les actions de la société dominante et celles de la société affiliée, la part de dividende qui pourrait revenir normalement aux actionnaires et associés externes.

Le règlement terminal et l'allocation compensatrice annuelle sont l'un et l'autre des charges de la société dominante. Le système proposé pourrait ainsi apporter une garantie sérieuse aux actionnaires et associés externes.

La suppression de l'intangibilité du patrimoine de la société affiliée dans le droit des groupes envisagé conduirait à l'anéantissement financier de cette dernière si n'était prévue l'obligation pour la société dominante de compenser annuellement et intégralement les pertes de la société dépendante. Tel est l'objet du «transfert compensateur» prévu par l'article 32.

Cette disposition est reprise du précédent projet. Les critiques auxquelles elle avait donné lieu pourraient avoir perdu de vue qu'elle est la contrepartie du pouvoir conféré à la société dominante de disposer du patrimoine des sociétés affiliées. Cela a été rappelé avec une particulière vigueur au cours du colloque international tenu à la faculté de droit de Liège les 20 et 21 octobre 1972 sur le droit des groupes. Supprimer la compensation des pertes, c'est permettre l'absorption par la société dominante de l'actif entier de la société affiliée sans dédommager les actionnaires externes demeurés dans cette dernière. Autant alors ne permettre cette absorption que par une franche fusion qui fait disparaître la société absorbée comme ses actionnaires, avec toutes les garanties qui sont celles de la fusion, plutôt que d'instituer un droit des groupes trompeur.

La proposition prévoit également une réglementation des comptes consolidés. L'énoncé du principe seul figure dans le texte, à l'article 45, mais cette disposition, qui répond à un besoin d'information essentiel et constitue en elle-même une autre forme de protection des actionnaires, des tiers et du public, peut s'appuyer sur le rapport approuvé par arrêté ministériel du 4 mars 1968 du Conseil national de la comptabilité, sur les recommandations de la commission des opérations de Bourse dont les exigences en matière de publication de comptes consolidés ont pris effet au 1er juillet 1971, et sur les travaux d'approfondissement des techniques comptables de consolidation qui ont été menés par le comité d'études du financement des entreprises et le Conseil supérieur de l'Ordre des experts-comptables et des comptables agréés, notamment à la lumière de la norme comptable internationale sur la consolidation (norme n° 3).

Il n'a pas été jugé utile de prévoir la désignation d'un commissaire de groupe, le ou les commissaires de la société dominante devant rendre compte annuellement à l'assemblée générale des actionnaires de celle-ci de l'exécution des clauses particulières du contrat d'affiliation et la même tâche incombant, en ce qui concerne la société affiliée, aux commissaires aux comptes de celle-ci (art. 41).

*
* *

A côté des actionnaires externes et au moins aussi dignes d'intérêt figurent les salariés de l'entreprise dépendante. L'entrée de celle-ci dans le groupe ne sera pas sans entraîner pour eux de graves conséquences: réduction éventuelle du personnel, fermeture d'ateliers sinon même d'usines entières, transfert d'une usine dans une autre qui doit d'ailleurs être autorisé s'il est effectué dans l'intérêt social du groupe.

Mais il a paru difficile de résoudre, dans le cadre de la présente proposition de loi, l'ensemble des problèmes que pose l'existence des groupes à l'égard de deux grands domaines:

- le maintien du contrat de travail et des avantages acquis dans le cadre de celui-ci et/ou des conventions collectives;
- la représentation des travailleurs des entreprises dépendantes auprès de la société dominante.

Les juristes n'ont porté leur attention que depuis peu à ces problèmes et les décisions de jurisprudence restent peu nombreuses et de portée limitée. Une recherche approfondie et une longue réflexion auraient conduit à retarder l'ensemble de la présente proposition de loi. Seules ont donc été retenues deux mesures:

- la représentation des travailleurs de la société dépendante au sein d'un comité d'entreprise du groupe dont le comité d'entreprise européen prévu par le statut de la société anonyme européenne peut laisser présumer la forme (art. 25);
- le sort des travailleurs qui ont reçu, au titre de la participation, des actions ou coupures d'actions provenant d'incorporations de réserves ou de rachat dans la société affiliée, et dont la qualité d'actionnaires est semblable à celle des autres actionnaires externes (art. 26).

*
**

La présente proposition de loi instaure pour base légale d'existence du groupe le contrat d'affiliation. Mais quelle est alors la situation du groupe de fait, autrement dit quel est le régime des sociétés liées par un rapport de dépendance sans avoir passé entre elles de contrat d'affiliation?

C'est à cette question que répond le titre VII de la proposition sur «l'exercice du pouvoir de décision sans contrat d'affiliation». Cette réponse, le discours du 9 juin 1971 l'avait déjà donnée. Ayant mentionné le caractère non obligatoire de la constitution du groupe de droit, le Ministre ajoutait: «. . . les sociétés pourraient constituer aussi, si elles le préféraient, des groupes de fait, mais alors elles resteraient sous la menace d'une application stricte des règles de la loi du 24 juillet 1966 et l'on peut penser que les tribunaux, s'ils ont pu se montrer libéraux dans l'application des textes qui paraissent difficilement compatibles avec la réalité des groupes, le seraient beaucoup moins le jour où les groupes auraient à leur disposition une possibilité légale d'y échapper».

Au sein du groupe de fait ne sauraient donc être admis les transferts patrimoniaux, soit implicites, soi ouvertement réalisés comme tels, qu'autorise pleinement le groupe de droit. A l'initiative des actionnaires externes de la société dépendante pourra être mise en œuvre la responsabilité des dirigeants de fait et de droit des sociétés du groupe de fait. Tel est l'objet des articles 34 à 37 de la proposition.

Cette incitation à passer sous le régime du groupe de droit devrait être décisive.

*
* *

C'est aux limites de la fusion que se situe la «société intégrée» (filiale à 100%) tirée du précédent allemand, réglé dans le titre IX de la proposition. Elle échappe à la critique exposée ci-dessus, puis qu'elle ne peut être instituée qu'à partir d'une société déjà dominée à 95% et cela par transfert à la société dominante des 5% restants.

Il est apparu souhaitable de ne pas la contraindre et inutile de l'obliger à fonctionner comme si elle comportait de multiples actionnaires, ni même nécessaire de continuer à exiger d'elle l'existence de sept actionnaires si l'actionnaire à 100% est une personne morale. On voit apparaître là le problème de la société unipersonnelle qui est posé depuis longtemps dans notre pays. Il convient à cet égard de signaler l'innovation importante apportée par la loi n° 66-537 du 24 juillet 1966, dont l'article 9 prévoit qu'une société peut subsister, ne serait-ce temporairement, avec un seul associé. Il serait donc plus conforme à la réalité des choses que la filiale à 100%, dont l'associé unique est une personne morale, puisse apparaître au grand jour, comme une société à main unique: tel est le but des articles 52 à 54 de la présente proposition. La solution proposée permet de simplifier le mécanisme actuel de la société anonyme, tout en laissant subsister la personnalité juridique de la société dépendante. L'existence d'un seul actionnaire est incompatible avec la notion d'assemblée: dès lors le plus grand nombre des décisions qui sont du domaine des assemblées d'actionnaires doivent être prises par le ou les représentants qualifiés de la société dominante, qui sont constitués entre eux en un comité de direction, qui jouit de tous les pouvoirs attribués par la législation sur les sociétés par actions aux organes d'administration, de direction ou de surveillance (art. 53).

Aucune disposition particulière n'est prévue pour limiter la responsabilité de l'actionnaire unique, il n'existe en effet aucune raison pour qu'un créancier reçoive plus de garanties en traitant avec une société ayant un seul actionnaire qu'avec une société en ayant plusieurs.

De même il n'a pas été créé d'obligation pour la société dominante de soumetre à l'approbation de ses actionnaires les comptes des filiales à 100%: si celles-ci sont nombreuses, il y aurait eu là une impossibilité pratique. Les obligations actuelles concernant les filiales permettent à ces actionnaires d'obtenir des renseignements suffisants sur la marche de ces filiales.

La filiale à 100% n'est pas le seul cas où les actionnaires externes n'ont plus aucun rôle dans la société dépendante. La même situation existe lorsque la participation majoritaire est presque totale. Cette situation a été prévue par certaines législations étrangères et, en Grande-Bretagne, si une société est amenée à détenir plus de 90% du capital d'une autre société, les actionnaires de celle-ci peuvent demander à la première de racheter leurs actions, et réciproquement la société dominante peut obliger les actionnaires externes de la société dépendante à lui vendre leurs propres actions.

L'adoption de dispositions de ce genre est apparue possible, dans le but de simplifier les structures de groupes qui sont souvent alourdies par de très faibles minorités. Pour tenir compte des réticences formulées à cet égard par le groupe «Droit et financement de l'entreprise» du VIe Plan, la limite inférieure de participation a été fixée à 95% (art. 47).

Il convient enfin de conférer un statut à la société dominée à 95%, qui soit une incitation à la société dominante de procéder à l'intégration. C'est pourquoi les actionnaires externes de la société dominée à 95% sont en droit à tout moment de réclamer un contrat d'affiliation rétroagissant, quant à l'allocation compensatrice et quant à l'évaluation de la parité, à la date où la participation de 95% a été atteinte, si elle ne remonte pas à plus de cinq ans (art. 55).

*
* *

En combinant le système de la présente loi avec les modifications proposées à la loi n° 66-537 du 24 juillet 1936 sur les sociétés commerciales qui ont été préparées par le Garde des Sceaux, ministre de la Justice (projet de loi n° 2510 déposé au cours de la précédente législature en juillet 1976), ou prévues dans une proposition de loi, il semble que l'on doive aboutir à un apurement de la situation actuelle en matière de groupes de sociétés, et à une régénération du droit des sociétés. L'ensemble de la présente proposition, en s'en tenant aux groupes de droit et en laissant jouer les dispositions actuelles, constitue une première étape vers un droit des groupes que la réalité économique appelle et que la Commission des Communautés européennes cherche à mettre en place.

La proposition laisse toutefois de côté un certain nombre de questions. Aucune mention n'est faite des groupes dits d'entreprises équivalentes, ou groupes horizontaux. Le problème de la concentration par liens d'égalité prend de plus en plus d'importance dans les pays du Marché commun. On peut se demander si ces «filiales communes» fonctionnent comme des «filiales» soumises à une unité de direction ou au contraire comme des sociétés anonymes typiques.[1] Le problème a fait l'objet d'une réflexion approfondie au cours des journées d'études tenues en février 1975 à l'initiative de l'Association des juristes d'entreprises. Rien n'empêchera de telles sociétés, dans un premier temps, de conclure entre elles un contrat d'affiliation qui, si la direction unique existe en fait, entraînera les dispositions prévues dans la présente proposition en faveur des actionnaires et associés externes.

La proposition ne traite que des groupes à la tête desquels se trouve une

[1] Voir *Memorandum de la Commission des Communautés européennes sur la politique industrielle* en date du 18 mars 1970, IIe partie, pp. 11-18 et suiv., notamment 11-22 à 28.

société et, pour les filiales à 100%, que de celles dont l'actionnaire unique est une personne morale. Elle laisse hors de son champ les cas des groupes dominés par une personne physique. Il est difficile de faire autrement aussi longtemps que le droit français n'aura pas évolué vers la notion de patrimoine commercial de la personne physique et de société unipersonnelle déjà rencontrée plus haut.

Ont été enfin volontairement laissés de côté, comme il a été dit déjà, tous les problèmes de nature fiscale, dont certains devront faire l'objet de mesures d'ensemble (tels ceux posés par la possibilité de transferts d'actifs), et d'autres trouveront facilement des solutions de détail, comme le sort fiscal de l'allocation compensatrice annuelle.

Tels sont les motifs pour lesquels nous vous demandons d'adopter la présente proposition de loi.

Proposition de loi

Titre Premier
Définitions

Article premier.

Quand une société dispose sur une autre société d'une influence lui permettant d'exercer sur celle-ci, directement ou indirectement, par des moyens de droit ou de fait, le pouvoir de décision, la première est dite société dominante et la seconde société dépendante.

Art. 2.

Une société est, sauf preuve contraire, présumée dépendante d'une autre société quand cette dernière dispose, directement ou indirectement, dans la première de plus de 50% des voix attachées à l'ensemble des droits sociaux.

Cette présomption ne pourra notamment être invoquée si les statuts de la société affiliée prévoient que certaines décisions de gestion des associés doivent être prises à une majorité supérieure au nombre de voix dont dispose, directement ou indirectement, la société dominante.

Art. 3.

Les sociétés dominante et dépendante forment un groupe quand elles sont réunies sous la direction unique de la société dominante.

Toute société dominante est présumée former un groupe avec la société dépendante, sauf à apporter la preuve qu'il n'y a pas exercice du pouvoir de décision.

Le groupe n'a pas la personnalité morale.

Art. 4.

Le lien de groupes inter-sociétés s'établit en droit par un contrat dit d'affiliation, conclu et publié en conformité des titres II et VII de la présente loi.

Chacune des sociétés dépendantes au sein d'une groupe est dite société affiliée.

Par le contrat d'affiliation, la société affiliée s'oblige, en contrepartie des garanties conférées en vertu des titres III, IV et V de la présente loi à ses actionnaires et associés, à son personnel et à ses créanciers, à obéir aux ordres de direction de la société dominante conformément aux dispositions du titre VI de la présente loi.

Art. 5.

Les actionnaires ou associés de la société affiliée qui n'ont pas de participation dans le capital de la société dominante sont dénommés actionnaires ou associés externes.

Toutefois, seront également traités comme tels ceux dont la participation dans le capital de la société dominante ne dépasse pas 1% du capital de celle-ci.

La qualité d'actionnaire ou d'associé externe est exclue pour ceux qui participent, en droit ou en fait, à la direction du groupe.

Art. 6.

Les groupes de sociétés non affiliées sont soumis aux dispositions du titre VII de la présente loi, sous réserve des dispositions du titre IX relatives aux sociétés intégrées.

Titre II
Le Contrat d'Affiliation

Art. 7.

Le contrat d'affiliation est, à peine de nullité, passé par écrit et établi en autant d'exemplaires que de parties contractantes.

Il doit être approuvé par les associés des sociétés contractantes dans les conditions prévues pour les modifications statutaires de celles- ci.

Art. 8.

Les commissaires aux comptes de la société dominante et de la société affiliée, assistés le cas échéant d'experts de leur choix, établissent et présentent un rapport sur les modalités du contrat d'affiliation et du règlement terminal prévu aux articles 13 à 23 de la présente loi, plus spécialement sur la parité proposée pour l'échange des actions ou parts sociales de la société affiliée contre les titres ou parts sociales de la société dominante, et sur le montant de l'indemnité en numéraire à verser en échange de la reprise de ces actions. A cet effet les commissaires aux comptes peuvent obtenir communication de tous documents utiles auprès de chaque société intéressée et des sociétés liées à elle par le lien défini à l'article premier de la présente loi.

Un commissaire aux comptes est désigné, dans les sociétés qui n'en comportent pas, par ordonnance du Président du tribunal de commerce ou à son défaut du Président du tribunal de grande instance de leur siège social rendue sur requête.

La mise en œuvre des dispositions du présent article sera précisée par décret.

Art. 9.

Avant la décision d'approbation, l'organe d'administration de la société dépendante adresse, à chaque actionnaire ou associé de celle-ci, en même temps que la proposition du contrat d'affiliation, le rapport des commissaires aux comptes, dans les conditions qui seront déterminées par décret.

Le projet de contrat d'affiliation est soumis pour avis, le cas échéant, aux comités d'entreprise de la société dominante et de la société dépendante.

Art. 10.

Le contrat d'affiliation entre en vigueur à la date de son inscription au registre du commerce, prévue à l'article 38 de la présente loi.

Art. 11.

La modification du contrat d'affiliation ne peut intervenir que dans la forme et selon la procédure prévues aux articles 7, 8 et 9 pour sa conclusion, le tout assorti des mesures de publicité prévues au titre VIII de la présente loi et par le décret à intervenir.

Art. 12.

Le contrat d'affiliation prend fin quand le lien défini à l'article premier de la présente loi disparaît.

Le contrat est susceptible de résiliation judiciaire pour manquement de la société dominante aux obligations qui y sont contenues, à la demande des actionnaires ou associés externes de la société affiliée dans les conditions prévues à l'article 21 de la présente loi.

Le juge des référés peut enjoindre à la société dominante de respecter et d'exécuter le contrat d'affiliation en tout ou en partie de ses dispositions, jusqu'à décision au principal. Il ordonne à cet effet toutes mesures provisoires appropriées, même d'office.

Titre III
Protection des Actionnaires ou Associés Externes

Art. 13.

Le contrat d'affiliation prévu à l'article 4 de la présente loi contient l'offre, aux actionnaires ou associés externes de la société affiliée, d'une option entre le droit de retrait aux conditions arrêtées dans un règlement terminal et le maintien aux droits dans la société affiliée assorti d'une allocation compensatrice annuelle.

Art. 14.

Le retrait offert par le règlement terminal s'opère selon les cas prévus à l'article 15 de la présente loi, soit par échange des actions ou parts de la société affiliée contre des titres ou parts de la société dominante, soit par paiement d'une indemnité en numéraire.

Si le nombre d'actions ou parts de la société affiliée dont l'échange est demandé ne permet pas d'obtenir un nombre entier de titres de la société dominante, celle-ci est tenue d'acheter les «rompus».

Art. 15.

I. — Si la société dominante est une société anonyme ou une société en commandite par actions ayant son siège social en France métropolitaine ou dans les départements et territoires d'outre-mer ou dans l'un des Etats membres de la Communauté économique européenne, ne dépendant elle-même d'aucune autre société, les titres de la société dominante proposés dans le règlement terminal sont des actions, des obligations convertibles en actions ou des obligations ordinaires.

II. — Si la société dominante dépend elle-même d'une autre société chef de groupe revêtant la forme de société anonyme ou en commandite par actions, ayant son siège social en France métropolitaine ou dans les Départements et Territoires d'outre-mer ou dans un des Etats membres de la Communauté économique européenne, le règlement terminal doit offrir le choix entre des titres de la société dominante du groupe visés à l'alinéa I ou une indemnité en numéraire.

III. — Si la société dominante est une société anonyme ou une société en commandite par actions ayant son siège dans un pays étranger autre que l'un des Etats membres de la Communauté économique européenne, le règlement terminal comprend les titres de la société dominante visés à l'alinéa I ou, en cas d'impossibilité, une indemnité en numéraire.

IV. — Si la société dominante est une S. A. R. L. ou une société de personnes, le règlement terminal comprend seulement une indemnité en numéraire.

Art. 16.

La société dominante est directement tenue des obligations du règlement terminal vis-à-vis des actionnaires ou associés externes de la société affiliée.

Art. 17.

Les conditions dans lesquelles la société dominante peut se procurer les titres à offrir pour le règlement terminal sont réglées par décret.

Art. 18.

Les actionnaires ou associés externes de la société affiliée qui n'ont pas réclamé l'application du règlement terminal dans les trois mois de l'inscription du contrat d'affiliation au registre du commerce, prévue à l'article 38 de la présente loi, ont droit, au lieu et place du dividende ou de leur part dans les bénéfices, ou en complément à ceux-ci, à l'allocation compensatrice annuelle.

Art. 19.

L'option pour l'allocation compensatrice annuelle est offerte aux actionnaires ou associés externes de la société affiliée conjointement avec le règlement terminal.

Elle est d'un montant déterminé établi selon le rendement passé de la société affiliée et les perspectives futures de celle-ci, aussi approché que possible du montant sur lequel l'actionnaire ou l'associé aurait pu compter si la société était demeurée indépendante.

Il peut être offert aussi un montant proportionnel aux futurs dividendes de la société dominante, ou encore un montant représentant une fraction fixe des bénéfices consolidés de l'exercice.

Art. 20.

Les actions de la société affiliée conservées par les actionnaires externes qui ont opté pour l'allocation compensatrice annuelle sont désormais privées du droit de vote qui leur était attaché.

Art. 21.

Les actionnaires externes représentant au moins un cinquième du capital de l'actionnariat externe de la société affiliée ont le droit de contester le règlement terminal et l'indemnité compensatrice annuelle, dans le délai de trois mois de l'inscription du contrat d'affiliation au registre du commerce prévue à l'article 38 de la présente loi. A cet effet, ils peuvent se grouper au besoin dans des conditions fixées par décret.

Dans les sociétés autres que les sociétés par actions, la même action en contestation peut être introduite, dans le même délai, par tout associé externe, quelle que soit sa part dans le capital de la société affiliée.

Art. 22.

L'exécution des clauses du contrat d'affiliation portant règlement terminal et fixation de l'allocation compensatrice annuelle est suspendue jusqu'à décision judiciaire entrée en force de chose jugée sur les actions visées à l'article précédent.

Art. 23.

La décision judiciaire rendue en application de l'article 21 et entraînant modification du contrat d'affiliation oblige les parties contractantes au même titre que ce contrat lui-même, à la date de son entrée en vigueur selon l'article 10 de la présente loi.

Titre IV
Protection des Créanciers

Art. 24.

La société dominante répond, solidairement avec la société affiliée, de toute dette de celle-ci, échue avant la clôture de l'exercice précédent et demeurée exigible trois mois après l'approbation des comptes dudit exercice.

Titre V
Protection des membres du personnel

Art. 25.

Il est créé auprès de la société dominante un comité central de groupe, dont l'avis doit être obligatoirement demandé par les organes de direction ou de gestion de cette société dans tous les cas où les décisions prévues dans l'ordonnance n° 455-280 du 22 février 1945 concernent une ou plusieurs sociétés affiliées et non la seule société dominante.

Le membre central de groupe est composé de membres désignés par les comités d'entreprise des sociétés affiliées et de la société dominante en fonction du nombre des salariés de cette société, dans des conditions qui sont fixées par décret.

Les avis et décisions du comité central de groupe s'imposent, dans le cadre des compétences de ce comité, aux comités d'entreprise des sociétés affiliées et de la société dominante.

Art. 26.

Lorsque les salariés de la société affiliée ont reçu des actions au titre de l'intéressement prévu par l'ordonnance n° 59-126 du 7 janvier 1959 ou de la participation aux fruits de l'expansion des entreprises prévue par l'ordonnance n° 67-693 du 17 août 1967 et la loi n° 73-1197 du 27 décembre 1973, des options de souscription ou d'achat d'actions prévues par la loi n° 70-1322 du 31 décembre 1970, des souscriptions ou des achats d'actions prévues par la loi n° 73-1196 du 27 décembre 1973, les actions de la société dominante qui leur seront remises en échange, conformément aux dispositions de l'article 14 de la présente loi, seront frappées de la même indisponibilité que les actions de la société affiliées qu'ils possédaient, et ce jusqu'à l'expiration du délai restant à courir pour celles-ci.

Si le règlement terminal prévoit un paiement en numéraire, les sommes revenant à ce titre aux salariés seront portées à un compte bloqué dans la société affiliée, qui portera intérêt, sauf convention contraire, à un taux fixé par décret. Ce compte restera bloqué jusqu'à l'expiration du délai restant à courir pour les actions de la société affiliée que possédaient lesdits salariés. Il en sera de même pour les sommes versées par la société dominante en cas d'application du second alinéa de l'article 14 de la présente loi.

Titre VI
Fonctionnement du groupe

Art. 27.

La société affiliée est tenue d'exécuter les ordres de direction que lui adresse la société dominante en vertu du pouvoir de décision à elle conféré par le contrat d'affiliation.

Elle doit toutefois opposer un refus aux ordres dont l'exécution constituerait une violation du contrat d'affiliation ou une infraction tombant sous les dispositions pénales dont la présente loi n'a pas pour effet d'écarter l'application.

Art. 28.

Les ordres de direction ne peuvent être donnés que par les organes qualifiés de la société dominante aux organes qualifiés de la société affiliée.

Art. 29.

Si l'exécution de l'ordre de direction requiert l'agrément du conseil d'administration ou de surveillance ou de l'assemblée générale ordinaire de la société affiliée, et que cet agrément ne soit pas accordé dans un délai raisonnable, la société dominante est en droit de réitérer l'ordre de direction, qui devra alors recevoir exécution même sans l'agrément.

Art. 30.

Les ordres de direction peuvent imposer à la société affiliée, tout transfert d'actifs, toute prestation ou livraison au profit de la société dominante ou d'autres sociétés du groupe. Ils peuvent inclure l'obligation de passer toutes conventions et d'accomplir tous actes, même si ces opérations sont susceptibles de porter préjudice à la société affiliée.

Art. 31.

Les ordres de direction peuvent également imposer à la société affiliée des tranferts des bénéfices de l'exercice, au profit de la société dominante ou d'autres sociétés du groupe.

Art. 32.

Si les comptes annuels de la société affiliée font ressortir une perte, la société dominante est tenue d'opérer, en faveur de la société affiliée, dans le délai d'un mois suivant l'approbation de ces comptes, un transfert compensateur égal au montant de cette perte, dans la mesure où celle-ci n'a pas été compensée par des prélèvements sur les réserves facultatives constituées pendant la durée du contrat d'affiliation.

Art. 33.

Les dirigeants de la société affiliée n'encourent aucune responsabilité du chef de l'exécution des ordres de direction, même si ceux-ci portent préjudice à la société affiliée, sauf dans les cas visés par l'article 27, alinéa 2, de la présente loi.

L'exécution des ordres de direction ne saurait constituer l'un des délits prévus par l'article 437, alinéas 3 et 4, de la loi n° 66-537 du 24 juillet 1966 sur les sociétés commerciales.

Titre VII
Exercice du pouvoir de décision sans contrat d'affiliation

Art. 34.

Sans préjudice de l'application de l'article 226 de la loi n° 66-537 du 24 juillet 1966 et des autres règles de droit commun assurant la protection de l'intérêt social, toute société dominante, au sens de l'article premier de la présente loi, qui exerce sur la société dépendante le pouvoir de décision sans conclusion et publication préalables d'un contrat d'affiliation, doit à la société dépendante réparation de tout dommage causé.

Elle ne pourra s'exonérer de cette responsabilité en invoquant l'intérêt du groupe fût-il réel, qui a déterminé l'exercice du pouvoir de décision.

Art. 35.

L'action tendant à la réparation du préjudice subi par la société dépendante et prévue par l'article précédent de la présente loi sera portée devant le tribunal de commerce ou, à défaut, devant le tribunal de grande instance du siège social de la société dépendante, ou, dans le cas d'une société dominante ayant son siège social à l'étranger, devant le tribunal compétent en vertu des dispositions du droit international privé.

A défaut d'être exercée par le représentant légal de cette société, ladite action sociale ne pourra l'être que par les actionnaires ou associés externes de celle-ci représentant au moins 10% du capital social, ou détenant des actions dont le montant représente au moins une valeur nominale de un million de francs, ou par mandataire de justice désigné par le Président du tribunal de commerce ou, à défaut, par le Président du tribunal de grande instance du siège social à la requête de tout actionnaire ou associé de la dite société. Ce dernier devra assortir sa requête de toutes justifications rendant vraisemblable la relation de dépendance invoquée ou la faisant présumer en vertu de l'article 2 de la présente loi. L'ordonnance nommant mandataire est susceptible d'opposition dans les quinze jours de sa signification. L'ordonnance rejetant l'exécution est exécutoire nonobstant appel. Elle ne fait pas préjudice au principal.

La même action tendant aux mêmes fins peut être exercée par le comité d'entreprise de la société dépendante dans des conditions qui sont fixées par décret.

En cas de règlement judiciaire ou de liquidation des biens de la société dépendante, l'action ne pourra être exercée que par le syndic.

Art. 36.

Devant le tribunal saisi de l'action visée à l'article précédent de la présente loi, pourra être portée, dans les mêmes conditions, concurremment ou après jugement y ayant fait droit, une action tendant à mettre à la charge des dirigeants de droit ou de fait de la société dominante tout ou partie de l'indemnité allouée ou à allouer à la société dépendante.

La même action pourra être dirigée, aux mêmes fins, contre les dirigeants de droit ou de fait de la société dépendante, si ceux-ci ont admis l'exercice du pouvoir de décision par la société dominante sans mettre cette dernière en demeure d'avoir au préalable à conclure et publier un contrat d'affiliation.

Ces dirigeants de droit ou de fait des sociétés dominante et dépendante ne pourront s'exonérer de leur responsabilité en arguant avoir agi dans un intérêt de groupe, fût-il réel.

Cette cironstance ne pourra non plus les exonérer de la responsabilité pénale par eux encourue à raison de ces opérations.

Art. 37.

Sous réserve des dispositions du dernier alinéa de l'article 35 de la présente loi, les créanciers de la société dépendante peuvent agir, dans leur intérêt propre, en responsabilité contre la société dominante et les dirigeants de celle-ci ainsi que ceux de la société dépendante elle-même, dans la mesure où ils ne sont pas parvenus, dans un délai qui sera fixé par décret, à se faire désintéresser par la société dépendante.

Titre VIII
Publicité et information des actionnaires ou associés

Art. 38.

Mention du contrat d'affiliation est inscrite au registre du commerce par les sociétés dominante et affiliée, dans les conditions qui seront prévues par décret.

Art. 39.

Le contrat d'affiliation, ainsi que les modifications de celui-ci, doivent être publiés au ***Bulletin des annonces légales obligatoires,*** dans les quarante-cinq jours qui suivent l'inscription au registre du commerce, et dans des conditions qui seront fixées par décret.

Art. 40.

Toute société est tenue de faire mention, dans le rapport annuel de ses organes d'administration ou de gestion, des contrats d'affiliation qu'elle a conclus, ou de l'établissement ou de la constatation par jugement de liens de dépendance, avec d'autres sociétés.

S'il n'est intervenu au cours de l'exercice ni contrat d'affiliation ni établissement ou constatation par jugement de liens de dépendance, le même rapport doit en faire mention.

Le rapport mentionnera également toute modification intervenue ou toute extinction ou cessation du contrat d'affiliation ou de liens de dépendance existant antérieurement.

Art. 41.

Dans toute société, les commissaires aux comptes sont tenus de présenter chaque année un rapport spécial sur l'exécution des contrats d'affiliation que la société a conclus, ou sur les conséquences au cours de l'exercice de l'établissement ou de la constatation par jugement de liens de dépendance qui sont venus à leur connaissance.

Art. 42.

Toutes actions introduites en vertu des dispositions des articles 21 à 23 de la présente loi et tous jugements et arrêts intervenus sur ces actions seront inscrits au registre du commerce dans les conditions qui seront fixées par décret.

Art. 43.

L'extinction du contrat d'affiliation fait l'objet de toutes mesures de publicité qui seront fixées par décret.

Art. 44.

Toute société est tenue d'annexer à son bilan, un tableau, dont le modèle sera fixé par décret, en vue de faire apparaître la liste et la nature des contrats d'affiliation qu'elle a conclus ainsi que l'établissement ou la constation par jugement de liens de dépendance qu'elle a avec d'autres sociétés.

Art. 45.

Toute société dominante au sens de l'article premier de la présente loi, qui a conclu des contrats d'affiliation, est tenue d'établir et de publier des comptes annuels consolidés et un rapport annuel sur le groupe ainsi constitué, dans les conditions qui seront fixées par décret. Ces mêmes comptes seront mis à la disposition des sociétés affiliées dépendant d'elle, selon les dispositions qui seront prises par décret.

Art. 46.

Toute société dépendante au sens de l'article premier de la présente loi, qui a conclu des contrats d'affiliation, est tenue de mettre à la disposition de ses actionnaires ou associés, dans des conditions qui seront fixées par décret, un exemplaire de ces contrats d'affiliation et, le cas échéant, des avenants correspondants, ainsi que le texte des jugements et arrêts intervenus sur toutes actions introduites en vertu des dispositions de la présente loi.

Titre IX
Sociétés intégrées

Art. 47.

Le présent titre s'applique aux sociétés, affiliées ou non, qui revêtent la forme de sociétés par actions, ont leur siège en France ou dans les Départements ou Territoires d'outre-mer et dont 95% au moins du capital est détenu, directement ou indirectement, par une autre société par actions, ayant son siège en France ou dans les Départements ou Territoires d'outre-mer.

Art. 48.

La société dépendante peut, aux conditions de quorum et de majorité définies pour la modification de ses statuts, décider son intégration à la société dominante.

Art. 49.

Après prise de la décision dont il est fait état à l'article précédent de la présente loi, la société dominante doit, dans un délai et selon les modalités qui seront fixées par décret, proposer aux actionnaires de la société dépendante l'échange de leurs actions contre ses propres actions. Le rapport d'échange est fixé dans les mêmes conditions qu'en cas de fusion.

Si la société dominante est elle-même affiliée à une autre société, l'offre portera soit sur des actions de cette dernière, soit sur une indemnité en numéraire.

A défaut d'accord entre la société dominante et les actionnaires de la société dépendante, le rapport d'échange ou le montant de l'indemnité en numéraire sera déterminé par un expert désigné en justice, dans des conditions qui seront fixées par décret.

Art. 50.

La décision d'intégration est inscrite au registre du commerce dans des conditions qui seront fixées par décret.

Elle porte effet à dater du jour de cette inscription.

Art. 51.

La dissolution de la société intégrée ne peut être demandée en application des dispositions de l'article 9 de la loi n° 66-537 du 24 juillet 1966 sur les sociétés commerciales.

Art. 52.

La société intégrée n'a qu'un seul actionnaire, la société dominante, par dérogation aux dispositions de la législation sur les sociétés exigeant un nombre minimum d'actionnaires.

Par dérogation aux dispositions de la loi, la société dominante dirige la société intégrée en nommant à sa tête un ou plusieurs représentants.

Art. 53.

Lorsque plusieurs représentants sont désignés par la société dominante à la tête de la société intégrée, ces représentants sont constitués en un comité de direction, qui jouit de tous les pouvoirs attribués par la législation sur les sociétés par actions aux organes d'administration, de direction ou de surveillance.

S'il n'existe qu'un représentant, celui-ci jouit des mêmes pouvoirs.

Art. 54.

La société dominante décide seule, le cas échéant, des modifications à apporter aux statuts de la société intégrée sans que la réunion d'une assemblée générale extraordinaire de cette dernière soit nécessaire.

Art. 55.

Si la société dépendante ne fait pas l'objet d'une décision d'intégration conformément aux dispositions des articles 48 à 50 de la présente loi, elle pourra à tout moment se voir réclamer par ses actionnaires externes la proposition d'un contrat d'affiliation répondant aux conditions du titre II de la présente loi.

L'allocation compensatrice sera rétroactivement due depuis la date où a été atteinte la participation de 95% de la société dominante, sans qu'elle puisse remonter au-delà du cinquième exercice ayant précédé l'exercice en cours à la date de la réclamation. Le règlement terminal sera fixé en prenant cette même date pour date de référence quant à la parité d'échange des titres ou à l'indemnité de retrait.

A défaut d'accord sur les termes du contrat, chaque actionnaire externe pourra assigner la société dominante en fixation des conditions du contrat d'affiliation.

Art. 56.

Un décret précisera les formes, modalités et conditions de l'intégration et le régime de la société intégrée.

Titre X
Dispositions communes

Art. 57.

Le présente loi est applicable à toutes sociétés dominantes et dépendantes ayant leur siège en France métropolitaine ou dans les Départements et Territoire d'outre-mer.

Art. 58.

Les effets que la présente loi attache à l'absence de contrat d'affiliation ne recevront application que si ce contrat n'a pas été conclu et publié dans un délai de dix-huit mois à partir de l'entrée en vigueur de la présente loi.

Art. 59.

La présente loi entrera en vigueur le premier jour du troisième mois qui suivra celui de sa publication au *Journal officiel.*

3. Sweden/Suède

3. a. The Swedish Companies Act 1975* (as of 1980)

Ch. 1 § 2, ch. 4 § 20, ch. 7 § 1, ch. 8 § 7, ch. 9 § 1 last para., § 12, ch. 10 §§ 4, 7, 8, 9, ch. 11 §§ 10, 11, 13, ch. 12 §§ 2, 7, ch. 14 §§ 9-13

Chapter 1
Introductory provisions

[§ 1 omitted]

2 § Where a company limited by shares is holder of such a number of shares or parts of a Swedish or a foreign legal person that the holding represents more than half of the votes of the shares or the parts, the company limited by shares is a parent company and the legal person a subsidiary. Where a subsidiary holds or where a parent company holds jointly with one or several subsidiaries or where several subsidiaries jointly hold such a number of shares or parts of a legal person as mentioned above, that legal person is also a subsidiary of the parent company.

Where a company limited by shares has otherwise, by virtue of its holding of shares or parts, or by virtue of agreement, a decisive influence itself alone over a legal person and a considerable share in its results, the company limited by shares is a parent company and the legal person a subsidiary.

A parent company and its subsidiaries, taken as a whole, constitute a group.

Chapter 4
Increase of the share capital through a new issue or a bonus issue

[§§ 1-19 omitted]

20 § A prospectus shall contain the balance sheets, the profit and loss statements and a summary of the information which had to be included in the directors' report for the last three financial years for which annual reports and auditors' reports have been rendered. Where these documents do not meet the requirements set forth in Chapter 11, section 5, paragraph two and section 9, paragraph four they shall be completed in accordance with those provisions.

Chapter 11, section 2, paragraph one, second sentence is correspondingly applicable to prospectuses.

Where the company is a parent company, the prospectus shall contain the

* Reproduced with the kind permission of the Federation of Swedish Industries. Taken form THE SWEDISH COMPANIES ACT 1975, WITH EXCERPTS FROM THE ACCOUNTING ACT 1976 (WITH CUMULATIVE SUPPLEMENT OF JUNE 1978) (Federation of Swedish Industries, Stockholm, 1976 and 1978). The 1980 amendments in Ch. 1 § 2 are inserted.

consolidated profit and loss statements and the consolidated balance sheets for the last three financial years. When financial statements and other information relating to the group are included in the prospectus, similar information concerning the parent company may be omitted to the extent that it may be considered without material importance for the assessment of the company's shares. The parent company's profit and loss statement and balance sheet for the last financial year as indicated in paragraph one may, however, not be omitted.

[§§ 21-26 omitted]

Chapter 7
Acquisition of own shares and raising of certain loans

1 § A company may not acquire its own shares or accept such shares as security. Nor may a subsidiary acquire shares in the parent company or accept such shares as security. An agreement which violates this prohibition is invalid.

Paragraph one does not prevent a company or its subsidiary from acquiring the company's own shares in connection with taking over a business, from redeeming the company's own shares pursuant to Chapter 13, section 3, or from acquiring at a public auction the company's own shares which have been seized to satisfy a claim of the company. Such shares shall be disposed of as soon as they can be sold without a loss, unless they have previously been withdrawn by a reduction of the share capital. Shares which have been acquired in connection with taking over a business shall, however, be disposed of not later than two years after the acquisition unless the Government or an authority appointed by the Government permits the company to keep the shares for a longer period.

Where a company has become a parent company and the subsidiary owns shares in the parent company, these shares shall be disposed of pursuant to the provisions of paragraph two dealing with own shares acquired in connection with taking over a business.

[§§ 2-3 omitted]

Chapter 8
Management of the Company

[§ 1-6 omitted]

7 § Where a company has become a parent company, its board of directors shall inform the management of the subsidiary accordingly. The management of the subsidiary is obliged to provide such information about the subsidiary as the board of the parent company needs for calculating the financial position and the results of the group.

[§ 8-15 omitted]

Chapter 9
General meeting of Shareholders

1 § [para. 1-3 omitted]
A share in the company which is owned by the company itself or by its subsidiary may not be represented at the general meeting. Such a share shall not be taken into account when the consent of the owners of a certain number of shares is required for the validity of a decision or for the exercise of a right.
As amended 1976:992
[§ 2-11 omitted]
12 § Upon request of a shareholder the board of directors and the managing director shall, if the board considers it possible without any material prejudice to the company, furnish such information to the general meeting of shareholders as may influence the assessment of the company's annual report and its financial position or a matter before the meeting. In a group company the duty to furnish such information covers also the relationship to other group companies and, where the company is a parent company, the consolidated accounts and such circumstances concerning subsidiaries as are mentioned in the first sentence.

Where the information requested is not available at the general meeting, it shall be held available in writing to the shareholders at the office of the company within two weeks thereafter and it shall also be sent to the shareholder who submitted the request for information.

Where the board of directors considers that the information requested can not be supplied without material prejudice to the company, the information shall instead be submitted to the auditors within two weeks thereafter provided that the shareholder requests it. The auditors shall, within a month after the general meeting, give their written opinion to the board of directors on whether they have received the information requested and whether, in their view, the information should give rise to an amendment of the auditors' report or, in case of a parent company, the auditors' report on the group, or whether it otherwise should result in a comment. Where this is the case, the amendment or the comment shall be specified in the auditors' opinion. The board of directors shall hold the auditors' opinion available to the shareholders at the office of the company and shall also send a copy thereof to the shareholder who submitted the request for information.
[§§ 13-18 omitted]

Chapter 10
Audit and special examination

[§§ 1-3 omitted]
4 § A person may not be auditor if he

1. is a director or the managing director of the company or of a subsidiary or assists the company in its book-keeping or the management of its assets or in the company's control thereof,

2. is employed by or is otherwise subordinated to or dependent on the

company or someone referred to in point 1, or is active in the same enterprise as someone who professionally assists the company in the chronological accounting or the management of its assets or the company's control thereof,

3. is married to or cohabits under circumstances similar to marriage with or is a brother or sister or a relative in the ascendent or the descendent line of someone referred to in point 1 or is related by marriage to such a person in the ascendent or the descendent line or related in such a way that one is married to the brother or sister of the other, or

4. is indebted to the company or another company in the same group or has obligations for which such a company has provided a security or a guaranty.

A person who pursuant to paragraph one may not be auditor of the parent company may not be auditor of a subsidiary company.

An auditor may not be assisted in the audit work by a person who pursuant to paragraph one or two may not be auditor. Where the company or the parent company has employees whose task is solely or primarily to handle the internal audit, the auditor may be assisted by such employees in the audit work to an extent compatible with generally accepted auditing standards.

[§§ 5-6 omitted]

7 § An auditor shall to the extent required by generally accepted auditing standards examine the annual report, the accounts and the board's and the managing director's administration of the company.

Where the company is a parent company, the auditor shall also examine the consolidated accounts and the relations between the group enterprises.

An auditor shall observe the special instructions given by the general meeting of shareholders provided that these instructions are not contrary to law, the articles of association or generally accepted auditing standards.

8 § The board of directors and the managing director shall allow an auditor to perform his examination to the extent he finds necessary and shall provide the information and the assistance he requires. The board of directors, the managing director and auditors of a subsidiary company have the same obligation towards auditors of the parent company.

9 § When an auditor has completed the examination he shall make a note on the annual report and, in a parent company, on the consolidated accounts with a reference to the auditors' report. Where the auditor is of the opinion that the balance sheet or the profit and loss statement should not be adopted he shall enter a remark to this effect on the annual report. In a parent company the same rule shall apply in respect of the consolidated balance sheet and the consolidated profit and loss statement.

[§§ 10-14 omitted]

Chapter 11
Reporting Requirements

[§§ 1-9 omitted]

10 § A parent company shall for each financial year prepare, in addition to its annual report, consolidated accounts consisting of a consolidated profit and loss

statement and a consolidated balance sheet. The accounts shall refer to the same date as the balance sheet date of the parent company.

Section 3 is correspondingly applicable to the consolidated accounts and the auditors' report on the group.

As amended 1976:992

11 § The consolidated profit and loss statement and the consolidated balance sheet shall be a summary of the profit and loss statements and the balance sheets of the parent company and its subsidiaries, prepared in conformity with generally accepted accounting principles and with observance of sections 2 and 5-8 where relevant.

The consolidated profit and loss statement shall show the group's profit or loss for the year, after deduction of intercompany dividends and after deduction or addition for increases or decreases of inter-company profits during the financial year. The consolidated balance sheet shall show the group's non-restricted equity capital or accumulated loss after deduction of inter-company profits. The term "inter-company profits" shall mean the portion accruing to the parent company of the profit resulting from a transfer of assets within the group, provided that the asset thereafter has not been transferred to a party outside the group or the group enterprise which made the acquisition has not consumed the asset or reduced its value.

Where the composition of the group or other special reasons lead to extraordinary difficulties in applying paragraphs one or two in preparing the consolidated accounts such exceptions may be made as are necessary under the circumstances. The reasons for such a deviation shall be stated in the directors' report on the parent company.

The directors' report on the parent company shall also contain the information on the group referred to in section 9, paragraphs one and two. The report shall describe the methods and valuation principles used in the preparation of the consolidated accounts. The report shall also specify the amount which according to the annual reports of the group enterprises shall be transferred from the non-restricted equity capital of the group to the restricted equity capital.

The directors' report of a subsidiary company shall specify the name of the parent company and, where applicable, also the name of the latter's parent company. A parent company and a subsidiary company shall also specify the portion of purchases and sales which relates to other companies in the same group.

The consolidated accounts shall contain information on the size of and change in the group's inventory reserves provided that the group is of the size mentioned in Chapter 10, section 3, paragraph four. In that case a statement of changes in the group's financial position shall also be attached to the consolidated accounts.

As amended 1977:1092

[§ 12 omitted]

13 § An interim report shall contain a brief description of the company's activities, results, the trends reflected by the company's results, investments, changes in working capital and financing during the period from the expiration

of the preceding financial year to the date of the interim report. Furthermore, for the period covered by the report the amount of gross sales and the profit or loss, before appropriations and taxes, shall be given. Where special reasons require it, an estimated profit or loss figure may be given. Section 6, paragraph one and section 9, paragraph one shall also apply to the interim report where relevant.

Where the group is of the size mentioned in Chapter 10, section 3, paragraph four, the parent company shall in its interim report furnish such information on the group as is mentioned in paragraph one in addition to information on itself. The information on gross sales and profit or loss shall refer to amounts after deduction of inter-company items and adjustment for inter-company profits.

As amended 1977:1092

[§ 14 omitted]

Chapter 12
Distribution of dividends and other use of the company's property

[§ 1 omitted]

2 § Dividends to the shareholders may not exceed the amount which according to the adopted balance sheet for the last financial year, and in respect to a parent company, the adopted consolidated balance sheet, has been reported as the company's or the group's net profit for the year, profit brought forward and free reserves less

1. the amount of reported losses,
2. the amount which shall be allocated to restricted equity capital under this Act or the articles of association or in respect to a parent company, the amount which according to the annual reports submitted by the group enterprises shall be transferred from non-restricted equity capital of the group to restricted equity capital.
3. the amount which according to the articles of association shall otherwise be used for a purpose other than for dividends to the shareholders.

Dividends may not be distributed to such an extent that in view of the company's or the group's consolidation needs, cash needs or financial position in other respects the distribution would be contrary to good business practices. Payment of dividends is under certain circumstances prohibited under Chapter 6, section 5.

[§ 3-6 omitted]

7 § A company may not grant cash loans to a person who owns shares in or who is a director or managing director of the company or of another company in the same group. The same rule shall apply with respect to cash loans to

1. a person who is married to a shareholder, director or managing director or who is a brother or sister or a relative in the ascendent or the descendent line of such a person,
2. a person who is related by marriage to such a person in the ascendent or the descendent line or related in such a way that one is married to the brother or sister of the other, or

3. a legal person where a person as mentioned above has a decisive influence over the activities of the legal person.

The provisions in paragraph one shall not apply where

1. the debtor is a municipality or a county council,

2. the debtor is a legal person within the same group as the lending company,

3. the deptor operates a business and the loan is given for business reasons and is intended solely for the deptor's business,

4. the debtor or any related natural or legal person covered by paragraph one, points 1-3 is a shareholder who owns less than one per cent of the share capital in the company and, where the company is part of a group, also less than one per cent of the total of the share capitals in the group companies. Paragraph one is, however, applicable where the debtor or a legal person over whose activity he has a decisive influence owns or they together own more than five hundred shares in the company or, where the company is part of a group, in the group companies.

A company may not grant a cash loan for the purpose of financing the acquisition of its shares or shares in another company in the same group by the debtor or any related natural or legal person covered by paragraph one, points 1-3.

The provisions in this section prohibiting cash loans shall be correspondingly applicable to the furnishing of a security or a guaranty.

In the application of this section, cohabitation under circumstances similar to marriage shall be held equal to marriage if the cohabiting parties previously have been married to each other or have or have had children together.

As amended 1977:1092

[§§ 8-9 omitted]

Chapter 14
Fusion, compulsory transfer of shares in a subsidiary

[§§ 1-8 omitted]

9 § Where a parent company alone or together with one or more subsidiaries owns more than nine-tenths of all the shares in a subsidiary company and these shares represent more than nine-tenths of the votes, the parent company is entitled to purchase the remaining shares in the subsidiary company. A person whose shares are subject to such a right of purchase may require the parent company to purchase his shares.

A dispute whether there is a right or obligation to purchase or a dispute regarding the price shall be submitted to arbitration by three arbitrators under the Arbitration Act (1929:145) unless otherwise provided in this Chapter. The provisions in section 18, paragraph two of that Act on the period within which the award shall be given shall not apply.

Where the parent company has acquired the larger portion of the shares it owns in the subsidiary company through an offer directed to a substantial number of persons, offering to acquire the shares for a certain consideration per share, the purchase price shall be the same as the consideration contained in the offer, unless there are special reasons for a different price.

The costs for the arbitration proceedings shall be borne by the parent company, unless the arbitrators should for special reasons order a shareholder to be wholly or partly responsible for them.

As amended 1977:1092

10 § Where a parent company wishes to acquire shares of a subsidiary company pursuant to section 9 and an agreement on the acquisition can not be reached, the parent company shall, naming its arbitrator, make a request in writing to the board of the subsidiary company that the dispute shall be referred to arbitration.

The board of directors of the subsidiary company shall, when a request under paragraph one has been received, without delay call the shareholders whose shares are subject to a right of purchase by announcement in the Swedish Official Gazette and one or more local newspapers as determined by the board, and request them to submit in writing the name of their arbitrator not later than two weeks from the announcement. The notice shall also be sent by letter to each such shareholder if his mailing address is known to the subsidiary company.

Unless all shareholders entered in the share register whose shares are subject to the right of purchase have named a common arbitrator within the prescribed period, the board of directors of the subsidiary company shall request the court in the municipality where the registered office of the company is located to appoint an administrator. The administrator shall ask the chief executory authority for the municipality in question to appoint the arbitrator, and he shall look after the interests of absent shareholders in the dispute.

As amended 1977:709

11 § Where a dispute relating to a purchase under section 9 is dealt with by arbitrators and the dispute does not concern the right of purchase as such, or where the arbitrators declare that such a right exists without determining the purchase price at the same time, the shareholders are under an obligation to deliver their share certificates to the parent company with a transfer, if the parent company pays the established purchase price or, as the case may be, furnishes a sufficient security or guaranty approved by the arbitrators for the price to be established and interest thereon.

The shareholders are entitled to reasonable interest on the purchase price from the time when the security is furnished until the purchase price is due.

12 § Where the shareholders have been offered the established purchase price and the share certificates have not been delivered, the parent company shall without delay deposit the purchase price in public custody according to the Act (1927:56) on payment of debts through deposit of funds in public custody. Such deposit may not be made subject to a provision that it can be withdrawn from public custody.

13 § Where a security has been furnished pursuant to section 11 or a deposit made pursuant to section 12, the parent company is owner of the shares to be purchased. Until the share certificates have been delivered to the parent company, they shall in such a case only entitle the holder to receive the purchase price and interest thereon against delivery of the certificates to the parent company or the chief executory authority.

Where a share certificate has not been delivered after one year from the time when the parent company became owner of the shares, a new share certificate may be issued to the parent company. The new share certificate shall state that it replaces an earlier certificate. Where the earlier share certificate is thereafter delivered to the parent company, the certificate shall be returned to the subsidiary company for cancellation.

3. b. Act on Annual Reports of Certain Enterprises 1980

Ch. 1 § 1

Chapter 1
Introductory provisions

1 § Where a trading partnership is holder of such a number of shares or parts of a Swedish or a foreign legal person that the holding represents more than half of the votes of the shares or the parts, the trading partnership is a parent enterprise and the other legal person a subsidiary. Where a subsidiary holds or where a parent enterprise holds jointly with one or several subsidiaries or where several subsidiaries jointly hold such a number of shares or parts of a legal person as mentioned above, that legal person is also a subsidiary of the parent enterprise.

Where a trading partnership has otherwise, by virtue of its holding of shares or parts, or by virtue of agreement, a decisive influence itself alone over a legal person and a considerable share in its results, the trading partnership is a parent enterprise and the legal person a subsidiary.

The provisions in the two preceding paragraphs concerning trading partnerships apply also to individual tradesmen and legal persons other than trading partnerships, companies limited by shares, economic associations or foundations, if the individual tradesman or legal persons are obliged to present annual accounts according to the Accounting Act (1976:125).

A parent enterprise and its subsidiaries, taken as a whole, constitute a group.

List of Abbreviations/Table des abréviations

A. 2d	Atlantic Reporter, Second Series
AB	Aktiebolag (Swedish: corporation)
AC	Appellate Court, Appeal Cases
AD	Arbetsdomstolens domar (Reports of Cases decided by the Swedish Labour Court)
AG	Aktiengesellschaft, Die Aktiengesellschaft
AktG	Aktiengesetz
al.	alinéa
All E. R.	All England Reports
Amend.	Amendment
AP	Arbeitsrechtliche Praxis/Nachschlagewerk des Bundesarbeitsgerichts
App. Cas.	Appeal Cases
ApS	Anpartsselskab (Danish: private company)
A. R.	Arrêté Royal (Belgium)
art.	article
A/S	Aksjeselskap (Norwegian: corporation) Aktieselskab (Danish: public company)
Ass. Nat.	Assemblée Nationale
Aust. H. C.	High Court of Australia
AWD	Außenwirtschaftsdienst des Betriebs-Berater
BAG	Bundesarbeitsgericht
BALO	Bulletin des annonces légales obligatoires
BayObLG	Bayerisches Oberstes Landesgericht
BB	Betriebs-Berater
Betrieb	Der Betrieb
BetrVG	Betriebsverfassungsgesetz
BGB	Bürgerliches Gesetzbuch
BGE/RO	Entscheidungen des schweizerischen Bundesgerichts Amtliche Sammlung/Receuil Officiel
BGH	Bundesgerichtshof
BGHZ	Entscheidungen des Bundesgerichtshofes in Zivilsachen
B. I. A. C.	Business and Industry Advisory Committee
BRDrS	Bundesrats-Drucksache
BTDrS	Bundestags-Drucksache
Bull.	Bulletin
Bull. (cass.) civ.	Bulletin des arrêts de la Cour de cassation, section civile
Bull. cons. nat. com. aux comptes	Bulletin du conseil national des commissaires aux comptes

c.	contra
C. A.	Court of Appeal(s)
Cass. civ.	Cour de cassation, section civile
Cass. com.	Cour de cassation, section commerciale
Cass. soc.	Cour de cassation, section sociale
C. C.	Code civil
C. com.	Code de commerce
C. D. C.	Caisse des dépôts et consignations
C. E. E.	Communauté Economique Européenne
cf.	confer
ch.	chapter; chapitre
cl.	clause
C. L. P.	Current Legal Problems
C. L. R.	Commonwealth Law Reports
C. M. L. R.	Common Market Law Reports
C. M. L. Rev.	Common Market Law Review
Cmnd	Command Papers (3rd Series)
C. O.	Code of Obligations
C. O. B.	Commission des opérations de bourse
col., cols.	column(s)
Co. Law	Company Lawyer
com., comm.	commercial
Comm.	Tribunal de commerce
comp.	comparez
const.	constitution
CREDA	Centre de recherche en droit des affaires
D.	Recueil Dalloz
DB	Der Betrieb
décr.	Décret
Dépt.	Department
Diss.	Dissertation (thesis)
D. L. R.	Dominion Law Reports
Doc.	Document
Doctr.	doctrine
Dr. soc.	Droit social
D. S.	Dalloz Sirey
E.C	European Communities
E. C. R.	European Court Reports (offical reports of the Court of Justice of the E. C.)
E. C. S. C.	European Coal and Steel Community (Treaty)
ed., éd., eds.	editor(s), éditeur(s); edition, édition; edited, édité
E. E. C.	European Economic Community (Treaty)
e. g.	for example
EGAktG	Einführungsgesetz zum Aktiengesetz
esp.	especially
EStG	Einkommenssteuergesetz
et seq.	following
et suiv., et s.	et suivants

E. U. A.	European Unit(s) of Account
EuR	Europarecht
fasc.	fascicule
Gaz. Pal.	Gazette du Palais
GbR	Gesellschaft des bürgerlichen Rechts
GmbH	Gesellschaft mit beschränkter Haftung
GmbH & Co. (KG)	GmbH & Co. (Kommanditgesellschaft)
GmbHG	Gesetz betreffend die Gesellschaften mit beschränkter Haftung
GmbH-Rdsch	GmbH-Rundschau
G. P.	Gazette du Palais
GroßK	Großkommentar (zum Aktiengesetz)
GWB	Gesetz gegen Wettbewerbsbeschränkungen
Harv. L. Rev.	Harvard Law Review
H. C.	High Court; House of Commons
H. L.	House of Lords
Hrsg., hrsg.	Herausgeber, herausgegeben
ibid.	ibidem
ICC	International Chamber of Commerce
I. C. F. T. U.	International Confederation of Free Trade Unions
I. C. R.	Industrial Cases Reports; Industrial Court Reports
id.	idem
i. e.	that is, equals
I. F. A.	International Fiscal Association
I. L. O.	International Labour Organization
I. M. E.	Committee on International Investment and Multinational Enterprises (O. E. C. D.)
Ind. L. J.	Indiana Law Journal
Industrial L. J.	Industrial Law Journal
I. R. L. R.	Industrial Relations Law Reports
I. T. F.	International Transport Workers' Federation
I. T. S.	International Trade Union Secretariat
J.	Judge, Justice
J. C. B.	Jurisprudence commerciale de Belgique
J. C. P.	Jurisclasseur périodique
J. C. P. – C. I.	Jurisclasseur périodique (édition commerce et industrie)
J. O.	Journal Officiel
J. O. doc. admin.	Journal officiel, édition des documents administratifs
J. O. C. E.	Journal Officiel des Communautés Européennes
Journal soc.	Journal des sociétés
J. T.	Journal des Tribunaux
JZ	Juristenzeitung
KG	Kammergericht, Kommanditgesellschaft
KGaA	Kommanditgesellschaft auf Aktien
KK	Kölner Kommentar (zum Aktiengesetz)

KStG	Körperschaftssteuergesetz
KStR	Körperschaftssteuer-Richtlinien
L.	Loi
LG	Landgericht
Lloyd's Rep.	Lloyd's Reports
L. T.	Law Times
McGill L. J.	McGill Law Journal
MitbestG	Mitbestimmungsgesetz (1976)
MitbestErgG	Gesetz zur Ergänzung des MontanMitbestG (1956)
MNE	Multinational enterprise(s)
mod.	modified, modifié
MontanMitbestG	Gesetz über die Mitbestimmung der Arbeitnehmer in den Aufsichtsräten und Vorständen der Unternehmen des Bergbaus und der Eisen und Stahl erzeugenden Industrie (1951)
M. R.	Master of the Rolls
n.	note
NJW	Neue Juristische Wochenschrift
N. L. R. A.	National Labour Relations Act
No., Nr., n°., n^{os}	number(s); numéro(s)
N. Z. L. R.	New Zealand Law Reports
obs.	observation
OECD (OCDE)	Organization for Economic Co-operation and Development
OHG	offene Handelsgesellschaft
O. J. E. C. C.	Official Journal of the E.C., C series
O. J. E. C. L.	Official Journal of the E.C., L series
OLG	Oberlandesgericht
Ont. H. C.	High Court of Ontario
O. P. A.	Offre public d'achat
op. cit.	cited work
O. P. E.	Offre public d'échange
O. R.	Obligationenrecht
Ord.	ordonnance
OY	Osakeyhtiö (Finnish: corporation)
p., pp.	page(s)
par., para(s)	paragraph(s)
par ex.	par exemple
P. & C. R.	Planning and Compensation Reports
Prés. comm.	Président du Tribunal de commerce
RabelsZ	Rabels Zeitschrift für ausländisches und internationales Privatrecht
R. C.	registre de commerce
R. C. J. B.	Revue critique de jurisprudence belge

RDS/ZSR	Revue de Droit Suisse/Zeitschrift für Schweizerisches Recht
réf.	référez
Rev. Banque	Revue de la Banque (belge)
Rev. de jurispr. com.	Revue de jurisprudence commerciale
Rev. Int. Belge	Revue du droit international et du droit comparé (belge)
Rev. prat. soc.	Revue pratique des sociétés
Rev. soc.	Revue des sociétés
Rev. trim. dr. com.	Revue trimestrielle de droit commercial (et de droit économique)
Riv. int. sc. econ.	Rivista internazionale di scienze economiche e commerciali
Riv. soc.	Rivista delle società
RiW	Recht der internationalen Wirtschaft
Rnr	Randnummer
Rz	Randziffer
s./sec.	section(s)
S.	Recueil Sirey
S. A. R. L.	Société à responsabilité limitée
spec.	spécialement
Sten. Bull.	Stenographischer Bulletin
t.	tôme
Trib. com.	Tribunal de commerce
Trib. corr.	Tribunal correctionnel
T. U. A. C.	Trade Union Advisory Committee
T. U. C.	Trade Union Congress
T. U. L. R. A.	Trade Union and Labour Relations Act
U. Chi. L. Rev.	University of Chicago Law Review
U. S. (L. Ed.)	United States Supreme Court Reports (Lawyer's Edition)
v.	voir, volume
Va. J. Int. L.	Virginia Journal of International Law
Va. L. Rev.	Virginia Law Review
vol.	volume
voy.	voyez
W. L. R.	Weekly Law Reports
WM	Wertpapier-Mitteilungen
WPg	Die Wirtschaftsprüfung
Yale L. J.	Yale Law Journal
ZGR	Zeitschrift für Unternehmens- und Gesellschaftsrecht
ZHR	Zeitschrift für das gesamte Handelsrecht und Wirtschaftsrecht
ZR	Blätter für Zürcher Rechtsprechung
ZSR	Zeitschrift für Schweizerisches Recht

Table of Cases and Enterprises/Table des décisions et des entreprises

I. Europe in general (and European Communities)
Europe en général (et les Communautés européennes)

II. Belgium/Belgique

III. Federal Republic of Germany/République fédérale d'Allemagne

further decisions:

IV. France

V. Scandinavia/Scandinavie

VI. Switzerland/Suisse

VII. United Kingdom (and Commonwealth)/Royaume Uni (et Commonwealth)

VIII. U.S.A./États-Unis

Index / Index alphabétique

(Numbers refer to pages, numbers in italics refer to Annex II with the text of relevant legal provisions. The English index basically refers to articles and legal texts in English language)

(Les chiffres correspondent aux pages, les chiffres en caractères italiques correspondent à l'annex II avec les textes des lois. L'index alphabéthique en langue française se réfère principalement aux articles et textes français)

Index

Index alphabétique